DECODING THE ACT®

The Unofficial, Comprehensive Teacher's Guide

1st Edition

MasteryPrep

Inquiries concerning this publication should be mailed to:

MasteryPrep
7117 Florida Blvd.
Baton Rouge, LA 70806

MasteryPrep is a trade name and/or trademark of Ring Publications LLC.
This publication, its author, and its publisher are in no way affiliated with or authorized by ACT Inc.

ACT® is a copyright and/or trademark of ACT Inc.

10 9 8 7 6 5 4 3 2 1

ISBN-13: 978-1-948846-15-8

TABLE OF CONTENTS

Math Test Mastery 175

Science Test Mastery 363

OVERVIEW

This overview is split into four sections:

- **Orientation**, which provides a broad overview of the ACT, what it measures, and how it is scored, as well as tips and strategies on motivating students to succeed both on the ACT and in academics in general.

- **Time Mastery**, which introduces the concept of time management and provides proven techniques for improving your students' ability to handle timed tests.

- **Test Mastery**, which covers fundamental test-taking strategies applicable to all of the subject areas on the ACT and provides a foundation for all subject-specific, test-taking strategies found later in this book.

- **Content Mastery**, which provides a framework for the content remediation strategies that boost ACT outcomes and prepares you to make the most of the content strategies provided later in this book for each test section.

The very best test preparation focuses on three factors: time management, test-taking strategies, and mastery of content (with a heavy emphasis on content). This book is organized around the same pillars: each major section of the book provides instruction on *time mastery*, *test mastery*, and *content mastery*. Consider taking the same approach with your students, interweaving elements from each area into your ACT prep lessons.

WHY THE ACT?

A Note From the Author

Not too many years ago, the ACT eclipsed the SAT to become the #1 college readiness exam. More than two million students take it each year, and almost as many college aspirations hinge on its outcome.

Standardized testing in general, not only of the three-letter college readiness variety, has gradually taken a dominant role in the world of education during the era of accountability.

In the past five years, we have seen a growing merger between these two facts of life in education. Many states now provide all of their students with the opportunity to take the ACT or SAT and have come to use the test for accountability purposes. The consensus is this lets the schools kill two birds with one stone: money is saved and the testing burden on teachers and students is lowered.

These policies create new dynamics. Many students are taking the ACT who might never have registered for the test on their own. Some of these students are surpassing their own expectations and earning both scholarships and entry into choice colleges by virtue of their scores. Many more are scoring far too low for that happy outcome. State departments of education are forcing the issue: districts must increase the percentage of students who are exiting high school "college ready" or face dire accountability consequences. A test that was once the worry only of parents, students, and guidance counselors is now one of the major performance indicators for core teachers and school administrators.

In many ways, these radical changes in the testing landscape are not radical at all. If there is one constant in the world of testing and accountability, it is *change*. In our professional development programs, we often ask for a show of hands from teachers who have been in education more than ten years. We then ask them how many times their accountability system or standardized test has changed. It's a rare teacher who doesn't give a number of changes equal to the number of years they have been in the system!

At MasteryPrep, we believe that the new emphasis high schools are placing on the ACT is more than just a new fad that will soon fade, more than the accountability flavor of the month, more than just the next test that gets in the way of instructional time. High school emphasis on the ACT presents a rare opportunity for educators and principals, an opportunity that should be seized.

At any given high school, there is now an unprecedented alignment of interests surrounding this college readiness exam. Parents and students have always had a vested interest in their ACT scores: the test directly affects their futures and their pocketbooks. Now, everyone has a vested interest, from the student all the way up to the state superintendent of education. The result is that more resources are provided to teachers who are working to improve students' ACT scores.

But that is only a sliver of the opportunity. It turns out that what works best to improve student ACT scores only has a little to do with time management and test-taking strategies. Yes, it's important that students be able to handle timed tests, both for the ACT in future college courses. It's also true that the critical thinking and logic skills that make a good test-taker are well worth teaching and can impact ACT scores. But what moves the dial on the ACT far and away more than anything else on the ACT is *content*, and not just any content, but the content that has been empirically proven to strongly correlate to students being ready to succeed in college.

Are you an English teacher who *knows* your students need help with grammar to be ready for life but are forced to stick with only literature in order to meet state mandates? Now, in order to improve ACT scores, you can make sure your students get the grammar help they need either in your class or during their RTI (Response to Intervention) time.

Are you a math teacher whose students are struggling with the basics? These weak fundamentals are exactly what is suppressing their math scores on the ACT. Because Johnny's mom wants him to earn a scholarship, Johnny will show up to that after-school ACT prep (read *math remediation*), and because the school needs Johnny's scores to go up, it will provide the resources *you* need to be successful with him.

We have seen time and again that if educators use ACT prep as an opportunity not to teach a test, but to provide meaningful remediation, dramatic improvements can be achieved at any school or district.

Our analysis of the ACT shows that students who do not have a college-ready score have not achieved competency in skills and concepts that are commonly taught by the ninth grade. In general, students just need more help, more practice, and more opportunities to master these subjects than they have been provided thus far. The time and resources you spend with your students in the name of ACT prep can fill that gap.

We ask you to consider joining us in redefining ACT prep as *college readiness remediation*. Let's get students ready for this test, sure, but let's also get them ready for life by teaching them the fundamentals in English, math, reading, and science that they need to succeed not only on the ACT but also in college.

If you are a school or district administrator, use the ACT as a rallying cry to bring your community together around a life event that makes a huge difference in your students' prospects. Their ACT scores can make or break them. Over the long term, the number of new college graduates could even make or break the future of your city. This is even in the best interests of local businesses and community partners, and they should get involved to help. When they do, see to it that what results is *meaningful remediation* instead of the fluff and tricks that qualifies as commercial test preparation.

This book is the blueprint for how to radically improve ACT scores at your schools. Your students could be earning millions of scholarship dollars each year. They could be routinely gaining entry into elite colleges. Your campus could become an academic center in your community, and if it already is, it could become even more so.

Systemically improving ACT scores isn't easy. It can't be done in a single year. There are many pieces to the puzzle: The intangibles (such as student motivation); effective remediation on topics that impact college readiness (English, math, reading, and science); and, yes, time management and test-taking strategies.

This book provides the roadmap for making that happen. Based on an analysis of over 50 actual ACT tests administered over the past two decades, more than 10 million student responses to ACT questions, and our experience in helping over 700 schools and school districts improve their ACT outcomes, we will provide you with guidance on exactly *what works* and *what doesn't* to get the results you want and need.

Much of the information that we provide has heretofore only been available to our product development team. Our business partners have advised heavily against us releasing this data, as it will undoubtedly enable competitors to "borrow" our techniques and begin to rival our results. But we feel strongly that each campus needs at least one on-site expert to present this content, someone who can advise the school on what needs to be done to improve student outcomes. That person, in case you haven't already picked up the not-so-subtle hint, is you. Or at least, *will* be you, after you finish this program.

MasteryPrep's goal is to double the number of students who are graduating from high school college-ready in English, math, reading, and science. Right now, only 25% of students in the U.S. meet this standard in all four subject areas. With our school and district partners, we are beginning to turn that tide. We need your help to make it happen.

It's an exciting time to be in education, helping students get ready for college and working with them to boost their ACT scores. It's a high-stakes game; if students don't get the remediation they need now, they'll have to get it at the community college, and we've all heard of the abysmal persistence rates of students forced to take remedial, not-for-credit college courses. However, the rewards match the stakes: there's nothing better than making a significant, measurable impact on a student's future. We're excited that you're in the game with us, helping students to succeed on the ACT, in education, and in life.

Best wishes,

Craig Gehring

ACT ORIENTATION
An Introduction to Impoving ACT Scores

Getting Students Motivated

Motivation is an essential factor to consider on any standardized assessment. Quite simply, if students don't care about the outcome of a test, they are unlikely to do well on it.

Regarding motivation there is a battle, and then there is a war. The battle is how students feel about the ACT in particular and whether or not they sustain what motivation they have throughout the three-hour testing ordeal. The larger war concerns the state of the student's level of academic motivation as a whole.

How important is school to your students? How important is it to them that they do well? Does school align with their life plans? Do your students feel like school will take them where they want to go?

If a large percentage of your students are blowing off the ACT, chances are that these same students blow off other tests and academic activities as well.

In this chapter, we provide some practical tips and ideas for getting students motivated to do well on the ACT. They all have a common thread: they remind students about what's in it for them—the benefit they receive from doing well on the ACT. These motivators also remind students that their efforts can be rewarded. It is possible for them to get a better score on the test if they put in the hard work and come to the test prepared and focused.

Use these ideas to get your students motivated for an ACT prep session or for an upcoming test date.

The next chapter provides ideas for motivating students academically across multiple dimensions, extrinsically and intrinsically.

In our final chapters on motivation, we delve into modern motivation theory and discuss big-picture strategy for motivating your students academically and thus transforming (or evolving) your campus culture. We also describe five motivation killers to avoid at all costs.

Let's first take a look at the battle and examine some arguments you can pose to your students to extract the extra effort you need in prep or before test day.

The Most Important Number

Ask your students to visualize all of the work they have put into their high school careers. That means all of their schoolwork for all 20+ courses. Ask them what is the latest they have stayed up to complete a project or study for a final exam. See how many of them have pulled all-nighters. Count up the study groups, hours spent cramming during lunch or on the bus, all of their homework. All of that effort is so they can graduate, and it's summarized by a single number: their GPA.

And yet, there is one number that scholarship committees and college admissions boards look at before they consider GPA. There is one number that is weighted more heavily. As a matter of fact, GPA is considered through the lens of this number. It's the most important number on your students' college or scholarship applications. This number is their ACT score.

Even the students who are the most intense about studying for the ACT don't seem to be in on this secret. They study for the ACT like they would study for an important final exam. In reality, in terms of future opportunities, your students' ACT is weighted more heavily than all of their final exams, combined.

If your students value the importance of the ACT, are diligent in studying for it, and take it seriously on test day, they'll have a major advantage over most of the two million students who take the test each year.

Student Loans

Students who have high ACT scores are more likely to earn scholarships and avoid student loans.

Do your students know that student loans are one of the only types of debt that stick with them even if they go bankrupt? If they don't pay them back by the time they retire, they'll even be taken out of their social security!

One eye-opening exercise is to have your students tally up their impending tuition costs, books, and housing, add interest, and then figure out the final cost of college without scholarships.

Other teachers have found success in telling their students to imagine that each point on the ACT is worth a thousand dollars in scholarships, money they don't have to pay back in student loans, a thousand *real* dollars (actually, each point is probably worth more like $5,000). Every time their attention wavers, students are reminded that ACT preparation is probably the highest-paying job they will have for quite some time. They just have to earn those points.

Finishing School

Students with higher ACT scores are better prepared for college, which means that they are more likely to actually *finish* school and get a degree. They're less likely to take a break that never ends.

The last thing students want is to accumulate a huge pile of student loan debt and then never get the added earning power from a college degree that they need in order to pay it off.

One Million Dollars

Students who complete college and get a degree on average earn over one million dollars more over the course of their lifetime than students who only complete high school. The higher students' ACT scores are, the more likely they will successfully complete college, not to mention how much easier it will be for them to get there.

M&Ms

A group of researchers did an interesting study with the IQ test. This test is supposed to give a score measuring intelligence on a scale of about 50 to 150, and this score should not change. According to psychologists, you would have the same IQ in third grade as in eleventh grade, even if you studied harder than anyone else during that time.

In this study, researchers gave a group of elementary school students an IQ test. Seven weeks later, they gave them another IQ test. They should have had the same score on the test, but they didn't. That's because the researchers told the students that they would get an M&M for each correct answer.

The average IQ of those students increased by 12 points!

Those were some powerful M&Ms. This study highlights the power of motivation. If an *IQ* can change by becoming more motivated about taking the test, your students' scores on the ACT can *definitely* change. In fact, the ACT was designed to be changeable: the more students learn, the better they perform.

That doesn't mean , necessarily, that you should feed your students an M&M after every correct answer they get. What it does mean is that it's a good idea to establish with your students a clear concept of *what's in it for them* when they take the ACT test. What do they have to gain? That's their M&M. Why do they want a high ACT score? What does a high ACT score mean for them in their life? The answers to these questions will vary from student to student, but it's worth the work to help each of your students understand what reward they can get for keeping their head in the game as they take the ACT.

Before they begin the ACT and at the start of each test section, remind your students to pull out their "M&M." They should do this when they're thinking about quitting and just guessing on the rest of the test. And tell them that if they *really* want their scores to increase, they need to focus on their M&M before each ACT prep session as well.

(This study is discussed in detail in *How Children Succeed* by Paul Tough.)

You Can Do It

The most fundamental, widespread, and yet nearly invisible motivation killer is your students' deep-seated suspicion that they can't do it: that no matter how hard they try, they won't get a good score on the ACT.

If students feel like their effort won't be rewarded, they won't make the effort. This is a completely logical response. What's more, "I didn't try," sounds a lot cooler than "I failed."

This is a difficult factor to address because students won't come out and tell you it's a problem.

There are few ways to combat this:

- **Social Proof:** As often as you can, celebrate peer accomplishment. When one student sees a classmate succeeding, particularly if those two students are in parity academically, it *proves* that it's possible. Anecdotes about other students succeeding on the ACT can also support this process, particularly if you take the time to prove the similarities between the students in the anecdotes and *your* students in the classroom.

- **Correct Difficulty:** Start with the easier questions that many students in the room know how to answer. Use scaffolding as necessary. Don't let ACT prep become defined in your students' minds as "that segment of time where we have no idea what is going on." If that happens, you are only reinforcing the "I can't do it" philosophy and *de-motivating* your students. Avoid working on the ACT practice questions that all of your students missed. By definition, these are the hardest questions and usually appear the most infrequently on subsequent tests. Focus first on the low-hanging fruit. Use early wins to build momentum.

- **Realistic, Valuable Goals:** All students want a "good score" on the ACT, but most aren't clear on what that means. Make sure that your students know what "good" is. If your student has a 17 on the ACT and feels like improvement is impossible because he can't reach 30, he doesn't understand how the ACT works. If he can get up to 21, he could earn college scholarships and totally change his future. He would only have to answer about half of the questions correctly to accomplish this! Ensure that your students have a goal they can achieve and that they understand the personal value they can obtain from reaching this goal.

Motivation Strategy

It can be helpful to view your strategy for motivating students through the lens of modern motivation theory. One major motivation model is called *self-determination theory*, which describes three needs and three motivation dimensions.

We are not motivation psychologists and recommend a thorough reading of Edward Deci and Richard Ryan's work on the subject as well as related texts, but some basic, broad strokes will serve us well here.

Three Needs

The three needs are as follows:

- **Autonomy:** Autonomy is the urge to be the causal agent of one's own life (I'm in charge of myself, you're not my boss, etc.) and to take actions in harmony with one's integrated self ("to thine own self be true").

- **Competence:** Competence refers to the urge to control the outcome (of anything and everything) and experience mastery (the result of having controlled an outcome or at least being able to do so). We want to learn how to drive, and it's a much more pleasant experience when the car listens to us than when it skids out of control.

- **Relatedness:** Relatedness is the urge to interact, to be connected to others, and to experience caring for others. It's communication and people. It causes society.

Three Motivation Dimensions

There are three major types of motivation:

- **Intrinsic:** Motivation to do (or not do) something based solely on how that thing satisfies or fails to satisfy needs. For example, taking an ACT test might violate *autonomy* ("I have to take this during school, and I didn't choose to be here to begin with."), *competence* ("I have no idea how to do this, and my score is just going to remind me how little I actually know."), and *relatedness* ("I don't get to talk with anyone but my bubble sheet for three hours."). If these were the only motivational factors involved, we could say this student is intrinsically motivated *not* to take the ACT.

- **Extrinsic:** Motivation to do (or not do) something based solely on how other, external factors related to the thing satisfy or fail to satisfy needs. To continue our example, if a student were to skip school when the ACT is being administered, he could be violating his need for *autonomy* since he knows that people who skip without a written excuse are forced to accept consequences. He might also be violating *relatedness*, because a teacher he admires might chide him or think less of him. Rewards and penalties fit squarely into the extrinsic motivation category.

- **Amotivation:** An absence of any connection between one's actions and the resulting outcomes. In the case of *amotivation*, we are dealing with a topic where it doesn't make sense to get motivated because motivation is what causes action. If one is convinced that there is no action that can be taken to affect the outcome, then even if the outcome could impact that person dearly, amotivation produces inaction. To round out our example, your student might be convinced that he can't improve his ACT score. He may have even taken the test a couple times, but nothing has improved. Your exhortations about how seriously he needs to take the ACT and about how the score will impact his future fall on deaf ears because he is amotivated. Yes, it's important. He'll even *agree with you* on that point. But without a pathway to cause change, he cannot be motivated to do the necessary work.

The Big Picture

For every student, preparing for and taking the ACT satisfies certain needs and frustrates others, often at the same time. They're teenagers, so the motivation picture is probably going to be as dramatic and complicated as possible.

If you want a campus that is motivated to do well in academics and on the ACT, your goal is to remove amotivation and create an environment where students feel that school, academics, and doing well on the ACT satisfy their needs more than frustrate them.

As part of your motivation plan, try to address all three needs in some way as well as include enhancements to both extrinsic and intrinsic motivation.

Here is a sample plan that covers all the points:

Intrinsic Motivation Plan

- **Autonomy:** Students do research on their own and select at least three colleges (a safety school, a goal, and a reach—a school they would really have to compete for). They will use their research on these schools to set a goal score for the ACT. After discussing school choices and ACT score goals with a guidance counselor, students can wear a jersey or T-shirt from one of these schools on the first Friday of each month.

- **Competence:** Conduct professional development with teachers to reinforce the concept of correctly sequencing ACT practice so that students have early wins. Praise loudly and often (bulletin boards, announcements, award ceremonies, etc.) any students who *improve* their ACT scores (instead of only recognizing students who achieve high scores).

- **Relatedness:** All students will participate in a *college club,* comprised of those students who plan on attending a particular school. Similar schools with only a few students in the club will be grouped together, and too large groups will be split up by grade. This allows students to make connections and feel that a community is moving with them beyond high school. Where possible, teachers or administrators who are alumni of these schools will lead the clubs, and during each club period they will help students explore different aspects of campus life, available classes and majors, notable graduates, etc. Arrange for campus visits to major destination schools and encourage students pursuing more exotic schools to make visits as well. Involve community partners to help defray the cost of visits for students who can't afford it.

Extrinsic Motivation Plan

- **Autonomy:** Any senior who reaches his or her score goal before the end of senior year and is accepted to college does not have to wear the uniform anymore (they still need to comply to a basic dress code).

- **Competence:** Any student who improves by two or more points on the ACT is recognized as a *rising star* and entered into a raffle to win an iPad donated by a community partner.

- **Relatedness:** Any student who participates fully in the ACT prep during Response to Intervention time and improves on the ACT gets to enjoy a pizza party.

Comments on Sample Plan

Note how the extrinsic blends with the intrinsic. For example, allowing students to wear a jersey at school upon completing their research project, in and of itself, is an extrinsic motivation—it is its own reward and has nothing to do with getting a good ACT score. And yet it has a powerful psychological impact because it reminds students of and reinforces the *intrinsic* value: they will get to attend a school that they themselves chose by achieving an ACT score that they personally set as a goal. This also sets the course to becoming their own person and deciding what life after high school will look like. Whenever possible, tie the extrinsic to the intrinsic; wearing a college T-shirt is a better reward than a doughnut party.

Missing Out

Keep in mind that having an incentive program in place can do double-duty because of how basic needs work. When students *miss out* on an incentive, they have a powerful motivation to take seriously the *next* opportunity to earn an incentive. Missing out jams all of their *autonomy, competence,* and *relatedness* buttons. They want to wear that jersey but aren't allowed to, and they feel incompetent because they didn't control the outcome, *and* they don't feel connected to their peers who *are* wearing jerseys. They will certainly have their research project done before the free dress Friday rolls around!

The *carrot* is less motivation than *missing out* on the carrot.

Tap into this fact by having your incentive programs trigger rewards early in the year. Once a group of students win, make sure that the incentive is *highly visible.*

One principal told me she likes to have her pizza parties in the hallway when the cafeteria serves mystery meat. She actually peruses the monthly menu and picks the day that looks like the food will be the worst! She makes sure all the pizza boxes are open so that the delicious, cheesy aroma permeates the school. Needless to say, everyone wants to get in to that pizza party!

Another thing to keep in mind is that you have to be ruthless about your incentives. If students miss by a fraction of a point on an incentive goal, no dice. Otherwise, you are weakening one of the most powerful aspects of extrinsic incentives that you can wield.

Five Motivation Killers

Beware of these five motivation killers. They happen all too often during ACT preparation courses.

1. Testing too much.

ACT prep often takes this form: students take a full-length practice test, then review the whole test with their teacher. After review, they take another full-length test, and another, and another. This kills motivation. It's exhausting and burns students out. What's more, most students find the experience to be overwhelming. It's very difficult for students to feel like they are making gains. A variant of this issue is when students take tons of actual tests without much prep. The parent thinks that if Johnny takes the ACT just one more time, he'll magically get the ACT score he needs. Chances are he'll just eventually quit and refuse to take any more without reaching his goal score.

2. Random ACT questions or bell ringers.

This is another common form of school-based ACT prep. The teacher has a *Real ACT Prep Guide* and through the *eeny meeny miney mo* method he selects an item of the day to start class with. Unfortunately, more than a third of the questions he selects are too advanced, which reinforces his students' suspicion that prepping for the ACT is a lost cause.

3. Moving too quickly.

The enormous scope of the ACT tends to induce frenzy on the part of the ACT prep instructor. She feels like she needs to cover *everything*, but in doing so, she covers *nothing*. The most likely reason students miss a question is because they have a skill deficiency; remedying this skill takes work and much *time*. Students need plenty of practice with the skill in isolation. Shortcutting this process will only cause you to lose your students. If you could have your students master just 20% more of the test, you would help them make *miraculous* score improvements. So don't try to blitz through all 100%—you'll only crush with confusion what motivation and goodwill you've managed to build up.

4. Not controlling the sequence of ACT prep.

From a pedagogical perspective, the sequence in which ACT questions appear on the test is random. The math test bounces from pre-algebra to trig to geometry with wild abandon. The English test might start with parallel structure and end with complete sentences. Curricular sequence is disregarded on the ACT, but it cannot be disregarded in ACT prep or else you risk losing your students. Group similar questions together, and then stick with one topic at a time. In as logical a sequence as possible, build from one idea to the next. Move through one subject area at a time (English, math, reading, science).

5. Assuming your students know the basics and skipping them.

You know that saying about what happens when you assume. The *basics* are preventing your students from scoring well on the ACT, but your students are not going to speak up about not having mastered the basics. It's embarrassing. But if you don't catch that your students need a review of the basics, or if you make assumptions about these basics when you give explanations, your students will nod their heads on the outside and nod off to sleep on the inside. Explanations that don't make sense to your students only reinforce their insecurities. To them, if they can't understand the ACT question even *after* the explanation, then they *know* the cause is lost. Mitigate against this by building from the basics (even briefly) with any explanation you engage in.

A common thread of the five motivation killers is that if you treat school-based ACT prep like commercial ACT prep, you'll lose. But if you take a more remedial approach, your students are more likely to stick with you.

What the ACT Measures

A simplistic but nonetheless accurate model of what the ACT measures can be represented by the "three R's." We add a fourth "R" for good measure:

- Reading

- Writing

- Arithmetic

- Reasoning

If you were to rank your students by their reading level, their ability to write (in grammatically correct sentences), their skill with arithmetic and mental math, and by their ability to reason and use logic, chances are you would also accomplish a roughly accurate ranking of your students by their ACT scores.

The ACT is a fundamentally sound test, empirically polished over decades. It does a fair job assessing the core competencies students need in order to do well in college. There are many more skills being tested than the *4R's*, but these form a core you can use to visualize your goal for ACT prep. Yes, you're working on individual skills and strategies, but your overall goal—the peak of the mountain you're scaling—is to help your students become stronger in these four core areas.

Many aspects of these competencies seem to have nothing to do with ACT prep at all, and yet they can have major positive impacts on ACT outcomes. For example, it may seem that increasing a student's reading level belongs to reading remediation, but it's also one of the best things you can do for a student struggling with a low ACT score.

Predictive Validity of ACT Scores

In 2008 ACT Inc. released a paper titled *The Relative Predictive Validity of ACT Scores and High School Grades in Making College Admission Decisions*. It is highly demonstrative of what the ACT assesses and our simplified *4R's* model fully aligns with it.

In the paper, data from over 200,000 students was analyzed to examine ACT scores and high school grade point averages, as well as the ability of these factors to predict five college success indicators:

- **First-Year College GPA:** What was the student's college GPA at the end of the first year?

- **Enrollment/Retention Status:** Did the student continue to a second year of college?

- **Collegiate Assessment of Academic Proficiency:** What were the student's scores on the CAAP test?

- **Final College GPA:** What was the student's GPA at the end of his or her college career?

- **Degree-Attainment Level:** Did the student attain a degree, and if so, what level of degree?

The paper reported that high school GPA was a much better predictor of final college GPA. In other words, if students could meet high school classroom expectations, they could probably meet college classroom expectations.

However, the ACT was a much better predictor of a student's degree-attainment level. In other words, a high ACT score was more accurate than a high GPA in predicting whether students actually finished college and received degrees, even whether they went on to even higher levels of learning.

High school GPA, it seems, is almost useless in predicting whether or not students will attain a college degree. Is it reasonable to expect anything different? Teachers are tasked to assess how students *did* in their class, not predict how they *will do* in college. For many decades the ACT has been working to accomplish just that: predict degree attainment.

The ACT is measuring something different than GPA. It is assessing core academic competencies that correlate to students persevering in college and obtaining a degree, the same competencies as those listed above.

By improving your students' ACT scores, you are helping them improve their core academic competencies and improving the likelihood that they will actually finish college and attain a degree.

How the ACT Is Scored

Most students enter the ACT possessing only the slightest clue about how the ACT is scored.

If you poll your classroom, most of your students will probably be able to tell you that it's scored from 1 to 36. A smaller number will tell you that four subject scores of 1–36 are averaged to give a composite score ranging between 1 and 36. Only a select few will be able to go into much more detail than that.

For exactly this reason, students who know how the ACT is scored have a huge advantage. These students will suffer less test anxiety, improve in time management, and even apply test-taking strategies with more efficiency. The road to becoming a better test taker begins with understanding the test and how it measures performance.

Likewise, you must know how the ACT is scored if you're going to set realistic goals for improvement.

Raw Score

Every question on the ACT is worth one raw point. There are a total of 215 questions spread over four subject areas. Every single question is worth the same: one raw point. If students answer the question correctly, they get the point. If they don't answer the question correctly, they don't get the point. There is no penalty for guessing. The consequence for leaving a question blank is identical to the consequence for answering it incorrectly (whether students guessed on it or not): they don't get the raw point.

These facts of ACT life form the foundation upon which many time management and test-taking strategies are built. First of all, students must *never leave an answer blank*. A guess is always *much* stronger than leaving a blank. Secondly, because they have the opportunity to hazard a penalty-free guess, students must be very clever in their guesses. And lastly, because every question is worth the same, students must be sure to *move through the entire test* within the time limit, allowing themselves the opportunity to consider *every question* and avoiding wasting time on questions that are too difficult.

Students receive a *raw score* for each subject area, which is simply the total number of raw points they earned on each subject test. For example, since there are 75 questions in English, 75 raw points are possible.

Conversion Tables and Scale Scores

Please refer to page 59 of *Preparing for the ACT 2015-16.*

The ACT uses a *conversion table* to convert raw scores into scale scores for each subject area. These scale scores range from 1 to 36, although in actual practice the lowest score, even for a student who makes random patterns on his bubble sheet, is around 9.

To arrive at the all-important composite score, the ACT averages the four scale scores. Scores are rounded to the nearest whole number, so a score of 25.25 is rounded to a 25 while a 25.5 is rounded to a 26. Yes, students can literally be 0.25 points away from the scholarship eligibility they are aiming for.

Every ACT test has a different *conversion table*. That means that a raw score of 30 in Math may garner a scale score of 20 on one test, but a 19 on another.

Essentially, the conversion table curves the test. Harder tests are given more forgiving conversion tables.

You may have had the experience of students telling you that a particular ACT test was more difficult or easier. This is possible. It's also possible that those same students might have scored the same or worse on the "easier" test because of the curve!

Scale Scores vs. Raw Scores

You'll notice that certain scale scores are associated with more than one raw score. This tends to happen especially in the middle ranges between 17 and 25. It might take two, three, or even four raw points to increase a scale score by one point.

This phenomenon has two effects. Because it takes fewer raw points to increase scale scores at higher score ranges, if students have a subject they are strong in, they should *prioritize* that subject in their ACT prep. This is counterintuitive: typically, we want to focus on where students are weak and help them improve. Actually, we still focus on students' weak areas within their stronger subject, but the point is for students to spend the most time and energy on the subject they do best in. Not only are students more likely to respond to prep in their strong subjects, but it is also easier to pick up scale points because it requires less improvement (less additional raw points) to do so.

The second effect of this phenomenon is that it makes scale scores a deceptive yardstick when teachers set growth goals. Suppose you have a group of students you are working with in Math. Their scale scores average a 15. You set a goal of 20% growth. It would seem that the goal scale score is 18, but that's not the case. First of all, moving a group of students from 15 to 18 is equivalent of improving them by about 27 performance percentiles (in other words, improving over 27% of their peers, from the 14th percentile to the 41st percentile), but that is beside the point. Look at the sample conversion table in *Preparing for the ACT 2015-16*. A scale score of 15 in this Math test is associated with a raw score as low as 13. To score an 18, students must answer at least 24 questions correctly. You are really asking for an 85% increase in the number of correct answers. When you say 20% growth, what you more likely mean is a 20% increase in the number of *questions* answered correctly. In this test, that would equal a one-point scale score increase.

When setting growth goals, scale scores can still be useful because they allow you to compare multiple tests. But if you use them, be sure to look at the *raw scores* and see what the scale score increases actually mean in terms of questions answered correctly.

As you can probably tell, the interaction between scale scores and raw scores can mask gains, especially in the eyes of students. A one-point increase on a 100-point midterm means almost nothing to a student, and so a one-point increase on a scale score might not feel like progress, either. However, depending on where the student has started, one extra point on a scale score could be quite significant, the fruit of a lot of hard work and effort on the part of the student.

By helping your students understand how the scoring process works, you are helping them measure their own progress and maintain a higher motivation level.

MasteryPrep Conversion Tables

When students set a goal for their scale score, they should also set a goal for their *raw score*—how many questions they need answer correctly in each of the four subtests on the ACT.

If students only have a scale score goal, they don't really have a goal. They know they need a 25, but they don't know what that means. No other test has the ACT's specific scale system. Your students are probably only familiar with tests on a percentage scale based on the number of questions answered correctly. A 25 is meaningless in terms of informing your students' strategy.

Students need to convert that 25 scale score into a raw score. They must to go into the test knowing exactly how many questions they need to answer correctly and how many questions they can afford to miss. This knowledge breeds confidence and naturally makes students better test takers. You would be amazed how many students go into the ACT with a goal score of 21 feeling like they need to get an "A" on the test: 90% right. If they think this way, even instinctively, their time management will be completely off. They'll stick with difficult questions way too long because every question feels like mission critical. Much more likely to succeed is the student going for 21 who knows she only needs to correctly answer 34 out of 60 questions on the Math test, for example. This student won't suffer anxiety from a few (or even 20) questions that stump her.

One problem with this approach, however, is that if you use a conversion table to help your students determine what raw scores they need, you are only giving them the raw scores for *one* test. It's totally possible that when your students take a real ACT test, they could achieve their raw score goal but miss their scale score goal because of differences in the conversion table (the curve of the test).

We have solved this issue by analyzing over 30 actual ACT conversion tables from the past two decades and creating two predictive conversion tables that are highly suited for setting raw score goals. One is designed for students, the other for educators.

Our *student* conversion table gives the raw scores that practically guarantee a given scale score. If students achieve the raw score given for a particular scale score, they are more than 97% likely to achieve that scale score (and will probably end up with a *higher* scale score than that).

In each section of this book (English, Math, Reading, and Science) we provide additional information about how to use the student conversion table to set goals for growth. Every student should have a raw score goal, their "number" they are trying to hit, for each test section.

Our *averaged* conversion table is suited for educators who want to understand the relationship between raw scores and scale scores and use that information to set goals for growth in their class. This conversion table represents the mathematical mean of all of the conversion tables we analyzed. In other words, the *averaged* conversion table represents the *most likely* conversion table to be used for any given test.

We recommend against using the *averaged* conversion table with students because, by the very fact that it is *averaged*, roughly half of all conversion tables represent a tougher curve than what is shown here. If your students use the averaged conversion table, they might reach their raw score goal but still miss their scale score goal, which defeats the purpose.

Please feel free to copy these conversion tables and distribute to students as you see fit. An easy-to-print PDF is also available for you at masteryprep.com/decode/resources.

SCALE SCORE	AVERAGED RAW SCORE CONVERSION TABLE				SCALE SCORE
	ENGLISH	MATH	READING	SCIENCE	
36	75.00	59.76	39.84	39.79	36
35	73.71	58.28	38.63	38.50	35
34	72.27	56.80	37.93	37.75	34
33	71.08	55.53	36.97	36.90	33
32	70.00	54.29	35.98	36.23	32
31	69.10	53.06	35.07	35.45	31
30	67.89	51.71	34.03	35.00	30
29	66.48	50.08	32.87	33.89	29
28	64.98	48.16	31.81	33.02	28
27	63.34	45.89	30.64	31.76	27
26	61.47	43.44	29.56	30.42	26
25	59.34	40.95	28.48	28.82	25
24	56.97	38.45	27.26	27.10	24
23	54.52	36.10	25.92	25.42	23
22	51.98	34.05	24.55	23.73	22
21	49.10	32.26	23.19	22.03	21
20	46.00	30.44	21.77	20.18	20
19	43.19	28.39	20.35	18.34	19
18	40.74	26.02	19.08	16.65	18
17	38.50	23.11	17.82	15.13	17
16	36.13	19.42	16.48	13.82	16
15	33.26	15.45	15.10	12.68	15
14	30.45	12.15	13.63	11.56	14
13	28.18	9.60	12.03	10.44	13
12	26.15	7.60	10.34	9.35	12
11	24.03	6.02	8.65	8.27	11
10	21.73	4.81	7.18	7.05	10
9	19.29	4.04	6.14	5.76	9
8	16.56	3.09	5.24	4.65	8
7	13.53	2.90	4.44	3.87	7
6	11.06	2.04	3.75	3.00	6
5	8.63	1.83	3.04	2.10	5
4	6.45	1.00	2.13	2.00	4
3	4.55	1.00	1.92	1.00	3
2	2.85		1.00	1.00	2
1	0.79	0.00	0.00	0.00	1

SCALE SCORE	STUDENT CONVERSION TABLE				SCALE SCORE
	ENGLISH	MATH	READING	SCIENCE	
36	75	60	40	40	36
35	74	59	39	39	35
34	73	58	39	39	34
33	72	59	38	38	33
32	71	57	37	38	32
31	71	55	37	38	31
30	69	53	36	37	30
29	68	52	35	36	29
28	67	50	34	36	28
27	65	47	33	34	27
26	63	45	32	33	26
25	61	42	31	31	25
24	59	40	30	30	24
23	57	37	29	28	23
22	54	36	27	27	22
21	52	34	26	25	21
20	49	32	24	23	20
19	46	30	22	21	19
18	43	28	21	19	18
17	41	25	19	17	17
16	38	20	18	15	16
15	35	17	16	14	15
14	33	14	15	13	14
13	31	12	13	12	13
12	29	9	12	11	12
11	26	7	10	10	11
10	24	6	8	8	10
9	21	5	7	7	9
8	18	4	6	6	8
7	15	3	5	5	7
6	12	3	4	4	6
5	9	2	4	3	5
4	7	1	3	2	4
3	5	1	2	1	3
2	3	-	1	1	2
1	0	0	0	0	1

TIME MASTERY
Time Management Strategies for the ACT

Introduction to Time Mastery

In this section we provide a brief overview of time management on the ACT and introduce two strategies that are applicable to all subject areas. We also introduce one of the most effective tools for coaching time management.

Each section of this book includes a wide variety of additional subject-specific time management strategies. This is only the first of five *Time Mastery* sections. The others are found on the pages given below.

The chart below provides the time limits for each test section on the ACT and a suggested pacing guide. More nuanced pacing guidance appears in each subject's *Time Mastery* section.

Subject	Items	Passages	Time Limit	Pace Guideline
English	75 questions	5 passages	45 minutes	8 minutes per passage
Math	60 questions	----	60 minutes	~1 minute per question
Reading	40 questions	4 passages	35 minutes	8 minutes per passage
Science	40 questions	6–7 passages	35 minutes	4–7 minutes per passage

Between the Math and Reading tests, students are given a short break (approximately 10 minutes).

Students should know this chart cold. The more familiar they are with the test, the less likely they are to experience test anxiety, and the more likely they are to make smart time management decisions.

A basic assumption of our time management strategies is that students have access to a clock or watch. Since there is no guarantee that the testing facility will have a functional clock on the wall (although it's in the ACT's testing specs, that doesn't mean it always happens), students should *always* wear a watch on test day. Students must ensure that their watch does not make sounds or have any alarms; if an alarm on a student's watch goes off, the test proctor will dismiss the student and his or her test will not be scored.

Time Management Skills

We break down time management into three distinct skills. There are actually many more than that, but these three broad categories can help you shape your overall strategy for improving time management with your students.

Pace

Pace is usually the easiest of the three skills to coach and can produce some phenomenal score gains when you do so. For some reason, it's also an area that receives short shrift in the test prep world.

Pace refers to your students' ability to be disciplined with their time and not allow one section of a test to eat into the time allocation of another. In English, Reading, and Science, this means that students who have mastered pace treat each passage like its own test. In Math, it means meeting specific question milestones within a given time limit. Students who are on-pace refuse to allow the third English passage, for example, to consume 12 minutes when they only have eight to give it.

Pace is largely a matter of discipline and practice. Students need to know how it feels to move through a passage in the time allotted, and they need enough practice to be able to do this naturally. Then, if a particular question threatens their pace, a ticking internal clock pressures them to move on.

In the end, pace is a decision. Even if students have a question left in a passage, *pace* dictates that they guess on the question and move to the next passage. Because of the random distribution of difficulty in English, Reading, and Science, students *have* to give themselves the opportunity to consider all the questions in each passage. The last passage might be the easiest.

Cherry-Picking

If pace puts the ACT under a magnifying glass to examine time management one passage at a time, then cherry-picking puts it under a microscope. This time management skill guides students through the decisions they will make on any one test question. If students have mastered pace, then they have a limited amount of time to work through each passage or group of questions. Usually they must cherry-pick to make the most of it.

By *cherry-picking*, we mean deciding to spend time on the sweetest questions, those most likely to yield points, and refusing to spend time on questions that will bear no fruit (no points) until all of the other questions associated with a given passage have been considered.

For example, let's say a student has just started her Reading test. Because she understands the importance of pace, she has allocated eight minutes for the first passage. After reading, she quickly answers questions #1 and #2. When she gets to question #3, she has to read the question a couple times and is drawing a complete blank. She recognizes that feeling: *this one is going to be a toughie.* So she bubbles in a guess, places an asterisk next to the question, and moves on to question #4, which she answers after scanning the passage a little. Once she gets to question #10, she checks her watch. She still has one minute, so she goes back to question #3 and gives it another shot. But if she *didn't* have that minute, if she had already reached the eight-minute mark, she would move on to the next passage. Good riddance, question #3!

The hallmark of good cherry-picking is quick decision-making. If students take more than a few seconds to decide whether to move past a question, much of the benefit of cherry-picking is lost. You'll notice that in the example above, because this student was good at cherry-picking, she ended up with an extra minute to go back and work on a question she skipped. If she had taken too long with the initial decision, she would have missed out.

Cherry-picking is necessary in part because students don't know how long it will take to answer the questions for a given passage or group of items until they reach the end of that set.

Stamina

Stamina looks at the big picture and answers this question: did students maintain their ability to *cherry-pick* and hit the correct *pace* throughout the entire test? Did they keep up a high energy level and a rapid clip from beginning to end? Or did they tire out and slow down as they approached the finish line?

Stamina is difficult to improve but a necessary aspect of test taking to consider. Can your students endure the ACT test marathon?

Stamina is built through a combination of practice and motivation. Your students must become competent at motivating themselves in order to do well; unfortunately, you can't magically appear over their shoulders and give them a rah-rah session before they start the Science test.

Stamina is also impacted by the "game day rituals" of your students. Did they sleep well the night (or week) before? Did they have breakfast that morning? Did they bring a snack, or are they starving by the end of the test? These seemingly small details can have an enormous impact on your students' ability to stick with it all three hours.

A Note on Sequence

We recommend coaching your students on time management roughly in the sequence provided in this chapter. *Pace* provides the context for all further time management skills; from there, *cherry-picking* helps students make additional time management gains. As you approach the upcoming ACT test date, give *stamina* its due.

Mark and Move

If students are correctly applying the concepts of pace and cherry-picking (see previous chapter), they will invariably encounter questions they don't know how to answer and must move past. If students have a definite routine they follow whenever they decide to move past a question for time management reasons, they are more likely not to linger unnecessarily and less likely to experience anxiety about not knowing the answer.

The Problem with Skipping

When students don't know an answer, the typical solution is to skip it. Students make a mark or asterisk near the question in their test booklets and move on to the next question.

Skipping poses at least two major problems. For one, students open themselves up to a transcription error. There's the risk that if they skip question #6, when they get to question #7, they'll bubble in the first available blank: #6. They don't discover their error until question #60 when they realize they have a blank left over, but by then it's too late. If you poll your class, you'll find that many students have made this mistake before. Even though the ACT alternates ABCDE and FGHJK on its bubble sheets, this error can still occur.

The second problem with skipping is that most students never have time to go back and consider the questions they skipped. Instead, when the proctor announces there are five minutes remaining (or worse, in the mad rush during the last ten seconds of the test), students blindly fill in guesses on the skipped questions. These are by definition the worst guesses possible. No eliminations are made. Students only have a 20% chance of guessing correctly in Math, and a 25% chance of guessing correctly in English, Reading and Science.

How to Mark and Move

Skipping causes errors and blind guesses. We recommend an alternative: *mark and move*.

When students apply the mark and move strategy, they never skip questions. They still place a mark or asterisk beside the question so they can come back to it if they have extra time, but they *mark* their best guess right then and there, making whatever eliminations they can.

The benefits of this simple technique are surprisingly significant. Even if students only make one accurate elimination with every guess, it can result in an entire scale point improvement on each subject area. Mark and move tilts the guessing game in your students' favor.

Making an educated guess on the fly takes some practice, so consider modeling this strategy for your students as well as leading some "we do" classroom activities, asking students to chime in about likely eliminations for a tough question.

To reinforce this skill, after an ACT practice test, ask your students if they remembered to mark and move. Then, ask if they got a question right by marking and moving.

You can also walk around the room and check for blank rows: if students are marking and moving, their answer sheets should never have a blank row between bubbled rows.

Head Down

Students must use every second that is available to them in order to maximize their scores. They should have their *heads down*, working, from the beginning of the test to the end.

It's amazing how many advanced students put their pencils down during a test section before time is up. Very rarely do these students answer every question perfectly. Instead, they should spend the remaining time double- and triple-checking their answers. They can also try to attack a problematic question from a different angle. They can scan the test document for anything that might help them solve a difficult problem (like grammar examples from earlier or later passages that show the right pattern). *Anything* is better and more fruitful than staring smugly into space! There is no blank on the answer document where the proctor marks how quickly students finished the test. They don't get any brownie points for finishing early.

Likewise, it's a common occurrence for students at every score range to stop before time is up, even if there are many questions that the student has *marked and moved* past. Their thinking goes something like this: "I have answered everything that I can. I guessed on all the rest. I've taken this as far as I am able."

The thing is, they *haven't* taken it as far as they are able, not by a long shot. It is time-consuming to eliminate answer choices, particularly when the question is difficult, but at the very least students can work on *that*. Every elimination, every wrong answer they knock out, is in fact worth a fraction of a point. By improving their guesses, they are improving their scores.

Get your students to commit to keeping their heads down as they work through every second of the test from beginning to end. Challenge them to practice like they want to perform and call out those who don't apply this strategy during practice tests. Commend those students who stay committed.

It can help to have your students visualize all of the students they are competing against. Some of them are quitting early, either out of cockiness or apathy. Your students can beat them just by working harder!

Mini-Tests

Mini-tests can be a powerful tool to develop your students' time management skills.

A mini-test is a portion of a full-length ACT test section. For example, a mini-test might be one Science passage and the seven questions that go with it.

Some test prep programs like to provide full-length ACT tests. While one full-length ACT at the outset of a prep class can be very beneficial, providing a wealth of data to the instructor and introducing students to the upcoming challenge, multiple full-length practice tests will result in diminishing returns.

The reason for this is that a full-length ACT test does not leave much room for coaching. By the end of it, students are exhausted. They don't remember what happened or what they were thinking at the beginning of the test. It's an assessment, not a coaching opportunity.

Much, much better for our purposes of test prep is the mini-test: a small segment, timed exactly at the pace you want your students to achieve, with coaching immediately afterward on relevant test-taking techniques, time management, and content. The mini-test closes the feedback loop that all too often is left wide open in ACT prep.

Practice makes permanent, so it is essential that students participate in the mini-tests the same way they want to perform on the ACT. They should apply all of the strategies they have learned. They should imagine they are actually in an ACT testing environment.

During the mini-test, you can and should provide verbal cues to help students understand whether or not they are on track. A best practice is to gradually reduce the verbal cues until students keep the correct pace without any cues at all.

In each of the subject-specific *Time Mastery* sections of this book, we provide detailed tips and strategies on how to maximize the value of this vital tool. We also provide sample mini-tests as well as links to sources of additional practice tests.

Used correctly, mini-tests can pave the road to better time management and better scores.

TEST MASTERY
Test-Taking Strategies for the ACT

Introduction to Test Mastery

Test mastery helps students become better thinkers and better test takers. Most of the strategies discussed in the *Test Mastery* sections of this book are applied once all else has failed. This is when students don't know the "right" way to answer a question, but through reasoning can arrive at the right answer anyway.

There is no such thing as a naturally good test taker. There are only naturally bad test takers. If students are good test takers, it's because somewhere along the way they learned the reasoning skills so essential to performing well on standardized tests.

If you have a class full of naturally bad test takers, take heart. By applying the strategies in this book, your classroom will be to the brim with test whizzes in no time.

Students need *many* opportunities to master a test-taking skill. Encourage the teachers on your campus to integrate some of these concepts into their classrooms for maximum impact. It can take a year or more for students to transform from awful test takers to strong ones, but along the way their standardized test scores will steadily rise.

This is the first of five *Test Mastery* sections. The others are found on the pages given below.

Process of Elimination

The process of elimination is *the* fundamental skill underlying all test-taking techniques.

Our analysis of over 10 million student responses to ACT questions shows that most students don't use the process of elimination on questions that are giving them trouble. Instead, the most common response to a difficult question is to guess blindly.

Students must learn to use the process of elimination even if they are confused or under pressure. They must become so familiar with this process that it occurs to them naturally.

Unfortunately, the process of elimination is not a naturally developing process. It must be learned. Psychologists call this skill by another name: falsification. *Falsification* is the mental act of proving something wrong.

The naturally developed process is the opposite of what would actually help a student on a test. Students naturally tend toward *confirmation bias*. Students who are using their confirmation bias on the ACT find an answer they like and then look for any evidence that proves their hunch was correct. Students with strong confirmation bias make bad test takers.

This falsification/confirmation bias dichotomy is the crux of whether a student is a "good test taker" or a "bad" one.

Since falsification is not a naturally developing skill, there really is no such thing as a natural test taker. Somewhere along the line, the "good test taker" had help learning logic. They learned how to prove something *wrong*.

Some students might find it useful to learn that this strategy can not only help them do well on a test but can also help them do better in life as well. Falsification will help them figure out whether or not a friend is really a frenemy. Falsification helps them avoid that dead-end job. Falsification helps them make a decision when Mr. Right turns out to be Mr. Wrong. In all of these examples, confirmation bias can only get them into deeper and deeper trouble.

If you are working with a classroom of "bad test takers," don't be discouraged. There is hope for them to learn falsification yet. Below are three strategies that will bolster your students' ability to use the process of elimination. Additionally, you'll find that many of the strategies and exercises described in this book tie into the process of elimination in some way.

Model

Students need to see what the process of elimination looks like before they can do it themselves. Some students have spent their entire high school careers answering constructed response questions and so applying the process of elimination to a test item is a foreign concept.

Whenever possible, take the opportunity to demonstrate not only why a correct answer is correct but also why the wrong answers are wrong.

Explaining why an answer is correct will help students with the one or two questions related to that topic, but the thinking process you model for them (for both correct and incorrect answer choices) will guide them on every test they ever take and will help them in life as well.

Ask for Eliminations

When you are discussing a question with the class, consider first asking students to provide you with eliminations *before* you discuss the correct answer. Be sure to have students justify their thinking.

This concept applies not only to multiple-choice questions. Consider sometimes taking the approach of asking students to *disprove* (rather than support) an idea, theory, or assertion. The logical progression students must work through to complete such an activity will bolster your students' skill with falsification.

Logic Puzzles and Games

Logic puzzles and competitive games such as chess have a strong positive impact on your students' test-taking skills because they reinforce the essential skill of falsification. If your school has a chess club or a logic course, encourage your students to participate.

A note to educators at elementary and middle schools: consider lobbying your school to introduce logic games and activities to students in lower grades. In many school districts, only students participating in gifted programs receive an early introduction to logic. However, the students who would stand to benefit the most from such activities might not be allowed to participate in a gifted program.

Don't Second Guess

Your students' first guesses are usually their best guesses.

A *second guess* is when students convert a guess into another guess. Usually, their second guess leads them astray. Their instincts had it right the first time.

By all means, if students have figured out the correct answer to a question, they should erase their guess and mark the correct answer instead.

But most erasures aren't because students have figured out the correct answer. Rather, they are the result of students doubting themselves and over-thinking.

Keep a sharp eye out for students who take mini-tests with their eraser pointed at the paper. Look for bubble sheets where it seems that students marked and erased half the available choices, where it seems like they wanted to bore a hole through their answer sheets with their eraser tips. Coach them to never second guess.

If you notice this problem is prevalent in your class, ask this question every few mini-tests: "How many of you chose a correct answer, then changed it to the incorrect answer?" When several students groan and raise their hands, remind the class, "That is second-guessing. Trust your instincts. Your first guess is usually your best guess."

Yards After Contact

Football commentators have a new statistic that they're fascinated with. It's called *yards after contact*, measuring the distance that a running back is able to travel after he gets hit. It's a metric that shows a combination of stability, toughness, and grit.

Anyone can run to the end zone if the opposing team never touches them. The true test of greatness is if you can continue on even after taking a few hits.

For the test-taking strategies in this book to work, students must be committed to earning yards after contact. These test-taking strategies are applied to the questions that students have no idea how to answer correctly. If students knew the correct answer, they would not need the strategies; they would just select the correct answer and move on. The strategies are designed to be used in an environment of confusion, stress, and bewilderment.

Most students give up when a question is confusing. Only a few are committed to wrest away every single point they can from the ACT's tightly-clenched fist.

If your students are willing to put in the extra effort when the test is proving to be difficult, then they can be taught the strategies they need to win. But it starts with them.

This metaphor can make for an excellent mantra. Recite it whenever your students are about to throw in the towel, when they moan and groan about that one extra mini-test you want them to take. The other test takers who are competing for the same scholarship dollars as your students are not going to give up. Are your students up for the challenge to do what it takes to win?

What it takes is yards after contact.

Get Pumped

Your students' attitudes have a massive effect on their aptitudes.

To continue the sports metaphor from the previous chapter, ask your students to imagine a team sitting in the locker room before a game, dolefully contemplating how miserable the game is going to be, how poorly they are going to play, and how they can't wait to just get it over with. What will be this team's outcome? Not too pretty.

Ask your students, "If you were the coach walking into that loser locker room, what would you do? What would you say? How would you turn things around?"

They might give a speech. They might get their players to encourage one another. They might play a boombox. They would do *something* to get their team pumped up. But in the end, who is in control of whether that team gets pumped up or not? The team, of course.

Your students cannot afford to participate in a loser locker room. They are in control of their attitudes, whether they believe it or not.

Your students have to pump themselves up about the ACT, not just at the beginning of the test, but through every test section. They have to make themselves look forward to the challenge. They have to look forward to *owning* that test.

It isn't that the ACT is an intrinsically exciting thing. But neither is a sports game where you are the underdog. In sports, it doesn't matter if you are the underdog. You know that you don't have a chance unless you get your mind right about the game. It's the same way with the ACT.

Students who pump themselves up, who get themselves excited and interested in how they perform and in how they can beat the test, will have a much easier time tapping into the mental energy they need to be successful on the three-hour marathon that is the ACT.

Two Rights Make a Wrong

There can only be one correct answer on any ACT test question. This, you could say, is the fundamental, inviolable law for all ACT test writers.

Therefore, *if two choices are equally correct, they must both be wrong.*

Students who are unfamiliar with this concept struggle and then finally guess one of the two equally *wrong* choices as their answer.

Students who know this strategy make two eliminations and are much closer to scoring a point. These students know that when two correct responses appear on an answer choice, they need to re-examine the question and their own assumptions. Chances are, after assuming a new perspective and pocketing two eliminations, they will be able to answer correctly.

> Refer to English question #52 on page 20 of *Preparing for the ACT 2015-16.*

In question #52, students may at first miss the point of the test item. Choices F, G, H, and J are all grammatically correct. They all seem to work. This fact should set off alarm bells in your students' brains. There must be only one correct answer.

At this point, students should take a step back and re-examine their assumptions. The question is not asking for a grammatically correct choice. It's asking for a choice that does not involve redundancy. With this new insight, students can select choice J, which is the only choice that does not repeat information already given in the paragraph.

> Refer to English question #75 on page 23 of *Preparing for the ACT 2015-16.*

Question #75 presents a subtler opportunity to use the same strategy. Let's say your students are uncertain about the definition of the 19th and 20th centuries. Is the 20th century the 1900s? Or is it the 2000s? Or something else entirely?

Even if your students are unsure about the definition, they can still narrow it down to choices C and D because the essay only discusses the contributions made by one woman, not multiple women. After this point, however, they would be stuck unless they remember that two rights make a wrong.

If the students know that choice D is correct but think that it's possible that choice C is also correct, they can confidently eliminate choice C. Why? Because there can only be one right answer. If the definition of the 19th century is correct in choice C, then there would be two right answers, and that simply isn't possible on the ACT.

Two wrongs don't make a right, but on the ACT, two rights do make a wrong. If two choices are equally correct, then neither can be.

Help Your Intuition

Have you ever had the answer to a problem that you struggled over for days come to you in a dream? Or ever notice that sometimes a solution to a difficult riddle seems to bubble up out of nowhere, almost inexplicably?

It is a well-known fact in the test prep world that if question #20 stumped you, the answer might magically occur to you as you worry over question #50.

This is your subconscious at work—your intuition, if you will. The subconscious excels at ruminating over impossible problems. It works in somewhat mysterious ways, and provides assistance when you least expect it.

Psychologists have dedicated a great deal of research to learning the properties of the subconscious, trying to understand what makes it tick. Research shows that your conscious mind fails to answer a question often because of a false assumption or a missed detail. Long after your conscious mind has given up, your subconscious continues to tinker, ignoring assumptions and free associating with details.

From this fact is derived a useful best practice for tapping into intuition during test.

If students take a problem as far as they can, until they are absolutely stuck, and then move on, their subconscious will keep working on it for them.

For this to be effective, they have to work hard on the problem and get to an impasse. If they just glance at a question and move on, their subconscious probably won't care.

Once they move on, they shouldn't even think about the problem again. The more completely they "walk away" from it, the more likely it is that the answer will come to them.

Students should let their subconscious minds earn their keep by helping them gain a raw point or two.

Game Day

Small details make big differences on game day, the day your students take the ACT.

Students who start or even end the test hungry aren't going to perform at their best. Tired students will have unnecessary difficulties. If students have an argument with a friend on their mind, their scores will suffer.

Review these game day tips with your students and do everything you can to reinforce them.

1. **Get enough sleep the entire week before the test.** Trying to get a good night's sleep the day before the test isn't enough. If students have been running on five hours sleep a night, chances are if they try to hit the sack early the night before the test, they will just lay there with their eyes open, worrying. It takes about a week to reset a sleep cycle. Teenagers need at least nine hours of sleep a night for peak mental performance. Students with home situations or work hours that prevent them from getting enough sleep might want to stay with a friend and/or ask for a reprieve from work for a few days.

2. **Eat well, especially on the days leading up to the test.** Students should avoid junk food, which can slow thinking and generally make them feel awful. They should also work to eat *enough*. The brain needs calories. Even if your students are in home situations where dinner is not a regular occurrence, they can still avail themselves of the cafeteria food for breakfast and lunch. Some schools provide a pre-ACT breakfast to make sure students are fed before the big event.

3. **Bring a snack on test day.** A healthy snack like a protein bar or some fruit (or both) can ensure that students don't get hungry during the Reading and Science tests. Students should avoid junk food (beware Honey-Buns!) that might fill them up but will put them to sleep.

4. **Try to reduce caffeine intake.** Students who take their daily dose(s) of energy drink are likely to be exhausted and suffer from disrupted sleep patterns. Encourage your students to minimize their caffeine intake during the month before their test. That being said, students should not quit cold turkey; if they are accustomed to an energy drink every morning, the morning of the ACT is not a good time to change things up!

5. **Reduce distractions.** Friends and social media pull students' attention from the task at hand, especially when they have upsetting news. Students should avoid checking social media the morning of the test; the last thing they need is a change in their crush's relationship status crushing their ACT score.

If your students follow these game day tips, they will avoid many of the issues that keep them from performing at their best.

Error Paranoia

Errors are the destroyers of ACT dreams. They are surprisingly difficult to catch and prevent.

Give your students the world's shortest IQ test, the Cognitive Reflection Test (CRT), to emphasize how they need to think more carefully and thoroughly on assessments like the ACT:

Question 1:

A bat and a ball cost $1.10 in total. The bat costs $1.00 more than the ball. How much does the ball cost?

Question 2:

If it takes 5 machines 5 minutes to make 5 widgets, how long would it take 100 machines to make 100 widgets?

Question 3:

In a lake, there is a patch of lily pads. Every day the patch doubles in size. If it takes 48 days for the patch to cover the entire lake, how long would it take for the patch to cover half of the lake?

(Note: it's best to give this as a timed bell ringer without any introduction. For maximum effect, don't give your students any tips or warnings.)

Correct answers:

1. $0.05

2. 5 minutes

3. 47 days

Studies show that if the text of the CRT is put in a font that is hard to read, participants will score better because the difficulty triggers the part of the brain that carefully analyzes.

In all three of these questions, the *intuitive* answer is not the *right* answer.

It's the same on the ACT. The test is full of trap answers for students who move too quickly or who forget a simple math function. They have a false *aha* moment when they see what looks like the right answer. The intuitive sense that they are correct actually leads them astray.

Students should adopt error paranoia in order to get themselves in the correct frame of mind to succeed on the ACT. Having a paranoid mindset about errors is akin to taking the CRT in an obscure font. It activates a different part of the brain, the correct part of the brain for the task.

If a question is worth answering, it's worth double-checking.

There are two parts of any test item that students should check.

1. *Check the question.* Make sure you are answering the exact question asked.

2. *Check the answer.* Make sure it's the one you meant.

In our boot camps, we tell students that to catch errors they must develop a sixth sense. It's like the horror movies where the creepy music starts playing as the heroine approaches the abandoned log cabin in the middle of a haunted forest. You hear the music and yell at the TV screen for her to not open that door. Can't she hear the music?

Creepy music plays behind every error. Students must listen carefully to catch it. To do this they have to become self-aware of the errors they are prone to. For example, if a student always messes up pronoun number, he needs to "hear the music" and tread slowly whenever he is working with a question involving pronouns.

This is one area where paranoia is a good thing. Help your students adopt error paranoia to boost their scores.

(Interested in learning more about studies involving the CRT? Check out Malcolm Gladwell's book *David and Goliath: Underdogs, Misfits, and the Art of Battling Giants.*)

Fluency Illusion

Learning psychologists have made an interesting discovery that sheds light on the topic of test anxiety and how to prevent it.

It turns out that much test anxiety is actually the result of what is called the *fluency illusion.*

When students read a text or receive classroom instruction on a topic multiple times, they gain a sense of familiarity with it. They feel that they know it because as they read the text they can almost predict what it will say next. They keep telling themselves, "Oh, yeah, I remember this!"

That feeling of familiarity is what most students consider to be *fluency*. Unfortunately, it is only an illusion.

Standardized tests don't assess your students' familiarity with topics. Fundamentally, they test your students' *retrieval strength*: how well students can *retrieve* information and skills they have learned to apply to the task at hand.

Students who reread texts or sit through a classroom review will feel like they are well-prepared for whatever test they are studying for. But these tasks do not move the needle on *retrieval strength*.

When these same students go into the test and the first question asks them to retrieve a grammar or math rule, they can't. Their memory doesn't have sufficient retrieval strength to do so.

The students think, "Oh no! I knew this! I spent all week preparing for this test, and now I'm blanking out!" Anxiety sets in with the realization that they may fail.

Students attribute these struggles to test anxiety, but actually, anxiety occurred *after* the students fell for the fluency illusion.

Test anxiety of this nature is self-reinforcing. Students who experience test anxiety as a result of the fluency illusion thereafter try to avoid tests of any form whenever possible (since bombing tests is not a pleasant experience), but the cure for the *fluency illusion* is self-assessment.

The best and simplest way to improve the *retrieval strength* of a memory is to *retrieve* it. Each time your students retrieve a memory, their brains note that this memory is somewhat important and make it progressively easier to access. For this reason, students must become skilled at self-assessment to defeat the fluency illusion. Flashcards are a great way to accomplish this. Students can also read a passage, then close their books and try to recite what they just read.

The concept of *intervals* or *spacing* is also important in the fight against the fluency illusion. Students should space out their self-assessment. After they work with a set of flashcards, they should wait a day and then try their flashcards again. Then again after three days, then a week later.

Likewise, if you cover the Pythagorean theorem with your students, test them on it a week later, then a month later, then three months later. Each time, you are improving their retrieval strength, *even if* your students get the question wrong and you have to explain the answer afterward.

Just because students feel good about a concept doesn't mean they'll do well when that concept is tested on the ACT. Until there has been some time between the your lesson and an assessment students answer correctly, you can't know that the fluency illusion won't hold your studnets back.

Coach your students on the fluency illusion so they can quash test anxiety and boost their scores.

(Interested in learning more about the fluency illusion? Read *How We Learn* by Benedict Carey.)

Blind Guessing Strategies

In rare circumstances, even when you have done everything you can to help your students achieve a fast pace and master the process of elimination, students must resort to blindly guessing.

When they do so, the following two strategies can help them have slightly better odds of success. It turns out that even a blind guess can be improved.

It's important to note that these strategies apply to *blind guessing*, where students can't make any eliminations or don't have time to do so. If students have made some eliminations, they should continue to use whatever test-taking strategy they are already applying.

Don't Charlie Out

Usually, if batch blind guessing occurs, it happens at the end of the test. We analyzed the prevalence of correct answer choices at the back of the ACT, and the results were somewhat surprising.

At the end of the test, students should avoid blindly guessing choices C and H (the third bubble on each row). The other choices are 30% more likely to be correct than C and H. The old adage of *when in doubt, Charlie out* is completely false on the ACT.

We theorize that this distribution is because most students, when blindly guessing, do go for the third bubble on each row, so the ACT compensates for this.

On the Math test, not only is choice C/H a poor guess on the last 10 questions, but choices B and G (the second bubble in each row) are bad guesses as well. Actually, on the Math test, B/G is an absolutely terrible choice: only 10% of the time is it the correct answer.

The best blind guess on Math is choice E/K (the fifth bubble in each row). 31% of the time choice E/K is the correct answer in the last 10 questions, more than choices B/G and C/H combined!

Column Counting

This strategy is more applicable to advanced students. It's akin to counting cards and becomes more powerful the closer a student gets to a perfect score.

The ACT has a remarkably even distribution of correct answer choices throughout its tests (except for the disruptions at the back of each test as described in the section above). Students can use this fact to determine what is the most likely answer for any blind guess.

Once students have answered all of the questions they understand, they count the number of bubbles they have made in each column (there are four columns in English, Reading, and Science; five columns in Math). One column is associated with two letters. Column 1, for example, corresponds to choices A and F. Don't count a bubble if it has an asterisk near it (indicating that the student *marked and moved* on that question).

Whatever column(s) have the least number of bubbles are the ones students should favor on their guesses. Because the distribution of correct answer choices on the ACT is relatively even, these guesses are more likely to be accurate.

The fewer the questions students have to guess on, the more powerful this strategy becomes. We know of several students who earned the last few raw points they needed to score a 36 by using this strategy.

Students should never want to blindly guess. But if they have to, applying these strategies will give them an advantage.

CONTENT MASTERY
Content Strategies for the ACT

Introduction to Content Mastery

Content is king on the ACT. Only by actually learning valuable skills associated with academic college readiness can students reliably make large gains on the test. Content mastery helps you navigate this diverse territory.

The *Content Mastery* sections of this book are oriented around the content that the ACT weights most heavily and explain exactly how the test assesses each college readiness standard. In this book we make the assumption that if we clarify exactly where your students need preparation in your subject area, you can then apply your expertise in that subject to help your students succeed.

The gap between *standards* and *assessed standards* can rival the Grand Canyon. Just because students can order fractions does not mean that they can order fractions the way the ACT asks them to. Content mastery helps you bridge this divide.

This is the first of five *Content Mastery* sections. The others are found on the pages given below.

In each section, you'll find extensive mention of the ACT College Readiness Standards and our ACT Standard Families.

ACT College Readiness Standards

The ACT College Readiness Standards are the official standards provided by the ACT. Every single test question on the ACT is tied to an ACT College Readiness Standard. These standards are grouped into categories and sorted by relative difficulty.

According to the ACT's website,

The standards are empirically derived descriptions of the essential skills and knowledge students need to become ready for college and career, giving clear meaning to test scores and serving as a link between what students have learned and what they are ready to learn next. Parents, teachers, counselors, and students use the standards to:

- *Communicate widely shared learning goals and expectations*

- *Relate test scores to the skills needed in high school and beyond*

- *Understand the increasing complexity of skills needed across the score ranges in English, mathematics, reading, science, and writing*

MasteryPrep uses the ACT College Readiness Standards to organize its analysis of released ACT tests and student answer responses. We also use them in this book to provide a framework for discussing essential content areas relative to the ACT.

Below is an example of ACT College Readiness Standards on the Science test. These standards are categorized under Interpretation of Data and are associated with an ACT score range of 13–15:

IOD 201. Select one piece of data from a simple data presentation (e.g., a simple food web diagram)

IOD 202. Identify basic features of a table, graph, or diagram (e.g., units of measurement)

IOD 203. Find basic information in text that describes a simple data presentation

Each standard has a code. The three letters indicate the category. The first number refers to relative difficulty. The other two numbers are used to give each standard a unique ID.

The first number always refers to a specific ACT score range. Students who score in a given range are likely able to correctly answer questions associated with that standard. For example, students who score 15 are likely to be able to answer questions associated with standards in the 200s but unlikely to be able to answer questions associated with standards in the 300s.

Code Range	ACT Score
200s	13–15
300s	16–19
400s	20–23
500s	24–27
600s	28–32
700s	33–36

ACT Standard Families

ACT Standard Families are a MasteryPrep invention. It can be quite challenging to use the ACT College Readiness Standards in lesson planning because related skills are spread across multiple difficulty codes.

Our ACT Standard Families group the ACT College Readiness Standards into logical clusters that can then be used for further analysis and planning. Typically, it's easier to discuss an ACT Standard Family than it is to discuss a set of unrelated College Readiness Standards grouped into difficulty categories.

The way standard families are organized means that simple and difficult versions of a similar standard are all gathered into the same family.

Below is an example of a Science standard family:

Select Data & Features
IOD 201. Select one piece of data from a simple data presentation (e.g., a simple food web diagram) **IOD 202.** Identify basic features of a table, graph, or diagram (e.g., units of measurement) **IOD 301.** Select two or more pieces of data from a simple data presentation **IOD 401.** Select data from a complex data presentation (e.g., a phase diagram)

Curriculum

Much of the curricula that we have developed (*ACT Mastery*, *ACT Essentials*, *ACT Elements Bell Ringers*) are designed to build content mastery. These are the only ACT prep curricula that take this approach.

These resources provide complete lesson plans, practice questions, student exercises, exit tickets, and assessments so that you can spend your time focusing on teaching instead of scrounging for resources.

More information about our curricula and free samples are available for request at masteryprep.com/decode/resources.

Four I's Framework

Coaching your students through the content we highlight in each subject-specific *Content Mastery* section is most effective when it follows the Four I's framework. These are essentially best practices in teaching with which you are already familiar, but we call attention to them because they are the exact opposite of what most drill-and-kill test prep looks like.

Inquiry

Wherever possible, include *inquiry-based activities* as you help students with an ACT subject area. Inquiry is the opposite of selected response, but it is closer to the optimum way the brain learns. Yes, ACT prep has to include selected response questions, but if it doesn't also include inquiry most of your students will quickly lose interest.

Isolation

If students don't know how to correctly answer a certain type of question on the ACT, then they need plenty of practice with this question *in isolation* to have the chance to master it. The questions need to be varied (since the ACT almost never asks the exact same question twice), but the question category needs to remain constant. Without working a question type in isolation, students lose the opportunity to adequately learn content; as soon as they start to understand, they're torn away to focus on a different subject. Inquiry and isolation are easily combined; if your class is deficient in a skill, provide an inquiry-based lesson end-capped with ACT practice of that skill in isolation. (This is the same way we format our *ACT Mastery* curriculum.)

Intervals

Even if you work hard to limit your focus to the most essential ACT content, it can be a challenge for students to retain everything before the test. Use *intervals* (spacing or time gaps) to increase the likelihood that your students will remember what you covered with them. Introduce a topic and coach students to mastery. A week later, do more work on the topic; return to it again a month later. These intervals force the brain to push your lessons into long-term memory.

Interleaving

Interleaving, in which students answer questions from multiple content categories, is the default in the world of test prep. It occurs every time you give your students mini-tests (see page 35). Since the ACT requires students to answer a wide variety of questions, sorted randomly in terms of both content and difficulty, you have to strengthen your students' ability to differentiate between questions and know when to apply particular rules or strategies. Use interleaving to make this happen. Interleaving is the opposite of isolation. One way to incorporate both is to provide inquiry-based activities with practice in isolation, then at later intervals provide interleaved practice. (Again, this is the way we format the *ACT Mastery* program and a large part of why it works.)

Mastery Cube

There are three dimensions across which you can improve your students' ACT scores through content mastery. They are represented on what we call the Mastery Cube.

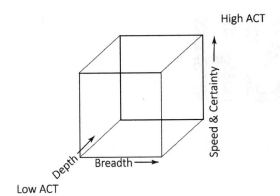

In this diagram, the lower left-hand corner represents a low ACT score, while the upper right-hand corner represents a high ACT score. All three paths are viable methods for improving performance. Almost all commercial test prep programs are one-dimensional in this regard, focusing only on breadth. This is probably one of the main reasons that commercial test prep programs average less than a one-point composite score improvement with their students.

Not surprisingly, since score gains are available across all three dimensions, the biggest score gains occur when students develop ability along the entire Mastery Cube.

Breadth

By *breadth*, we mean a shallow introduction or review of a topic or rule. Students who have never heard of a nonrestrictive phrase or who have completely forgotten what a control is would benefit from this approach. One example of content mastery through this dimension would be giving students a practice test with a wide variety of questions and then reviewing the answers. MasteryPrep's *ACT Boot Camp* (a one-day student workshop) follows this method.

Depth

By *depth*, we mean an in-depth examination of a particular topic or rule. Students may know the Pythagorean theorem, but can they apply it to find the length of telephone poles or shadows? Can they put the length of one side in terms of another? Can they use it to determine the dimensions of compound shapes? In ACT prep, teaching along the depth dimension means preparing students for each major variant of how the ACT asks questions about a given content area. This approach is almost nonexistent in the test prep world but is similar to the approach you take with a typical Math or Literature unit in your classroom. MasteryPrep's *ACT Mastery* and *ACT Essentials* curricula are examples of this approach.

Speed and Certainty

The most-neglected of all content mastery dimensions is speed and certainty. By *speed and certainty*, we mean working on a content area with which your students are already familiar, with the goal of improving their ability to answer questions quickly and without second-guessing. No new content is introduced. There's only practice, and it's usually timed. Since the ACT is a timed test, improving speed and certainty with core topics and skills can have a marked impact. Speed practice works best when you scaffold from isolation to interleaving (see previous chapter). This isn't time mastery: you aren't trying to improve your students' time management skills. You are just making them naturally faster because they have learned the content cold. An example of speed and certainty practice is the typical approach taken in elementary school to help students learn times tables. MasteryPrep's *ACT Elements Bell Ringers* curriculum addresses ACT test prep through this dimension.

In the chapters that follow, we will discuss many methods for improving mastery along all three dimensions.

ENGLISH

The English section of this book, like the other sections, is broken into three segments:

- **English Time Mastery**, where we discuss how to get students on pace for the 45-minute, 75-question ACT English test.

- **English Test Mastery**, where we detail effective test-taking techniques, guessing strategies, and rules of thumb that can help students navigate through their uncertainties to get the correct answer by hook or by crook. Some of these strategies may seem to overlap with the next segment, Content Mastery. As a general rule, if a content rule is not applicable to the entire English language or constitutes a shortcut, we address it in Test Mastery.

- **English Content Mastery**, where we provide guidance on which English content areas need the most focus. We also share winning strategies that help students gain rigorous mastery of this content.

Time Mastery, Test Mastery, and Content Mastery represent the three major areas where students can make improvement on their ACT scores. The most balanced, effective approach to test preparation is to work each day to help your students make progress in all three areas.

ENGLISH TIME MASTERY
Time Management Strategies for the ACT English Test

Even Difficulty Distribution

The basic fact that underlies any time management strategy on the ACT English test is that English questions are not rigidly ordered by difficulty. The questions *do not* become gradually more difficult in any way that is discernible to the student.

The basic goal of time management is to ensure that students have time to consider every single question on the English test.

It's entirely probable that the last passage, with its 14 to 16 questions, may contain several of the easiest questions on the entire test.

It is true that some of the "gotcha" questions and test items that evoke obscure grammar rules appear near the back of the test, but the great majority of the difficulty increase that the student perceives has more to do with running low on time than with any intrinsic qualities of the questions themselves. As a matter of fact, a student who happens to be familiar with the topic covered in the final passage might actually consider it to be the easiest of all!

Easy questions, questions you know how to answer, appear in the last passage of the English test.

Some students have time management problems because they don't believe this. They think that if they are having trouble with editing an essay, there is no point in trying to get to the next one since that one will only be harder. Nothing could be further from the truth. If a passage is giving a student fits, chances are that the next passage will be easier.

If many of your students have trouble getting through the English test, you may want to consider proving this concept to them. Provide your students with a mini-test that consists of a "Passage V" from a full-length ACT. When the students do just as well as they did on other mini-tests, make a big deal of the fact that this was a *final passage*. Ask your students if they noticed any difference in difficulty between the mini-test they just took and other mini-tests they had taken in the past. After this exercise, you'll find that some students take time management more seriously. They now have a rationale for getting through to the end within the time limit provided.

The Time Management Heat Map

Below is what we call a "heat map" showing the performance of over 20,000 students on an ACT English test. This is a powerful tool for understanding your students' level of time mastery.

Each vertical bar represents one of the 75 questions on the test. A light shade means that most of the students answered the question correctly. A darker shade means that fewer students answered right. When the color is completely black, it means that students would have done better if they had just blindly guessed.

We use heat maps to understand at a glance how students in a class are handling time management.

On the ACT Math test, for example, we expect the heat map to get darker and darker as we read from left to right. There is a very clear reason for this: the questions become more and more complex.

On the English test, however, if students are managing their time correctly, there should be only a very minor shift in color from left to right. The stronger the shift, the more likely it is that students failed to manage their time and felt rushed at the end of the test. We call this characteristic of the graph *color shift*. If you see a strong color shift with your students, you should work with them on their *pace*. By pace, we mean your students developing the discipline to spend only a certain amount of time on a given section of the test (such as eight minutes per passage in English).

This graphic tells us that the typical class of students has a relatively strong *color shift* in English. In the absence of any specific data about your students, you should assume they will be rushed by the fourth or fifth passage, and you should work with them on rationing time to each passage to avoid this outcome.

It should be noted here that students are a relatively bad judge of whether they felt rushed towards the end of the test. It's hard for anyone to give their all on a test and also analyze on the level of metacognition. For this reason, we recommend using the hard data, the color shift, rather than surveying students about whether or not they felt like they had enough time.

We also look for *contrast* when we read a time management heat map. There should be a strong contrast in the colors between any two questions. The reason for this is that students who are managing their time correctly, and who are quickly moving past confusing questions to retain their time, are able to identify the easy questions sprinkled throughout the test and answer them correctly. Students who are unable to cherry-pick the easiest questions get rushed and guess on questions they should know how to solve. A class of students who are failing to cherry-pick (in other words, manage their time on individual questions) will have a heat map without much contrast. Each question will have a similar color, one to the next. Good time managers have very bright spots scattered throughout the test, even toward the end.

This graphic also tells us that a typical group of students is able to cherry-pick obviously easy questions toward the end of the test, but still has a long way to go on this important time management skill. Every third or fourth question should look relatively bright when students attain a high degree of competence in time management.

MasteryPrep provides a very affordable practice testing service that can give you these pre-made heat maps specific to your students. You can also accomplish similar insights by gathering your student practice test data, looking at the percentage of students who correctly answered each question, and laying this information out in a spreadsheet. Use Excel's "Conditional Formatting / Color Scales" feature to visualize the data in a way similar to the graphic we have provided.

Pace

In the context of test preparation, we use the term *pace* to mean a specific aspect of time management. By *pace* we mean *how well the student is moving through each of the four tests*. Pace is largely a matter of familiarity and discipline. Improving pace is not a question of speeding the student up with a single question or type of question. Rather, we improve pace by helping students move through an entire passage within a specified time allotment.

Students who pace themselves well have a good sense of where they are in a test and whether or not they are running behind. Students who can't pace themselves have no idea how much time is left and often are surprised when the proctor calls out, "Five minutes left!"

Students' sense of pace is one of the primary sources of information they use to determine whether or not to spend time on a particular question. If students sense they are running ahead of schedule, they can afford to pause and think. If they sense they are behind, they look for opportunities to *mark and move* and catch up.

For that reason, we recommend working with your students on pace first, then following that up with specific strategies that are designed to help students move more quickly through particular items or question types.

Below is the pacing summary for English.

ACT ENGLISH

75 Questions
5 Passages
45 Minutes
Pace: 8 minutes per passage, 5 minutes for review

Students should spend a maximum of eight minutes on each passage. That allows for five minutes at the end to double back and review challenging questions. If students balance the time they spend with each passage, they are more likely to be able to consider every question and earn a better score.

One of the best ways to improve pace is through mini-tests. We discuss English mini-tests in more detail on page 59.

More than on any other test section, focusing on pace on the English test can resolve most of the time management issues that students suffer from.

Fairness

Every single one of the five passages in the ACT English test contains questions that students can answer.

If your students never get to the last passage, they'll never have a shot at the last of those questions.

This is an important point to consider when you are reviewing a practice test with students. If students missed most of the questions at the back of the English test, it doesn't make sense to review the content of those questions. The fact that students missed a batch of questions at the back doesn't point to content problems; it tells you that they ran out of time.

Students must be totally fair to their passages and conserve their time so that they can work through the last passage without being rushed.

I explain to my students that I have twins. One of my very first lessons in twin fatherhood concerned the fact that twins have a strong, innate sense of justice. Everything must be fair. If you deign to give one purple shoes and another the same brand in pink, you may as well have committed a crime against humanity. For a long time, we had to be sure to get them the same gifts.

English passages are the same way. Students should treat them like jealous quintuplets. If students spend more time on one passage, the others will know and they'll make trouble because of it!

(The exception here is during the last five minutes before time runs out, when students are allowed spend time with their "problem child" *after* all passages have been given eight minutes.)

Be fair to your passages, and they'll be fair to you and give you more points.

English Mini-Tests Coaching Instructions

Refer to page 35 of this book for general information about mini-tests.

One of the best ways to improve pacing on the ACT English test is through the administration of *mini-tests*.

A mini-test in English is one passage from the test and the 14-16 questions that come with it.

Time each passage eight minutes. Project a full-screen timer using a website such as online-stopwatch.com so that students can refer to it as they need. We also recommend you call out the time remaining every two minutes and clue students in on what question number they should be past.

"Six minutes left. You should be past question #4 by now."

"Four minutes left. You should be past question #8 by now."

"Two minutes left. You should be past question #12 by now."

Eventually, call out time only at the halfway point, and then not at all. Finally, remove the giant timer and have your students pace themselves entirely on their own steam.

After you run the mini-test, it's best to immediately provide the students with the answers as well as explanations for the questions they are most curious about.

Some teachers have successfully structured entire test prep programs around mini-tests. You provide a mini-test, then segue into a lesson with learning objectives based on one or more of the standards that were tested. Our ACT Boot Camp follows an abbreviated version of this model.

Mini-tests can be a powerful tool for drawing student interest and dramatically improving time management skills.

English Mini-Tests

What follows are five English mini-tests. You are allowed to photocopy these mini-tests and provide them to your students.

Printable PDFs of these mini-tests with answer keys and explanations, as well as links to four full-length ACT tests that you can use as fodder for additional mini-tests, are available at this address: masteryprep.com/decode/resources

Mini-Test 1

PASSAGE I

Attempts: _____ Correct: _____

Grandmother's Scarves

[1]

When I was very young, my grandmother would
sew, knit and crochet. She made
1

my siblings and I scarves for the winter. She liked
2

to use our favorite colors in the scarves she made for us,
3
sometimes she would combine multiple colors to create more
3
diverse patterns.

[2]

My grandmother's hand-made scarves came in handy in
the winter when it would snow owing to the fact that they were
4
warm. When I would get ready to go outside in the cold, my
mother would always remind

me of the scarf my grandmother has made me. My siblings
5
and I would play outside or go sledding wearing our scarves
around our necks.

[3]

One year, Nana tried to teach some of the
6
grandchildren how to knit and crochet. She let everyone
pick out the colors of yarn they wanted. We

1. A. NO CHANGE
    B. sew and knit and crochet.
    C. sew, knit, and crochet.
    D. sew, knit and crochet,

2. F. NO CHANGE
    G. my siblings, and I
    H. my siblings and me
    J. me and my siblings

3. A. NO CHANGE
    B. scarves, sometimes,
    C. scarves. And sometimes,
    D. scarves. Sometimes

4. F. NO CHANGE
    G. and
    H. for the reason that
    J. because

5. A. NO CHANGE
    B. made
    C. makes
    D. make

6. F. NO CHANGE
    G. year; Nana
    H. year. Nana
    J. year—Nana

GO ON TO THE NEXT PAGE

all laughed as each <u>other's</u> fingers fumbled over the needles
₇
and yarn.

[4]

    <u>Hence,</u> my grandmother remained patient. After a few
₈
days of lessons, some of my cousins were able to knit and
crochet on their own.

<u>The scarves were not very long, but they were good to start.</u>
₉
My grandmother was very proud to share her talents with her
grandchildren.

[5]

    My grandmother's <u>scarves means</u> a lot to me
₁₀
because they remind me of all the wonderful things

she <u>does</u> for us while we were growing up.
₁₁

She <u>was always</u> there to make us smile with her warm
₁₂

welcomes and unceasing love. I am a better person <u>today,</u>
₁₃
<u>because</u> I grew up with her in my life.
₁₃

7.   **A.** NO CHANGE
        B. others's
        C. others'
        D. others

8.   **F.** NO CHANGE
        G. Therefore,
        H. Nevertheless,
        J. Although

9.   **A.** NO CHANGE
        B. Although the scarves were not very long, they were a good start.
        C. The scarves were a good start even if they were not as long.
        D. The scarves were not very long, but the cousins had a good start.

10.   **F.** NO CHANGE
        G. scarves meant
        H. scarves mean
        J. scarves, mean

11.   **A.** NO CHANGE
        B. did
        C. had did
        D. had does

12.   **F.** NO CHANGE
        G. were always
        H. is
        J. are

13.   **A.** NO CHANGE
        B. today, since
        C. today because
        D. today therefore

GO ON TO THE NEXT PAGE

One <u>day, when</u> I become a grandparent, I hope to give my
                14
grandchildren the same amount of love and care that my

grandmother gave me. 15

14. **F.** NO CHANGE
    G. day when
    H. day, when,
    J. day when,

15. The writer is considering adding the following
    sentence to Paragraph 1:

    > My grandmother made us these scarves to show
    > us how much she loved us.

    Would this addition help the writer's piece?

    A. Yes, because it makes the passage flow more
    smoothly and fits with the overall theme of the
    passage.
    B. Yes, because it would give the reader a better
    visual idea of the writer's grandmother.
    C. No, because it is irrelevant to the rest of the
    passage.
    D. No, because it is stylistically different from
    the rest of the passage.

END OF MINI-TEST ONE
STOP! DO NOT GO ON TO THE NEXT PAGE
UNTIL TOLD TO DO SO.

Mini-Test 2

PASSAGE II   Attempts: _____   Correct: _____

Ride a Bike

[1]

Each and underline{everyday} carbon dioxide emissions
16

from automobiles underline{affect} our atmosphere and
17

underline{attribute} to the deterioration of the ozone layer.
18

underline{Using public transportation is a significant way to decrease
19
daily carbon dioxide emissions.}
19

[2]

For instance, imagine if all the people underline{who ride}
20
the subway in New York City tried to drive to work.
They would sit in traffic all morning, alongside the
thousands of people who already drive, with their
underline{vehicles release} fumes into the atmosphere.
21

16. **F.** NO CHANGE
    G. every-day,
    H. every day
    J. every day,

17. **A.** NO CHANGE
    B. affects
    C. effect
    D. effects

18. **F.** NO CHANGE
    G. contribute
    H. attributes
    J. is contributed

19. **A.** NO CHANGE
    B. It is important for public transportation to reduce the number of people driving cars.
    C. Public transportation increases carbon dioxide emissions, as well as the number of cars on the roads.
    D. The use of public transportation will significantly decrease the number of people driving.

20. **F.** NO CHANGE
    G. whom ride
    H. that ride
    J. which ride

21. **A.** NO CHANGE
    B. vehicles releasing
    C. vehicles released
    D. vehicle releasing

GO ON TO THE NEXT PAGE

[3]

That being said, the most environment-conscious way
to travel from point A to point B is to ride a bike.
                        22

22. How would omitting this phrase change the sentence?

    F. It would remove an unrelated detail.
    G. It would affect the tone of the overall paragraph.
    H. The writer would improve conciseness and clarity.
    J. The sentence would lose meaning.

[4]

Riding a bicycle has many benefits. Not only is it good
for the environment but it also helps the rider stay fit. In a
          23
country with obesity rates at an all-time high, physical activity
should be a top priority. Riding

23.   **A.** NO CHANGE
     B. environment and
     C. environment, but
     D. environment, yet

a bicycle instead of driving a car is great exercise that works
                                                      24
multiple muscles at one time. Bicycling also exercises the

24.   **F.** NO CHANGE
     G. exercise works
     H. exercise working
     J. exercise, and working

heart making the rider altogether more physically fit.
  25

25.   **A.** NO CHANGE
     B. heart, which makes,
     C. heart and makes
     D. heart, and making

[5]

While on a bike, the rider is more aware of his
or her surroundings then when driving a car. Too many
                        26
people drive while distracted, whether they are texting,
changing the radio, or eating. A cyclist

26.   **F.** NO CHANGE
     G. than during driving
     H. than while driving
     J. then while driving

GO ON TO THE NEXT PAGE

is <u>significantly</u> less likely to be distracted on the road. If more
27
people rode bicycles, there would be fewer

accidents and fatalities because <u>people who ride bikes are safer</u>
28
<u>when compared to</u> drivers.
28

[6]

Why wouldn't you choose to ride a bike instead of
driving a car? A car can definitely get you to your destination
faster—but at substantial risk. A bike, on the other hand, is
environmentally friendly, good for your <u>health, and</u> safer than
29
a car. 30

27. **A.** NO CHANGE
B. being significantly
C. are significantly
D. is more significantly

28. **F.** NO CHANGE
G. bike riders are generally safer than
H. people who ride bikes are safer then
J. people who bike are compared to

29. **A.** NO CHANGE
B. health while
C. health and,
D. health while,

30. Which of the following choices is the best way for the writer to make a more convincing argument for the passage as a whole?

F. NO CHANGE
G. The writer could include a paragraph about the financial benefits of riding a bike.
H. The writer could mention famous bike riders.
J. The writer could describe a city where a lot of people ride bikes.

END OF MINI-TEST TWO
STOP! DO NOT GO ON TO THE NEXT PAGE
UNTIL TOLD TO DO SO.

PASSAGE III

Religious History in Rome

[1]

Rome, known worldwide as the heart of Christianity, housing Vatican City and the Pope. For thousands of years,
31

however, people worshipped the gods and goddesses of
32
Roman mythology. Through their worship, the Romans were able to make sense of the world around them and build the unique culture the Roman Empire.
33

[2]

Rome today still has roots in these traditional
34

values as evidenced the prominent architecture that continues
35
to stand in the city, such as the Pantheon and various pagan statues.

[3]

The reformation of Rome from the ancient Roman religion to Christianity happened within only a few generations with or without the consent of the Roman
36
public.

31. A. NO CHANGE
     B. Christianity because it houses
     C. Christianity, is home to
     D. Christianity; housing

32. F. NO CHANGE
     G. although,
     H. therefore,
     J. however;

33. A. NO CHANGE
     B. culture; the
     C. culture, the
     D. culture of the

34. F. NO CHANGE
     G. Rome, today
     H. Rome today,
     J. Today, Rome

35. A. NO CHANGE
     B. values, as evidenced by
     C. values, that can be seen
     D. values, as evidence by

36. F. NO CHANGE
     G. generations, with
     H. generations; with
     J. generations with,

GO ON TO THE NEXT PAGE

[4]

When Christianity first came to Rome,

<u>implemented largely by Emperor Theodosius in 391</u>
                                              37
<u>C.E.,</u> not all Romans accepted the conversion. Many
  37
people in Rome, particularly the

37. The writer is thinking about removing the following information:

> implemented largely by Emperor Theodosius in 391 C.E.,

If the writer would delete this, how would it affect the essay?

A. It would have no effect on the essay.
B. The essay would lose historical context.
C. The essay would lose irrelevant information about a Roman emperor.
D. The essay would lose the writer's opinion about a Roman emperor.

senatorial <u>elites,</u> protested the removal of
          38

38. **F.** NO CHANGE
G. elites',
H. elite's,
J. elite;

<u>pagan non-Christian</u> altars and statues.
      39

39. **A.** NO CHANGE
B. pagan and non-Christian
C. pagan, non-Christian
D. pagan

While Christianity was sweeping across the <u>nation many</u>
                                                    40
<u>Romans</u> were asking not only for more respect for
  40

40. **F.** NO CHANGE
G. nation the Romans
H. nation; Romans
J. nation, many Romans

traditional <u>altars; but</u> freedom of religion.
          41

41. **A.** NO CHANGE
B. altars but
C. altars, but also for
D. altars, but for also

[5]

<u>Hence,</u> religious tolerance was not implemented
  42
until many years

42. **F.** NO CHANGE
G. However,
H. Therefore,
J. Although

GO ON TO THE NEXT PAGE

<u>later, the</u> Roman protests against the removal of pagan altars
43

<u>was</u> revolutionary at that time in history. 45
44

43. **A.** NO CHANGE
    B. later the
    C. later; the
    D. after Roman

44. **F.** NO CHANGE
    G. were
    H. continues to be
    J. is

45. Suppose the writer intended to write on the history of ancient Roman mythology and gods. Would this essay as a whole have fulfilled her intention?

    A. Yes, because the essay covers religion in Roman history.
    B. Yes, because the essay mentions religious tolerance in ancient Rome.
    C. No, because the essay focuses more on the introduction of Christianity than specific Roman gods.
    D. No, because the essay does not mention the Roman goddess Athena.

END OF MINI-TEST THREE
STOP! DO NOT GO ON TO THE NEXT PAGE
UNTIL TOLD TO DO SO.

PASSAGE IV   Attempts: _____   Correct: _____

Zion National Park

[1]

In a plateau region of Utah that was once a <u>desert,</u>
                                                      46
<u>lays</u> a beautiful
46

national <u>park which span</u> nearly 150,000 acres. The Zion
              47
National Park features the Virgin River, which

engraves <u>it's</u> long trail through Navajo sandstone. One of the
           48
features of the park is Zion Canyon, a narrow gorge so deep
that sunlight barely reaches the bottom.

[2]

<u>Along the floor of this canyon which contains</u>
                                              49
<u>vegetation, it is abundant.</u> The park sits at an
                            49
intersection of ecosystems, which allows a variety of
more than 800 different kinds of plants to flourish at
any one time. ⬚50

46. **F.** NO CHANGE
    G. desert lies
    H. desert, lies
    J. desert lays

47. **A.** NO CHANGE
    B. park which spans
    C. park, that spanning
    D. park, spans

48. **F.** NO CHANGE
    G. one's
    H. its
    J. the

49. **A.** NO CHANGE
    B. It is quite abundant at the floor which is this canyon containing vegetation.
    C. Vegetation along this abundant canyon floor is contained.
    D. Vegetation is abundant along this canyon floor.

50. The author is considering adding a sentence here to convey relevant information concerning vegetation variety. Assuming all of the following are true, which addition best accomplishes this goal?

    F. The widest plant diversity in Utah can be seen at Zion National Park.
    G. Zion National Park also has hanging gardens.
    H. A lot of flowers can be seen in the spring and summer.
    J. A lot of these plants were useful to the Native Americans who once inhabited the area.

GO ON TO THE NEXT PAGE

[3]

The terrain rises nearly a mile <u>high then</u> different
                                        51
vegetation can be seen with changes in elevation. The
park is home to a variety of

<u>animals, that can be seen,</u> by hikers and other nature lovers.
      52

Along the river, live bank beavers and many different birds.
                            53
Throughout the rest of the canyon, birds such as eagles,
hawks, falcons, and vultures can be spotted. Foxes, deer, and
mountain lions also live within the park.

[4]

The Zion National <u>Park being</u> a popular site
                          54

for climbers even though the sandstone <u>makes</u> it a challenge.
                                            55
The same techniques and gear that would work on granite do
not work on sandstone because the rock is too loose.

[5]

There are many hiking trails throughout the
<u>park that visitors</u> can explore at a leisurely pace. Hiking
      56
is a great alternative to climbing for those who are
inexperienced.

[6]

The climate at Zion National Park changes
throughout the year and at different <u>elevations. Visitors</u>
                                          57
must be prepared for fluctuating

51. **A.** NO CHANGE
    B. high, then
    C. high, and
    D. high and

52. **F.** NO CHANGE
    G. animals, that can be seen
    H. animals. That can be seen
    J. animals that can be seen

53. **A.** NO CHANGE
    B. Along the river, live bank beavers and many
       different birds:
    C. Bank beavers and many different birds, live
       along the river.
    D. Bank beavers and many different birds live
       along the river.

54. **F.** NO CHANGE
    G. Park is
    H. Park was
    J. Park,

55. **A.** NO CHANGE
    B. make
    C. would make
    D. had made

56. **F.** NO CHANGE
    G. park where visitors
    H. park; and visitors
    J. park, visitors

57. **A.** NO CHANGE
    B. elevations, and, visitors
    C. elevations; therefore, and visitors,
    D. elevations, and visitors

GO ON TO THE NEXT PAGE

temperatures, <u>thunderstorms and even</u> wintery snow storms.
                58

The best time to visit the park <u>being</u> spring or fall. 60
                                59

58. **F.** NO CHANGE
     G. thunderstorms, and even,
     H. thunderstorms and even,
     J. thunderstorms, and even

59. **A.** NO CHANGE
     B. would being
     C. is
     D. in

60. To enhance the logical progression of the essay, the last paragraph should go:

     F. before paragraph 2.
     G. before paragraph 3.
     H. before paragraph 4.
     J. where it is now.

END OF MINI-TEST FOUR
STOP! DO NOT GO ON TO THE NEXT PAGE
UNTIL TOLD TO DO SO.

PASSAGE V

Attempts: _____   Correct: _____

German Brother

[1]

When I was a freshman, there <u>were</u> two foreign
61
exchange students attending our high school. My school
was very small, and all of the students had known each
other since the first <u>grade, so having</u> two new students
62
from a different country was intriguing.

[2]

Both of the foreign exchange students were boys.

<u>One, named Zuka,</u> was from Georgia, and the other, named
63

<u>Bjorn, he was</u> from Germany. [65]
64

[3]

Halfway through his year at my high <u>school,</u>
66
<u>Bjorn</u> came to live with my family because he did not
66
get along with his first host family.

61. **A.** NO CHANGE
    B. was
    C. is
    D. be

62. Which of the following alternatives to the underlined portion would NOT be acceptable?

    F. NO CHANGE
    G. grade. To have
    H. grade. So to have
    J. grade. Having

63. **A.** NO CHANGE
    B. One named Zuka
    C. One was named Zuka,
    D. One, were named Zuka,

64. **F.** NO CHANGE
    G. was
    H. is
    J. he is

65. The writer is considering adding a sentence to the preceding paragraph in order to provide more information about the exchange students. Which of the following sentences best accomplishes this goal?

    A. Both boys were seniors in high school.
    B. At the time, Germany had stricter laws than Georgia.
    C. Some people thought that Georgia was the state in the U.S. rather than the country.
    D. I had always wanted to learn German.

66. **F.** NO CHANGE
    G. school; Bjorn
    H. school. Bjorn
    J. school, Bjorn,

GO ON TO THE NEXT PAGE

It was not a good fit for Bjorn. Over the rest of the year, Bjorn
67
became like a brother to me.

[4]

At first, he was very quiet and shy in his new

home, but eventually he opened up to my family and fit

in perfect. Since Bjorn was the same age as my older
68
brother, he was able to relate to him easily, and they

became close friends.

He told us all about Germany and we helped him break
69
down the language barrier. The single most important German

phrase that he taught us was

"Ich liebe dich", which is German for *I love you.*
70

[5]

Bjorn had left at the end of the summer after
71
graduating from our high school. He has yet to return

to the United States, but he keeps in contact with my family
72
and I over the Internet.
72

[6]

One day when I travel to Germany, he will be my
73
host and help me navigate the new culture, just as we

67. **A.** NO CHANGE
    B. The first family was
    C. They was
    D. It were

68. **F.** NO CHANGE
    G. in perfect!
    H. in more perfect.
    J. in perfectly.

69. **A.** NO CHANGE
    B. Germany. And
    C. Germany; and
    D. Germany, and

70. **F.** NO CHANGE
    G. "Ich liebe dich," which
    H. "Ich liebe dich" which
    J. Ich liebe dich, which

71. **A.** NO CHANGE
    B. left
    C. had gone
    D. leaving

72. **F.** NO CHANGE
    G. my family, and I,
    H. us, my family
    J. my family and me

73. **A.** NO CHANGE
    B. One day, when,
    C. One day, when
    D. One day when,

GO ON TO THE NEXT PAGE

<u>did</u> for him. He will forever be in my heart and a part of my
74
family. 75

74. **F.** NO CHANGE
G. had did
H. done
J. were doing

75. Which of the following details could the writer add to the last paragraph of the passage in order to improve the development of her conclusion?

A. Mention what happened to Zuka.
B. Give details about when the writer expects to visit Germany.
C. Explain the differences between the cultures of the United States and Germany.
D. Discuss the language barrier the writer might face in Germany.

END OF MINI-TEST FIVE
STOP! DO NOT GO ON TO THE NEXT PAGE
UNTIL TOLD TO DO SO.

Other Time Management Strategies

By helping your students improve their pacing abilities through mini-tests, you will alleviate most of their time management woes. That being said, many of the time mastery techniques covered in other sections of this book also work quite well when applied to the English test. Consider using these strategies:

- Mark and Move (page 33)

- Head Down (page 34)

- Time Management Skills: Cherry-Picking (page 31)

- Answer Awareness (page 146)

ENGLISH TEST MASTERY

Test-Taking Strategies for the ACT English Test

Orientation

The English test is always first on the ACT. If your students have trouble remembering the sequence of the tests, tell them that the tests are always in alphabetical order:

ACT TEST SEQUENCE
1. English
2. Math
3. Reading
4. Science
5. Writing (Optional)

How things go on the English test can set the tone for the entire day. Students who feel rushed and flustered during the English test might find it difficult to regain their cool and do their best on the later sections.

Help your students become test-savvy by orienting them to the major categories of questions that appear on the ACT English test.

USAGE AND MECHANICS	Grammar Questions: Punctuation, Sentence Structure, and Usage	40 out of 75 questions
RHETORICAL SKILLS	Composition Questions: Topic Development, Organization, and Style	35 of 75 questions

The simple rule of thumb for telling the difference between the two types of questions is that grammar questions present alternatives that are grammatically incorrect because of punctuation, usage, or sentence structure errors. Composition questions typically have no issues with grammar; instead, students must identify the best choice in terms of style, topic development, and organization.

There are actually three types of questions within each category. Your more advanced students will appreciate being looped in on the test structure at this level. Students going for a score higher than 30 might even find the benefit in taking a look at the ACT Standard Families document (found on masteryprep.com/decode/resources), which includes the weight of each standard on the test.

USAGE AND MECHANICS

Punctuation (10-15% of Questions)

- Unnecessary Commas
- Parenthetical Elements & Commas
- Commas for Ambiguity & Series
- Apostrophes
- Colons & Semicolons

An example of a Punctuation question is English question #66 on page 22 of *Preparing for the ACT 2015-16.*

Usage Conventions (15-20% of Questions)

- Adjectives & Adverbs
- Comparative & Superlative
- Confusing Pairs
- Forming Verbs
- Idiom
- Prepositions
- Pronoun-Antecedent Agreement
- Pronouns
- Subject-Verb Agreement

An example of a Usage Conventions question is English question #61 on page 21 of *Preparing for the ACT 2015-16.*

Sentence Structure & Formation (20-25% of Questions)

- Sentence Structure Disturbances
- Faulty Coordination & Subordination
- Fragments & Run-Ons
- Misplaced Modifiers & Phrases
- Parallelism
- Participial Phrases
- Relative Pronouns
- Verb Tense & Pronoun Person

An example of a Sentence Structure & Formation question is English question #69 on page 22 of *Preparing for the ACT 2015-16.*

What is another example of a Punctuation question on the English Test?

_____

_____

What is another example of a Usage Conventions question on the English Test?

_____

_____

What is another example of Sentence Structure and Formation on the English Test?

_____

_____

RHETORICAL SKILLS

Topic Development (15-20% of Questions)

- Accomplish Purpose
- Identify Purpose
- Relevance
- Writer's Goal

An example of a Topic Development question is English question #51 on page 19 of *Preparing for the ACT 2015-16.*

Organization, Unity, and Cohesion (10-15% of Questions)

- Introductions & Conclusions
- Paragraph Division
- Paragraph Sequence
- Sentence Placement
- Sentence Sequence
- Transitions

An example of an Organization, Unity, and Cohesion question is English question #57 on page 20 of *Preparing for the ACT 2015-16.*

Knowledge of Language (15-20% of Questions)

- Conjunctions
- Redundancy
- Style & Tone
- Vague & Clumsy Writing
- Word Choice

An example of a Knowledge of Language question is English question #59 in page 21 of *Preparing for the ACT 2015-16.*

What is another example of a Topic Development question on the English test?

_____

_____

What is another example of an Organization, Unity, and Cohesion question on the English test?

_____

_____

What is another example of a Knowledge of Language question on the English test?

_____

_____

Setting Goals

Below is provided the AVERAGED CONVERSION TABLE for the ACT English test. This is the average number of questions that need to be answered correctly to achieve a certain scale score.

We averaged 30 actual ACT conversion tables in order to determine this table.

Teachers should use the averaged conversion table to set their own goals for class progress. Scaled scores can be deceptive. An apparent growth of 10% or 20% in a scaled score might correspond to a raw score growth of 50% or as much as 100%. When you set your goals for classroom growth, consider this averaged conversion table and the actual number of questions your students will need to answer correctly to reach your goal.

Teachers and students have an easier time preparing when their goal is stated by the number of questions they want answered correctly. That is because a scale score is a very nebulous concept, but a raw score (the number of correct answers) is concrete and easy to calculate. If you want your students to earn two more scale points, it's a more definite goal to say that you want your students to answer five more questions correctly.

ENGLISH - AVERAGED CONVERSION TABLE			
Scale Score	**Correct Questions**	**Scale Score**	**Correct Questions**
36	75.00	18	40.74
35	73.71	17	38.50
34	72.27	16	36.13
33	71.08	15	33.26
32	70.00	14	30.45
31	69.10	13	28.18
30	67.89	12	26.15
29	66.48	11	24.03
28	64.98	10	21.73
27	63.34	9	19.29
26	61.47	8	16.56
25	59.34	7	13.53
24	56.97	6	11.06
23	54.52	5	8.63
22	51.98	4	6.45
21	49.10	3	4.55
20	46.00	2	2.85
19	43.19	1	0.79

It's important to keep in mind that this conversion table shows the *average*. That means a student could aim for a target number of questions according to this table and still not reach their goal scaled score. For this reason, show them instead the STUDENT CONVERSION TABLE.

In the student conversion table, we provide the number of questions a student needs to answer correctly in order to practically guarantee a given scale score. If students achieve this raw score, they won't score lower than the given scale score, and they might even score higher.

Provide your students with the student conversion table to avoid the problem of achieving a goal raw score but still not getting the scale score needed.

Using the student conversion table, students determine their "number" for the English test. This is how many questions they need to answer correctly. They should write this number at the top of their test booklet when the test begins. Some students might find it helpful to think of this in reverse: they can afford to miss 15 questions, for instance, and still achieve their target scale score.

When students know their goal in terms of questions right, they are less likely to waste time on difficult questions and won't panic if they miss a few. This can be a big step toward reducing test anxiety and helping students become smarter test-takers.

Please feel free to copy this page and distribute it to your students. An easy-to-print PDF is also available for you at masteryprep.com/decode/resources.

ENGLISH - STUDENT CONVERSION TABLE

Scale Score	Correct Questions	Scale Score	Correct Questions
36	75	18	43
35	74	17	41
34	73	16	38
33	72	15	35
32	71	14	33
31	71	13	31
30	69	12	29
29	68	11	26
28	67	10	24
27	65	9	21
26	63	8	18
25	61	7	15
24	59	6	12
23	57	5	9
22	54	4	7
21	52	3	5
20	49	2	3
19	46	1	0

Read the Passage and Edit as You Go

Refer to English question #15 on page 14 of *Preparing for the ACT 2015-16*.

Students should read the English passages, editing them as they go, much in the way they would edit a friend's paper.

The directions to the ACT English test say, "Read each passage through once before you begin to answer the questions that accompany it." This is not good advice because it takes a lot of time to do and is unnecessary. Students should read for comprehension as they go.

Throughout each passage, students will use their comprehension of the meaning of each sentence and paragraph to arrive at the correct answers, so why should they do one read-through for comprehension and then a separate one for answering questions?

However, students will run into difficulties if they adopt the opposite extreme and skip reading entirely, moving to each underlined portion and making edits in isolation.

Questions like #15 are designed to punish students who aren't reading for comprehension as they proof. These students won't catch the author's overall concept, so they won't be able to easily answer this question. Instead, these students will have to do *another* read-through just to answer this question, which will eat up more time than if they had read and proofed as they went along.

Don't Fear NO CHANGE

You have heard it said that people fear change. On the ACT, it's the opposite. Students fear NO CHANGE. They feel like it's a trick answer.

Reassure students that NO CHANGE is a perfectly legitimate choice. It is just as likely that NO CHANGE will be the correct answer as any other.

Refer to English question #21 on page 15 of *Preparing for the ACT 2015-16.*

In question #21, students will do best to leave the sentence as it is. Choices B, C, and D are all awkward, and most students can *hear* that choice A is best. Despite this, they might hesitate to go with choice A even if the answer is obvious because they fear NO CHANGE.

Just because a sentence has an underlined portion doesn't mean the sentence is incorrect and needs to be changed.

Refer to English question #38 on page 17 of *Preparing for the ACT 2015-16.*

Question #38 is another classic example of how students fearing NO CHANGE can trip themselves up. Only choice F has a meaning that satisfies the question asked, making this one of the simplest questions in this passage. Yet some students will resist choosing F simply because they feel that they are being tricked.

This problem is compounded by the fact that the correct answer to question #37 is also NO CHANGE. Not to mention question #36 is correctly answered by choice F (although it does not have a NO CHANGE option), which creates three identical answers in a row on the test sheet! This kind of pattern can also make students paranoid that they have missed a crucial error somewhere.

In the English test included in *Preparing for the ACT 2015-16*, there are 56 questions that include NO CHANGE as an answer choice. 23.2% of these questions are answered correctly with NO CHANGE, which means that, statistically speaking, this ACT test does not have a preference for or against NO CHANGE as a choice.

Don't fear NO CHANGE.

Tune Out

Tune out nonrestrictive phrases that aren't underlined.

A nonrestrictive phrase is not essential to the meaning of the sentence. The trick to decide whether or not a phrase is essential is to check whether the sentence makes sense without it. If the sentence makes logical sense without the phrase, then it should be surrounded with commas or em dashes.

In terms of the ACT, this fact is important for two reasons. One, the English test will directly assess this. Questions will ask students to punctuate (or un-punctuate) a certain phrase based on whether or not the phrase is nonrestrictive.

Secondly, this concept can simplify English questions with complex sentence structures. Since a nonrestrictive phrase is surrounded by punctuation and is *unnecessary*, students can tune it out when it's not underlined for the question being considered.

Refer to English question #22 on page 15 of *Preparing for the ACT 2015-16*.

In question #22, we are dealing with a complicated sentence:

> "As we neared the summit, the whole group of hikers—thinly spread across the mountain for most of the route—condensed, <u>forming</u> an illuminated line along the trail."

This question is difficult to grasp because the phrase *thinly spread across the mountain for most of the route* interrupts the sentence. Since the phrase in question is surrounded by dashes, however, students can *tune it out*. Now the sentence becomes more manageable:

> *As we neared the summit, the whole group of hikers condensed, <u>forming</u> an illuminated line along the trail.*

Considering the alternatives without this phrase, some of the problems created by the incorrect answer choices are much more obvious.

Students might find it easier to tune out a phrase by covering it with their fingers or lightly scratching through it with their pencils. Students should be warned not to scratch heavily through anything because they still might need to read it to answer another question!

Refer to English question #33 on page 17 of *Preparing for the ACT 2015-16*.

Question #33 is made unnecessarily complicated by a nonrestrictive phrase set off with a comma.

Check Your Understanding: Circle the part of this sentence that students can tune out.

Fascinated by the geometric designs, Quezada <u>wondered, if he could make pots like these?</u>

Sounds Wrong

If it sounds wrong, it probably *is* wrong.

The reverse isn't necessarily true.

Refer to English question #37 on page 17 of *Preparing for the ACT 2015-16.*

In question #37, how the answer *sounds* won't get students to the correct answer. What sounds right to them often isn't right.

Choices B and C may *sound* right because the student might pronounce *lead* as the noun for the metal rather than as the present-tense verb.

For this reason, instead of trying to get students to find what *sounds right*, emphasize that they should *trust themselves on what sounds wrong or awkward.*

This strategy results in some quick eliminations on otherwise difficult questions. The student doesn't need to know why it's wrong. It *sounding wrong* is enough. This technique combines well with the *secret service move* detailed on page 88.

For example, in question #37, the use of the reflexive pronoun *himself* in choices B and C just *sounds wrong.* It's awkward, and students can eliminate this usage even if they aren't sure of the rule that governs it.

Sound won't get students all the way to the answer, but it will narrow down the available choices. In question #37, this strategy gives them a 50-50 chance at the correct answer.

Refer to English question #54 on page 20 of *Preparing for the ACT 2015-16.*

Question #54 is another case where the sound of the choices might not reveal the correct answer, but it can certainly help make a couple eliminations.

Choices G and H stick out like sore thumbs and can easily be eliminated based on how awkward *elegantly chandeliers* sounds.

However, students should avoid using sound to get themselves all the way to the correct answer. Because the singular noun *theater* appears earlier in the sentence, some students won't have any objection to the singular verb *illuminates* and will choose J.

It's important to slow down and find the actual subject of the sentence, which is *chandeliers.* If students have trouble finding the subject, remind them that they can *tune out* the prepositional phrase *inside the theater itself* since it is set off by a comma and not part of the underlined portion.

Once they have identified the plural subject, they can choose F with its plural verb, *illuminate.*

The Grammar Book You Can Bring to the Test

Use the passages for grammar examples.

Except for the underlined portions, ACT English passages are grammatically correct, so they are great models to use to verify that you are thinking correctly about grammar rules. Students who are good at this technique basically treat the ACT English test like a grammar book!

This is an advanced technique. For those students who have a good grasp of grammar but struggle with being certain about a particular rule or construction, this technique can make a difference.

Refer to English question #16 on page 14 of *Preparing for the ACT 2015-16.*

In question #16, the sentence starts with the participial phrase *bundled up in wool sweaters and thick coats.* Imagine that at this moment, in the rush of getting through the test in 45 minutes, a student blanks out on how to punctuate this phrase. Questions flurry in his or her mind: *Is there supposed to be a comma there? How does this work? Am I even allowed to have this construction? What's that rule about introductory phrases?*

To gain clarity, students can scan the passages they have read thus far for similar constructs. It turns out that this construction appears in the sentence associated with question #7 on page 13:

> *Bypassing the liquid water phase, those molecules condense directly onto the established hexagonal pattern.*

Now students have a model of how a participial phrase should be punctuated. Students can then select choice H for question #16 with more confidence.

If a student has no idea what the correct choice is, he or she should mark and move but remain on the lookout for an exemplar in a later passage that can demonstrate the right answer.

Refer to English question #48 on page 19 and question #67 on page 22 of *Preparing for the ACT 2015-16.*

Question #67 tests student knowledge of an arcane punctuation rule involving reflexive pronouns. Many students will feel they are on shaky ground answering this question, but not the students who use the English test as a grammar book. It turns out that a reflexive pronoun has appeared in an earlier passage, and they can use this as a guide.

Consider the sentence that is referred to by questions #48 and #49:

> *Most are there to attend a performance; a few, however, are likely to be architecture buffs there to admire the stunning building itself.*

This sentence ends with the reflexive pronoun *itself.* It isn't set off by any punctuation, which can be used as evidence to surmise that the best choice in question #67 also has no commas. In this case, students would be surmising correctly.

Use the English test like a grammar book.

Replace Semicolons with Periods

To test whether a semicolon is being used correctly, replace it with a period.

On the ACT, if a semicolon can't be replaced with a period, it's likely incorrect.

This rule works because the most common use of semicolons on the ACT is to join independent clauses.

Refer to English question #50 on page 19 of *Preparing for the ACT 2015-16*.

In question #50, this rule would eliminate choice G. If the semicolon is replaced with a period, it becomes clear that *into which are carved…* cannot stand on its own as a complete sentence. It is not an independent clause.

This rule also interacts well with the *two rights make a wrong* technique on page 42. If two choices are identical except that one uses a semicolon and the other a period, they are both wrong. In question #50, this means that choices G and H are *both* incorrect and can be knocked out.

Refer to English question #64 on page 21 of *Preparing for the ACT 2015-16*.

Question #64 follows a similar pattern as question #50. When the semicolon in choice H is replaced with a period, the result is an incomplete sentence: *for the autobiography isn't about the life of Mary Harris Jones.*

What's more, since choices G and H are the same, except one has a period in place of a semicolon, the *two rights make a wrong* technique eliminates both choices.

Refer to English question #69 on page 22 of *Preparing for the ACT 2015-16*.

Question #69 again presents an alternative that includes a semicolon.

Check Your Understanding: What questions would you ask your students to coach them toward applying the *replace semicolons with periods* strategy to question #69?

_____

_____

_____

_____

Colons and Fire Extinguishers

Students are often confused about when they *can* and *can't* use a colon.

Refer to English question #9 on page 13 of *Preparing for the ACT 2015-16.*

For example, on question #9, students might feel uncomfortable about going with choice C if they are only familiar with the use of colons to introduce lists. However, this choice correctly uses a colon to introduce more information about what was discussed earlier in the sentence. *Dust* defines what the *significant addition* was.

By broadening their understanding of how to use colons, you can help your students pick up an extra raw point on the English test.

Refer to English question #12 on page 13 of *Preparing for the ACT 2015-16.*

It's also important that students be sensitive to when they *can't* use a colon. Colons can only be used when they come after an independent clause.

In question #12, choice J is incorrect because *although these snowflakes appear to have a triangular shape* is a dependent clause.

To test a colon, students can imagine replacing the colon with a period. If what comes before the colon cannot stand on its own as a complete sentence, ending in a period, then the colon is being used incorrectly.

Refer to English question #24 on page 15 of *Preparing for the ACT 2015-16.*

In question #24, we can make a similar elimination. Choice F is incorrect because what comes before the colon, *in the half-light of the rising sun*, is not an independent clause.

Refer to English question #62 on page 21 of *Preparing for the ACT 2015-16.*

In question #62, students may be tempted to go with choice J because they recall that colons can be used to introduce lists, and choice J seems to be doing just that. It even uses the word *listing*! As it turns out, the ACT rarely uses colons to introduce lists and instead employs this trick answer quite commonly.

Students can handily eliminate choice J by recalling that colons must come after independent clauses. *Jones even fudges her date of birth, falsely listing* is not a complete sentence. The idea started by the phrase *falsely listing* is interrupted by the colon.

Students can apply a second rule to eliminate this choice: if the sentence is grammatically correct *without* the colon, you can't include the colon there. Colons are like fire extinguishers. Only use them if you really need them.

Refer to English question #72 on page 23 of *Preparing for the ACT 2015-16.*

Question #72 is the rare punctuation question where every answer choice includes a colon.

Check Your Understanding: What do the three incorrect answer choices have in common?

_____

_____

What rule would you introduce to your students to help them eliminate these choices?

_____

_____

How would you explain it to your students?

_____

_____

Secret Service Move

Some students treat commas like sprinkles. The more commas, the better! Their goal seems to be to create a veritable ice cream sundae of punctuation in their sentences.

Particularly, students often fall for the trap of adding a comma whenever they hear a pause. Reader breathing habits do not dictate punctuation; the English language doesn't account for lungs.

Pauses don't cause commas. That being said, commas *do* tend to cause pauses, and your students can use this fact to their advantage on the ACT.

Commas cause pauses.

By listening for awkward pauses occasioned by misplaced commas, students can make a number of eliminations. To help themselves actually *hear* the pauses, students should try the *secret service move*:

Cover one ear with a finger. Whisper very quietly. With your ear covered, you can hear yourself loud and clear without disrupting anyone else around you.

By using the part of the brain that processes the written word as well as the part of the brain that processes the spoken word, students will have an easier time eliminating answers.

To use the *secret service move* to eliminate commas, students should pause their reading every time they come across a comma. Look for choices that sound like cheesy, overly-dramatic movie trailers. Those are the ones you can eliminate easily.

Refer to English question #1 on page 12 of *Preparing for the ACT 2015-16.*

The *secret service move* provides two easy eliminations on question #1. To illustrate this strategy, read the sentence aloud with each choice plugged in, pausing dramatically at each comma.

> B. Snowflakes form (pause) from tiny (pause) water droplets (pause) following a specific…

> C. Snowflakes form from tiny (pause) water (pause) droplets following a specific…

While reviewing this concept, resist the urge to pause naturally and instead rigidly follow the rhythm insinuated by the commas for maximum effect.

The secret service move can usually eliminate one or two choices with commas.

Some students may also find it helpful to verbalize what they're reading when they have trouble concentrating during the math, reading, and science tests. They can use the secret service move to focus and get back on track.

No Solo Commas

Refer to English question #10 on page 13 of *Preparing for the ACT 2015-16.*

Students who are struggling with difficult punctuation questions will do well to remember this rule:

No solo commas. There can never be just one comma between the subject and the verb.

There can be two commas or no commas, but never just one comma between the subject and verb.

To use this strategy, take care to identify the subject and the verb. Then count commas. Eliminate any choices that use a solo comma between the subject and verb.

In question #10, students may struggle to eliminate choice F until they use the *no solo commas* rule. The subject is *pressure*, and the verb is *causes*. Choice F has a solo comma between the subject and verb, so it can be eliminated.

Refer to English question #31 on page 16 of *Preparing for the ACT 2015-16.*

In question #31, two choices can be eliminated by using this rule. The subject of the sentence is *boy*, and the verb is *gathered*. Count the commas between the subject and the verb. Choices C and D both have a solo comma, and so both can be eliminated.

Refer to English question #47 on page 19 of *Preparing for the ACT 2015-16.*

Check Your Understanding: What two choices can students eliminate by applying the no solo comma rule to question #47?

_____

_____

_____

_____

When in Doubt, Commas Out

If you must guess, lean toward the choices with fewer commas.

It is rare that a choice loaded down with commas ends up being the correct answer.

Refer to question #33 on page 17 of *Preparing for the ACT 2015-16*.

While a knowledge of how to punctuate a dependent clause that follows an independent clause will help students arrive at the correct answer for question #33, this guessing rule can also help them win:

When in doubt, commas out.

If forced to guess, students can use this rule to eliminate choices A and C. If they remember that question marks are only for direct questions, they would then arrive at the correct answer, choice B, even though they weren't sure of the exact rules.

Apply *when in doubt, commas out* to any questions where commas appear in several choices.

If students are careful to eliminate any obvious run-ons before choosing the option with the fewest commas, this guessing technique will work over 80% of the time.

For example, in the English test in *Preparing for the ACT 2015-16*, the correct choice for 70% of the comma questions is to take them out. Removing run-ons, this technique's success rate increases to 90%.

Refer to question #67 on page 22 of *Preparing for the ACT 2015-16*.

Question #67 presents quite a challenge for students, requiring them to recall a relatively obscure rule about punctuating reflexive pronouns.

What's more, this question appears towards the back of the test, at a point where students tend to run out of time.

Fortunately, *when in doubt, commas out* swings in to the rescue. It turns out that choice D, devoid of commas, is correct.

Don't apply this rule to questions that require choosing between commas and other punctuation marks. Do not choose colons, semicolons, dashes, and parentheses over commas when guessing on these questions.

The Least Terrible Answer

Some students over-think questions.

They shouldn't think they are alone in this test-taking plight. Everyone's brain is built to ponder and worry over things that don't make sense. When an ACT question, particularly on the English, Reading, and Science tests, establishes a premise that does not jive with what the student understood from reading a passage, it can trigger over-thinking.

That's because the correct answer is not going to feel great to the student. It isn't going to "click," and the student is going to feel like he or she needs to spend more time figuring things out, when really he or she needs to move on.

The ACT establishing a disagreeable premise (particularly an over-simplification) is one of the primary reasons students over-think questions.

> Refer to English question #30 on page 16 of *Preparing for the ACT 2015-16*.

The premise of question #30 is that the *writer's primary purpose had been to describe the experience of doing something difficult.*

Choices H and J can quickly be eliminated because the details in the passage do not support the reasoning in either alternative. As a result, students are stuck with agreeing that the writer accomplished his or her purpose.

The problem is that if students were asked to provide a free response about what was the writer's purpose in writing this essay, answers would probably be drastically different from the premise given in the question. When students narrow the answers down to *yes*, it doesn't sit well.

It's likely that the writer had a purpose much more specific than describing *the experience of doing something difficult.*

Advise your students that on some tough questions such as this one, they should not be looking for the *correct* answer. Instead, they should be looking for the *least terrible* answer choice.

Choice F is not the correct answer so much as it is the *least terrible* answer.

Remove indecision by seeking the least terrible answer choice.

> Refer to English question #60 on page 21 of *Preparing for the ACT 2015-16*.

In question #60, the generalization of the writer's purpose might cause some students to pause. A more direct statement of the purpose may have been, "to provide a positive illustration of the Beaux Arts architectural style by describing the Lyceum Theatre." While this echoes the purpose stated in the question, some students will feel like they should answer *no* because the purpose given does not seem specific enough.

Students should avoid over-thinking and approach this question by seeking *the least terrible answer*. Choices H and J can be eliminated because they contain factual inaccuracies. Students are stuck with saying *yes*! Instead of wallowing in the uncertainty of it all, students should be glad they found their *least terrible answer* and move on with their testing lives.

Introduction to Grammar and the Three C's

The ACT English test rarely asks questions. Rather, it tends to pose a set of four alternatives and require students to deduce what is being tested.

Students can alleviate most of the challenge intrinsic to this format by checking each answer against *grammar and the three C's.*

If only one choice is grammatically correct, it must be the answer. If more than one choice is grammatically correct, students can use the three C's to figure out what the ACT considers to be the best choice. What follows is a detailed description of the three C's.

Introduction to Grammar and the Three C's

Grammar and the Three C's: Consistent

The best answer choice is *consistent*. After eliminating any answer choices that have or create grammar errors, students should remove any alternative that is inconsistent with the sentence or passage.

Refer to English question #6 on page 12 of *Preparing for the ACT 2015-16*.

In question #6, choice H is incorrect because it uses the past tense *bumped*, which is inconsistent with the present tense in the rest of the passage. The correct answer maintains a consistent tense.

Refer to English question #17 on page 14 of *Preparing for the ACT 2015-16*.

Question #17 is a little more challenging. Students have to combine a search for consistency with an understanding of what the author is trying to communicate.

Choice D is easily eliminated, however, purely on the basis of consistency. The present-tense verb sticks out like an inconsistently sore thumb.

Refer to English question #35 on page 17 of *Preparing for the ACT 2015-16*.

In question #35, choices B and C can be eliminated quickly because it does not make sense to say that Quezeda is *selling a dedication to teaching* or that he is *selling a teacher of*.

It comes down to choosing the answer that is most consistent in terms of verb tense.

Check Your Understanding: In question #35, how can the concept of consistency help students arrive at the correct answer choice?

_____

_____

_____

_____

Refer to English question #36 on page 17 of *Preparing for the ACT 2015-16*.

It's also important that a choice be consistent in terms of the positive or negative statements that surround it.

The sentence after the underlined portion in question #36 explains that Spencer MacCallum's search *led him to Mata Ortiz and an eventual partnership with Quezeda*. This indicates a *positive* relationship between MacCallum and Quezeda.

It is therefore inconsistent to choose an answer that communicates a negative relationship between MacCallum and Ortiz. Choices G and J have a negative, critical tone, so they can be eliminated.

Refer to English question #63 on page 21 of *Preparing for the ACT 2015-16*.

In question #63, the verb tense varies in the answer choices. Mainly, students have to determine whether past or present tense is the most appropriate alternative.

Check Your Understanding: What questions could you ask your students to help them identify the tense most consistent with the paragraph?

_____

_____

_____

_____

Grammar and the Three C's: Concise

The best answer choice is concise.

Concise means brief but comprehensive. A *concise* writer says much in as few words as possible.

An answer choice that says the same thing as the underlined portion, but in fewer words, is the better choice. An answer choice that gives *less* information in fewer words is NOT the better choice.

For example:

> *I proceeded to endeavor to the retail location premise that goes by the name of Wal-Mart, and there I managed to make a purchase of a T-shirt of the green variety.*

This sentence would be much more *concise* if it were written like this:

> *I bought a green T-shirt at Wal-Mart.*

However, this sentence is *not* more concise:

> *I bought a green T-shirt.*

It is not as concise because it has lost information: the name of the store.

The best answer choice is not the shortest answer choice. *Sometimes* it's the shortest answer, but *always* it's the most concise answer.

Refer to English question #18 on page 15 of *Preparing for the ACT 2015-16.*

In this question, choices F, G, and H are incorrect because they are less concise than choice J. Since they present information that has already been communicated in the paragraph, they are unnecessary and so can be eliminated.

Refer to English question #39 on page 18 of *Preparing for the ACT 2015-16.*

In question #39, it appears at first glance that there are two viable answer choices: B and C. Choice A can be quickly eliminated because the United States is a *place*, not *places*. Choice D can also be knocked out because it creates a comma splice. Choices B and C, however, both communicate the same meaning.

This is the point where students should remember *grammar and the three C's*. They should choose the most *concise* option, the answer that says the most in the fewest words. Since choices B and C say the same thing, choice C is the best answer.

Refer to question #52 on page 20 of *Preparing for the ACT 2015-16.*

Check Your Understanding: Three of the choices in question #52 are redundant. How would you explain to your students why they are incorrect?

_____

_____

_____

Refer to question #41 on page 18 of *Preparing for the ACT 2015-16.*

In question #41, the concept of concise writing can also cause students to add meaning, not just remove words.

Choices A and B are vague, provide little information, and taken literally seem be saying that there are very few potters or artists in the world.

Choice D, while it is the shortest choice, provides the least information of all—four hundred *what* is anyone's guess.

Choice C is the best answer because it provides the most information in the shortest form. It's the most concise.

Specific writing tends to be better than general writing because specific writing conveys more information, and is thus *brief but comprehensive*, the very definition of concise.

> *I drove a vehicle.*

> *I drove a bus.*

In this example, *I drove a bus* is more concise. It's more specific and provides more information in the same number of words. It answers more questions.

Grammar and the Three C's: Communicates Meaning

What an answer choice *means,* what it *communicates,* actually matters on the ACT. In these cases, students can't solely look for the answer that is grammatically correct. They must find the one that makes sense and fits the meaning of the sentence and paragraph.

Refer to English question #7 on page 13 of *Preparing for the ACT 2015-16.*

In question #7, choices C and D can be eliminated because they communicate meanings that do not match the underlined portion. The *meaning* has to work for the choice to be valid.

Choice C is incorrect because *bypassing the liquid water phase* is not a *visual description.*

Choice D is incorrect because *bypassing the liquid water phase* does not mention *various air temperatures.*

Refer to English question #5 on page 12 of *Preparing for the ACT 2015-16.*

In question #5, students considering what is actually *communicated* can make a somewhat subtler elimination. Choice A indicates that the water is freezing something, which is not the intended meaning of the sentence. Instead, the sentence makes more sense if the water *itself* is being frozen, so choice A can be eliminated.

Refer to English question #2 on page 12 of *Preparing for the ACT 2015-16.*

Question #2 tests the meaning of transition words. The key to reaching the correct answer is understanding what the sentence and each transition word is communicating. If your students don't understand some of the nuances of transition words, they can miss out on as many as six raw points on the English test (including this one).

Refer to English question #19 on page 15 of *Preparing for the ACT 2015-16.*

Check Your Understanding: The answer choices in Question #19 feature two prepositions: *with* and *on.*

_____

_____

What two choices can your students eliminate based on what is *communicated* by one of these prepositions?

_____

_____

Questions Over Answer Choices

When you see a question over a set of alternatives, shift gears. Focus on the question being asked.

For most of the English test, students are responsible for figuring out what the ACT is asking. When presented with an underlined portion and three choices, students must work out what, if anything, is wrong and how to fix it. It's as though students are writers for the ACT.

We have already covered how students should first check for grammar on "questionless questions," then go with the choice that is *consistent*, *concise*, and clearly *communicates* the intended meaning.

However, all of this should be thrown out the window when the ACT deigns to ask a question. For English test items that include questions above the alternatives, students must laser-focus on what is being asked.

No longer are they trying to find the best fit for the passage. No longer are they seeking what sounds best. Instead, they have to find the choice that satisfies the criteria set forth in the question, and this can be *very different* from which alternative sounds best or makes the most sense in the passage.

> Refer to English question #23 on page 15 of *Preparing for the ACT 2015-16.*

In question #23, students need an alternative that *emphasizes…slowness…and supports the idea that [they]…did not set their own pace.*

Every choice must be examined based on these criteria: slowness and not controlling the pace.

Often, the question is *so important* that students don't even need the passage. Imagine that your students didn't have the passage, just question #23 and the answers. They could still figure out the correct answer: only one choice conveys slowness and not being able to set one's own pace: choice B.

> Refer to question #28 on page 16 of *Preparing for the ACT 2015-16.*

In question #28, many students might think that choice F sounds better in the context of the sentence. As a matter of fact, if it weren't for the question above the alternatives, choice F might very well be the best choice.

However, choice F must be eliminated because the question asks for a dramatic emphasis to the *ruggedness of the landscape. Squelched out* is dramatic, but it emphasizes qualities of the sunlight, not the landscape, so it is incorrect. Choice H is likewise eliminated since it also emphasizes the qualities of the light rather than the landscape.

Choice J is the opposite of *dramatic* and can also be eliminated. This leaves only choice G as a viable option, even though it sounds a bit awkward compared to choice F. At least it is making a statement about the landscape and not the sunlight.

Extremes

Refer to English question #13 on page 13 of *Preparing for the ACT 2015-16.*

Extreme statements in answer choices make for easy eliminations. If a statement stretches beyond what is supported in the passage, it should be dropped from consideration, even if it is partially backed up.

Take extreme statements literally. Eliminate them liberally.

In question #13, choice B is tempting but in the end can be eliminated because certain words and phrases are extreme and are not backed up by the passage.

> *Scientists can be <u>certain</u> that a solution to <u>even the most confusing event</u> will be found.*

Can scientists really be *certain* about this? That's strong language, especially considering this assertion is based on scientists figuring out the mystery of the triangular snowflake.

Does this essay provide evidence that *even the most confusing event* can be solved? This is also an extreme statement, particularly because triangular snowflakes do not necessarily qualify as the deepest of the universe's conundrums.

Use Related Questions and Answers to Focus

Refer to questions #13 and #15 on pages 13 and 14 of *Preparing for the ACT 2015-16*.

Some answers to ACT test questions interact with one another. For example, the correct answer to question #13, *the basic laws of chemistry still apply*, directly contradicts choice A in question #15, which states that scientists' *understanding of the basic laws of chemistry is flawed*.

Students should be aware that they can use answers from previous test items as clues to solve tough questions.

What's more, if students run into a question that seems to fit with an earlier question that they *marked and moved*, they should double back to consider both questions in the context of each other.

For example, say your students *marked and moved* past question #13. When they get to question #15 and consider the answer choices, they might notice that there are choices in both questions #13 and #15 that discuss the *basic laws of chemistry* and whether or not these laws were violated. This gives students an area of focus for their reading and will help them make eliminations more quickly. By concentrating on how the passage discusses the *basic laws of chemistry*, both correct answers might click into place in the student's mind!

Common Errors to Avoid in English

A major part of scoring well on the ACT is avoiding careless errors. Here are the top 10 errors to watch out for on the English test. If your students choose an incorrect alternative because they made one of these errors, take particular care to reinforce their practice in that area.

1. Making a verb agree with a noun that is not the subject

2. Making a pronoun agree with a noun that is not the antecedent

3. Accepting verbals as verbs

4. Adding commas like sprinkles on an ice cream sundae

5. Deleting essential information (choosing short over concise)

6. Choosing an answer because it contains an unfamiliar word or punctuation mark

7. Mixing up punctuation on restrictive and nonrestrictive phrases

8. Mixing up homonyms (their vs. they're, led vs. lead, it's vs. its)

9. Not considering every aspect of a choice to eliminate it (focusing instead on the aspect that is confusing and thus missing obvious eliminations)

10. Reading too much into questions instead of taking them literally

---

Check Your Understanding: What three errors are your students most likely to make?

_____

_____

What will you do to help your students quash these errors?

_____

_____

Passage Statistics

Below you will find the word counts, estimated grade levels, and ATOS complexity levels of the grammatically correct versions of the five passages in the English test provided in *Preparing for the ACT 2015-16.*

It is worth pointing out that the difficulty level of these passages is roughly equal to the ACT Reading test passages. A major challenge in the English test is applying middle school grammar concepts to college reading level sentence structures.

If you have your students peer edit one another's papers, it's important to consider that this activity might not be enough to fully prepare students for the editing they are required to do on the English test. Unless students are writing at a sufficient complexity level, it's unlikely that the sentence structures of their peers will come close to the difficulty of the ACT English passages.

	GRADE LEVEL	WORD COUNT	ATOS LEVEL
Passage 1	College	304	10.5
Passage 2	10th Grade	331	7.4
Passage 3	12th Grade	337	8.4
Passage 4	12th Grade	257	11.3
Passage 5	11th Grade	312	10.2

ENGLISH CONTENT MASTERY

Content Strategies for the ACT English Test

Content Area #1: Transitions

Focus on what occurs *before and after* a transition to determine which choice is most appropriate.

Refer to question #2 on page 12 of *Preparing for the ACT 2015-16.*

Question #2 asks for the most appropriate transition word. A transition word describes a relationship between what comes before it and what comes after it, so the correct answer will be the word that best describes the relationship in this particular sentence.

Compare the following selections:

Snowflakes form from tiny water droplets, following a specific process of chemical bonding as they freeze, which results in a six-sided figure.

The rare "triangular" snowflake confounded scientists for years because it apparently defied the basic laws of chemistry.

Confounding scientists is not similar to or an example of the formation of snowflakes, so choices F and G are a poor fit.

Two choices are left: *additionally* or *however*.

At this point, students can check in with themselves: does the sentence that comes after the transition agree or disagree with what comes before? Is it adding on or contradicting?

In this question, the earlier sentence describes *a specific process*, while the latter sentence describes an unknown process that *apparently defied the basic laws of chemistry*. These two sentences seem to conflict with one another. For that reason, choice J is the better pick.

Refer to question #27 on page 16 of *Preparing for the ACT 2015-16.*

In question #27, the best way to determine which transition word is most appropriate is to again look before and after the transition.

Compare the following selections:

We crouched down on jutting pieces of rock and waited for the shifting clouds to clear. We waited for the sun.

A sudden gap in the clouds left us blinking as the sunlight squelched out the severe landscape of gray volcanic rock.

Choice A can be eliminated because *generally* indicates that what comes next will speak in general terms, but instead the sentence provides specific information about a gap in the clouds.

Choice B doesn't make sense because the selection that follows the transition word does not add to the concept presented in the first selection.

Choice C doesn't fit because *once again* indicates that the passage has a previous description of a gap opening up in the clouds, which isn't the case.

Choice D correctly indicates the passage of time between the first selection and the second. The relationship between these selections is that they occurred one after another in a sequence, and this transition communicates that.

If students are having trouble identifying the correct transition, they should take a moment to find the selections they are comparing and consider the relationship between the two.

Refer to question #48 on page 19 of *Preparing for the ACT 2015-16.*

Check Your Understanding: Consider the selections that come before and after the transition in question #48.

Before: *Most are there to attend a performance*

After: *a few are likely to be architecture buffs there to admire the stunning building itself.*

How could you help your students determine the relationship between the *before* and *after* phrases and select the choice that best captures this relationship?

_____

_____

_____

_____

CATEGORY: ORGANIZATION, UNITY & COHESION

Family: Transitions

Weight: 8-15%

Standards:
ORG 201. Determine the need for transition words or phrases to establish time relationships in simple narrative essays (e.g., then, this time)
ORG 401. Determine the need for transition words or phrases to establish straightforward logical relationships (e.g., first, afterward, in response)
ORG 501. Determine the need for transition words or phrases to establish subtle logical relationships within and between sentences (e.g., therefore, however, in addition)
ORG 601. Determine the need for transition words or phrases to establish subtle logical relationships within and between paragraphs
ORG 701. Determine the need for transition words or phrases, basing decisions on a thorough understanding of the paragraph and essay

Example: English question #2 on page 12 of *Preparing for the ACT 2015-16.*

Content Area #2: Sentence Structure Disturbances

This category of questions includes a wide variety of different sentence structure disturbances that cause major problems in sentence construction.

The six major types of Sentence Structure Disturbances are as follows:

- Fragments & Run-Ons

- Faulty Coordination & Subordination

- Relative Pronouns

- Participial Phrases

- Misplaced Modifiers & Phrases

- Parallelism

It should be noted that many ACT questions fall into two or more of these categories, since each incorrect answer choice could potentially involve a different sentence structure disturbance. In our "ACT English Decoded" section, we label each question with its most prominent type, but this does not mean that other types don't apply.

One of the common denominators of sentence structure questions is that one or two alternatives involve incomplete sentences that are lacking verbs.

Work with your students to clear up the difference between a *verbal* and a *verb*. The pathway to a high score in the English test is paved by an ability to identify verbals.

Verbal: a verb form which functions as a noun or adjective.

Verbals include gerunds, participles, and infinitives.

One characteristic of a verbal is that it often appears in a different tense than the verbs in the passage, ending in *-ing* or beginning with *to.*

Refer to English question #47 on page 19 of *Preparing for the ACT 2015-16.*

In question #47, choices A and B include the verbal *filling.* One giveaway that this is not a verb is that none of the other verbs in the passage end with *-ing.* Unless the passage is written in present tense (which is quite the rare occurrence on the ACT English test), verbs in general will not end with *-ing.*

Students should always seek to eliminate incomplete sentences to narrow down their options.

Refer to English question #49 on page 19 of *Preparing for the ACT 2015-16.*

Another source of easy eliminations is to look for choices that create run-ons or comma splices. In these cases, the sentences have too many subjects and verbs or lack necessary conjunctions.

In question #49, choices A and D create run-on sentences. Both the clause *a few, for example, are likely to be architecture buffs* and the clause *they (come to) admire the stunning building itself* are independent clauses. Two independent clauses need proper punctuation and conjunctions to be joined together.

Refer to English question #53 on page 20 of *Preparing for the ACT 2015-16.*

Check Your Understanding: In question #53, one choice includes a verbal that may camouflage an incomplete sentence. Which choice is this?

What choice can be eliminated because it forms a comma splice?

_____

_____

_____

_____

CATEGORY: SENTENCE STRUCTION & FORMATIONS

Family: Sentence Structure Disturbances

Weight: >15%

Standards:
SST 201. Determine the need for punctuation or conjunctions to join simple clauses
SST 301. Determine the need for punctuation or conjunctions to correct awkward-sounding fragments and fused sentences as well as obviously faulty subordination and coordination of clauses
SST 401. Recognize and correct marked disturbances in sentence structure (e.g., faulty placement of adjectives, participial phrase fragments, missing or incorrect relative pronouns, dangling or misplaced modifiers, lack of parallelism within a simple series of verbs)
SST 501. Recognize and correct disturbances in sentence structure (e.g., faulty placement of phrases, faulty coordination and subordination of clauses, lack of parallelism within a simple series of phrases)
SST 601. Recognize and correct subtle disturbances in sentence structure (e.g., danglers where the intended meaning is clear but the sentence is ungrammatical, faulty subordination and coordination of clauses in long or involved sentences)
SST 701. Recognize and correct very subtle disturbances in sentence structure (e.g., weak conjunctions between independent clauses, run-ons that would be acceptable in conversational English, lack of parallelism within a complex series of phrases or clauses)

Example: English question #3 on page 12 of *Preparing for the ACT 2015-16.*

Content Area #3: Redundancy & Wordiness

An entire ACT College Readiness Standard Family is dedicated to conciseness, which is covered in more detail in *Grammar and the Three C's* on page 92. We call this standard family *Redundancy & Wordiness.* This standard family makes up 8-15% of your students' English scores, so it's one of the biggest categories of questions on the test.

CATEGORY: SENTENCE STRUCTION & FORMATIONS

Family: Sentence Structure Disturbances

Weight: >15%

Standards:
KLA 301. Delete obviously redundant and wordy material
KLA 401. Delete redundant and wordy material when the problem is contained within a single phrase (e.g., "alarmingly startled," "started by reaching the point of beginning")
KLA 502. Delete redundant and wordy material when the meaning of the entire sentence must be considered
KLA 602. Delete redundant and wordy material that involves fairly sophisticated language (e.g., "the outlook of an aesthetic viewpoint") or that sounds acceptable as conversational English
KLA 701. Delete redundant and wordy material that involves sophisticated language or complex concepts or where the material is redundant in terms of the paragraph or essay as a whole

---

Example: English Question #59 on page 21 of *Preparing for the ACT 2015-16.*

Content Area #4: Identify Purpose

The most common phrasing of the "identify purpose" question type is as follows:

If the writer were to delete the preceding sentence, the paragraph/passage would primarily lose:

This is one of the few questions that the ACT recycles for every single test. Your students should anticipate it appearing with this exact wording.

The convoluted way the question is asked often trips up students, so it's worth helping them decode it.

Refer to English question #26 on page 16 of *Preparing for the ACT 2015-16.*

This question is a double negative. It's really asking this:

What is the purpose of the preceding sentence?

Or:

Why did the author put this sentence here? What was he or she trying to accomplish with this sentence? What is the purpose of this sentence?

You will find that if you rephrase the question like this, some students who answered incorrectly will suddenly be able to get the right answer.

When students are asked about the consequences of deleting a sentence, they should ask themselves *what is the purpose of this sentence?*

Refer to English question #56 on page 20 of *Preparing for the ACT 2015-16.*

Check Your Understanding: What is the ACT actually asking in question #56?

_____

_____

_____

_____

CATEGORY: TOPIC DEVELOPMENT

Family: Identify Purpose

Weight: 4-8%

Standards:
TOD 302. Identify the purpose of a word or phrase when the purpose is simple (e.g., identifying a person, defining a basic term, using common descriptive adjectives)
TOD 402. Identify the purpose of a word or phrase when the purpose is straightforward (e.g., describing a person, giving examples)
TOD 502. Identify the purpose of a word, phrase, or sentence when the purpose is fairly straightforward (e.g., identifying traits, giving reasons, explaining motivations)
TOD 602. Identify the purpose of a word, phrase, or sentence when the purpose is subtle (e.g., supporting a later point, establishing tone) or when the best decision is to delete the text in question
TOD 701. Identify the purpose of a word, phrase, or sentence when the purpose is complex (e.g., anticipating a reader's need for background information) or requires a thorough understanding of the paragraph and essay

Example: English question #7 on page 13 of *Preparing for the ACT 2015-16*.

Content Area #5: Word Choice

Students are required to make word choices that accomplish a given style or purpose.

There are actually three ACT Standard Families that fit into this question type and look quite similar when they appear on the test. These are *Word Choice* and *Style & Tone* from Knowledge of Language and *Accomplish Purpose* from Topic Development.

Vocabulary tends to be the main obstacle that makes these questions particularly challenging. Help your students manage tough vocabulary and work through confusion to arrive at the correct answer.

Refer to English question #55 on page 20 of *Preparing for the ACT 2015-16*.

This question asks for words that are *positive* and *elaborate*. For some students, the answer jumps off the page. A student who finds this question challenging is likely stumped by the vocabulary in the answer choices.

Elaborate, mimics, décor, embellished, myriad, marred, and *gaudy* are all words not commonly used by high school students.

In order to break through the confusion, students should assign an emotion to each difficult term. Even if students do not understand the definition of a word, they have probably heard it before, read it in some context, or it may look similar to a word that they *are* familiar with. These connotations can help students arrive at the correct answer.

For example, to the students *marred* may have a negative connotation. It sounds like an ugly word, and it is quite similar to *scarred*, which happens to be its synonym. Since the question asks for a *positive* word choice, they can eliminate C.

Another trick is to use context to understand what is being asked. Question #55 hinges on the meaning of the word *elaborate*. If students don't know what this word means, they won't understand what is being asked of them. That being said, if students put the unfamiliar term *elaborate* into a *lock box* (see page 300), they may still get the idea from the rest of the question that they are looking for a choice that is similar to the descriptions that are nearby in the essay. From there, they can go with the choice that sounds the fanciest and is positive: B.

Students who persevere through confusing vocabulary and who are willing to play detective will do better on word choice questions.

CATEGORY: TOPIC DEVELOPMENT

Family: Accomplish Purpose

Weight: 4-8%

Standards:
KLA 404. Use the word or phrase most appropriate in terms of the content of the sentence when the vocabulary is relatively common
KLA 505. Use the word or phrase most appropriate in terms of the content of the sentence when the vocabulary is uncommon
KLA 604. Use the word or phrase most appropriate in terms of the content of the sentence when the vocabulary is fairly sophisticated
KLA 702. Use the word or phrase most appropriate in terms of the content of the sentence when the vocabulary is sophisticated

CATEGORY: KNOWLEDGE OF LANGUAGE

Family: Word Choice

Weight: 4-8%

Standards:
TOD 403. Use a word, phrase, or sentence to accomplish a straightforward purpose (e.g., conveying a feeling or attitude)
TOD 504. Use a word, phrase, or sentence to accomplish a fairly straightforward purpose (e.g., sharpening an essay's focus, illustrating a given statement)
TOD 603. Use a word, phrase, or sentence to accomplish a subtle purpose (e.g., adding emphasis or supporting detail, expressing meaning through connotation)
TOD 703. Use a word, phrase, or sentence to accomplish a complex purpose, often in terms of the focus of the essay

Example: English question #38 on page 17 of *Preparing for the ACT 2015-16.*

CATEGORY: KNOWLEDGE OF LANGUAGE

Family: Style & Tone

Weight: 1-2%

Standards:
KLA 302. Revise expressions that deviate markedly from the style and tone of the essay
KLA 402. Revise expressions that deviate from the style and tone of the essay
KLA 503. Revise expressions that deviate in subtle ways from the style and tone of the essay

Example: English question #55 on page 20 of *Preparing for the ACT 2015-16.*

Content Area #6: Unnecessary Commas

We have covered several strategies for determining when a comma is necessary or unnecessary. These tips include the *no solo commas* rule, the *secret service move*, and *when in doubt, commas out*.

Three entire standard families are dedicated to comma usage, including two that have made our Top Ten Content Areas: *Unnecessary Commas* and *Parenthetical Elements*. Below is the information for the most heavily weighted of these standard families.

CATEGORY: PUNCTUATION

Family: Unnecessary Commas

Weight: 4-8%

Standards:
PUN 201. Delete commas that create basic sense problems (e.g., between verb and direct object)
PUN 301. Delete commas that markedly disturb sentence flow (e.g., between modifier and modified element)
PUN 401. Delete commas when an incorrect understanding of the sentence suggests a pause that should be punctuated (e.g., between verb and direct object clause)
PUN 501. Delete commas in long or involved sentences when an incorrect understanding of the sentence suggests a pause that should be punctuated (e.g., between the elements of a compound subject or compound verb joined by and)

Example: English question #1 on page 12 of *Preparing for the ACT 2015-16*.

Content Area #7: Parenthetical Elements

The crux of the most difficult punctuation questions is telling the difference between *restrictive* and *nonrestrictive* phrases.

A *restrictive phrase* limits or restricts the meaning of what it is modifying.

A *nonrestrictive phrase* gives more information about what it modifies, but it does not restrict or limit it.

Nonrestrictive phrases should be set off with commas. An easy way to remember this is to think that the longer word, *nonrestrictive*, gets the commas and pauses.

Restrictive phrases are too essential to the meaning of what they modify to be separated by commas.

Many students find this type of question to be challenging because it's easy to mix up restrictive and nonrestrictive phrases.

Refer to English question #31 on page 16 of *Preparing for the ACT 2015-16*.

Named Juan Quezada limits the meaning of the word *boy*. Without this phrase, the sentence could be talking about *any* twelve-year-old boy from the early 1950s. With this phrase, *boy* is restricted to referring to only one person, *Juan Quezada*. This is a restrictive phrase. For that reason, no commas are necessary.

It should be noted that students could eliminate their way to the correct answer in this question without being clear on restrictive and nonrestrictive phrases. Choice A inserts an awkward pause between *named* and *Juan*, while choices C and D can be eliminated using the *no solo commas* rule (there can never be only one comma between the subject and the verb).

Refer to English question #32 on page 17 of *Preparing for the ACT 2015-16*.

In question #32, choices F and G place punctuation around the phrase *along with an occasional complete pot*.

Check Your Understanding: Is this phrase restrictive or nonrestrictive?

_____

_____

What questions could you ask your students to guide them to this conclusion?

_____

_____

CATEGORY: PUNCTUATION

Family: Parenthetical Elements

Weight: 4-8%

Standards:
PUN 404. Use commas to set off simple parenthetical elements
PUN 503. Use punctuation to set off complex parenthetical elements
PUN 602. Use punctuation to set off a nonessential/ nonrestrictive appositive or clause
PUN 701. Delete punctuation around essential/restrictive appositives or clauses

Example: English question #31 on page 16 of *Preparing for the ACT 2015-16.*

Content Area #8: Verb Tense & Pronoun Person

Verb Tense & Pronoun Person is a heavily weighted ACT Standard Family, accounting for 4-8% of the student's English score. The *Three C's: Consistent* section on page 92 has strategies that can help students answer more questions correctly in this category.

CATEGORY: SENTENCE STRUCTURE & FORMATION

Family: Verb Tense & Pronoun Person

Weight: 4-8%

Standards:
SST 202. Recognize and correct inappropriate shifts in verb tense between simple clauses in a sentence or between simple adjoining sentences
SST 302. Recognize and correct inappropriate shifts in verb tense and voice when the meaning of the entire sentence must be considered
SST 502. Maintain consistent and logical verb tense and pronoun person on the basis of the preceding clause or sentence
SST 602. Maintain consistent and logical verb tense and voice and pronoun person on the basis of the paragraph or essay as a whole

Example: English question #63 on page 21 of *Preparing for the ACT 2015-16*.

Content Area #9: Pronoun-Antecedent Agreement

When a question offers two or more pronoun alternatives, students should take care to identify the pronoun's antecedent. Often, the noun that is closest to the pronoun or the noun that appears in the same phrase or clause as the pronoun is *not* the antecedent.

When a distractor noun appears near a pronoun, it can make the pronoun's number (singular or plural) *sound* correct even when this number does not actually agree with the antecedent.

Refer to English question #46 on page 19 of *Preparing for the ACT 2015-16*.

In question #46, *it's* and *they're* can be eliminated right away because these contractions don't make sense in the context of the sentence. Students are left to choose between *their* and *its*.

Unfortunately, *their* will sound right to many students. *Buildings* is a plural noun that appears in the same phrase as the underlined portion, and so the plural *their* seems to work.

Only if students pause to identify the actual antecedent, *Lyceum Theatre*, will they be able to determine that the singular *its* is more appropriate.

CATEGORY: USAGE CONVENTIONS

Family: Pronoun-Antecedent Agreement

Weight: 2-4%

Standards:
USG 303. Ensure straightforward pronoun-antecedent agreement
USG 502. Ensure pronoun-antecedent agreement when the pronoun and antecedent occur in separate clauses or sentences
USG 503. Recognize and correct vague and ambiguous pronouns

Example: English question #46 on page 19 of *Preparing for the ACT 2015-16*.

Content Area #10: Sequence

Two to three times throughout the English test, students will be asked to find the optimum placement for a sentence (or occasionally, a paragraph).

There are a few ways that the ACT asks this question, and it's a good idea to review these wordings with your students so they are prepared.

Which of the following sequences of sentences makes Paragraph X most logical?

For the sake of the logic and coherence of this paragraph, Sentence X should be placed:

Upon reviewing the essay and finding that some information has been left out, the writer composes the following sentence incorporating that information…The sentence would most logically be placed:

Coherence, logically, following, and *incorporating* are terms that often give students trouble, and they occur frequently in this question type.

> Refer to English question #29 on page 16 of *Preparing for the ACT 2015-16.*

This question is a simplified version of the third question variant described above.

Students should look for three major clues to find the correct sequence.

The first clue to look for is *time.* Is there a specific reference to time or to signs of the passage of time?

In the case of question #29, the addition mentions *the sun dipped below the trees.* This is a clue that tells students the addition should be placed in the part of the passage that occurs during sunset.

The second clue is to look for parts of the passage that are similar to the addition. Sentences that are about the same topic should be grouped together in the same paragraphs.

> Refer to English question #14 on page 14 of *Preparing for the ACT 2015-16.*

The third and most important clue to look for is a *specific reference.* Is there a specific reference made in the addition that won't make sense if it appears too early in the passage?

In question #14, the addition begins with *This growth.* It wouldn't be logical to place this addition before the growth is introduced. Likewise, the addition should not be placed too far from the introduction of the growth because such a specific reference wouldn't be relevant. By looking for the location closest when growth is introduced, the best placement is in choice H.

> Refer to English question #34 on page 17 of *Preparing for the ACT 2015-16.*

This strategy doesn't apply to sequence questions only. Students can use *specific references* to make sense of transitions as well.

In question #34, *he dug the clay* makes a specific reference to *the* clay, which indicates that it should have already been introduced by this point in the passage.

Only choice H introduces the clay, making the specific reference that follows logical.

> Refer to English question #44 on page 18 of *Preparing for the ACT 2015-16.*

Check Your Understanding: What is the specific reference being made in Sentence 5?

_____

_____

What two choices can be eliminated because they place a specific reference _before_ the reference has been introduced?

_____

_____

CATEGORY: UNITY & COHESION

Family: Sentence Sequence

Weight: 2-4%

Standards:
ORG 405. Rearrange the sentences in a straightforward paragraph for the sake of logic
ORG 503. Rearrange the sentences in a fairly straightforward paragraph for the sake of logic
ORG 604. Rearrange the sentences in a fairly complex paragraph for the sake of logic and coherence

Example: English question #29 on page 16 of _Preparing for the ACT 2015-16_.

The Four Toughest Questions and Why

Please refer to Preparing for the ACT 2013-14. *For the bulk of this book, we have been referring to a later edition of* Preparing for the ACT, *but in this chapter we are referring to the earlier 2013-14 edition so that we can provide information about student response data that we have gathered. Please note that if you refer to the* Preparing for the ACT 2015-16 *booklet, this chapter won't make sense.*

In this section of the book, we have covered the ten most heavily weighted content areas on the ACT English test. Here, we will discuss the three types of questions that give students the most trouble.

Restrictive vs. Nonrestrictive

Far and away, our data shows that students of all ability levels have the most trouble with differentiating restrictive and nonrestrictive phrases and punctuating them correctly.

> Refer to English question #22 on page 15 of *Preparing for the ACT 2013-14.*

Question #22 is the most missed question on this test. In our database, only 11% of students have answered it correctly, which is much worse than the students just guessing! The most common answers are choices F and G, both of which try to get at least one comma around what the student feels is a nonrestrictive phrase. It's interesting to note that students feel so sure about needing to punctuate this phrase that they opt for awkwardly including only one comma rather than dropping the punctuation.

The key to answering this question is recognizing that *William Barclay Parsons* is restrictive and so should not be punctuated at all. For that reason, J is the best choice.

> Refer to English question #63 on page 21 of *Preparing for the ACT 2013-14.*

Question #63 echoes the same challenge presented in question #22. In this case, *or constellation* is nonrestrictive, providing relevant information that is not necessary to the sentence's meaning. The most popular answer for this question is choice C, which leaves an awkward comma between the subject and the verb and puts *pattern* and *constellation* in parity.

Choice A is the best choice because it surrounds the phrase with commas, but some students may shy away from it simply because there are so many commas in a very small space.

Colons

> Refer to English question #17 on page 14 of *Preparing for the ACT 2013-14.*

Students are often challenged by the way the ACT tests colons. Most students are familiar with the use of a colon to introduce a list, and this familiarity is often their downfall. On the ACT, colons are usually used to introduce more information about a previous statement, not to introduce lists. Students typically gravitate toward the choice that most looks like it provides a list, or they will eliminate any choices that use a colon because they don't see a list.

In question #17, the most common answers are choices A and B. Students would rather create a sentence fragment or a comma splice than use a colon to introduce something other than a list. The correct answer is choice C, which clues in the reader that what follows will provide more information about the *incredible engineering feat.*

Sentence Structure Disturbances

Refer to English question #12 on page 13 of *Preparing for the ACT 2013-14*.

Sentence Structure Disturbances is a massive ACT Standard Family and one of the most difficult to coach. To reliably answer these questions correctly, students must be familiar not only with identifying subjects and verbs and therefore complete sentences, but they also must master coordinating and subordinating conjunctions and their intended meanings.

In question #12, for instance, the most popular answer is choice G, which incorrectly uses *however* as a coordinating conjunction. It is an easy mistake for students to make unless they are quite familiar with *however* and its usage.

The correct answer is choice H, which uses a period to separate two complete sentences. It's interesting to note that choice H is a completely safe and obvious choice, yet choice G by and large wins in the popularity contest.

English Standard Families

ACT provides College Readiness Standards that are essential to understanding the structure of the test. At MasteryPrep, we have taken it one step further by grouping these standards into logical, teachable categories and providing data on how frequently each standard family is assessed on the ACT. Below is a preview of one of the standard families. Feel free to download this resource, print it, and use it as you see fit.

PUNCTUATION CONVENTIONS (13%)

AMBIGUITY & SERIES (1-2%)

PUN 302. Use appropriate punctuation in straightforward situations (e.g., simple items in a series)

PUN 403. Use commas to avoid obvious ambiguity (e.g., to set off a long introductory element from the rest of the sentence when a misreading is possible)

PUN 601. Use commas to avoid ambiguity when the syntax or language is sophisticated (e.g., to set off a complex series of items)

APOSTROPHES (2-4%)

PUN 402. Delete apostrophes used incorrectly to form plural nouns

PUN 504. Use apostrophes to form simple possessive nouns

PUN 603. Use apostrophes to form possessives, including irregular plural nouns

COLONS & SEMICOLONS (<1%)

PUN 502. Recognize and correct inappropriate uses of colons and semicolons

PUN 604. Use a semicolon to link closely related independent clauses

PUN 702. Use a colon to introduce an example or an elaboration

PARENTHETICAL ELEMENTS (4-8%)

PUN 404. Use commas to set off simple parenthetical elements

PUN 503. Use punctuation to set off complex parenthetical elements

PUN 602. Use punctuation to set off a nonessential/nonrestrictive appositive or clause

PUN 701. Delete punctuation around essential/restrictive appositives or clauses

UNNECESSARY COMMAS (4-8%)

PUN 201. Delete commas that create basic sense problems (e.g., between verb and direct object)

PUN 301. Delete commas that markedly disturb sentence flow (e.g., between modifier and modified element)

PUN 401. Delete commas when an incorrect understanding of the sentence suggests a pause that should be punctuated (e.g., between verb and direct object clause)

PUN 501. Delete commas in long or involved sentences when an incorrect understanding of the sentence suggests a pause that should be punctuated (e.g., between the elements of a compound subject or compound verb joined by and)

Visit masteryprep.com/decode/resources to download a printable PDF of MasteryPrep's ACT English Standard Families.

Recommended Reading

There are thousands of books that can help students improve their grammar skills.

As a matter of fact, that's a very limiting statement. Indeed, just about *any* book that is written in standard English will help a student with the English test. To the bookworms go the spoils. There is no substitute for the intimate familiarity of the English language afforded by a vast experience in reading books.

That being said, there are a couple books that wefeel can help students with their ACT English scores disproportionate to the time spent reading them—these are short reads with big payoffs. Any student who aims to score higher than 27 on the ACT English test should read them:

The Elements of Style by Strunk and White

The Elements of Grammar by Margaret Schertzer

The first is the bedrock for understanding the Rhetorical Skills questions that appear on the test. The second is akin to drinking grammar orange juice concentrate and thus can boost student outcomes on Usage and Mechanics questions.

They are both classics and quick reads. We would argue that students should be familiar with them regardless of whether or not it helps them with the ACT.

Common Core Alignment

Visit masteryprep.com/decode/resources to find the Common Core alignment to ACT standards.

DECODING ENGLISH TEST 72-C
Answer Explanations and Standard Families

1. Punctuation >> Unnecessary Commas

Choice B is incorrect because *from tiny water droplets* is a prepositional phrase modifying the verb *form*, and so it should not be separated from the verb by a comma.

Choice C is incorrect because *water droplets* is a single concept that should not be interrupted by a comma.

Choice D is incorrect because *from tiny water droplets* is a prepositional phrase modifying the verb *form* and should not be separated from the verb with a comma. Furthermore, without a comma after *droplets*, the meaning of the sentence is confused—it seems that the *droplets* are *following* a process, not the snowflake formation.

The correct answer is A. The comma correctly separates the prepositional phrase *from tiny water droplets* from the participial phrase *following a specific process*, indicating that this process modifies *snowflake formation* and not the *water droplets*.

2. Organization >> Transitions

Choice F is incorrect because *snowflakes form from tiny water droplets* is not similar to *snowflakes confounded scientists,* so *similarly* is a poor word choice.

Choice G is incorrect because the *rare "triangular" snowflake* is not an example of what is discussed in the previous sentence.

Choice H is incorrect because *additionally* infers that information is being added to the point made in the previous sentence, but a triangular snowflake is *different* from a six-sided snowflake.

The correct answer is J. *However* is used to introduce information that is in contrast with a previous statement. In this case, the previous sentence talks about *six-sided* snowflakes, while this sentence talks about *triangular* (three-sided) snowflakes.

3. Sentence Structure & Formation >> Relative Pronouns

Choice A is incorrect because the clause following *that* is incomplete, lacking a subject.

Choice B is incorrect because it creates an incomplete thought: *the manner in which formation through a different process of chemical bonding.* The sentence ends abruptly. This choice also makes the sentence wordy.

Choice C is incorrect because *which had formed through a different process of chemical bonding* does not explain what the shape of these snowflakes *suggests*.

The correct answer is D. *That they form* creates a complete dependent clause with a subject and verb; it also tells us what the triangular shape *suggests*.

4.   Sentence Structure & Formation >> Misplaced Modifiers & Phrases

Choices F and G are incorrect because the phrase *by re-creating snowflake formation* modifies *discovery*, rather than the *scientists*.

Choice J is incorrect because the phrase *by re-creating snowflake formation* modifies *cause* instead of *scientists*.

The correct answer is H. It places *scientists* close to the phrase that modifies it, *by re-creating snowflake formation*. For that reason, it is the clearest alternative.

5.   Sentence Structure & Formation >> Fragments & Fused Sentences

Choice A is incorrect because the intended meaning of this sentence is that the water is being frozen, not that the water is freezing the snowflake, as this choice suggests.

Choices C and D are incorrect because they form comma splices.

The correct answer is B. The comma correctly separates *freezes* from the participial phrase *causing the water molecules to bond*.

6.   Usage >> Subject-Verb Agreement

Choices F and G are incorrect because the subject *molecules* is plural, but *bumps* and *has bumped* are singular verbs.

Choice H is incorrect because *bumped* is a past tense verb, which is inconsistent with the present tense verbs in the rest of the passage.

The correct answer is J. *Bump* is a plural verb, which agrees with the plural subject *molecules*. *Bump* is also in the present tense, which is consistent with the tense of the passage.

7.   Topic Development >> Identify Purpose

Choice A is incorrect because this sentence describes *bypassing the liquid water phase*, but it does not talk about going *from liquid to vapor to solid*.

Choice C is incorrect because the underlined portion does not provide a *visual description*.

Choice D is incorrect because the underlined portion does not mention or refer to *various air temperatures*.

The correct answer is B. *Bypassing the liquid water phase* has a similar meaning to *mentions a step some water molecules skip*. *Skip* and *bypass* are synonyms.

8.   Usage >> Subject-Verb Agreement

Choice F is incorrect because *forms* is a singular verb, which does not agree with the plural subject *snowflakes*. Even though the singular nouns *process* and *bonding* are close to the verb, neither are the subject.

Choices G and H are incorrect because they create incomplete conditional statements and are not consistent with the compound predicate, *begin with the same process of chemical bonding*.

The correct answer is J. The plural verb *form* is consistent with the construction of the compound predicate started earlier in the sentence and agrees with the plural subject *snowflakes*.

9. Punctuation >> Colons & Semicolons

Choices A and B are incorrect because they create a run-on sentence.

Choice D is incorrect because the semicolon is used in this context to join two independent clauses. *Dust* is not an independent clause, so a semicolon cannot be used here.

The correct answer is C. The colon lets the reader know that additional information follows. The information before the colon is an independent clause, which means that a colon can properly be used here.

10. Sentence Structure & Formation >> Fragments & Fused Sentences

Choice F is incorrect because the comma after *wind* unnecessarily separates the subject from the verb. A single comma can never come between the subject and the verb. This choice also starts the construction of an introductory phrase, *the greater the pressure*, but the sentence does not complete the idea.

Choices G and H are incorrect because they form incomplete sentences. Choice G creates the fragment *which causes bonds to form*, while Choice H creates the dependent clause *as the wind causes bonds to form*, neither of which can stand alone.

The correct answer is J. This choice creates a complete sentence without any unnecessary punctuation.

11. Usage >> Comparatives & Superlatives

Choice A is incorrect because *quick* modifies the verb *form* and so should be in the form of an adverb, not an adjective.

Choice C is incorrect because the superlative *most quickly* is inappropriately used to compare two things.

Choice D is incorrect because *quickest* modifies the verb *form* and so needs to be in the form of an adverb, not a superlative adjective.

The correct answer is B. This choice uses the comparative adverb phrase *more quickly*, which is the best fit for the sentence since only two speeds are being compared.

12. Punctuation >> Colons & Semicolons

Choice F is incorrect because an em dash is used for parenthetical information, not for punctuating an introductory dependent clause.

Choice H is incorrect because the semicolon joins two independent clauses, but *although these snowflakes appear to have a triangular shape* is a dependent clause.

Choice J is incorrect because the colon must come after an independent clause, but *although these snowflakes appear to have a triangular shape* is a dependent clause.

The correct answer is G. It correctly uses a comma to separate the dependent clause in the beginning of the sentence from the independent clause that follows.

13. Organization >> Introductions & Conclusions

Choice B is incorrect because it contains an extreme statement that is not fully supported by the essay.

Scientists cannot be *certain that a solution to even the most confusing event will be found* simply because they figured out the mystery of the triangular snowflake.

Choice C is incorrect because the conclusion does not match the focus of the essay. The topic of the essay is not "the conditions for when snowflakes will fall," but rather a discussion of the nature of triangular snowflakes and whether they follow the basic laws of chemistry.

Choice D is incorrect because it does not logically follow the previous phrase, *even when impurities interfere*. The essay explained that impurities cause snowflakes to have a different shape, so *even when* does not make a logical transition.

The correct answer is A. This conclusion ties nicely to the introductory paragraph, which stated that triangular snowflakes *confounded scientists for years because it apparently defied the basic laws of chemistry*. This choice captures the meaning of the essay and logically follows the beginning of the sentence.

14. Organization >> Sentence Placement

Choices F and B are incorrect because at points [A] and [B] in the passage, the growth has not been introduced, and so *this growth* is out of place.

Choice J is incorrect because this sentence interrupts the description in paragraph 4. The growth has been introduced earlier in the essay, and it would be better to place this statement closer to the first reference.

The correct answer is H. In this placement, the new sentence directly refers to the preceding statement, *As a result, the flake grows outward into bigger and more complex hexagonal arrangements surrounding the original hexagonal shape at the center of the flake.*

15. Topic Development >> Writer's Goal

Choice A is incorrect because the essay makes clear that despite appearances, the triangular snowflake still follows the basic laws of chemistry, not that the scientists had a flawed understanding of these laws.

Choice B is incorrect because the essay does not support that scientists have applied their newfound knowledge to other areas of chemistry.

Choice C is incorrect because the last three paragraphs of the essay show that the scientists did in fact determine how triangular snowflakes are formed: *the triangular shape was an illusion…they actually have a hexagonal pattern.*

The correct answer is D. The essay did not accomplish the stated purpose because it did not describe scientists changing how they viewed the basic laws of chemistry. Furthermore, the last paragraph establishes that the triangular snowflakes did not *violate the basic laws of chemistry*.

16. Sentence Structure & Formation >> Participial Phrases

Choice F is incorrect because *bundled up in wool sweaters and thick coats* is not an independent clause, so a comma with a coordinating conjunction does not work.

Choices G and J are incorrect because they create incomplete sentences that lack subjects.

The correct answer is H. The subject and verb *we watched* create a complete sentence, and the participial phrase is properly set apart from what it modifies by a comma.

17. Sentence Structure & Formation >> Verb Tense & Pronoun Person

Choice A is incorrect because *would have needed* creates a conditional statement that is not logical in this paragraph.

Choices C and D are incorrect because they are inconsistent with the tense of the passage.

The correct answer is B. *Would* is the past tense form of *will*, which is consistent with the past tense in the passage.

18. Knowledge of Language >> Redundancy & Wordiness

Choice F is incorrect because *jumbled rocks* and *slipping* are mentioned earlier in the paragraph, so this wording is redundant.

Choice G is incorrect because *walking sticks* are already mentioned in the sentence, so this second mention is redundant.

Choice H is incorrect because *efforts to remain steady* repeats the earlier phrase in the sentence, *we tried to steady ourselves.*

The correct answer is J. This option gives necessary information concisely without repeating earlier content.

19. Usage >> Prepositions

Choices A and D are incorrect because the preposition *on* indicates that the roof is *on top of* the fallen rocks, which does not make sense when the roof is later described as protecting from falling rocks.

Choice B is incorrect because the roof is not actively and continuously *piling* rocks, but rather, the rocks had already *piled high* by the time the narrator saw them.

The correct answer is C. This choice conveys the intended meaning that rocks had *piled high* atop the roof. The phrase *piled high with* means that many objects are stacked on top of something, which is a good fit for the meaning of this sentence.

20. Sentence Structure & Formation >> Fragments & Fused Sentences

Choice F is incorrect because using *which* and *it was* in the same modifying phrase is unnecessarily wordy and confusing.

Choice G is incorrect because it creates a comma splice. *It was proof of our progress through the darkness* needs a conjunction after the comma in order to be joined with the other independent clause in the sentence.

Choice J is incorrect because it creates an illogical sentence.

The correct answer is H. This choice correctly sets off the appositive from the sentence by a comma.

21. Usage >> Adjectives & Adverbs

Choice B is incorrect because it is wordy and redundant.

Choice C is incorrect because the proper format would be *the majority*, not *majority* by itself. In this context, *majority* requires an article, such as *the* or *a*.

Choice D is incorrect because this sentence is not comparing anything, so the comparative *more* is not logical.

The correct answer is A. *Most* clearly and smoothly conveys that for a large part of the route, the hikers were *thinly spread across the mountain*. *Most* in this sense is not used as a superlative, but rather to mean *nearly all of*.

22. Sentence Structure & Formation >> Fragments & Fused Sentences

Choices G, H and J are incorrect because they form run-on sentences. Each choice also needs a conjunction following the comma.

The correct answer is F. The participial phrase, *forming an illuminated line along the trail*, is properly punctuated by a comma, setting it apart from the independent clause.

23. Topic Development >> Accomplish Purpose

Choices A and D are incorrect because *progressing along the trail* and *climbing higher in altitude* do not convey the *slowness of the ascent*.

Choice C is incorrect because *moving forward with each step* does not show that the group *did not set their own pace*.

The correct answer is B. *Able to advance only a few steps at a time* clearly communicates *slowness* while also indicating that the group of friends did not control *their own pace*. Even if the friends wanted to move more quickly, the adverb *only* emphasizes that they were limited.

24. Punctuation >> Colons & Semicolons

Choice F is incorrect because *in the half-light of the rising sun* is not an independent clause, so a colon cannot come after this phrase.

Choice G is incorrect because an em dash is used to punctuate parenthetical phrases, not introductory phrases.

Choice J is incorrect because a semicolon joins two independent clauses. *In the half-light of the rising sun* is not an independent clause, so the semicolon cannot be used.

The correct answer is H. A comma properly separates the introductory phrase, *in the half-light of the rising sun*, from the rest of the sentence.

25. Punctuation >> Apostrophes

Choices A and B are incorrect because *cliffs* is the object of the preposition *of* and is not possessing anything, so an apostrophe cannot be used.

Choice D is incorrect because the *edge* belongs to the *crater*, so an apostrophe is needed to show possession.

The correct answer is C. The plural noun *cliffs* is plural and not possessive, so an apostrophe is not needed. The singular noun *crater* is possessive, so it uses an apostrophe.

26. Topic Development >> Identify Purpose

Choice G is incorrect because the hikers waiting has already been introduced in the previous sentence.

Choice H is incorrect because there is no information earlier in the paragraph that contradicts the statement *we waited for the sun*.

Choice J is incorrect because *we waited for the sun* does not describe what the hikers saw at the summit.

The correct answer is F. Since *waiting* has already been introduced in the previous sentence, *we waited for the sun* is a restatement of a point already made. This restatement emphasizes what the hikers were anticipating.

27. Organization >> Transitions

Choice A is incorrect because *generally* means *speaking in non-specific terms*, but the sentence that follows is very specific in its description.

Choice B is incorrect because *furthermore* means that what comes next builds on the previous statement. However, the sudden gap in clouds does not logically add to the previous sentence: *we waited for the sun*.

Choice C is incorrect because *once again* means that what comes next repeats what has already been discussed. *A sudden gap in the clouds* has not been previously described.

The correct answer is D. *Finally* can be used to show that something anticipated has occurred, so this word choice echoes the theme of waiting and anticipation that the essay has developed.

28. Topic Development >> Accomplish Purpose

Choices F, H, and J are incorrect because *squelched out, smothered,* and *went over* do not convey *the ruggedness of the landscape*.

The correct answer is G. Saying that the sunlight figuratively *shattered over* gives a strong visual image of the landscape as sharp and rugged.

29. Organization >> Sentence Placement

Choice B is incorrect because this addition describes the beginning of hiking, but this placement occurs after the group has started hiking.

Choices C and D can be eliminated because the addition talks about the sun setting, but these placements in paragraph 4 take place during dawn.

The correct answer is A. Because the addition describes the group starting their hike as the sun sets, it is logical to place this sentence in the beginning of the essay, when the hiking group sets out.

30. Topic Development >> Writer's Goal

Choice G is incorrect because although the passage does mention walking sticks, the entire essay does not focus on walking sticks and tools but rather on the hikers' journey.

Choice H is incorrect because the essay *does* describe the hike as challenging in several places, such as *we tried to steady ourselves with our walking sticks but slipped and stumbled with each step* in paragraph 2, and *we leaned against each other, spent* in paragraph 5.

Choice J is incorrect because as a whole, the essay does not describe the beauty of the landscape but rather focuses more on the hikers.

The correct answer is F. Throughout the essay, the author describes various challenges on the hike. This answer may not feel like a great fit, but according to the premise set by the question, choice F is the only choice that can't be eliminated.

31. Punctuation >> Parenthetical Elements

Choice A is incorrect because *named Juan Quezada* is a complete thought that cannot be interrupted with a comma.

Choices C and D are incorrect because one comma alone cannot come between the subject, *boy,* and the verb, *gathered*.

The correct answer is B. *Named Juan Quezada* is restrictive, defining *which* boy. For this reason, no commas can be used around it.

32. Punctuation >> Parenthetical Elements

Choice F is incorrect because it correctly uses em dashes to set off the parenthetical phrase *along with an occasional complete pot.*

Choice G is incorrect because it correctly uses commas to set off the parenthetical phrase from the rest of the sentence.

Choice J is incorrect because it correctly uses parentheses to set off the parenthetical phrase.

The correct answer is H. This alternative is not acceptable because commas and parentheses cannot be used together to set apart a parenthetical phrase. Only one or the other can be used. Because the question asks which alternative is NOT acceptable, a grammatically correct answer is incorrect in this case.

33. Punctuation >> Unnecessary Commas

Choices A and D are incorrect because this sentence is not a direct question, so a question mark cannot be used.

Choice C is incorrect because *if he could make pots like these* is a dependent clause. No comma is necessary between an independent clause and the dependent clause that follows it.

The correct answer is B. This sentence correctly ends with a period since it is not a direct question, and it refrains from punctuating the dependent clause with a comma after the independent clause.

34. Organization >> Transitions

Choice F is incorrect because a description of the village does not transition from Quezada wondering if he could create similar pots to his experimental process.

Choices G and J are incorrect because although they do connect from the preceding phrase *fascinated by the geometric designs*, they do not logically connect to the sentence that follows, which describes Quezada attempting to create clay pots.

The correct answer is H. Explaining that Quezada *began working with clay from the mountains* offers a logical transition between Quezada wondering if he could create similar pots to the process of making his own.

35. Sentence Structure & Formation >> Verb Tense & Pronoun Person

Choices B and C are incorrect because it does not make sense for Quezeda to be *selling a dedication to teaching* or *selling a teacher of*. These are not things that can be sold.

Choice D is incorrect because the present perfect tense of *has taught* is not consistent with the past tense in the essay.

The correct answer is A. The past perfect tense of *had taught* is consistent with the tense and meaning of the paragraph.

36. Topic Development >> Identify Purpose

Choices G and J are incorrect because Quezada's *technique as a potter* not being *very well developed* and his *style* being *outmoded* are negative statements that are not consistent with Spencer MacCallum joining in an *eventual partnership with Quezeda* in the next sentence.

Choice H is incorrect because the designs that Quezada used are described as *intricate* and *complex*, which contradicts the statement that his pots were *strikingly simple*.

The correct answer is F. The anthropologist thought that the pots were prehistoric because, the essay explains, Quezada followed the same processes as his ancestors in creating his pottery.

37. Usage >> Confusing Pairs

Choices B and C are incorrect because the reflexive pronoun *himself* is only used when the subject and object of the sentence refer to the same thing, but in this sentence the subject is *search*.

Choice D is incorrect because the present tense verb *lead* is inconsistent with the past tense of the passage. Because the noun *lead* sounds the same as the past tense verb *led*, this choice can be mistaken for correct.

The correct answer is A. *Led him* matches the past tense of the paragraph and uses the correct objective pronoun for MacCallum.

38. Topic Development >> Accomplish Purpose

Choices G and H are incorrect because they imply that the partnership did not last for long, not that there was a delay in forming the partnership.

Choice J is incorrect because it says that the partnership had good timing, but it does not indicate that the partnership *was not formed right away*.

The correct answer is F. *Eventual* means *occurring at the end of or as a result of a series of events*. Only this adjective communicates that a partnership was not immediately formed between MacCallum and Quezada.

39. Knowledge of Language >> Redundancy & Wordiness

Choices A and B are incorrect because they are unnecessarily wordy and awkward.

Choice D is incorrect because it creates a run-on sentence.

The correct answer is C. *Where* correctly and concisely connects *United States* to what follows.

40.   Usage >> Idiom

Choice F is incorrect because *so* begins a new clause that is interrupted by a period instead of being completed.

Choice G is incorrect because it uses *then,* which is a word that indicates a time period, rather than *than,* which would be used to compare.

Choice H is incorrect because it uses a vague pronoun, *them,* for which the antecedent is not clear.

The correct answer is J. *More* modifies *to do* and correctly conveys the idea that Quezeda wanted his contribution to his village to be larger.

41.   Knowledge of Language >> Vague & Clumsy Writing

Choice A is incorrect because it is vague. It also seems to communicate that there are only four hundred potters on Earth because *around* is a very general word.

Choice B is incorrect because it is vague, also. It seems that the author is claiming there are only four hundred people creating art in the world, which is a statement even more problematic than that created by choice A.

Choice D is incorrect because we are left with the unanswered question, *four hundred what?*

The correct answer is C. This choice is much more specific than the other choices and provides relevant, specific information.

42.   Sentence Structure & Formation >> Relative Pronouns

Choice F is incorrect because the pronoun *which* is not used when the antecedent is a person or persons.

Choice H is incorrect because it creates a comma splice. *All of them make their pots by hand* is an independent clause that would need to be joined to the previous independent clause by a comma and a conjunction.

Choice J is incorrect because *who* is the subjective form of the pronoun, but an objective pronoun is needed.

The correct answer is G. The objective pronoun *whom* is correctly used as the object of the preposition *of.*

43.   Usage >> Pronouns

Choice A is incorrect because *they're* is the contraction for *they are,* which does not make sense in this sentence.

Choice B is incorrect because *herselves* is not a word. The reflexive pronoun *herself* can in normal contexts only be singular.

Choice C is incorrect because the pronoun *hers* takes the thing that is being owned as its antecedent, but in this sentence, a possessive pronoun is needed.

The correct answer is D. The phrase *his or her* modifies the noun *creations* and matches the singular subject.

44.   Organization >> Sentence Sequence

Choice F is incorrect because each artist making unique pottery does not logically follow the discussion of the village and museums.

Choices G and H are incorrect because they give a specific reference to *each artist* before the artists have been introduced.

The correct answer is J. Sentence 2 introduces the artists, the *people from Mata Ortiz* to whom Quezada taught pottery. It is logical to follow this with more detail about these artists.

45. Topic Development >> Writer's Goal

Choice A is incorrect because discussing the pottery of the *Paquimé Indians* does not accomplish the purpose of summarizing the entire history of pottery making in Mexico.

Choice B is incorrect because discussing *the quality of ancient pottery* does not summarize the history of pottery making.

Choice D is incorrect because each paragraph focuses on Quezada, not on the various aspects of the *Casas Grandes culture in ancient Mexico.*

The correct answer is C. Each paragraph focuses on Quezada, his work with pottery, and his teaching others to do the same.

46. Usage >> Confusing Pairs

Choice F is incorrect because *it's* is a contraction for *it is*, which does not make sense in this sentence.

Choice G is incorrect because *they're* is a contraction for *they are*, which also does not work in this sentence.

Choice H is incorrect because *their* is a plural possessive pronoun, but its antecedent, *Lyceum Theatre*, is singular.

The correct answer is J. *Its* is a singular possessive pronoun that agrees in number with *Lyceum Theatre.*

47. Sentence Structure & Formation >> Fragments & Fused Sentences

Choices A and B are incorrect because the sentence is incomplete—*filling* is a verbal, not a verb.

Choice C is incorrect because a comma interrupts the subject and the verb. There can never be just one comma between the subject and verb.

The correct answer is D. The sentence is complete because it includes the verb *fill*, and there is no unnecessary punctuation.

48. Organization >> Transitions

Choice F is incorrect because *architecture buffs* coming *to admire the stunning building* is not an *example* of most people being *there to attend a performance.*

Choice G is incorrect because *architecture buffs* coming *to admire the stunning building* is not a *consequence* of most people being *there to attend a performance.*

Choice J is incorrect because *in fact* means *actually, really, or indeed.* This transition word indicates that the second half of the sentence further emphasizes the first half of the sentence. However, only a few *are likely to be architecture buffs*, whereas the first half of the sentence discusses *most* people.

The correct answer is H. The transition *however* indicates a contrast or contradiction. Because there is a contrast between the first and second parts of the sentence, this is the best choice.

49. Sentence Structure & Formation >> Fragments & Fused Sentences

Choices A and D are incorrect because they create run-on sentences by joining two independent clauses without punctuation or conjunction.

Choice C is incorrect because *whom* is the subject of the clause and so should be in the subjective form, *who*, rather than the objective form, *whom*.

The correct answer is B. *There to admire the stunning building itself* modifies *buffs* and avoids creating a run-on sentence.

50. Punctuation >> Colons & Semicolons

Choice G is incorrect because, in this context, a semicolon is used to join two independent clauses, but *into which are carved the classical theatrical masks that represent comedy and tragedy* is not an independent clause.

Choice H is incorrect because *into which are carved…* is an incomplete sentence.

Choice J is incorrect because it creates a comma splice.

The correct answer is F. The semicolon shows a connection between two independent clauses. Although *carved into it are the classical theatrical masks that represent comedy and tragedy* may not appear to be an independent clause, it is simply inverted with the predicate first.

51. Topic Development >> Relevance

Choice A is incorrect because the paragraph does not make a point about theatrical masks, but only briefly mentions them, and the main subject of the essay is the Lyceum Theatre, not *classical Greek theater*.

Choice B is incorrect because this addition is not relevant to the essay, which is focused on describing the Lyceum Theater.

Choice C is incorrect because even if the addition included information about Roman theater, it would not be relevant to this essay.

The correct answer is D. The essay focuses on the Lyceum Theatre, and every paragraph describes some aspect of the building's architecture. It is not relevant to discuss in detail how *masks figured prominently in classical Greek theater performances*.

52. Knowledge of Language >> Redundancy & Wordiness

Choices F, G, and H are incorrect because *gray* and *limestone* are already mentioned in the preceding sentence.

The correct answer is J. It is the only option that is not redundant.

53. Sentence Structure & Formation >> Fragments & Fused Sentences

Choice B is incorrect because the clause beginning with *which is a stone railing* is a dependent clause and cannot stand on its own as a complete sentence.

Choice C is incorrect because the sentence is incomplete—*being supported* is a verbal phrase, not a verb.

Choice D is incorrect because it forms a comma splice between the two independent clauses.

The correct answer is A. The comma sets apart the appositive from what it modifies, *balustrade*.

54. Usage >> Adjectives & Adverbs

Choices G and H are incorrect because the adverb *elegantly* modifies the noun *chandelier*, but it should be in the adjective form, *elegant*.

Choice J is incorrect because the verb *illuminates* is singular and does not agree with the plural subject *chandeliers*.

The correct answer is F. This choice correctly uses the adjective *elegant* to modify the noun *chandeliers*, and the plural verb *illuminate* agrees in number with the subject, also *chandeliers*.

55. Knowledge of Language >> Word Choice

Choices A and D are incorrect because they do not involve an *elaborate style*.

Choice C is incorrect because the word *marred* is negative, a synonym of *ruined* or *scarred*, and so does not maintain a *positive* tone.

The correct answer is B. *Embellished* and *myriad* are the most elaborate word choices that still maintain a *positive* tone.

56. Topic Development >> Identify Purpose

Choice F is incorrect because the sentence begins *in keeping with sumptuous Beaux Arts style*, which means that the *features* do not deviate *from Beaux Arts architecture*.

Choice H is incorrect because the essay does not make this claim.

Choice J is incorrect because this sentence does not define or clarify any architectural terms.

The correct answer is G. This paragraph describes the interior of the theater, and this sentence adds specific details about the furniture inside.

57. Organization >> Paragraph Division

Choices A and B are incorrect because dividing the paragraph in either of these two positions will group details about the *exterior balcony* with details about the *indoor features* that appear later in the paragraph.

Choice D is incorrect because it groups a sentence about the interior with earlier details about the building's exterior features.

The correct answer is C. All of the sentences before this point discuss *outdoor features*, while all of the sentences after this point discuss *indoor features*.

58. Organization >> Transitions

Choice G is incorrect because *patrons* crediting an *aesthetic* is not acting *in the same manner* (in the same way) as *rows of plush purple chairs* embracing the stage.

Choice H is incorrect because *on the one hand* introduces a discussion about two items, but a second item is not mentioned.

Choice J is incorrect because *patrons credit the handsome…* is not an *instance* (example) of *rows of plush purple chairs embrace the stage.*

The correct answer is F. It is the only choice that does not include an inappropriate transition. No transitional words are needed to change topics in this paragraph.

59.   Knowledge of Language >> Redundancy & Wordiness

Choices A is incorrect because *adding enhancement to* is wordy and unnecessary.

Choices B and C are incorrect because the word *experience* is stated later in the sentence, so it is redundant to repeat it here.

The correct answer is D. *Enhancing* is the most concise choice, communicating the same meaning as choices A, B, and C in a single word.

60.   Topic Development >> Writer's Goal

Choice F is incorrect because the essay does not focus on any other theater buildings in New York besides the Lyceum Theatre.

Choice H is incorrect because the essay does not give any details about set design.

Choice J is incorrect because the essay only focuses on the Beaux Arts architectural style.

The correct answer is G. In each paragraph, the passage *enumerates* the *Lyceum Theatre's Beau Arts features.* The title of the essay, *Beaux Arts Architecture in the Spotlight,* gives us a clue that the author seeks to *illustrate a particular architectural style*: Beaux Arts. The passage describes one building, the Lyceum Theatre, to accomplish this.

61.   Usage >> Adjectives & Adverbs

Choices A and D are incorrect because *inaccurate* is the object of the preposition *with* and so should be in the noun form, *inaccuracies.*

Choices B is incorrect because the adverb *factually* modifies the noun *inaccuracies,* but it should be in the adjective form, *factual.*

The correct answer is C. This choice correctly uses the adjective *factual* and the noun *inaccuracies.*

62.   Punctuation >> Colons & Semicolons

Choice F is incorrect because it creates a comma splice, joining two independent clauses without a conjunction.

Choice H is incorrect because what comes after the semicolon is not an independent clause. Semicolons are used to join two independent clauses.

Choice J is incorrect because what comes before a colon must be an independent clause.

The correct answer is G. The colon comes after the independent clause and what follows gives further information about how Jones *fudges her date of birth*.

63. Usage >> Subject-Verb Agreement

Choice A is incorrect because the singular verb *matters* does not agree in number with the plural subject *untruths*.

Choices B and C are incorrect because these are past tense verbs and are inconsistent with the present tense in the paragraph.

The correct answer is D. The present tense plural verb *matter* agrees in number with the plural subject *untruths* and is consistent with the tense of the paragraph.

64. Sentence Structure & Formation >> Faulty Coordination & Subordination

Choice G is incorrect because the meaning of the new sentence beginning with the coordinate conjunction *for* is unclear .

Choice H is incorrect because using a semicolon causes the same error as using the period in choice G.

Choice J is incorrect because it forms a comma splice between two independent clauses.

The correct answer is F. A comma and the coordinate conjunction *for* correctly join the two independent clauses in a coherent way.

65. Organization >> Transitions

Choices A and B are incorrect because they continue to discuss the *the life of Mary Harris Jones*, which contradicts the previous sentence.

Choice D is incorrect because this essay is less about why Jones is important in history and more about the public persona "Mother Jones."

The correct answer is C. This choice logically follows the preceding sentence and naturally connects to second paragraph, which discusses how *Mary Harris Jones got involved in labor politics* in the next sentence.

66. Punctuation >> Apostrophes

Choice F and G are incorrect because as the object of a preposition, *advocate* should be in noun form. Because it is not possessing anything, an apostrophe is unnecessary.

Choice J is incorrect because Jones did not become a *movement*. Rather, *movement* needs an apostrophe to show possession of *advocates*.

The correct answer is H. An apostrophe is correctly given to *movement*, which is possessing the noun *advocates*.

67. Punctuation >> Unnecessary Commas

Choice A and C are incorrect because they use a single comma to interrupt the subject and verb.

Choice B is incorrect because reflexive pronouns such as *herself* should not be punctuated with commas.

The correct answer is D. Since no punctuation is necessary around a reflexive pronoun, the best choice has no commas.

68. Topic Development >> Relevance

Choice F is incorrect because the essay has not established the personal style of the audience.

Choice H is incorrect because information about how Jones crafted her speech, dress, and mannerisms are *not* unrelated to her creating the persona of "Mother Jones."

Choice J is incorrect because the context of the paragraph does not suggest that an addition about *the effect Jones's public persona had on audiences* is necessary.

The correct answer is G. Two sentences earlier in the essay, we learn that Mother Jones adopted a *public persona*. It makes sense to include relevant details about how she did so.

69. Sentence Structure & Formation >> Fragments & Fused Sentences

Choices A and B are incorrect because they form comma splices.

Choice C is incorrect because it forms a run-on sentence.

The correct answer is D. The semicolon appropriately shows a connection between the two independent clauses.

70. Topic Development >> Identify Purpose

Choice F is incorrect because this quote does not bring into question a *distinction between Mary Harris Jones and her public persona, Mother Jones.*

Choice G is incorrect because the essay not characterized Mother Jones as a *vagabond* (someone who travels from place to place without job or home.)

Choice H is incorrect because the other paragraphs do not show that Jones enjoyed traveling for her work, so this quote cannot be a reiteration.

The correct answer is J. The previous sentence stated that *Jones subversively redefined the boundaries of home and family.* In this quote, Jones says that her address—her home—is always with her while she travels.

71. Knowledge of Language >> Word Choice

Choice B is incorrect because the essay does not support the concept that *Jones cared most about workers who were family relatives.*

Choice C is incorrect because the essay does not elsewhere mention a *family of workers*.

Choice D is incorrect because the familial comparison *is* related: the same sentence describes Jones as a *matriarch* (the female head of a family).

The correct answer is A. Describing Jones as a *matriarch* is a metaphor; she was not actually the workers' mother. It completes the metaphor to describe the workers as her family.

72. Punctuation >> Colons & Semicolons

Choices G, H, and J are incorrect because, with these alternatives, what comes before the colon cannot stand on its own as a complete sentence.

The correct answer is F. *And protect them she did* is a complete sentence that can stand on its own. What comes after the colon provides more information about how Jones protected them.

73. Knowledge of Language >> Conjunctions

Choice A is incorrect because *these tireless efforts* and the workers trusting Jones are not in contrast to one another, which is implied by the phrase *instead of*.

Choice C is incorrect because it is illogical to say that the workers trusted Jones because she did not make tireless efforts on their behalf.

Choice D is incorrect because *despite* is similar in meaning to *even though*. It does not logically follow that workers would trust Jones *even though* she made tireless efforts.

The correct answer is B. Mother Jones's tireless efforts were the reason why workers trusted her, so *because of* is the best fit.

74. Usage >> Confusing Pairs

Choices F and G are incorrect because *there* and *they're* are not in the possessive form. *They* possess the *behalf*, so *their* is the better choice.

Choice J is incorrect because *behalve's* is not a word.

The correct answer is H. The plural possessive *their* is appropriately used, and the singular noun *behalf* shows that this group of people have a singular interest.

75. Topic Development >> Writer's Goal

Choice A is incorrect because although the essay does show *that Mother Jones was a well-known and respected labor agitator*, the essay does not summarize *women's contributions to early-twentieth-century labor law reform*.

Choice B is incorrect because introducing one *prominent figure in labor history* does not summarize the contributions women as a whole made to labor law reform.

Choice C is incorrect because the essay focuses more on Mother Jones than on specific labor law reforms.

The correct answer is D. The essay focuses only on Mother Jones's work in the labor movement, so it does not accomplish the goal of summarizing *women's contributions to early-twentieth-century labor law reform*.

ACT QUESTION INDEX

Category Breakdowns for ACT English Test 72-C

MAIN CATEGORY	STANDARD FAMILY	QUESTION NUMBER
Punctuation	Unnecessary Commas	1, 33, 67
	Colons and Semicolons	9, 12, 24, 50, 62, 72
	Apostrophes	25, 66
	Parenthetical Elements	31, 32
Organization	Transitions	2, 27, 34, 48, 58, 65
	Introductions and Conclusions	13
	Sentence Placement	14, 29
	Sentence Sequence	44
	Paragraph Division	57
Sentence Structure and Formation	Relative Pronouns	3, 42
	Misplaced Modifiers and Phrases	4
	Fragments and Fused Sentences	5, 10, 20, 22, 47, 49, 53, 69
	Participial Phrases	16
	Verb Tense and Pronoun Person	17, 35
	Faulty Coodination and Subordination	64

Usage	Subject-Verb Agreement	6, 8, 63
	Comparatives and Superlatives	11
	Prepositions	19
	Adjectives and Adverbs	21, 54, 61
	Confusing Pairs	37, 46, 74
	Idiom	40
	Pronouns	43
Topic Development	Identify Purpose	7, 26, 36, 56, 70
	Writer's Goal	15, 30, 45, 60, 75
	Accomplish Purpose	23, 28, 38
	Relevance	51, 68
Knowledge of Language	Redundancy and Wordiness	18, 39, 52, 59
	Vague and Clumsy Writing	41
	Word Choice	55, 71
	Conjunctions	73

MATH

The Math portion of this book is split into three sections:

- **Math Time Mastery**, which focuses on how to help students make the most of the 60 minutes provided to answer the 60 questions on the Math test.

- **Math Test Mastery**, which centers on proven test-taking techniques and strategies that can help students get to the right answer, even if they aren't clear on the "right way" to solve a problem.

- **Math Content Mastery**, which provides a guide on the skills and standards most likely to be tested on the ACT Math test. This section also includes some content-related strategies for maximizing your students' Math scores.

When you work with your students on the ACT Math test, consider taking a balanced approach. In each lesson, try helping your students improve in terms of Time Mastery, Test Mastery, and of course, Content Mastery.

MATH TIME MASTERY
Time Management Strategies for the ACT Math Test

Time Management on the ACT Math Test

The Math portion of the ACT is the only test section with a clear-cut, easily observed difficulty distribution. As a general rule, questions gradually become more difficult as students progress from the front of the test to the back. All effective time strategies for the Math test center around two facts: each question on the Math test is worth the same (one raw point), and the difficulty gradually increases throughout the test.

The following tips apply to students who are aiming for a scale score up to 24 on the ACT Math test. Students who are aiming for higher scores should follow the *blitz* approach that appears in the next chapter.

Don't Rush

Students who are aiming for a 24 or less should not be in a hurry to get to the last question of the Math test. What's the point of rushing through the first 40 questions (questions these students are most likely able to answer), only to waste time being stumped on the difficult final 20? The path to success for these students is paved by accurately answering the first 40 questions and making reasonable guesses on the final 20 when the correct answer isn't evident.

One Minute per Question

With 60 minutes and 60 questions, students should plan to spend about one minute per question. Many students find that they can answer the first 30 questions in less than half an hour; they should use any extra time to double- and triple-check their answers.

It's okay if students spend *more* than one minute per question, as long as they are quickly *marking and moving* past questions they have no idea how to solve.

Cherry-Picking

The essential time management skill in Math is *cherry-picking*. By *cherry-picking*, we mean students are choosy and spend their time with the *very best* questions, those questions most likely to yield points, marking and moving past questions that confuse them.

Imagine a delicious ice cream sundae, and then imagine someone who deigns to eat only the cherry, the very best part. The rest isn't good enough for him!

If students have a goal score of 24 or lower, then there are many questions they don't have to solve. A third or more can be answered incorrectly and students can still reach their goal. Students should be on the lookout for their 25–35 cherries, the "gimmes" that they *know* they can answer correctly. It's okay if they spend more than a minute on a cherry because they are intentionally giving the other questions short shrift in the time department.

The toughest part of cherry-picking is being ruthless with the questions that aren't cherries. If your students only spend a few seconds looking at a question before moving on, they save a lot of time; so much time, in fact, that if they need to come back to the question, they can. If your students spend half a minute staring at a question before deciding that it is not a cherry, they have lost all the benefit of this strategy.

Give your students practice with cherry-picking by providing them five minutes to highlight 25 questions on an ACT Math test that look the easiest to them. Then, give them 35 minutes to answer *only the questions they circled.*

On the actual ACT test, we do not want students to spend any time just screening questions. They need to answer a cherry as soon as they find it. But this exercise isolates the skill of cherry-picking so your students can develop it into a natural habit.

Focus on the Front

When you are reviewing retired ACT Math practice tests with students who are aiming to score up to a 24, you should concentrate your review and prep work on the first 30 questions. Once students show marked improvement in this range, you can consider adding questions 31–40.

By focusing on the front, you concentrate your efforts on the questions that are more heavily weighted and more likely to yield to prep and practice. All of the low-hanging fruit is at the front of the test, so exhaust this supply of points before attempting to harvest from the higher branches.

Focus on the front also holds true for more advanced students. They should focus on the first 40 questions in an ACT practice test until they can reliably answer more than 85% correctly before they move on to the last 20 questions.

Blitz

Students aiming for a 25 or higher on the ACT Math test should blitz the front half of the ACT Math test.

By *blitz*, we mean finish as quickly and accurately as possible. The goal is to finish the first 30 questions in 20 minutes.

Most students will not feel comfortable at this pace. It's something that has to be practiced. But once they achieve this pace, the entire game has changed. Now students have 40 minutes for the last 30 questions. They have a much better shot at answering some of the most challenging questions the ACT can throw at them.

Part of achieving a rapid pace at the outset of the Math test has to do with familiarity. If students aren't used to the way the ACT asks its questions, they will tend to be careful because they are wary of traps and mistakes.

Refer to Math question #2 on page 24 of *Preparing for the ACT 2015-16.*

Students must find a straightforward average in order to answer question #2. Students can blitz through this sort of question if they are prepared. They add up the five fees, divide by five, select their answer, and move on.

If your students haven't practiced blitzing, though, then they might hesitate after finding the answer. It seems too easy! Maybe it's a trick.

Worse, some students who haven't practiced blitzing actually make a nervous mistake on a question like this.

If you are going to introduce the Math blitz to your students, make sure you give them enough practice (at least four half-tests) to get them accustomed to how the pace feels. It seems counterintuitive to give high-performing students practice only on the easier front half of the test, but consider that by teaching your students to squeeze out every available second from the easier questions, they are making the back half easier as well because they will have more time to work the harder questions.

To achieve a 25 or higher on the ACT Math test, students must have enough time for the tougher, more complex questions at the end of the test. By accurately blitzing the first 30 questions, students can pick up the extra time they need.

Answer Awareness

Answer choices limit possibilities. This can save your students valuable time, but only if they are *aware* of the answer choices.

Refer to Math question #1 on page 24 of *Preparing for the ACT 2015-16*.

Question #1 asks for a probability. There are two places where students can avoid adding 62, 67, 15, and 6 together to find the total number of possible outcomes. Many students miss both of them.

The first appears in the first line of text of the question. It flat out says there are a total of 150 people. In addition to this, all the answers clearly have the same denominator of 150.

The second, more common mistake that students make on this question is that they consider simplifying the fraction. They try working out whether or not 73 and 150 have a common factor (they don't; 73 is prime). *Or* they convert the fraction into a decimal or percentage on their calculator.

Once they have their percentage, they finally look up at the answer choices and realize that they don't need a percentage. They don't need a decimal. They just need a fraction. Then they have to backtrack, which takes up even more time.

Once they see the answer choices, they also realize that the question wasn't really asking about the denominator at all. Really, the ACT was asking, "What should be the numerator for this probability?"

Students should be particularly sensitive to answer awareness when a question seems unduly complicated in the first half of the Math test. If it seems complex, there is probably a simpler way to solve it. The answer choices often give a clue as to how.

Refer to question #36 on page 28 of *Preparing for the ACT 2015-16*.

In question #36, your students are asked to graph a set of inequalities. There is one (usually important) step that they *don't* need to take, however.

Check Your Understanding: How can answer awareness save your students some time on question #36?

_____

_____

What step in graphing the inequalities can they skip based on the characteristics of the answer choices?

_____

_____

Math Time Management Heat Map

Below is what we call a "heat map" showing the performance of over 20,000 students on an ACT Math test. This is a powerful tool for understanding your students' level of time mastery.

Each vertical bar represents one of the 60 questions on the test. A light shade means that most of the students answered the question correctly. A darker shade means that fewer students answered right. When the color is completely black, it means that students would have done better on that item if they had just blindly guessed.

We use heat maps to understand at a glance how students in a class are doing with time management.

On the ACT Math test, we expect the heat map to get darker and darker as we read from left to right. There is a very clear reason for this: the questions become more and more complex. We call this *color shift*. The stronger the color shift, the more difficulty your students had with the advanced concepts and multiple-step problems that appear in the back of the test.

This graphic tells us that the typical class of students has a relatively strong color shift in Math. In the absence of any specific data about your students, you should assume that you need to apply the time management strategies detailed for those students who are aiming for a 24 or lower on the ACT Math.

We also look for *contrast* when we read a time management heat map. There should be some contrast in the colors between any two questions. Even though difficulty gradually increases on the Math test, there is a significant variance between each question. If your students are successful in their cherry-picking, then they can pick out the easier questions, even near the end of the test. A class of students who are failing to cherry-pick (in other words, manage their time on individual questions) will have a heat map without contrast between individual items. Each question will have a similar color, one to the next. Good time managers have very bright spots scattered throughout the test, even toward the end.

This graphic tells us that a typical group of students is not able to cherry-pick the easier questions toward the end of the test. There should be some lighter lines than their surroundings among the last 20 questions.

MasteryPrep provides a very affordable practice testing service that can give you these pre-made heat maps specific to your students. You can also accomplish similar insights by gathering your student practice test data, looking at the percentage of students who correctly answered each question, and laying this information out in a spreadsheet. Use Excel's "Conditional Formatting/Color Scales" feature to visualize the data in a way similar to the graphic we have provided.

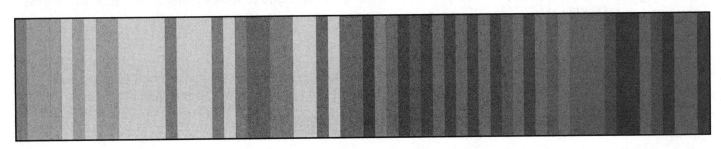

Mental Math

Students who are strong at mental math have a major advantage on the Math test. Conversely, students who are weak at mental math will struggle, make mistakes, and run out of time.

Many questions on the Math test yield to mental math *much more quickly* than when students try to "solve them the right way." What's more, the mental solutions to many of these problems are simpler, more elegant, and less prone to error than the calculator solution.

Also, students who are weak at mental math often find it impossible to finish the Math test in enough time, no matter how disciplined they are with their pace. They just can't solve the questions quickly enough.

> Refer to Math question #3 on page 24 of *Preparing for the ACT 2015-16.*

The "right" way to solve question #3 is to set up a proportion. This gets rough quickly, though, since the result is fractions inside of fractions. Even very advanced students can make a careless mistake on this sort of set up.

The faster, easier way to solve this is to have a solid understanding of arithmetic and skill in mental math. A student who solves this problem using mental math thinks along these lines:

I need to know how many half inches there are between those two towns. I'll divide $2\frac{1}{2}$ by $\frac{1}{2}$. Dividing by $\frac{1}{2}$ is the same as multiplying by 2. So there are $2\frac{1}{2} \cdot 2 = 5$ half inches. Which means there are $5 \cdot 18 = 90$ miles.

Although it seems counterintuitive, giving students speed drills on addition, subtraction, multiplication, and division can help them tremendously on the ACT, particularly if students show deficiencies in these fundamentals. It's hard to solve problems intuitively, as with the question referenced above, if students are struggling with the basic tools of arithmetic.

One way to reinforce the use of mental math is to select one question from the first 10 on an ACT Math test and ask your students to choose the correct answer without using their calculators or pencils. This isn't necessarily the way you want them to attack the problems on the actual test, but it can serve to emphasize to students that they can get the better of these questions, comprehend them, and solve them.

> Refer to Math question #5 on page 24 of *Preparing for the ACT 2015-16.*

This is a great example of a question that your students can be challenged to solve mentally. Their thought process might run something like this:

I swap out the 1 for the x. 3 times 1 is 3 plus 7 is 10. 10 squared is 100!

Tackling problems in this way has another nice side effect: it prepares your students for mentally juggling several concepts and data at once, which is essential for solving the multistep problems that appear later in the test.

> Refer to Math question #45 on page 29 of *Preparing for the ACT 2015-16.*

Question #45 certainly requires more than mental math skills to solve. Yet it is a great illustration of how an advanced problem can require so many small, mental calculations that students who struggle with these lose sight of the big picture.

Check Your Understanding: Solve problem #45 and take careful note of each calculation that needs to be made. Put yourself in the shoes of a student who can't work without a calculator and who struggles to isolate variables in an equation. Make notes of any realizations or observations you made while completing this exercise.

_____

_____

_____

_____

Eyes Only

Eyes only is an advanced exercise that you should use only with your strongest math students. This is *not* a strategy. We don't intend for students to tackle the ACT Math test in this way. Instead, this exercise helps your students think about the ACT in a new light and will improve their confidence and their ability to work out word problems.

In this exercise, students take an ACT Math test without using a calculator. They can't show their work; the only thing they can do with their pencil is bubble answer choices. Challenge your students to correctly answer as many questions as they can using only their wits, the questions, and the answer choices.

For advanced students, this can have a dramatic effect on how they view the ACT Math test. It also greatly increases their ability to use reasoning and the process of elimination on questions that they struggle with.

After students answer the questions, have them share with their classmates how they figured out the solutions.

You may be surprised how many questions can be answered by eyes only.

> Refer to Math question #6 on page 24 of *Preparing for the ACT 2015-16.*

At first blush, question #6 needs a calculator, but students can also arrive at the correct answer eyes only through this line of thinking:

6% of $12.00 is going to be 72-something since 6 times 12 is 72. I'm starting with a whole number of dollars, and I'm adding 72-something. Only one answer choice has 72 cents. Must be G.

Again, this is not necessarily how we want students to attack an actual ACT Math test. But as an exercise, *eyes only* greatly increases your students' mental flexibility regarding the assessment.

If students have a hard time with eyes only on question #6, this exercise is probably not appropriate for your class.

With tougher questions that students can't solve on their own, consider scaffolding with a series of questions. For example, on question #6 you might ask the following:

Okay, what's 6% of $12? Well, what's 1% of $12? Nobody? Okay, well, what's 1% of $1?

That's right. One cent. Then what's 1% of $12?

Good. Twelve cents. Now, what's 6% of $12? In other words, I have six of those 1% of $12. Right. $0.72.

I'm going to add $12.00 to $0.72. How many cents am I going to have? 72 cents, that's right. Which answer choice must it be?

> Refer to Math question #58 on page 31 of *Preparing for the ACT 2015-16.*

Check Your Understanding: How would you attempt to solve question #58 eyes only?

_____

_____

_____

Take One Path

Students have time to answer a question "the right way" or with a test-taking strategy like *plug and chug* (see page 188). They don't have time to do both.

When students encounter a fork in the road, they must quickly choose a branch and stick with it.

Students tend to be distrustful of the answers they get from using test-taking strategies. They then spend the time to try to solve the question "the right way." Preach to your students to take one path.

These is no point in trying to verify an answer another way after you have *assumed values* (see page 194) and eliminated every choice except one. There can be no other correct answer at that point. Once your students have eliminated the impossible, whatever is left must be true, no matter how improbable it seems.

Refer to Math question #26 on page 27 of *Preparing for the ACT 2015-16*.

Correctly answering question #26 requires that students not become confused by the variable in the measure of and then mistakenly subtract that measure from 90°.

Immediately after reading the question, students encounter a fork in the road. Either they clearly see that they need to subtract, or the whole thing seems foggy. If the solution is foggy, students cannot waste time trying to sort it out. They must trust their instincts and move quickly to a test-taking strategy: in this case, *assuming values* (see page 194). Speed is necessary because most test-taking strategies consume time; if your students will use one, they need to get started right away.

With this strategy, your students *assume* that the value of x is 30°. If that is the case, then has a measure of 30° + 20° = 50°. Therefore, has a measure of 90° – 50° = 40°. The student looks for an answer choice that yields a measure of 40°.

F. $(30 - 70)° = -40°$

G. $(70 - 30)° = 40°$

H. $(70 + 30)° = 100°$

J. $(160 - 30)° = 130°$

K. $(160 + 30)° = 190°$

Only choice G works.

Here is the crucial point: if your students apply the *assume values* strategy, they won't know *why* choice G works. That's the whole point of test-taking strategies: use it when you are confused or don't know how something works.

When your students arrive at choice G with this strategy, they might still feel confused and a bit doubtful. That's okay. Time to move to the next question. What students can't do at this point is try to solve it again, the "right way," or doubt themselves and assume another value, or put a star next to it so they can come back to it and worry about it later.

On the ACT Math test, students must take one path.

Refer to Math question #49 on page 30 of *Preparing for the ACT 2015-16*.

There are multiple pathways to a correct answer on question #49. One way involves a fundamental understanding of how inequalities work on the coordinate plane. Other methods incorporate guessing and checking.

Check Your Understanding: Solve question #49 in at least two ways

_____

_____

Why would it be important for your students to solve this problem only one way?

_____

_____

How might you hit that point home with your students?

_____

_____

Math Mini-Test Coaching

Refer to page 35 of this book for general information about mini-tests.

Math mini-tests provide your students with the timed practice they need to succeed on the ACT Math test.

A mini-test in Math is one or two pages (about 5–10 questions) from a retired ACT test.

Project a full-screen timer using a website such as online-stopwatch.com so that students can refer to it as they need. Before starting the mini-test, remind students about their pacing strategy. Vary the time limit according to their pacing strategy and the segment of the test the mini-test questions are pulled from.

For example, you would allot 40 seconds per question for questions 11–17 if your students were practicing the Math blitz strategy, but you would give students 80 seconds per question if they're working on questions 51–57.

Give students a verbal cue about their remaining time every two minutes. Gradually decrease the use of verbal cues until students are can keep pace without them.

Once the mini-test is complete, immediately call out the answers and explain difficult questions that your students are most confused about. If students have a concern about a particular aspect of one question, consider taking the time to explain the question in full, from beginning to end, for the benefit of all students instead of just answering the specifics asked about.

If you are working on particular skills, select a mini-test that includes that skill as well as others so that your students have practice identifying what approach to use for each question. The ACT will never throw the student 10 similar triangles problems in a row, so mini-tests are a great way to inject some realism after a few days of working on skills in isolation.

Students who are using the Math blitz strategy may benefit from gradually increasing the size of their mini-test until they are hitting the blitz pace with a full set of 30 questions.

Since cherry-picking, not pace, is the most important time management concept in Math, be sure to emphasize it whenever you can during mini-tests. For example, if the majority of your students miss a question, ask for a show of hands from those who immediately recognized they wouldn't be able to get it, used a guessing strategy, and moved on. Congratulate these students. Doing well on the ACT isn't just about knowing how to answer questions correctly; it's also about knowing what to do when you *don't* know the answer. Wasting time is never an option.

Use mini-tests to get your students on pace for the ACT Math test.

Math Mini-Tests

What follows are six Math mini-tests. You are permitted to photocopy these mini-tests and provide them to your students.

Printable PDFs of these mini-tests with answer keys and explanations, as well as links to four full-length ACT tests that you can use as fodder for additional mini-tests, are available at this address: masteryprep.com/decode/resources.

Mini Test 1

Attempts: _____   Correct: _____

DO YOUR FIGURING HERE.

1. If $5x + 2 = 7x - 7$, then $x = $?

    A. $\dfrac{2}{9}$

    B. $\dfrac{1}{3}$

    C. $\dfrac{2}{3}$

    D. $\dfrac{3}{2}$

    E. $\dfrac{9}{2}$

2. The expression $x[(y - w) + z]$ is equivalent to:

    F. $xy - xw + xz$
    G. $xy - w + z$
    H. $xy + xw + xz$
    J. $xy - xw - xz$
    K. $xy + w + z$

3. The toxicity level of a lake is found by dividing the amount of dissolved toxins the lake water currently has per liter by the maximum safe amount of dissolved toxins that the water can hold per liter and then converting it to a percentage. If the river currently has 0.86 milligrams of dissolved toxins per liter of water and the maximum safe amount of dissolved toxins is 1.04 milligrams per liter, what is the toxicity level of the lake water, to the nearest percentage?

    A. 86%
    B. 84%
    C. 83%
    D. 80%
    E. 79%

GO ON TO THE NEXT PAGE

DO YOUR FIGURING HERE.

4. A rectangular pasture that measures 250 meters by 300 meters is completely fenced around its borders. What is the approximate length, in meters, of the surrounding fence?

F. 75,000
G. 1,100
H. 750
J. 600
K. 550

5. So far, Michael has earned the following scores on five 100-point tests this semester: 72, 94, 85, 83, 97. What score must he earn on the sixth 100-point test of the semester if he wants to make an 88-point average for the six tests?

A. 100
B. 97
C. 88
D. 85
E. He cannot make an average of 88.

6. Which two numbers should be placed in the blanks below so that the difference between consecutive numbers is the same?

19, __, __, 55

F. 20, 53
G. 27, 50
H. 30, 48
J. 31, 43
K. 34, 42

7. Mrs. Cook is a teacher whose salary is $23,125 for a 185-day school year. In Mrs. Cook's school district, substitute teachers are paid at a rate of $90 per day. If a substitute is paid to teach Mrs. Cook's class in her absence one day, how much less does the school district pay in salary by paying a substitute teacher instead of paying Mrs. Cook for that day?

A. $215
B. $125
C. $ 90
D. $ 45
E. $ 35

GO ON TO THE NEXT PAGE

DO YOUR FIGURING HERE.

8. If a marble is randomly chosen from a bag that contains exactly 6 purple marbles, 4 blue marbles, and 10 green marbles, what is the probability that the marble will NOT be green?

F. $\frac{1}{5}$

G. $\frac{3}{10}$

H. $\frac{1}{3}$

J. $\frac{1}{2}$

K. $\frac{3}{5}$

9. Zach has 3 pairs of shoes, 8 shirts, and 5 pairs of jeans. How many distinct outfits—each consisting of a pair of shoes, a shirt, and a pair of jeans—can Zach select?

A. 240
B. 120
C. 40
D. 16
E. 8

10. $4x^2y \cdot 2x^3y \cdot 3xy^2$ is equivalent to:

F. $9x^6y^2$

G. $9x^6y^4$

H. $12xy^{10}$

J. $24x^6y^2$

K. $24x^6y^4$

END OF MINI TEST ONE
STOP! DO NOT GO ON TO THE NEXT PAGE
UNTIL TOLD TO DO SO.

Mini Test 2

Attempts: _____ Correct: _____

DO YOUR FIGURING HERE.

11. Which of the following is a solution to the equation
$x^2 - 25x = 0$?

    A. −25
    B. −5
    C. 5
    D. 25
    E. 125

12. Craig ran $2\frac{2}{3}$ miles on Wednesday and $3\frac{1}{4}$ miles on Thursday. What was the total distance Craig ran during those two days, in miles?

    F. $5\frac{3}{12}$

    G. $5\frac{2}{7}$

    H. $5\frac{3}{7}$

    J. $5\frac{9}{12}$

    K. $5\frac{11}{12}$

13. The ratio of the side lengths for a triangle is exactly 9:12:15. In another triangle, which is similar to the first, the shortest side is 18 inches long. To the nearest hundredth of an inch, what is the length of the longest side of the other triangle?

    A. 18.25
    B. 24.00
    C. 25.50
    D. 30.00
    E. Cannot be determined from the given information

GO ON TO THE NEXT PAGE

DO YOUR FIGURING HERE.

14. The formula for the volume V of a sphere with radius r is $V = \frac{4}{3}\pi r^3$. If the radius of a spherical rubber ball is $2\frac{3}{4}$ inches, what is its volume, to the nearest cubic inch?

F. 8
G. 11
H. 56
J. 77
K. 87

15. For the triangle $\triangle PQR$ shown below, what is sin R ?

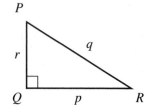

A. $\dfrac{r}{q}$

B. $\dfrac{r}{p}$

C. $\dfrac{p}{r}$

D. $\dfrac{q}{r}$

E. $\dfrac{p}{q}$

16. If x and y are positive integers such that the greatest common factor of x^2y^2 and xy^3 is 50, then which of the following could equal y ?

F. 50
G. 25
H. 10
J. 5
K. 2

GO ON TO THE NEXT PAGE

DO YOUR FIGURING HERE.

17. If x is a real number such that $x^3 = 729$, then $x^2 + \sqrt{x} = ?$
    A. 738
    B. 732
    C. 90
    D. 84
    E. 12

18. A circle in the standard (x,y) coordinate plane is tangent to the x-axis at 4 and tangent to the y-axis at 4. Which of the following is an equation of the circle?
    F. $(x - 4)^2 + (y - 4)^2 = 16$
    G. $(x + 4)^2 + (y + 4)^2 = 16$
    H. $(x - 4)^2 + (y - 4)^2 = 4$
    J. $x^2 + y^2 = 16$
    K. $x^2 + y^2 = 4$

19. What expression must the center cell of the table below contain so that the sums of each row and each column are equivalent?

$4x$	$4x$	$2x$
x	$?$	$6x$
$5x$	$3x$	$2x$

    A. $2x$
    B. $3x$
    C. $4x$
    D. $5x$
    E. $6x$

20. At a plant, 160,000 tons of petrochemicals are required to produce 100,000 tons of plastic. How many tons of petrochemicals are required to produce 5,000 tons of plastic?
    F. 8,000
    G. 10,000
    H. 16,000
    J. 80,000
    K. 100,000

END OF MINI TEST TWO
STOP! DO NOT GO ON TO THE NEXT PAGE
UNTIL TOLD TO DO SO.

Mini Test 3

Attempts: _____   Correct: _____

DO YOUR FIGURING HERE.

---

21. A chord 20 inches long is 4 inches from the center of a circle, as shown below. What is the radius of the circle, to the nearest tenth of an inch?

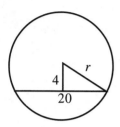

- **A.** 4.0
- **B.** 10.7
- **C.** 10.8
- **D.** 11.0
- **E.** 21.6

22. Workers for a roofing company lean a 20-foot ladder against a building. The side of the building is perpendicular to the level ground so that the base of the ladder is 5 feet away from the base of the building. To the nearest foot, how far up the building does the ladder reach?

- **F.** 5
- **G.** 10
- **H.** 18
- **J.** 19
- **K.** 20

23. Point C is to be graphed in a quadrant of the standard (x,y) coordinate plane below.

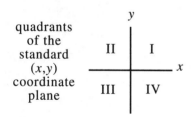

If the x-coordinate and the y-coordinate of point C are to have the same signs, then point C must be located in:

- **A.** Quadrant I or II.
- **B.** Quadrant I or III.
- **C.** Quadrant I or IV.
- **D.** Quadrant II or IV.
- **E.** Quadrant III or IV.

GO ON TO THE NEXT PAGE

DO YOUR FIGURING HERE.

24. What is the x-coordinate of the point in the standard (x,y) coordinate plane at which the two lines $y = 2x - 1$ and $y = x + 2$ intersect?

   F. −2
   G. 0
   H. 1
   J. 3
   K. 4

25. A square is circumscribed about a circle with a 6 foot radius, as shown below. What is the area of the square, in square feet?

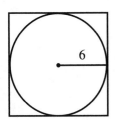

   A. 12
   B. 36
   C. 72
   D. 144
   E. 288

26. If a rectangle measures 12 meters by 16 meters, what is the length, in meters, of the diagonal of the rectangle?

   F. 14
   G. 18
   H. 20
   J. 22
   K. 28

27. Which of the following is a set of all real numbers x, such that $x + 1 > x + 8$?

   A. The set containing zero
   B. The set containing all real numbers
   C. The set containing all positive numbers
   D. The set containing all negative numbers
   E. The empty set

GO ON TO THE NEXT PAGE

DO YOUR FIGURING HERE.

28. For all pairs of real numbers P and Q where $P = 2Q + 9$, $Q = ?$

   F. $2P - 9$

   G. $\dfrac{P + 9}{2}$

   H. $\dfrac{P}{2} + 9$

   J. $\dfrac{P}{2} - 9$

   K. $\dfrac{P - 9}{2}$

29. The ratio of the radii of two circles is 5:12. What is the ratio of their circumferences?

   A. 5:12
   B. 5:12π
   C. 10:12π
   D. 10:24
   E. 25:144

30. Of the 777 graduating seniors in a certain high school, approximately $\dfrac{1}{3}$ are going to a trade school, and approximately $\dfrac{2}{7}$ of those going to a trade school are going to an art or design institute. Which of the following is the closest estimate for the number of graduating seniors going to an art or design institute?

   F. 74
   G. 75
   H. 110
   J. 219
   K. 256

END OF MINI TEST THREE
STOP! DO NOT GO ON TO THE NEXT PAGE
UNTIL TOLD TO DO SO.

Mini Test 4

Attempts: _____ Correct: _____

DO YOUR FIGURING HERE.

31. What is the slope-intercept form of $4x - y + 7 = 0$?

  A. $y = -4x - 7$

  B. $y = -4x + 7$

  C. $y = x + \dfrac{4}{7}$

  D. $y = 4x - 7$

  E. $y = 4x + 7$

32. Parallelogram *PQRS*, with dimensions in feet, is shown in the diagram below. What is the area of the parallelogram, in square feet?

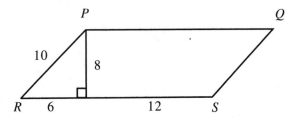

  F. 48
  G. 96
  H. 120
  J. 144
  K. 180

33. The distance *D*, in feet, that a ball can be catapulted is given by the equation $D = \dfrac{2}{3}T + 10$, where *T* is the applied torque in newtons. What amount of torque, in newtons, must be applied for the ball's distance to be 170 meters?

  A. 160
  B. 200
  C. 240
  D. 320
  E. 480

34. If $a = b - 3$, then $(b - a)^3 = $?

  F. −81
  G. −27
  H. −9
  J. 9
  K. 27

GO ON TO THE NEXT PAGE

DO YOUR FIGURING HERE.

35. Points B and C lie on line segment $\overline{AD}$, as shown below. Line segment $\overline{AD}$ is 40 units long, line segment $\overline{AC}$ is 15 units long, and line segment $\overline{BD}$ is 30 units long. How many units long, if it can be determined, is line segment $\overline{BC}$?

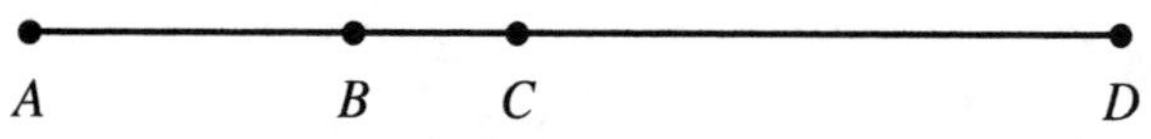

```
●————————●———●——————————————●
A         B   C              D
```

A. 20
B. 15
C. 10
D. 5
E. Cannot be determined from the given information

Use the following information to answer questions 36–37.

English Enrollment

Course	Section	Period	Enrollment
Composition	A	1	12
English I	A	1	21
	B	4	19
	C	5	20
English II	A	2	15
	B	3	16
English III	A	2	14
English IV	A	3	19

36. What is the average number of students enrolled per section in English I ?

F. 17
G. 18
H. 19
J. 20
K. 21

GO ON TO THE NEXT PAGE

DO YOUR FIGURING HERE.

37. The school owns 35 anthologies, which students are required to have during their English classes. There are 4 anthologies currently being re-covered, and 1 anthology is currently missing. For which of the following class periods, if any, are there NOT enough anthologies available for each student to have his or her own anthology?

A. Period 1
B. Period 1 & 2
C. Period 1 & 3
D. Period 2 & 3
E. There are enough anthologies for each class period.

38. After polling a class of 30 science students by a show of hands, you find that 12 students enjoy chemistry while 17 students enjoy biology. Given that information, what is the maximum number of students in this class who enjoy both chemistry and biology?

F. 0
G. 5
H. 12
J. 17
K. 29

39. For all positive integers X, Y, and Z, which of the following expressions is equivalent to $\dfrac{Y}{Z}$?

A. $\dfrac{Y}{Z} + \dfrac{X}{Y}$

B. $\dfrac{Y \cdot Z}{Z \cdot Y}$

C. $\dfrac{Y + X}{Z + X}$

D. $\dfrac{Y \cdot X}{Z \cdot X}$

E. $\dfrac{Y \cdot Y}{Z \cdot Z}$

40. If 120% of a number is 360, what is 50% of the number?

F. 120
G. 150
H. 260
J. 300
K. 480

END OF MINI TEST FOUR
STOP! DO NOT GO ON TO THE NEXT PAGE
UNTIL TOLD TO DO SO.

Mini Test 5

Attempts: _____ Correct: _____

DO YOUR FIGURING HERE.

41. The hypotenuse of the right triangle ΔLMN shown below is 18 feet long. The sine of angle L is $\frac{5}{6}$. About how many feet long is line segment $\overline{MN}$?

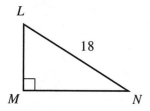

A. 11
B. 12
C. 15
D. 18
E. Cannot be determined from the given information

42. If $x = 3t - 8$ and $y = 4 + t$, which of the following equations expresses y in terms of x ?

F. $y = 4x - 4$

G. $y = \dfrac{x - 20}{3}$

H. $y = \dfrac{x + 3}{20}$

J. $y = \dfrac{x}{3 - 4}$

K. $y = \dfrac{x + 20}{3}$

43. Hexagons have 9 diagonals, as illustrated below. How many diagonals do octagons have?

Hexagon   Octagon

A. 8
B. 16
C. 20
D. 32
E. 40

GO ON TO THE NEXT PAGE

DO YOUR FIGURING HERE.

44. Jennifer wants to draw a circle graph showing the favorite candies of her friends. When she polled her friends, asking each his or her favorite candy, 30% of her friends said chocolate, 25% of her friends said peppermint, 15% of her friends said licorice, 15% of her friends said gum, and the remaining friends said some other type of candy. If she groups the other candies chosen by the remaining friends in the same sector, what will the degree measure of this sector be?

F. 12°
G. 24°
H. 26°
J. 48°
K. 54°

45. The number of students participating in afterschool programs at a certain high school can be shown by the following matrix.

Quizbowl   Band   Chorus   Debate
[30   60   40   30   ]

The principal estimates the ratio of the number of program awards that will be earned to the number of students participating with the following matrix.

$$\begin{bmatrix} \text{Quizbowl} : 0.2 \\ \text{Band} : 0.3 \\ \text{Chorus} : 0.5 \\ \text{Debate} : 0.4 \end{bmatrix}$$

Given this data, what is the principal's estimate of the number of programs awards that will be earned for these afterschool programs?

A. 60
B. 56
C. 52
D. 48
E. 36

GO ON TO THE NEXT PAGE

DO YOUR FIGURING HERE.

46. After a hurricane, coastal workers removed an estimated 8,000 cubic yards of sand from the downtown area. If this sand was spread in an even layer over a rectangular segment of beach, as shown below, about how many yards deep would the new layer of sand be?

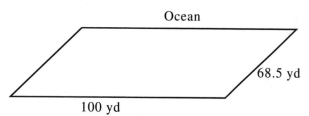

F. Less than 1
G. Between 1 and 2
H. Between 2 and 3
J. Between 3 and 4
K. More than 4

47. What is the distance in the standard (x,y) coordinate plane between points $(1,2)$ and $(4,6)$?

A. 4
B. 5
C. 7
D. 10
E. 13

48. In the figure below, $VWXY$ is a trapezoid, Z lies on line $\overrightarrow{VY}$, and angle measures are as marked. What is the measure of $\angle WYX$?

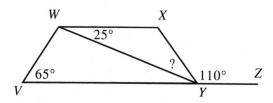

F. 25°
G. 30°
H. 45°
J. 55°
K. 65°

GO ON TO THE NEXT PAGE

DO YOUR FIGURING HERE.

51. An abandoned area of town has the shape and dimensions of the blocks given below. All borders run either north-south or east-west. A surveyor has set up his equipment halfway between point M and point O. Which of the following is the location of the surveyor from point L ?

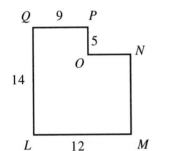

A. $9\frac{1}{2}$ blocks east and $4\frac{1}{2}$ blocks north

B. 9 blocks east and 5 blocks north

C. $10\frac{1}{2}$ blocks east and $4\frac{1}{2}$ blocks north

D. $10\frac{1}{2}$ blocks east and $5\frac{1}{2}$ blocks north

E. 12 blocks east and 9 blocks north

52. Which of the following systems of inequalities is represented by the shaded region of the graph below?

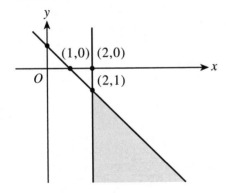

F. $y \le x$ and $x \ge 1$
G. $y \le -x + 1$ and $x \ge 2$
H. $y \le -x + 1$ and $x \ge 1$
J. $y \le x - 1$ and $x \ge 2$
K. $y \le x + 1$ and $x \ge -2$

GO ON TO THE NEXT PAGE

53. If $\sin \theta = \dfrac{4}{5}$ and $\dfrac{\pi}{2} < \theta < \pi$, then $\cos \theta = ?$

DO YOUR FIGURING HERE.

   A. $-\dfrac{4}{5}$

   B. $-\dfrac{3}{4}$

   C. $-\dfrac{3}{5}$

   D. $\dfrac{3}{5}$

   E. $\dfrac{5}{3}$

54. A triangle, ΔPQR, is reflected across the x-axis to have the image $\Delta P'Q'R'$ in the standard (x,y) coordinate plane; thus, P reflects to P'. The coordinates of point P are (a,b). Which of the following coordinates best describes the location of point P'?

   F. (a,b)
   G. $(a,-b)$
   H. $(-a,b)$
   J. $(-a,-b)$
   K. Cannot be determined from the given information

GO ON TO THE NEXT PAGE

55. What is cos $\frac{\pi}{12}$, given that $\frac{\pi}{12} = \frac{\pi}{3} - \frac{\pi}{4}$ and $\cos(\alpha - \beta) = (\cos \alpha)(\cos \beta) - (\sin \alpha)(\sin \beta)$?

(Note: You may use the following table of values.)

θ	Sin θ	Cos θ
$\frac{\pi}{6}$	$\frac{1}{2}$	$\frac{\sqrt{3}}{2}$
$\frac{\pi}{4}$	$\frac{\sqrt{2}}{2}$	$\frac{\sqrt{2}}{2}$
$\frac{\pi}{3}$	$\sqrt{\frac{3}{2}}$	$\frac{1}{2}$

A. $-\frac{1}{2}$

B. $\frac{1}{2}$

C. $\frac{\sqrt{2}}{2}$

D. $\frac{\sqrt{2} - \sqrt{6}}{4}$

E. $\frac{\sqrt{2} + \sqrt{6}}{4}$

DO YOUR FIGURING HERE.

56. The larger of two numbers exceeds twice the smaller number by 6. The sum of twice the larger number and 4 times the smaller number is 70. If x is the smaller number, which equation below determines the correct value of x ?

F. $2(2x - 4) + 6x = 70$
G. $2(2x + 6) + 4x = 70$
H. $2(2x - 6) + 4x = 70$
J. $4(2x + 6) + 2x = 70$
K. $4(2x - 6) + 2x = 70$

GO ON TO THE NEXT PAGE

57. In the figure shown below, each pair of intersecting line segments meets at a right angle, and all the lengths given are in inches. What is the perimeter, in inches, of the figure?

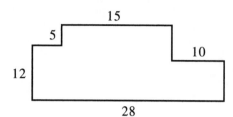

A. 70
B. 75
C. 80
D. 90
E. 95

DO YOUR FIGURING HERE.

58. Which of the following statements describes the total number of dots in the first n rows of the triangular arrangement illustrated below?

1st row
2nd row
3rd row
4th row
5th row

F. The total is equal to $2n$, where n is the number of rows.
G. The total is equal to n^2, where n is the number of rows.
H. The total is equal to $n!$, where n equals number of rows.
J. The total is equal to 2^n, where n is the number of rows.
K. The total is equal to $2^n - n!$, where n is the number of rows.

GO ON TO THE NEXT PAGE

DO YOUR FIGURING HERE.

59. A certain parabola in the standard (x,y) coordinate plane opens downwards and has a vertex NOT at the origin $(0,0)$. Which of the following equations could describe the parabola?

A. $x = 5y^2$
B. $y = 2(x + 3)^2 + 5$
C. $x = -2(y + 2)^2 + 4$
D. $y = -3x^2$
E. $y = -4(x + 1)^2 - 3$

60. The graph below shows the 2012 estimate of the five largest cities in the United States, to the nearest 1 million. According to the graph, the population of Houston makes up what fraction of the total population living in all five cities? Key: ☺ = 1 million people.

City	Population
New York	☺ ☺ ☺ ☺ ☺ ☺ ☺ ☺
Los Angeles	☺ ☺ ☺ ☺
Chicago	☺ ☺ ☺
Houston	☺ ☺
Philadelphia	☺ ☺

F. $\dfrac{1}{11}$

G. $\dfrac{1}{10}$

H. $\dfrac{2}{19}$

J. $\dfrac{3}{19}$

K. $\dfrac{4}{19}$

END OF MINI TEST SIX
STOP! DO NOT GO ON TO THE NEXT PAGE
UNTIL TOLD TO DO SO.

Other Time Management Strategies

In addition to the Math test-specific time management strategies we covered in this section, there are several time management strategies that appear in the General section of this book that can benefit students when applied to the Math test:

- Mark and Move (Page 33)

- Head Down (Page 34)

MATH TEST MASTERY
Test-Taking Strategies for the ACT Math Test

Math Orientation

The ACT Math test comes second during every ACT test, immediately after the English test.

A simple yet accurate way to describe the Math test is that it measures your students' ability to use math to solve problems. Students who are strong in math tend to do quite well on the ACT Math test. Students who have taken part in competitive math programs such as MATHCOUNTS, Mu Alpha Theta, or Math Olympiad, tend to do even better: the types of questions these programs use in their contests bear some resemblance to what appears on the ACT.

Because of the strong correlation between math skill and ACT Math scores, we recommend that if you are working with students with low ACT Math scores, you should first assume that your students have *math* issues, not *test-taking* issues. It may be the case that these students are simply unfamiliar with the ACT's format, but it's much more likely that some essential, un-mastered math skills are the source of your students' difficulties.

For that reason, our Math section on *Content Mastery* goes into explicit detail about the 10 most essential content areas. While all students will benefit from many of the test-taking strategies we cover in this book, at the end of the day on the Math test, content is king.

There are six major categories of question on the ACT Math test. It's worth reviewing this with your students. Anything you can do to make the test seem more familiar, structured, and predictable will help your students by reducing their anxiety and fear of the unknown. You can't know exactly what questions will be on the test, but you can share with your students what *categories* of questions always appear.

In addition to the information provided in the table below, advanced students may find it helpful to refer to our ACT Math Standard Families document, found on masteryprep.com/decode/resources, which includes a detailed look at each and every standard that the ACT Math test could possibly assess as well as how frequently each standard is tested.

ACT MATH QUESTION CATEGORIES

Pre-Algebra **(20–25% of Questions)**	**Elementary Algebra** **(15–20% of Questions)**	**Intermediate Algebra** **(15-20% of Questions)**
• Operations • Factors • Ratios • Proportions • Percent • Linear equations • Counting • Probability • Data interpretation • Mean, median, and mode	• Exponents • Square roots • Evaluating expressions • Creating expressions • Algebraic operations • Factoring quadratic equations	• Quadratic formula • Radical expressions • Absolute value • Inequalities • Patterns and sequences • Systems of equations • Functions • Matrices • Complex numbers
An example of Pre-Algebra is question #1 on page 24 of *Preparing for the ACT 2015-16.*	An example of Elementary Algebra is question #4 on page 24 of *Preparing for the ACT 2015-16.*	An example of Intermediate Algebra is question #48 on page 30 of *Preparing for the ACT 2015-16.*
What is another example of Pre-Algebra on the Math test? _____ _____	**What is another example of Elementary Algebra on the Math test?** _____ _____	**What is another example of Intermediate Algebra on the Math test?** _____ _____

ACT MATH QUESTION CATEGORIES

Coordinate Geometry (15-20% of Questions)	**Plane Geometry** (20-25% of Questions)	**Trigonometry** (5-10% of Questions)
The following topics all concern the standard (x, y) coordinate plane: • Graphing equations • Lines • Polynomials • Circles • Inequalities • Slope • Parallel and perpendicular • Distance • Midpoints	• Angles • Circles • Triangles • Polygons: rectangles, parallelograms, and trapezoids • Transformations • Proofs • Volume • 3-dimensional geometry	• Trig functions • Trig function graphs • Trig identities • Trig equations
An example of Coordinate Geometry is question #49 on page 30 of *Preparing for the ACT 2015-16.*	An example of Plane Geometry is question #53 on page 30 of *Preparing for the ACT 2015-16.*	An example of Trigonometry is question #30 on page 27 of *Preparing for the ACT 2015-16.*
What is another example of Coordinate Geometry on the Math test? _____ _____	**What is another example of a Plane Geometry question on the English test?** _____ _____	**What is another example of a Trigonometry question on the English test?** _____ _____

Setting Goals

Below is provided the AVERAGED CONVERSION TABLE for the ACT Math test. This is the average number of questions that need to be answered correctly to achieve a certain scale score.

We averaged 30 actual ACT conversion tables in order to determine this table.

Teachers should use the averaged conversion table to set their own goals for class progress. Scaled scores can be deceptive. An apparent growth of 10% or 20% in a scaled score might correspond to a raw score growth of 50% or as much as 100%. When you set your goals for classroom growth, consider this averaged conversion table and the actual number of questions your students will need to answer correctly to reach your goal.

Teachers and students have an easier time preparing when their goal is stated by the number of questions they want answered correctly. That is because a scale score is a very nebulous concept, but a raw score (the number of correct answers) is concrete and easy to calculate. If you want your students to earn two more scale points, it's a more definite goal to say that you want your students to answer five more questions correctly.

MATH - AVERAGED CONVERSION TABLE

Scale Score	Correct Questions	Scale Score	Correct Questions
36	59.76	18	26.02
35	58.28	17	23.11
34	56.80	16	19.42
33	55.53	15	15.45
32	54.29	14	12.15
31	53.06	13	9.60
30	51.71	12	7.60
29	50.08	11	6.02
28	48.16	10	4.81
27	45.89	9	4.04
26	43.44	8	3.09
25	40.95	7	2.90
24	38.45	6	2.04
23	36.10	5	1.83
22	34.05	4	1.00
21	32.26	3	1.00
20	30.44	2	--
19	28.39	1	0.00

It's important to keep in mind that this conversion table shows the *average*. That means a student could aim for a target number of questions according to this table and still not reach their goal scaled score. For this reason, show them instead the STUDENT CONVERSION TABLE.

In the student conversion table, we provide the number of questions a student needs to answer correctly in order to practically guarantee a given scale score. If students achieve this raw score, they won't score lower than the given scale score, and they might even score higher.

Provide your students with the student conversion table to avoid the problem of achieving a goal raw score but still not getting the scale score needed.

Using the student conversion table, students determine their "number" for the English test. This is how many questions they need to answer correctly. They should write this number at the top of their test booklet when the test begins. Some students might find it helpful to think of this in reverse: they can afford to miss 15 questions, for instance, and still achieve their target scale score.

When students know their goal in terms of questions right, they are less likely to waste time on difficult questions and won't panic if they miss a few. This can be a big step toward reducing test anxiety and helping students become smarter test-takers.

Please feel free to copy this page and distribute it to your students. An easy-to-print PDF is also available for you at masteryprep.com/decode/resources.

MATH - STUDENT CONVERSION TABLE

Scale Score	Correct Questions	Scale Score	Correct Questions
36	60	18	28
35	59	17	25
34	59	16	20
33	59	15	17
32	57	14	14
31	55	13	12
30	53	12	9
29	52	11	7
28	50	10	6
27	47	9	5
26	45	8	4
25	42	7	3
24	40	6	3
23	37	5	2
22	36	4	1
21	34	3	1
20	32	2	--
19	30	1	0

Be Negative about Negatives

Negative signs cause more mischief and steal more points than anything else on the ACT Math test.

We tell our students to imagine that whenever they see a minus or a negative sign, they should begin to hear creepy background music—the kind that plays in horror movies to let you know the villain is waiting on the other side of the door. (Also see *error paranoia* on page 45.)

Any time your students encounter negative signs, they need to double- and triple-check their work.

ACT test writers know that this is a weak point for most students and so they make sure to include answer choices that students who slipped up on negatives would arrive at.

There is no partial credit on the ACT. If you are in the habit of giving your juniors and seniors partial credit for math answers where they have swapped up the negatives, you may want to reconsider. It's better for students to feel the pain from one of your exams than to feel the pain of coming up a few points short on the ACT Math test because they never kicked the habit of being careless with negativity.

Whenever you are reviewing a math question that involves negatives, consider asking your students, "What would happen if we messed up the negatives, here?" If the question is multiple choice, ask your students what choice represents getting the negative confused. This will help students build awareness of the fact that just because their answer showed up as a choice doesn't mean it's right!

Refer to Math question #23 on page 26 of *Preparing for the ACT 2015-16*.

In question #23, the whole expression simplifies down nicely to one term. But if your students drop the minus on the last $2y$ when they distribute y^2, they would end up with two terms and erroneously select choice D.

It's a simple mistake to make, but one that all too often costs your students points.

Refer to Math question #39 on page 29 of *Preparing for the ACT 2015-16*.

Question #39 is relatively straightforward, but there is one major opportunity for students to drop a point.

Check Your Understanding: How would you coach your students to avoid a costly error on question #39?

_____

_____

_____

_____

Popularity Contest

When students get stuck and they need to *mark and move*, they should always try to inform their guess using the *popularity contest* strategy.

This is a powerful way to use the ACT test writers' tricks against them and make two or three solid eliminations.

It doesn't always work and should only be used as a guessing strategy. But as a guessing strategy it can make the difference of a point or more on your students' Math scores.

> Refer to Math question #4 on page 24 of *Preparing for the ACT 2015-16.*

You may notice that all the answer choices look similar on question #4. They are variations on the numbers 45 and 15. There is a very good reason for that: on a typical multiple choice math test, students *know* they have arrived at an incorrect answer because their answer doesn't show up as a choice. They are then free to try again! For that reason, ACT Math test writers include answer choices that match what students would arrive at if they made mistakes. They can catch the students in their errors and cost them points.

For example, choice H is for students who treat the 3 as a coefficient instead of an exponent.

Choices G and J are there in case students mess up resolving the exponent or get the place value wrong in their division.

Choice K is there because, well, who knows how students would get there, but maybe it's possible.

The test writers' method, which costs many students precious points, can be used to the advantage of a student in the know, because *the correct answer will have numbers that are similar to it.*

The reverse is also true: *the outlier, the answer that looks completely different, is probably wrong.*

To apply the popularity contest strategy, go with an answer choice that looks similar to most other answer choices.

In the case of question #4, there are three answer choices with the digits 4 and 5, but only two answer choices with the digits 1 and 5. For a student blindly guessing, she would go with choice F, G, or J.

> Refer to Math question #3 on page 24 of *Preparing for the ACT 2015-16.*

When your students are considering what answer choice wins the popularity contest, it does not matter whether the numbers are numerically close. It only matters if the numbers look similar or have a relationship in some way.

For example, in question #3 choice C is twice the amount of choice A. Likewise, choice E is twice the amount of choice D, which is twice the amount of choice B. Choices B, D, and E win the popularity contest, so an educated guess would go to one of them.

> Refer to Math question #6 on page 24 of *Preparing for the ACT 2015-16.*

With question #6, the popularity contest is rather obvious: three choices (F, G, and H) involve $12, so students should go with one of them if forced to blindly guess.

> Refer to Math question #11 on page 25 of *Preparing for the ACT 2015-16.*

Check Your Understanding: If you had to apply the popularity contest to make a better guess on question #11, what choices would you eliminate? What would be your reasoning?

_____

_____

_____

_____

Walk Through the Open Door

Most ACT Math problems are multi-step, which means that students are often left with the daunting question, "Where do I begin?" It can be challenging to visualize all of the processes that are needed to get to the right answer.

Fortunately, ACT Math questions are designed with minimal distractors. This is a matter of necessity: the test writers have to pack a lot of punch in a few lines of text.

This means that if there is an equation your students can set up or a formula they can use, chances are it will be useful in solving the problem.

Even if your students don't see all the way to the end of a solution, if they see a step they *can* take, they should go ahead with it.

We call this *walking through the open door.*

Refer to Math question #9 on page 25 of *Preparing for the ACT 2015-16.*

Question #9 has an open door. It states that the top and bottom layers are each 0.03 cm thick, and they don't count as inner layers, so students can remove them from the total thickness of 0.32 cm. It's not guaranteed that this step will bring them all the way to the answer, but this step has to be taken to make any headway, so they should walk through the open door.

$$0.32 - 0.03 - 0.03 = 0.26$$

Now students are faced with only one more step between them and the solution: how many 0.02 cm inner layers can fit inside of 0.26 cm? At this point, students can divide or, if they want to be extra careful, draw it out.

This strategy gradually increases in importance as students near the more complicated questions in the back of the test.

Refer to Math question #54 on page 30 of *Preparing for the ACT 2015-16.*

Question #54 requires several steps and some skill in creating expressions that model real-world situations.

Check Your Understanding: What is an open door that students can walk through to start solving question #54?

_____

_____

_____

_____

Make the Pictures Yours

It's a minor point but one that deserves at least a small mention. The figures the ACT provides are not holy. No one will smite the students if they touch them or mark them up.

Some students are very careful with figures and avoid writing on them. This wastes time and hurts their scores. When the ACT provides information about a figure, but that information does not appear on the figure, students should mark it up. Tell them, *Make the pictures yours*.

Ideally, once they add the information to the figure, students should no longer have to refer to the question and can instead just look at their figure.

> Refer to Math question #27 on page 27 of *Preparing for the ACT 2015-16*.

Question #27 gives the length of the hypotenuse, so students should go ahead and clearly write the length of hypotenuse on their figure. They should also make single marks on each leg to show that the lengths of the legs are equal (because this is an isosceles triangle). Although it isn't necessary on this problem, it also isn't a bad idea to write that the lower angles are each 45°.

> Refer to Math question #26 on page 27 of *Preparing for the ACT 2015-16*.

There are two facts in question #26 which do not appear on the figure.

Check Your Understanding: How might your students mark up the figure on question #26 to help them solve the problem?

_____

_____

_____

_____

Don't Compute Word Problems

Students often have the bad habit of instantly computing as soon as they begin reading a word problem.

The issue is that math isn't designed to solve word problems. It's designed to solve math problems.

Students must engage in *computational thinking* to convert the word problem into math that either they or their calculator can solve. The actual computation should be almost effortless and comes at the very end.

Trigger-happy students who love to start computing the moment they see a number should pause and force themselves to write out what they need to solve before relying on their calculators.

Setup should always be your students' first thought in a word problem. Not solution. They can't solve a word problem unless they set it up. Seconds spent trying to solve word problems outright without setting them up first are seconds wasted.

Refer to Math question #46 on page 29 of *Preparing for the ACT 2015-16.*

Question #46 appears at first to be a proportion problem, only such a question occurring so late in the test should arouse the student's suspicions. The Math test does gradually get more difficult, after all.

Students trying to multiply any of the fractions by 10 soon find themselves up a creek without a paddle. The only way forward is to set the problem up.

Students should be thinking from the initial read-through of the question, "What is the equation that I can write that expresses what this word problem is saying?" Once they can get an equation, they can solve the problem.

In this case, the equation is , where *x* is the volume of the container. Now your students can compute.

Computation is for math problems, not word problems! Your students' job is to convert word problems into math problems, *then* compute.

Draw It Out

When the ACT Math test describes a figure but does not show it , students must *draw it out*. To avoid wasting time, students should do this automatically, as though they are taking notes during a lecture. It's not ideal for students to read the question, realize they need to draw it out, then read the question again and start drawing. They should start drawing at the outset.

We tell our students to imagine that the Math test writers were being lazy, and now it's up to the students to do their jobs for them: if the writers forgot to add a figure, the student must draw one in.

It's important that students take care to draw the figure somewhat accurately and to scale. Incorrect drawings can cause students to reach false conclusions. It doesn't need to be a work of art, but it should be a reasonable attempt to represent what the question describes.

Some questions are extremely challenging without a figure but become quite simplistic once students draw them out.

Refer to Math question #17 on page 26 of *Preparing for the ACT 2015-16*.

Question #17 perfectly proves this point. Once students draw out the two lines and place point *A* at the intersection, they can see clearly that the two angles in question are supplemental to one another.

If students only try to visualize the question, they are making the question as hard as possible to solve. It's like trying to juggle with their hands tied behind their backs!

Whenever a question refers to a figure that isn't depicted, students should draw it out.

Refer to Math question #50 on page 30 of *Preparing for the ACT 2015-16*.

This question has one of the more complicated variants of a volume problem. It also involves the most text of any single question on this Math test, weighing in at nine lines.

 Check Your Understanding: Draw the figure described in question #50.

What questions could you ask your students to help them be successful in drawing out this question and solving the problem?

_____

_____

_____

Objects in Mirror

Near the climax of the Spielberg classic *Jurassic Park,* an enormous dinosaur gives chase to a jeep along a stormy, muddy trail. It is one of the most intense moments in the movie. The monster's teeth flash in the side-view mirror. And then, a quiet moment. The camera zooms in. At the bottom of the mirror is the customary warning: *objects in mirror are closer than they appear.*

Every ACT Math test has a similar warning: *illustrative figures are NOT necessarily drawn to scale.* In other words, what you see is not necessarily what you get.

Our analysis of ACT Math figures, however, tells another story than what this warning insinuates. Figures are nearly *always* drawn close to or exactly to scale. If students must guess, they should use the figure.

Two tools can help with guessing. They are our MacGyver versions of a ruler and a protractor. Students can't bring the real thing into the test room, but the ACT can't keep them from having these substitutes.

Pencils can be used as rulers. Students can hold the pencil up against any line and mark where the line ends using their thumbs. Now they can compare the length of the line to any other line by moving their pencils around, carefully leaving their thumbs in place.

The corner of a piece of paper (such as a bubble sheet) can become a protractor. The corner is a perfect 90° angle. Students can compare this to any other angle they are working on.

Refer to Math question #13 on page 25 of *Preparing for the ACT 2015-16.*

Imagine that your students are unable to solve question #13. It has come time for them to mark a guess and move on. If they place the corner of their paper into *BAC,* they will discover that the angle is slightly more than 90°. If they guess choice B, with an angle measure just above 90°, they will be answering correctly!

Even if students are unsure about their pick, they can use *objects in mirror* to definitively eliminate choice A. The angle in question is surely larger than the corner of their paper.

Refer to Math question #41 on page 29 of *Preparing for the ACT 2015-16.*

Question #41 is probably the most challenging question that has appeared up to this point in this test, and one that many students may feel bewildered by.

Check Your Understanding: Describe how you could coach your students to use a little logic and the objects in mirror strategy to arrive at the correct answer for question #41.

_____

_____

_____

_____

Plug and Chug

Plug and chug, or less colorfully, *guess and check*, occurs in its most basic form when students put the number in each answer choice into the equation in the question and see which one works.

Mastery of the plug and chug strategy in all its flavors can make a massive difference on your students' scores.

Refer to Math question #11 on page 25 of *Preparing for the ACT 2015-16*.

Some questions, such as question #11, seem to be written for plug and chug. Hardly any mental work is required.

When applying plug and chug, students should always start with the choice in the middle unless there is an overwhelming reason to begin elsewhere. The ACT Math test sequences its answer choices from least to greatest or vice versa, so if students start with a middle value they can also gain a clue as to whether they should move up or down in value for their second guess.

The best way to use plug and chug on question #11 is to select a value set from the table. Let's say $t = 5$ and $d = 44$. Plug these values into the equation for choice C. It works out just fine.

When students use plug and chug with a pair of points and find an equation that works, they should always verify with one more pair. This is because a line could run through one set of coordinates but still not be the line that the student needs. In question #11, let's say the second set of points are $t = 0$ and $d = 14$. This checks out as well, so C is the answer we go with.

The beauty of the plug and chug strategy is that your students can still get the correct answer on many questions, despite not knowing how to solve them.

Refer to Math question #15 on page 26 of *Preparing for the ACT 2015-16*.

This question requires students to convert a word problem into a system of equations. Or does it? Actually, students can plug and chug their way to points.

Application of this strategy here is a little more nuanced than in the previous example because students must take gsome extra steps.

Students should start in the middle with choice C. If there were 35 large figurines, then there were 70 – 35 = 35 small figurines. Next, students check out the dollar values of each of these figurine sets to determine if they are equal.

$35 \cdot 8 = 280$

$35 \cdot 12 = 420$

They are not equal, so choice C is incorrect. Before moving on to the next choice, students should ask themselves, "Do I need to *decrease* or *increase* the number of large figurines?" In choice C, there was too much money from the large figurines, so the best choice is to decrease them.

This one little step allows students to nearly double their plug and chug speed. At most, they need to try out three choices rather than five. After the first step, they know that choices D and E are incorrect.

Based on this reasoning, students should move to choice B. If there are 28 large figurines, then there are 70 – 28 = 42 small figurines.

$28 \cdot 12 = 336$

$42 \cdot 8 = 336$

This checks out, so choice B is the correct answer.

This example highlights the fact that students need to practice plug and chug with a number of questions before they can do so quickly and easily. It takes some logic to figure out how to test the answer choices against the information presented in the question. It isn't always provided cleanly in a formula where it's easy to plug in the values. To get the most mileage out of this strategy, students must be creative in the way they verify each choice.

Refer to Math question #55 on page 31 of *Preparing for the ACT 2015-16.*

Question #55 asks students to determine what set of students are situated in the overlap between the set of students who ski downhill and the set of students who ski cross-country.

Check Your Understanding: How could students use plug and chug to solve this problem?

_____

_____

_____

_____

Process of Elimination: Sign and Size

The *process of elimination* is the most fundamental, most powerful, and most under-used test-taking strategy on the ACT.

Test-taking strategies are there for students when they don't know the answer to a question. And yet for many, their first reaction when encountering a difficult question is to blindly guess. The confusion brought about by the test item causes students to shy away from it. They don't feel like they can get a grip on it, they sense the clock ticking away, and so they randomly bubble an answer.

This is particularly true on the ACT Math test, where it is possible that students could have *no idea* what a question is asking. Even in circumstances such as these, it is important that students use the process of elimination and try to figure their way to the correct answer anyway.

If students can eliminate three choices, they have more than doubled their odds of guessing correctly, from 20% to a healthy 50-50 shot.

There are several ways that students can eliminate choices, but two methods deserve particular attention: by *sign* and by *size*.

> Refer to Math question #7 on page 25 of *Preparing for the ACT 2015-16.*

Most of your students should have no difficulty answering this question, but for the purpose of illustration let's imagine they have forgotten all about what a *geometric sequence* is.

There are still some eliminations they can make, even if students can't puzzle out the pattern.

Students should notice that some answer choices are negative while some are positive. They can use the *sign* to make eliminations one way or another.

Should the seventh term by positive or negative? In the sequence given it seems to be alternating between the two signs:

1: Positive

2: Negative

3: Positive

4: Negative

5: Positive

6: Negative

7: Positive

The seventh number has a positive sign, so students can eliminate choices A and B.

> Refer to Math question #14 on page 25 of *Preparing for the ACT 2015-16.*

Size can also be the clue that students need to eliminate their way to the correct answer. In question #14, students must find the central angle measure of the *core subjects* sector.

Some students may be at a loss for solving this question because it combines an eclectic mix of math skills that were not likely covered in the same year of high school: proportions and central angles. Furthermore, sometimes it's more challenging to correct something wrong than to figure out the right way to do it the first time.

Before students guess, they should use the process of elimination. All answer choices are positive, so *sign* won't help. Let's take a look at *size*. Currently, *core subjects* takes up half the circle, or about 180°. There are a total of nine hours in the figure, so this piece with four hours shouldn't take up a whole half.

Once students start thinking about four hours out of nine, they should realize that 200° and 288° are *too big*. Those answers are saying that the *core subjects* piece should be even bigger, which does not make sense. At the very least, students can make these two eliminations.

If students carry their consideration of *size* further, choices F and G are a drastic reduction in the size of the *core subjects* sector. That does not seem likely because four out of nine is *close* to half. The best guess is therefore H, which also happens to be the correct answer.

Students should consider both *sign* and *size* when using the process of elimination.

Refer to Math question #44 on page 29 of *Preparing for the ACT.*

Question #44 is a sophisticated twist on finding a midpoint.

Check Your Understanding: Assume that your students are stumped on this question. How can they use the process of elimination to get close to the right answer?

_____

_____

_____

_____

Solve It All the Way

One of the most frustrating experiences in math is figuring out the crux of a problem but not answering the actual question and missing out on points.

Students seem to love leaving math problems half-solved.

This one bad habit can bring your students' ACT scores down by two points or more.

Drill it into your students' heads that they need to *solve it all the way* and double-check the question (always the last sentence in the text) to make sure they actually answered it.

> Refer to Math question #8 on page 25 of *Preparing for the ACT 2015-16*.

The ACT Math test writers are quite aware of students' propensity for half-answers and exploit it in the answer choices whenever they can. In question #8, after students calculate the price per pound to be $9.75, they are tempted to mark F.

There is a certain magical allure to seeing the number that you just wrote down on your worksheet match a choice on a test. It seems it *must* be right! It's a *eureka* moment! The lightbulb goes off.

Only, in this case, it's a booby-trapped lightbulb. $9.75 is only part of the answer. Students must add the $10.00 fee to get the *total* shipping rate for the box.

If your students have ever seen *Who Wants to Be a Millionaire?*, they should mimic Regis and ask themselves before moving on to the next question, "Is that your final answer?"

They need to be certain that they have solved it all the way.

Students who leave points on the table during the first 30 questions commonly do so because of this bad habit. The only way to break students of this habit is to practice again and again, pointing out each time students have fallen for the trap, until they no longer do so.

Another way to help students improve in this area is to take a question like #8 and solve it in a "we do" activity. Afterward, ask your students, "Why did the ACT test writers include choice F? How could a student accidentally arrive at $9.75 as their answer?"

> Refer to Math question #12 on page 25 of *Preparing for the ACT 2015-16*.

Question #12 is another example of how important solving it all the way can be in the front half of the ACT Math test.

In this question, students must find the width and then the perimeter. As they work the problem, they will be tempted to choose F, which gives the width they found, and H, which gives the sum of the length and width, but not the perimeter of the rectangle.

> Refer to Math question #27 on page 27 of *Preparing for the ACT 2015-16*.

Check Your Understanding: How might your students fail to solve it all the way on question #27?

_____

_____

What trap answers might catch students in their mistakes?

_____

_____

Assume Values

To apply *plug and chug* (aka *guess and check*) to some problems, you must assume some values.

Students often feel quite tentative about doing this. They are afraid that the conclusions they reach with a certain set of values won't be true for all values. Or they just don't know where to start.

The primary danger of assuming values is using it to validate an answer. Assuming a value can't usually prove an answer is right, but it can *definitely* prove the other answer choices wrong.

Once students have assumed values, they use their calculators to compute the results and look for an answer choice that is consistent with their results.

Students should clearly note what their assumed values are so they don't get them confused as they compute.

When assuming values, students should avoid numbers like 0 and 1 (these can create false positives) and select numbers that evenly divide into one another if fractions or ratios are involved. Students should also be careful to follow the rules for the possible values given in the question.

> Refer to Math question #22 on page 26 of *Preparing for the ACT 2015-16.*

In question #22, students can use mathematical proofs to reach the answer, but some may find that assuming values works faster and better for them.

The question says that the values of variables *a, b,* and *c* must be positive integers. Let $a = 3$, $b = 2$, and $c = 4$. Then, compute that into the equations given: $x = 3^2 = 9$. Also, $y = 4^2 = 16$. So $xy = 9 \cdot 16 = 144$.

Check each answer choice against the assumption.

F. $3 \cdot 4^2 = 3 \cdot 16 = 54$

G. $3 \cdot 4^4 = 3 \cdot 256 = 768$

H. $(3 \cdot 4)^2 = 12^2 = 144$

Choice H looks correct, but it's possible that more than one choice works for this set of assumed values. Students need to check all of them. If they get two possible correct answers, they then try some more values.

J. $(3 \cdot 4)^4 = 12^4 = 20,736$

K. $(3 \cdot 4)^4 = 12^4 = 20,736$

Only choice H works for this set of assumed values, so it must be the correct answer. For an answer to be correct, it would need to work for *all* assumed values, so a choice not working for *one* set of assumed values is enough to invalidate it.

> Refer to Math question #43 on page 29 of *Preparing for the ACT 2015-16.*

Question #43 requires either clear insight or tricky algebraic manipulation of the expression to solve it "the right way."

Check Your Understanding: Describe how a student could use the assume values strategy to solve this problem.

_____

_____

_____

_____

Breadcrumbs

Hansel and Gretel knew a thing or two about the ACT.

Particularly they knew about *breadcrumbs*, evidence they left behind so they could pick up their trail.

On the ACT Math test, it's important that students make note of their work, especially when they complete a step. The reason for this is that students never know when they will get stuck. They never know when they will need to put a mark near the question, make a guess, and move on.

If they mark and move but don't leave any breadcrumbs behind, when they return to the problem, they will be starting from scratch.

Many students do their work on a calculator, and with the numbers *right there* staring them in the face, they feel like they are showing their work. But once they hit the CLEAR button, it's all gone with the wind. Their test document is as blank it was when the proctor said, "Begin."

Students should write down anything they figured out about a math problem as part of their mark and move procedure

Sometimes, as students approach the end of the test, a new way to solve a previous question will flash into their minds. When they come back to this question with a new perspective, their breadcrumbs will help them quickly pick up the trail.

Refer to Math question #19 on page 26 of *Preparing for the ACT 2015-16.*

Question #19 illustrates this concept. Suppose a student adds the two numbers, but then gets stuck. He's scratching his head about what rule to apply. He feels like he needs to move on and come back later if he has time. It doesn't look like it's one of his cherries (see *cherry-picking* on page 143).

At this point, right before he marks his guess and moves on, he should write down the number he computed: 1,370,000,000. This is his *breadcrumb*. He's already solved half the problem! Why should he have to solve it all again when he comes back to it?

Question Sets: Don't Panic

Students are prone to panic when they encounter the only format variation on the ACT Math test: the "set" of three questions that relate to a block of text and one or more figures.

These sets occur twice on the Math test and usually feature much more text than other questions, with introductory text blocks often encompassing 10 lines or more. And that's before students even arrive at the actual questions!

Despite the added challenge from so many words, the level of difficulty on these questions is always *easier* than that of the questions surrounding the set.

In other words, sets contain pockets of *easy, simple* questions that often entail *pre-algebra*.

The ACT likes to embed pre-algebra questions into the latter half of the test by including them in complicated-looking sets.

Students should always be on the lookout for these and rejoice when they find them, for here reside easy points for the picking.

The questions within a set tend to be sequenced by difficulty, so the first of the three questions is usually the easiest and the last is the most difficult.

Even when students are focused on the front half of the math test, they should take care to give themselves time for the question sets at the back of the test. They'll have a good chance of getting most of these questions correct.

Refer to Math questions #33-35 on page 28 of *Preparing for the ACT 2015-16*.

Questions #33 through #35 is an example of a question set. Some students avert their eyes at once from the evil text, but those who don't give in to their fear are rewarded with the first question, which requires a straightforward proportion.

How to tackle a set is a matter of personal preference. Students who prefer math to reading might find it easier to read the question, *then* the introductory text. Students who are strong readers will probably do better if they read the introductory text and review the figure first.

Check Your Understanding: What are the question numbers of the other set in the Math test provided in Preparing for the ACT 2015-16?

_____

_____

_____

_____

Use a Graph

Coordinate geometry problems often yield to students either *graphing* the equation on a calculator or *drawing out* a rudimentary graph using the information provided.

Each ACT Math test includes 9 coordinate geometry problems. If students don't know how to solve them, they should always try to figure out the correct answer, anyway, by using a graph.

Refer to Math question #40 on page 29 of *Preparing for the ACT 2015-16.*

While it's much simpler for students to simply know what happens to a coordinate when it is reflected over an axis, if they aren't sure or don't remember the rule, they students can use the (much more time-consuming) *make a map* strategy for this question.

Students draw an axis with 12 grid marks to the right along the horizontal axis and 1 up the vertical axis. Next, they mark the reflection across the *y*-axis, counting the grid marks to the left and positioning the point. They then check their graph to determine the coordinate of the reflected point: (–12,1). Of course, it *is* much quicker and simpler for students to simply know the rule. However, test jitters can cause students to doubt themselves or suddenly forget the basics, and manually mapping out the coordinates in a situation like this can put them back on track.

Refer to Math question #28 on page 27 of *Preparing for the ACT 2015-16.*

In some cases, it's merely a matter of using the graph that the ACT has already provided. The graph in question #28 provides a ton of information about the nature of the function, if students recall how to read it. It's rare that so much work is already done for the student.

The question is asking, in a very convoluted way, for a description of the two *x*-intercepts on the graph. One is positive, and one is negative. Students must simply find the *x*-intercepts to choose the correct answer.

We strongly recommend that if your students miss a number of the coordinate geometry problems on the ACT, give them this question. It does an excellent job of assessing whether your students have a fundamental understanding of what a graph can tell them. If the majority of students miss it, you would do well to provide your students a comprehensive review of the coordinate plane and graphing.

Calculator Strategies

While "calculator" is a dirty word in some classrooms and student dependence on them can inhibit the development of mental math muscles, it *is* true that judicious, rapid, and accurate use of calculators can earn students extra points on the ACT Math test.

Viable calculator strategies fall into several categories:

Swapping Fractions for Decimals

If the ACT asks students to sequence fractions or find a value that involves a fraction, they can simplify the problem by converting the fraction to a decimal.

Refer to Math question #18 on page 26 of *Preparing for the ACT 2015-16.*

While question #18 can be solved by logic and understanding common denominators and the relationship between numerators and denominators, it can be answered almost as quickly by converting each of the three fractions into decimals.

To do the conversion, students divide each numerator by its denominator on their calculator. Students can then more comfortably identify which decimal value is least and which value is greatest.

Guessing and Checking

Use your calculator to *plug and chug* and compute possible values for the answer.

Refer to Math question #19 on page 26 of *Preparing for the ACT 2015-16.*

The way to answer this question with a calculator is as follows: First, students add the two numbers in the question. $670,000,000 + 700,000,000 = 1,370,000,000$. Then, with their calculators, they try out each answer choice until they find a match, always starting with the middle.

$1.37 \cdot 10^8 = 137,000,000$

Almost there, but too small. Students try one number higher, choice D.

$1.37 \cdot 10^9 = 1,370,000,000$

Bingo! Choice D must be the correct answer.

Graphing

Sometimes a complicated problem can be simplified just by making a graph on a graphing calculator and then using the arrow keys to learn more about particular points.

Refer to Math question #24 on page 26 of *Preparing for the ACT 2015-16.*

While this problem does work quite well with the plug and chug strategy, another way to solve is to graph the equation $y = 500x - x^2$ on a graphing calculator.

Then, it's simply a matter of pressing the arrow button to find that the first point where the line exceeds $60,000 is close to an *x* value of 200.

It often takes some finagling to convert an equation into slope-intercept form, but once that is done several problems will melt in your students' hands.

Refer to Math question #32 on page 27 of *Preparing for the ACT 2015-16.*

Check Your Understanding: How can you coach your students to use their calculators to solve question #32? Describe the steps you would walk them through.

Common Errors to Avoid in Math

Precision is key to a high ACT Math score. Just by avoiding costly errors, without improving any other math skill, students can increase by two points or more! Below are the most common errors to look out for. We recommend that you take every opportunity to remind your students about these pitfalls and spend time rectifying these common errors when they appear in your students' class work so that they can learn to avoid them.

Below are the 11 most common errors to avoid on the Math test:

1. Dropping a negative or otherwise incorrectly handling a negative number.

2. Answering only one step of a problem instead of the actual question.

3. Using an incorrect order of operations (particularly when exponents or absolute values are involved).

4. Incorrectly drawing out a problem, then making conclusions based on the incorrect drawing.

5. Subtracting (from 180°, from 90°, etc.) incorrectly.

6. Incorrectly transposing numbers from the question to your scratch work.

7. Incorrectly transposing numbers from your solution to the answer choice.

8. Pointing an inequality sign the wrong way or failing to reverse it when necessary.

9. Forgetting to count one or more matching sides on a polygon.

10. Only counting one occurrence of a number when it appears twice.

11. Reversing trig definitions (placing the *adjacent* length in the numerator in the *tan* function, especially).

Check Your Understanding: What three errors are your students most likely to make?

_____

_____

What will you do to help your students avoid these errors?

_____

_____

MATH CONTENT MASTERY
Content Strategies for the ACT Math Test

Red Herrings

When reviewing content, it's very important that you avoid pursuing the especially rare or tricky questions that appear on a particular Math test.

We call these *red herrings*. We strongly recommend that you use the skill weights that provided in this section to prioritize your review. If you review red herrings instead of these essential skills, chances are that your students' scores won't budge. Even if your students do manage to master the irksome herring, the likelihood that the skill will be assessed on their next ACT Math test is minimal.

This is because the ACT Math test has a broad set of standards with an enormous number of associated question variants. As a matter of fact, there are over 100 skills that could be tested on any given ACT Math test. Usually only 40 of those skills show up on any one assessment. This means that many of the challenging questions that appear on an ACT Math test are *interesting*, but reviewing them won't increase your students' scores.

This section helps you avoid red herrings and review the content that will positively boost your students' ACT outcomes.

Refer to Math question #29 on page 27 of *Preparing for the ACT 2015-16.*

Question #29 deals with complex numbers. This is a very interesting subject, particularly for math teachers. What's more, the problem is very neat. The product works out cleanly to cancel out the imaginary numbers. It's a sort of work of art as far as ACT Math problems go.

If your testing data only includes one ACT Math practice test that your students have taken, this question looks important. It might be one of only 15 questions a student missed. It seems like a must-review.

According to our research, however, complex numbers show up only once out of every three tests. In other words, most ACT tests don't have a single *i* in them! This skill is a red herring that can eat up a massive amount of valuable prep time without giving your students any improvement on their scores.

Refer to Math question #57 on page 31 of *Preparing for the ACT 2015-16.*

Trigonometric functions on the coordinate plane such as those presented in question #57, only appear in one ACT Math test out of three.

Check Your Understanding: How would you explain the red herring concept to another math teacher in the context of question #57?

_____

_____

_____

_____

Just Learn the Math

On the ACT Math test, there is no substitute for knowing the math.

The best prep for this ACT subject area looks similar to *teaching math*. Identify skills where students have deficiencies, then work to remedy those deficiencies. Focus on the 10 content areas we detail in the following chapters, and you and your students will win.

Students who score poorly on the ACT Math test are probably doing so because they don't know the math. This can manifest itself in students complaining that they "didn't have enough time." This is a true statement, and if students had unlimited time their Math scores could be as many as seven points higher. But since you can't change the time limits for these students, focus on what you can change. "I don't have enough time," is very similar to saying, "I don't know the math well enough to answer the questions quickly."

Students who have fully mastered the fundamentals of pre-algebra, algebra, geometry, and trigonometry finish the Math test with time to spare.

The ACT Math test is brutal, in that it will only yield a little to test-taking strategies. Students must know the math to succeed. That being said, if your students to the point where they know the math cold, they will do well. This is a test that will reward you for keeping content king.

In the end, students just have to learn the math.

Content Area #1: Solving Equations

The most heavily weighted standard family on the ACT Math test is *Solving Equations*. If only these questions were as straightforward as they sound!

Many of these problems require students to convert a word problem into one or more equations, then solve to find a value. In some cases, the value requires more manipulation before students can determine the answer.

These are the major test items associated with this standard family:

- Evaluating expressions

- Linear equations

- Quadratic equations

- Systems of equations

Practice Makes Perfect

Refer to Math question #46 on page 29 of *Preparing for the ACT 2015-16.*

Question #46 is one of the more difficult questions of this type. The item sounds like it wants students to set up a proportion, and this signal can cause students to miss the fact that what they really need to do is convert the word problem into an equation.

Students must be very comfortable with converting word problems into equations in order to arrive at the correct answer on this question. The only way they can reach that level of skill is through a high quantity of practice.

It can be difficult to find enough practice questions of this type, so one exercise we recommend is to take word problems that involve arithmetic (including ACT Math problems) and ask your students to solve the problems using algebra. Ask them, "How could we express this word problem as an equation?"

Your students may have no idea how to proceed at the beginning, especially when the option to solve with arithmetic is staring them in the face. Eventually, they will get to the point where they naturally think about word problems in terms of equations.

This has the added benefit of focusing your students on setting up word problems before they compute the solution, which reinforces the *don't compute word problems* strategy (page 185).

CATEGORY: ALGEBRA & FUNCTIONS

Family: Solving Equations

Weight: 8-15%

Standards:
A 202. Solve equations in the form $x + a = b$, where a and b are whole numbers or decimals
A 301. Substitute whole numbers for unknown quantities to evaluate expressions
A 302. Solve one-step equations to get integer or decimal answers
A 401. Evaluate algebraic expressions by substituting integers for unknown quantities
A 403. Solve routine first-degree equations
A 501. Recognize that when numerical quantities are reported in real-world contexts, the numbers are often rounded
A 502. Solve real-world problems by using first-degree equations
A 506. Identify solutions to simple quadratic equations
A 507. Solve quadratic equations in the form $(x + a)(x + b) = 0$, where a and b are numbers or variables
A 508. Factor simple quadratics (e.g., the difference of squares and perfect square trinomials)
A 604. Solve systems of two linear equations
A 605. Solve quadratic equations
A 703. Apply the remainder theorem for polynomials, that $P(a)$ is the remainder when $P(x)$ is divided by $(x - a)$

Content Area #2: Area, Perimeter, Volume, and Circumference

This broad geometry category begins with assessing students' knowledge of key formulas for area, perimeter, volume, and circumference, but it doesn't end there. Students must be conversant with determining measures for parts or segments of shapes. They must also be prepared to use algebra to determine the dimensions of the shapes, and from there be able to determine the shapes' properties.

This standard family includes the following topics:

- Line segments

- Area of triangles and rectangles

- Perimeter of polygons

- Perimeter of composite shapes

- Circles

- Dimension relationships

The ways that the ACT can assess this content area are wide and varied, so we recommend giving your students as much practice with these types of problems as possible. That way a question format can't throw them off guard.

Subtraction

Refer to Math question #34 on page 28 of *Preparing for the ACT 2015-16.*

Question #34 provides a typical example of a test item from this standard family. Students are required to make several area calculations and select the operations that will bring them all the way to the correct answer.

Many geometry problems of this type rely on the ability to subtract the area of one shape from that of another shape. If students are not familiar with this math strategy, the steps to solving questions like this might not be clear.

In some cases, it is not so clear that subtraction is needed. Typically in these situations, students will have to compute the area of a larger, complete shape and *then* subtract what is missing in order to determine the area of a composite figure.

CATEGORY: GEOMETRY

Family: Area, Perimeter, Volume & Circumference

Weight: 8-15%

Standards:

G 201. Estimate the length of a line segment based on other lengths in a geometric figure

G 202. Calculate the length of a line segment based on the lengths of other line segments that go in the same direction (e.g., overlapping line segments and parallel sides of polygons with only right angles)

G 302. Compute the perimeter of polygons when all side lengths are given

G 303. Compute the area of rectangles when whole number dimensions are given

G 403. Compute the area and perimeter of triangles and rectangles in simple problems

G 505. Compute the perimeter of simple composite geometric figures with unknown side lengths

G 506. Compute the area of triangles and rectangles when one or more additional simple steps are required

G 507. Compute the area and circumference of circles after identifying necessary information

G 601. Use relationships involving area, perimeter, and volume of geometric figures to compute another measure (e.g., surface area for a cube of a given volume and simple geometric probability)

G 702. Compute the area of composite geometric figures when planning and/or visualization is required

Content Area #3: Arithmetic

Believe it or not, *Arithmetic* is the third most heavily weighted content area on the Math test. And with good reason: many of the problems students will face in college and their careers can be solved by simple arithmetic.

All arithmetic problems on the ACT are couched in (sometimes quite challenging) word problems, and most require a combination of two or more steps.

There are four major types of arithmetic questions:

- Operations

- Percent

- Proportions

- Ratios

Of these, percent is weighted most heavily.

Refer to Math question #16 on page 26 of *Preparing for the ACT 2015-16.*

Question #16 is an excellent illustration of an arithmetic operations problem. Students must first subtract 88 from 220 to find the total change in speed, then divide by 3 to determine the acceleration.

This question is typical of others in this standard family: the computation is trivial, especially if students are using a calculator. The major challenge posed by this question is converting words into math that can actually be computed.

Students will ace these questions only when they have a strong fundamental understanding not only of how to do arithmetic, , but also of what the purpose of each arithmetical tool, and how to use each one.

One Step at a Time

Since most arithmetic questions are multiple-step word problems, students can lose easy points by mixing up the steps in their problem solving. It's of the utmost importance that they take one step at a time.

Refer to Math question #21 on page 26 of *Preparing for the ACT 2015-16.*

To solve question #21, students must perform two conversions and two operations. First, they must find the number of students who pass the written test. Then, they must find what number of those students also pass the driving test.

This is a relatively straightforward question, but if students don't read carefully and answer one question at a time, they won't pick up the raw point.

Refer to Math question #35 on page 28 of *Preparing for the ACT 2015-16.*

Check Your Understanding: What questions would you use to walk your students through question #35 one step at a time?

_____

_____

_____

_____

CATEGORY: ALGEBRA & FUNCTIONS

Family: Arithmetic

Weight: 8-15%

Standards:
AF 201. Solve problems in one or two steps using whole numbers and using decimals in the context of money
AF 301. Solve routine one-step arithmetic problems using positive rational numbers, such as single-step percent
AF 302. Solve some routine two-step arithmetic problems
AF 401. Solve routine two-step or three-step arithmetic problems involving concepts such as rate and proportion, tax added, percentage off, and estimating by using a given average value in place of actual values
AF 501. Solve multistep arithmetic problems that involve planning or converting common derived units of measure (e.g., feet per second to miles per hour)
AF 601. Solve word problems containing several rates, proportions, or percentages
AF 701. Solve complex arithmetic problems involving percent of increase or decrease or requiring integration of several concepts (e.g., using several ratios, comparing percentages, or comparing averages)

Content Area #4: Slope, Midpoint, and Distance

Determining slope, midpoints, and distance on the coordinate plane are definitely make-or-break skills on the ACT Math test. The bulk of the easier points that students can pick up out of the test's nine coordinate geometry questions are related to this content area.

The most important skill in this content area is the ability to use and interpret the slope-intercept form, followed closely by the ability to use the midpoint formula. The slope formula is also a key concept in this standard family.

The most difficult questions in this family require students to use the midpoint formula to find the coordinates of an *endpoint*, rather than the midpoint.

Refer to Math question #39 on page 29 of *Preparing for the ACT 2015-16.*

Question #39 represents one of the more straightforward varieties of questions assessing this content area. Students must divide the change in *y* by the change in *x* and be careful not to drop the negative sign.

CATEGORY: GEOMETRY

Family: Slope, Midpoint & Distance

Weight: 4-8%

Standards:
G 510. Determine the slope of a line from points or a graph
G 511. Find the midpoint of a line segment
G 605. Use the distance formula

Content Area #5: Angles & Shapes

This is one content area where memorization is non-negotiable. Students must be able to apply the rules concerning parallel lines, intersecting lines, transverse angles, and the interior and exterior angles of shapes in order to maximize points from this heavily weighted standard family.

Practice and drilling make all the difference. Once students are conversant and practiced with the rules, these angle problems become relatively straightforward.

There are four major variants of *Angles & Shapes* problems:

- Parallel lines

- Interior angles of triangles

- Exterior angles of shapes

- Angle relationships and proofs

Refer to Math question #13 on page 25 of *Preparing for the ACT 2015-16.*

To solve question #13, students must be familiar with solving for angles in order to identify that *BCA* is equivalent to *DCE*. Some students, even advanced ones, can get hung up trying to prove that the two triangles are similar (they are, but this fact does not bring them any closer to the solution).

When looking for an angle measure, students should be particularly attuned to finding intersecting or parallel lines, even if the nature of the lines must be deduced because it hasn't been explicitly stated.

It should be noted that the ACT Math test will sometimes avoid declaring the relationship between two lines and leave it to the student to make the deduction.

Extend the Lines

Refer to Math question #20 on page 26 of *Preparing for the ACT 2015-16.*

Question #20 is quite similar to question #13, but the trapezoid shape can obfuscate the relationship between the two angles being considered. and are supplementary, so the measure of must be $(180 - x)°$.

On angle problems such as these, we recommend that you coach your students to *extend the lines*. If you demonstrate how each line segment in the trapezoid can be extended in both directions, you will find that some of your students who were stumped are now able to answer the question. Extending the lines brings an unfamiliar shape into more familiar territory.

CATEGORY: GEOMETRY

Family: Angles & Shapes

Weight: 4-8%

Standards:
G 301. Exhibit some knowledge of the angles associated with parallel lines
G 401. Use properties of parallel lines to find the measure of an angle
G 402. Exhibit knowledge of basic angle properties and special sums of angle measures (e.g., 90°, 180°, and 360°)
G 501. Use several angle properties to find an unknown angle measure
G 705. Solve multistep geometry problems that involve integrating concepts, planning, and/or visualization

Content Area #6: Triangles

There is a wide range of question variants the ACT Math assesses under the *Triangles* standard family. Students need to know cold the Pythagorean theorem and special triangle rules (30°-60°-90° and 45°-45°-90°). They will also move more quickly if they know their Pythagorean triples, which the test favors heavily for its side lengths.

The *Triangles* standard family includes the following topics:

- Similar triangles

- Pythagorean theorem

- Special triangles

- Isosceles symmetry

The more difficult problems combine elements from two or more topics.

Refer to Math question #27 on page 27 of *Preparing for the ACT 2015-16*.

Students *could* solve #27 using either algebra in conjunction with the Pythagorean theorem (setting up the equation $2x^2 = 128$ to solve for the sides of the triangle) or trigonometry, but they'll move much more quickly if they have their special triangle rules down pat. Knowing these rules transforms this question into a simple perimeter problem.

CATEGORY: GEOMETRY

Family: Triangles

Weight: 4-8%

Standards:
G 404. Find the length of the hypotenuse of a right triangle when only very simple computation is involved (e.g., 3-4-5 and 6-8-10 triangles)
G 503. Use symmetry of isosceles triangles to find unknown side lengths or angle measures
G 508. Given the length of two sides of a right triangle, find the third when the lengths are Pythagorean triples
G 603. Apply properties of 30°-60°-90°, 45°-45°-90°, similar, and congruent triangles
G 602. Use the Pythagorean theorem

Content Area #7: Inequalities & Absolute Value

In order to maximize points in this standard family, students must be able to simplify inequalities, match inequalities to number lines, and solve absolute value problems.

Some of the most difficult questions on the ACT Math test incorporate absolute value either into algebra or coordinate geometry.

This content area includes the following topics:

- Absolute value equations and inequalities

- Solving linear inequalities

- Inequalities on the number line

Picking Points

Refer to Math question #36 on page 28 of *Preparing for the ACT 2015-16.*

Technically, question #36 is classified in our *Function Graphs—Coordinate Plane* standard family, but since this question involves an inequality and a figure, this strategy works for it as well.

Picking points is a variation of *plug and chug* for inequalities. Select a point from the represented as shaded region (either on the number line or the coordinate plane) in an answer choice, then check whether that point works with the inequality provided in the question.

Try to select points that can eliminate multiple answer choices.

This strategy allows students to avoid manipulating the inequality. For example, question #36 can be solved in this way:

Select a point that would eliminate multiple graphs. The origin, (0,0), is inside of the shaded region on two graphs, so that is a good place to start. Plug in the values:

$$1 < 0 + 0 < 2$$

Since 0 is not between 1 and 2, choices F and K can be eliminated. Choices H and J both have the point (1.5,0) inside the shaded region, so it's a good choice for further elimination.

$$1 < 1.5 + 0 < 2$$

This inequality is true, so choice G can be eliminated. The next point should make it possible to eliminate either choice H or J. The point (0,−1.5) is inside the shaded region of only choice H.

$$1 < 0 + (−1.5) < 2$$

This is false, so the correct graph must be choice J.

CATEGORY: ALGEBRA & FUNCTIONS

Family: Inequalities & Absolute Value

Weight: 4-8%

Standards:
A 405. Match simple inequalities with their graphs on the number line (e.g., $x \geq -35$)
A 503. Solve first-degree inequalities when the method does not involve reversing the inequality sign
A 504. Match compound inequalities with their graphs on the number line (e.g., $-10.5 < x \leq 20.3$)
A 602. Solve linear inequalities when the method involves reversing the inequality sign
A 603. Match linear inequalities with their graphs on the number line
A 606. Solve absolute value equations
A 701. Solve simple absolute value inequalities
A 702. Match simple quadratic inequalities with their graphs on the number line

Example: Math Question #52 on page 30 of *Preparing for the ACT 2015-16.*

Content Area #8: Exponents & Roots

The topic of exponents and roots tends to be a sore subject for students. The rules regarding these two math elements seem to be some of the first that flee their brains once the semester is over and done with. Students tread lightly on these questions and guess much more frequently than they ought to because, without a refresher on the rules, the questions and answer choices may as well be filled with hieroglyphics to them.

It's definitely worth providing your students with a crash course on exponents and roots, particularly about what happens when they're used in operations, when they appear in fractions, etc.

These are the three major categories in this standard family:

- Multiplying and dividing exponents

- Exponents of exponents

- Roots and irrational numbers

Refer to Math question #48 on page 30 of *Preparing for the ACT 2015-16.*

To answer question #48, students need to be comfortable with manipulating fractions that have radicals in their denominators.

Many correct answers in ACT Math leave radicals in the denominators. If you have been coaching your students to simplify so that radicals are only in the numerator, we strongly recommend you let them know about this fact. Some students will select an answer choice solely because it does not have a radical in the denominator, which is a big mistake on the ACT Math test.

CATEGORY: ALGEBRA & FUNCTIONS

Family: Exponents & Roots

Weight: 4-8%

Standards:
A 509. Work with squares and square roots of numbers
A 510. Work with cubes and cube roots of numbers
A 511. Work with scientific notation
A 512. Work problems involving positive integer exponents

Content Area #9: Functions—Understanding & Evaluating

In this standard family students find the values of functions, which are sometimes embedded inside one another or involve two variables.

Part of what makes this standard family so interesting is that it includes some of the ACT's simplest items (requiring students to simply substitute a value for *x* in order to compute a function) all the way to some of its most difficult.

Below is a list of the major question topics in this standard family:

- Function variable substitution

- Embedded and composite functions

- Coordinate functions

- Functions on the coordinate plane

Refer to Math question #42 on page 29 of *Preparing for the ACT 2015-16*.

Question #42 is typical of the more sophisticated function questions that appear on the ACT. The key to answering questions with multiple functions is to *take one step at a time*, the same strategy we recommend for arithmetic questions (see page 209). First, students must compute the value of the inner function, then the value of the outer function. Some of your students may be tempted to find the pure composite function $f(g(x))$, but there is no reason to go to such lengths on this question (or just about *any* of the function problems the Math test will throw at them).

CATEGORY: ALGEBRA & FUNCTIONS

Family: Functions—Understanding & Evaluating

Weight: 2-4%

Standards:
F 401. Evaluate linear and quadratic functions, expressed in function notation, at integer values
F 501. Evaluate polynomial functions, expressed in function notation, at integer values
F 507. Interpret statements that use function notation in terms of their context
F 511. Use function notation for simple functions of two variables
F 604. Evaluate composite functions at integer values
F 708. Write an expression for the composite of two simple functions

Content Area #10: Trig Geometry

Trig Geometry barely makes the top 10 list of content areas, but the way that the ACT assesses this skill is so predictable that it is definitely worth coaching with your students.

Nearly always, two out of the four trigonometry questions on ACT Math will test your students' ability to apply the basic definitions of core trig functions: SOHCAHTOA. Even if your students haven't taken a trigonometry course yet, it's immensely valuable to briefly teach the basics and encourage them to write SOHCAHTOA at the top of their Math tests when time begins.

Refer to Math question #30 on page 27 of *Preparing for the ACT 2015-16*.

Question #30 is an excellent example of this concept. So long as students can recall and apply the SOHCAHTOA rule, the question is an easy point.

CATEGORY: GEOMETRY

Family: Trig Geometry

Weight: 2-4%

Standards:
G 509. Express the sine, cosine, and tangent of an angle in a right triangle as a ratio of given side lengths
G 604. Apply basic trigonometric ratios to solve right-triangle problems

The Three Toughest Math Questions and Why

Please refer to Preparing for the ACT 2013-14. *For the bulk of this book, we have been referring to a later edition of* Preparing for the ACT, *but in this chapter we are referring to the earlier* 2013-14 *edition so that we can provide information about student response data that we have gathered. Please note that if you refer to the* Preparing for the ACT 2015-16 *booklet, this chapter won't make sense.*

At this point, we have discussed the 10 most important question categories on the ACT Math test. In this section, we have selected three questions that stumped most students relatively early in an ACT Math test. This information can provide you with additional insight into what causes students difficulties.

Functions–Understanding & Evaluating

Please refer to Math question #14 on page 25 of **Preparing for the ACT 2013-14.**

Question #14 is the first question in this Math test where the percentage of students answering correctly dipped below 40%. Many of the questions that come after it have a higher correct answer rate, so this stands out as an anomaly, especially when you consider that Math questions tend to gradually get more difficult as the test progresses.

Solving the problem is a relatively straightforward matter of substituting −3 for *x* and then computing. However, this question provides several opportunities for accuracy errors.

A small number of students miss this question because, at a basic level, they don't know how a function works. Most, however, fall prey to simple errors.

25% of students chose G, which means they either dropped the negative that appears to the left of the 8 or they kept the negative after squaring −3.

19% of students chose H, which means they applied the exponent to −8*x* and got −64*x*, then substituted in the −3. Or they decided to randomly guess the middle number.

17% of students chose either J or K, which means that they multiplied before they resolved the exponent.

Over 50% of the responses can be tied to accuracy errors. This highlights how a basic problem can become a major stumbling block for students: by providing multiple opportunities for calculation mistakes.

Expressions

Refer to Math question #21 on page 26 of *Preparing for the ACT 2013-14.*

Once more we see error with negatives rearing its ugly head.

In question #21, students are required to subtract the second group of terms from the first, including subtracting the −5*c*.

Fewer than half of students selected a response that indicated that they successfully subtracted −5*c* from 3*c* in order to get 8*c*. Choice B is virtually tied in terms of student response with the correct answer, E.

It seems that a significant portion of students correctly subtracted 4*a*, but then they used the other terms in the second group as-is (adding 6*b* and subtracting 5*c*).

Thus far, we have seen a matter as apparently simple as managing negative numbers reduce most student scores by an entire scale point.

Triangles

Refer to Math question #31 on page 27 of *Preparing for the ACT 2015-16.*

Question #31 provides contrast in terms of the cause of error. This is a case of not *solving it all the way* (see page 192). The most common response is choice B, garnering more than 33% of student answers. Only 18% of students selected the correct answer, choice E, which is a worse statistic than if students had blindly guessed.

Students arrive at choice B by squaring x, per the Pythagorean theorem, but failing to square 4. A smaller sample of students might also arrive at choice B because they fail to square the lengths of either leg and so are looking for , and choice B is the closest in appearance.

Students also tend to be confused by this question because they are unsure about what it means by *in terms of*. Unfamiliar vocabulary can radically increase the difficulty of problems.

Essential Formulas

These are the most essential formulas that will help your students succeed on the ACT Math test. The formulas listed in the "Need to Know" category are not provided by the ACT. The formulas that the ACT *does* provide are listed in the "Don't Need to Know" category. Students will still use these formulas on the test, but they do not need to have them memorized.

Need to Know

Area of a Square: $A = s^2$

Area of a Rectangle: $A = lw$

Area of a Triangle: $A = \frac{1}{2} bh$

Area of a Circle: $A = \pi r^2$

Area of a Parallelogram: $A = bh$

Area of a Trapezoid: $A = \frac{b_1 + b_2}{2} h$

Circumference of a Circle: $C = 2\pi r$

Volume of a Cube: $V = s^3$

Volume of a Rectangular Prism: $V = lwh$

Volume of a Cylinder: $V = \pi r^2 h$

Pythagorean Theorem: $c^2 = a^2 + b^2$

Equation of a Line: $y = mx + b$

Equation of a Circle: $(x - h)^2 + (y - k)^2 = r^2$

Sine: $\sin\theta = \frac{\text{opposite}}{\text{hypotenuse}}$

Cosine: $\cos\theta = \frac{\text{adjacent}}{\text{hypotenuse}}$

Tangent: $\tan\theta = \frac{\text{opposite}}{\text{adjacent}}$

Cosecant: $\csc\theta = \frac{\text{hypotenuse}}{\text{opposite}}$

Secant: $\sec\theta = \frac{\text{hypotenuse}}{\text{adjacent}}$

Cotangent: $\cot\theta = \frac{\text{adjacent}}{\text{opposite}}$

Don't Need to Know

Volume of a Sphere

Volume of a Cone

Volume of a Pyramid

Surface Area of a Sphere

Law of Cosines

Law of Sines

Math Standard Families

ACT provides College Readiness Standards that are essential to understanding the structure of the test. At MasteryPrep, we have taken it one step further by grouping these standards into logical, teachable categories and providing data on how frequently each standard family is assessed on the ACT. Below is a preview of one of the standard families. Feel free to download this resource, print it, and use it as you see fit.

STATISTICS & PROBABILITY (8%)

AVERAGES, MEDIAN & MODE (2-4%)
S 201. Calculate the average of a list of positive whole numbers
S 301. Calculate the average of a list of numbers
S 302. Calculate the average given the number of data values and the sum of the data values
S 401. Calculate the missing data value given the average and all data values but one
S 501. Calculate the average given the frequency counts of all the data values
S 601. Calculate or use a weighted average
S 701. Distinguish between mean, median, and mode for a list of numb

COUNTING (1-2%)
S 405. Exhibit knowledge of simple counting techniques
S 603. Apply counting techniques

STUDIES & MODELS (<1%)
S 505. Recognize that when data summaries are reported in the real world, results are often rounded and must be interpreted as having appropriate precision
S 506. Recognize that when a statistical model is used, model values typically differ from actual values
S 703. Understand the role of randomization in surveys, experiments, and observational studies
S 705. Recognize that part of the power of statistical modeling comes from looking at regularity in the differences between actual values and model values

DATA INTERPRETATION (1-2%)
S 202. Extract one relevant number from a basic table or chart, and use it in a single computation
S 303. Read basic tables and charts
S 304. Extract relevant data from a basic table or chart and use the data in a computation
S 402. Translate from one representation of data to another (e.g., a bar graph to a circle graph)
S 502. Manipulate data from tables and charts
S 504. Use Venn diagrams in counting
S 602. Interpret and use information from tables and charts, including two-way frequency tables
S 702. Analyze and draw conclusions based on information from tables and charts, including two-way frequency tables

PROBABILITY (1-2%)
S 305. Use the relationship between the probability of an event and the probability of its complement
S 403. Determine the probability of a simple event
S 404. Describe events as combinations of other events (e.g., using and, or, and not)
S 503. Compute straightforward probabilities for common situations
S 604. Compute a probability when the event and/or sample space are not given or obvious
S 605. Recognize the concepts of conditional and joint probability expressed in real-world contexts
S 606. Recognize the concept of independence expressed in real-world contexts
S 704. Exhibit knowledge of conditional and joint probability

Visit masteryprep.com/decode/resources to download a printable PDF of
MasteryPrep's ACT Math Standard Families.

Recommended Reading

There is a book series that can be extremely helpful to your students on their journey to higher ACT Math scores.

Since content is key to improving on the ACT Math, any of a thousand well-written math books could conceivably boost scores, but we recommend one series that provides a benefit all out of proportion to the time spent working on the materials. This is especially true for advanced students.

That series is *The Art of Problem Solving*. We recommend starting with *Competition Math for Middle School* by J. Batterson.

Common Core Alignment

Visit masteryprep.com/decode/resources to find the Common Core alignment to ACT standards.

DECODING MATH TEST 72-C
Answer Explanations and Standard Families

1. Statistics & Probability >> Probability

The correct answer is D. We find probability by dividing the number of desired outcomes by the number of possible outcomes. According to the chart, 67 people have Type A blood and 6 people have Type AB blood. 67 + 6 = 73 people have either Type A or Type AB blood. The text states that the total number of people is 150, so that is our number of possible outcomes. We divide the desired outcomes by the possible outcomes to find the probability: $\frac{73}{150}$.

2. Statistics & Probability >> Averages, Mean & Mode

The correct answer is H. To find the mean, we add up the terms and then divide by the number of terms.

$$\frac{\$370+\$310+\$380+\$340+\$310}{5} = \frac{\$1,710}{5} = \$342$$

3. Algebra & Functions >> Arithmetic: Proportions

The correct answer is E. Since $\frac{1}{2}$ inch represents 18 miles, and we need to find what $2\frac{1}{2}$ inches represent, we set up a proportion.

$$2\frac{1}{2} = \frac{5}{2}$$

$$\frac{\frac{1}{2}}{18} = \frac{\frac{5}{2}}{x}$$

The denominators in the numerators get brought down to the bottom denominators.

$2x = 180$

$x = 90$

A simpler way to solve this is to ask, "How many 0.5 inches fit into 2.5 inches?" Division tells us that the answer is 5. Since each half inch represents 18 miles, we multiply.
$5 \cdot 18 = 90$

4. Algebra & Functions >> Solving Equations

The correct answer is F. Substitute the known values of f and d, then solve for c.

$f = cd^3$

$450 = c(10)^3$

$450 = 1,000c$

$c = \dfrac{450}{1,000} = 0.45$

5. Algebra & Functions >> Functions: Understanding & Evaluating

The correct answer is E. Substitute 1 for x.

$f(1) = (3(1) + 7)^2$

$f(1) = (3 + 7)^2$

$f(1) = (10)^2$

$f(1) = 100$

6. Algebra & Functions >> Arithmetic: Percent

The correct answer is H. Find the amount of Jorge's pay increase by multiplying the percentage times his pay rate, then add that increase amount to his hourly wage.

$6\% = 0.06$

$0.06 \cdot \$12.00 = \$0.72$

$\$12.00 + \$0.72 = \$12.72$

7. Algebra & Functions >> Patterns & Sequences

The correct answer is E. In a geometric sequence, each term is multiplied by a coefficient to arrive at the next term. In the sequence 1, –3, 9, –27, … the coefficient is –3. If we continue the pattern, multiplying by –3 each time, we get 1, –3, 9, –27, 81, –243, 729. The seventh term is 729.

8. Statistics & Probability >> Data Interpretation

The correct answer is H. The box weighs 15 pounds. According to the table, the fee for a box weighing between 10 and 25 pounds is $10.00 plus $0.65 per pound.

$\$10.00 + (15 \cdot \$0.65)$

$\$10.00 + \$9.75 = \$19.75$

9. Geometry >> Area, Perimeter, Volume & Circumference

The correct answer is A. The question is only asking us about inner layers, so we first remove the top and bottom layers from the total thickness of the computer chip.

$0.32 - 0.03 - 0.03 = 0.26$

Each inner layer is 0.02 cm thick, so divide by this thickness to find the number of layers that will fit.

$$\frac{0.26}{0.02} = 13$$

10. Statistics & Probability >> Averages, Mean & Mode

The correct answer is K. To find the median, arrange the terms from least to greatest, then select the middle term.

13, 15, 16, 19, 19, 22, 25, 25, 26, 27, 28, 29

The middle terms are 22 and 25. When 2 terms make up a median, we average the two. Thus the median is

$$\frac{22+25}{2} + \frac{47}{2} = 23.5$$

A faster way to solve this question is to scratch through the largest and smallest number on the table, then do so again, repeating until there are just two numbers left. These two numbers are used to calculate the median.

11. Algebra & Functions >> Creating Expressions, Functions & Equations

The correct answer is C. The distance increases by 6 at each time interval, so the slope (coefficient of t) must be 6. At $t = 0$, the distance is 14, so the y-intercept is 14. Therefore, the equation is $d = 6t + 14$.

Another way to solve this is to plug in values for t and d from the table and see which equations work. For $t = 0$ and $d = 14$, only choices A and C work. Of those two choices, only choice C works for $t = 1$ and $d = 20$.

12. Geometry >> Area, Perimeter, Volume & Circumference

The correct answer is K. To find perimeter, we need the length and width of the rectangle. Use the area formula to solve for the width of the rectangle.

$54 = 9w$

$w = 6$

A rectangle has two sets of equal sides. Add the sides together to find the perimeter.

$9 + 9 + 6 + 6 = 30$

13. Geometry >> Angles & Shapes

The correct answer is B. *ABC* forms a triangle. Since the sum of the interior angles of a triangle is always 180°, if we can find the measure of ∠BCA, then we can determine the measure of ∠BAC. Because $\overline{AD}$ intersects $\overline{BE}$, ∠BCA ≅ ∠ECD . Therefore, ∠BCA = 45°. Subtract the two known interior angles in △ABC from 180° to find the measure of ∠BCA.

180° − 35° − 45° = 100°

14. Geometry >> Circles – Plane Geometry

The correct answer is H. The central angle measure of each sector of the circle graph should be proportional to the number of hours associated with each sector. There are a total of 9 hours and 360° in the figure. We are seeking the central angle measure associated with 4 hours. Set up a proportion and solve.

9x = 1,440°

x = 160°

15. Algebra & Functions >> Solving Equations

The correct answer is B. Set up a system of equations and solve for the number of large figurines. Let *y* represent the number of small figurines and *x* represent the number of large figurines. We know that the total number of figurines is 70, and we know that *x* multiplied by $12 is equal to *y* multiplied by $8.

x + y = 70

12x = 8y

Put the first equation in terms of *y*.

y = 70 − x

Substitute this expression for *y* into the second equation to solve for *x*.

12x = 8(70 − x)

12x = 560 − 8x

20x = 560

x = 28

16. Algebra & Functions >> Arithmetic: Operations

The correct answer is H. Acceleration is defined as the change in velocity. We find this value by dividing the change in speed by the amount of time over which the speed changed. In this case, we subtract to find the change in speed. 220 − 88 = 132. We then divide by the number of seconds in which this change took place.

$$\frac{132}{3} = 44$$

17. Geometry >> Angles & Shapes

The correct answer is D. Draw out the lines described. $\angle BAC$ and $\angle BAD$ are supplementary to one another (their measures add up to 180°). If the measure of $\angle BAC$ is 47°, then the measure of $\angle BAD$ is $180° - 47° = 133°$.

18. Number & Quantity >> Fractions

The correct answer is F. Find the decimal values for the fractions on your calculator.

$$\frac{1}{2} = 0.5$$

$$\frac{5}{6} \approx 0.833$$

$$\frac{5}{8} = 0.625$$

Now it is simple to arrange them in *ascending* (increasing) order.

$$\frac{1}{2} < \frac{5}{8} < \frac{5}{6}$$

19. Number & Quantity >> Exponents & Place Value

The correct answer is D. Add the two numbers, then count how many places the decimal must be moved to the left to put the number in scientific notation.

That count gives the exponent for the 10.

$670,000,000 + 700,000,000 = 1,370,000,000.$

The decimal must be moved 9 places over, so $1,370,000,000 = 1.37 \cdot 10^9$.

20. Geometry >> Angles & Shapes

The correct answer is F. Since $\overline{AB}$ is parallel to $\overline{CD}$, then $\angle A$ and $\angle D$ are supplementary to one another. Their measures must total 180°. Since the measure of $\angle D = x°$, the measure of $\angle A$ must be $(180 - x)°$.

21. Algebra & Functions >> Arithmetic: Percent

The correct answer is B. If we start with 1,000, and 80% pass the written test, then $1,000 \cdot 0.8 = 800$ students pass the written test. If, of those 800 students, 60% pass the driving test, then $800 \cdot 0.6 = 480$ students pass the driving test and get a license. In order to solve this problem, you must convert the percentages into decimals by dividing by 100.

22. Algebra & Functions >> Exponents & Roots

The correct answer is H. Assume that $b = 3$. Then $xy = a^3c^3 = aaaccc = acacac = (ac)^3$. For all positive integers b, $xy = (ac)^b$.

23. Algebra & Functions >> Expressions

The correct answer is A. Distribute $\frac{1}{2} y^2$ to the terms in parentheses.

$$\frac{1}{2} y^2(6x + 2y + 12x - 2y) = 3xy^2 + y^3 + 6xy^2 - y^3$$

Combine like terms.

$9xy^2$

24. Algebra & Functions >> Solve Equations

The correct answer is H. Set up an equation with the given expression equal to $60,000 and solve for *p*.

$500p - p^2 = 60,000$

$p^2 - 500p + 60,000 = 0$

$(p - 200)(p - 300) = 0$

$p = 200 \text{ or } 300$

Since we are looking for the *fewest* number of paintings, 200 is the best choice.

25. Algebra & Functions >> Arithmetic: Percent

The correct answer is B. At $254, clothes are Lucie's greatest expenditure. Divide by the total amount of expenditures, $900.

$$\frac{\$254}{\$900} = 0.282$$

Multiply by 100 to express as a percent, then round to find the answer.

$0.282 = 28.2\% \approx 28\%$

26. Geometry >> Angles & Shapes

The correct answer is G. $\angle BAC$ plus $\angle CAD$ must equal 90°, since these two angles make up $\angle BAD$. We subtract the measure of $\angle BAC$ from 90° to find the measure of $\angle CAD$.

$90° - (x + 20)° = 90° - x° - 20° = 70° - x° = (70 - x)°$

27. Geometry >> Triangles

The correct answer is E. The sides of an *isosceles right triangle* adhere to the following proportionality:

$x, x, x\sqrt{2}$. Since the hypotenuse has a length of $8\sqrt{2}$, the lengths of the other two sides must each be 8. Add the sides to find the perimeter.

$8 + 8 + 8\sqrt{2} = 16 + 8\sqrt{2}$

28. Algebra & Functions >> Function Graphs – Coordinate Plane

The correct answer is H. There are two points on the graph where $y = 0$. These are the points where the line touches the x-axis. One of these points corresponds to a negative x value, the other to a positive x value. Therefore, *1 positive real solution and 1 negative real solution* is the best description for the solutions for x.

29. Number & Quantity >> Complex Numbers

The correct answer is C. Use the FOIL method and combine like terms.

$(-3i + 4)(3i + 4) = -9i^2 - 12i + 12i + 16 = -9(-1) + 16 = 25$

30. Geometry >> Trig Geometry

The correct answer is G. is defined as the length of the opposite side divided by the length of the adjacent side, $\dfrac{\text{opposite}}{\text{adjacent}}$. The opposite length is 7, and the adjacent length is 5, so $\tan \theta = \dfrac{7}{5}$ gives the equation that, if solved, provides the value of θ.

31. Statistics & Probability >> Probability

The correct answer is D. To find the probability, determine the number of desired outcomes and divide by the number of possible outcomes. There are 5 desired outcomes (extra pieces) and $750 + 5 = 755$ possible outcomes, so the probability of selecting one of the extra pieces is $\dfrac{5}{755}$.

32. Number & Quantity >> Fractions

The correct answer is K. Convert the two fractions to share a common denominator.

$\dfrac{2}{3} = \dfrac{8}{12}$ and $\dfrac{3}{4} = \dfrac{9}{12}$. The numerator between 8 and 9 is 8.5, which is not an available answer choice, so convert the fractions to sharing denominators of 24. $\dfrac{8}{12} = \dfrac{16}{24}$ and $\dfrac{9}{12} = \dfrac{18}{24}$. Now it is clear that the number between the numerators is 17, so the fraction that lies exactly halfway between $\dfrac{2}{3}$ and $\dfrac{3}{4}$ is $\dfrac{17}{24}$.

33. Algebra & Functions >> Arithmetic: Proportions

The correct answer is B. The first paragraph of the text states that *0.25 inch represents 2 feet*. Set up and solve a proportion to determine the length of the wall in the scale drawing.

$\dfrac{0.25}{2} = \dfrac{x}{15}$

$2x = 3.75$

$x = 1.875$

34. Geometry >> Area, Perimeter, Volume, & Circumference

The correct answer is H. Find the area of the room.

$15 \cdot 12 = 180$

Subtract the area covered by the cabinets. The four middle cabinets are each 2 by 2, so their total area is $4(2 \cdot 2)$.

$180 - (12 \cdot 2) - 4(2 \cdot 2) = 180 - 24 - 16 = 140$

35. Algebra & Functions >> Arithmetic: Operations

The correct answer is D. Find the charge per cabinet. First subtract the labor charge from the total charge, then divide by the total number of cabinets. There were 4 cabinets in the middle, and, since each cabinet is 2 feet wide, $12 \div 2 = 6$ cabinets along the side of the wall: 10 cabinets total.

$\$2,150 - \$650 = \$1,5000$

$\dfrac{\$1,500}{10} = \$150$

Each cabinet costs $150. So if there were twice as many cabinets, $10 \cdot 2 = 20$, then there would be the $650 labor cost plus $20 \cdot \$150 = \$3,000$ for the cabinets, for a total charge of $\$650 + \$3,000 = \$3,650$.

36. Algebra & Functions >> Function Graphs – Coordinate Plane

The correct answer is J. The inequality $1 < x + y < 2$ is actually two inequalities: $1 < x + y$ and $x + y < 2$. Convert both of these to *slope-intercept* form so that you can visualize the lines (or graph them on your calculator).

$1 < x + y$

$y > -x + 1$

and

$x + y < 2$

$y < -x + 2$

So we are looking for two lines with a slope of -1 and y-intercepts of 1 and 2. The only two graphs that have y-intercepts of 1 and 2 are choices G and J. Only choice J has lines with negative slopes.

37. Statistics & Probability >> Averages, Median & Mode

The correct answer is A. To find the mean of the data set, add the terms, then divide by the number of terms.

$\dfrac{3 + 8 + 10 + 15}{4} = \dfrac{36}{4} = 9$

To find the mean, sort the terms, then take the middle term. Since two terms, 8 and 10, make up the middle, find their average.

$\dfrac{8 + 10}{2} = \dfrac{18}{2} = 9$

Subtract the median from the mean to find the difference.

$9 - 9 = 0$

38. Algebra & Functions >> Function Graphs – Coordinate Plane

The correct answer is F. Since $g(x)$ intersects with $f(x)$ at exactly two distinct points on the graph, $f(x) = g(x)$ for exactly two values of x.

39. Geometry >> Slope, Midpoint & Distance

The correct answer is B. The slope formula is $\dfrac{y_2 - y_1}{x_2 - x_1}$. Insert the coordinates for C and D into the formula to determine the slope.

$$\frac{1-4}{12-9} = \frac{-3}{3} = -1$$

40. Geometry >> Translation, Rotation, Reflection & Relative Equations

The correct answer is F. Since point D is being reflected across the y-axis, its x-coordinate will become negative while its y-coordinate remains the same. Therefore, the coordinates of D' are $(-12, 1)$.

41. Geometry >> Area, Perimeter, Volume & Circumference

The correct answer is E. Cut the shape into three figures: the left triangle, the rectangle, and the right triangle. The left triangle has a base of $3 - 2 = 1$ and a height of $4 - 1 = 3$, so its area is $\dfrac{1}{2}(1)(3) = \dfrac{3}{2}$. The right triangle has a base of $12 - 9 = 3$ and a height of $4 - 1 = 3$ so its area is $\dfrac{1}{2}(3)(3) = \dfrac{9}{2}$. The rectangle has a length of $9 - 3 = 6$ and a width of $4 - 1 = 3$ so its area is $6 \cdot 3 = 18$. The next step is to figure out where to cut the rectangle in two so that the left side of the rectangle plus the left triangle has the same area as the right side of the rectangle plus the right triangle. Set up an equation. Let x be the length of the new rectangle on the left side.

$$\frac{3}{2} + 3x = \frac{9}{2} + 3(6 - x)$$

$$\frac{3}{2} + 3x = \frac{9}{2} + 18 - 3x$$

$$6x = 21$$

$$x = \frac{7}{2}$$

Since the length of the left rectangle is $\dfrac{7}{2}$, we add that length to the x-coordinate of the left rectangle's lower left vertex to find the x-coordinate of the dividing line.

$$3 + \frac{7}{2} = \frac{13}{2} = 6.5$$

42. Algebra & Functions >> Functions – Understanding & Evaluating

The correct answer is K. First find $g(\frac{1}{2})$.

$$g\left(\frac{1}{2}\right) = \frac{1}{\frac{1}{2}} = 2$$

Then find $f(2)$.

$$f(2) = 2 - \frac{1}{2} = \frac{3}{2}$$

43. Algebra & Functions >> Expressions

The correct answer is D. Let x be the coefficient of p that will describe the effect of doubling a.

$$xp = \frac{\frac{1}{2}(2)ary + (2)a}{12y}$$

We can take the twos in the numerator.

We use the original equation to substitute p.

$xp = 2p$

$x = 2$

p is multiplied by 2.

44. Geometry >> Slope, Midpoint & Distance

The correct answer is G. Since the length of $\overline{EF}$ is 4 times the length of $\overline{DE}$, and both line segments lie across the same line, we know that point D will have an x-coordinate and a y-coordinate that are $\frac{1}{4}$ of the way from 6 to 14 and from 4 to 12, respectively. Find the x distance between E and D, then add the starting x value of E to get the x-coordinate of D.

$$14 - 6 = 8 \cdot \frac{1}{4} = 2$$

$6 + 2 = 8$

The x-coordinate is 8. Repeat this procedure with the y-coordinate.

$$12 - 4 = 8 \cdot \frac{1}{4} = 2$$

$4 + 2 = 6$

The y-coordinate is 6. Therefore the coordinates of D are (8,6).

45. Number & Quantity >> Matrices

The correct answer is D. When a matrix is multiplied, all of the terms of the matrix are multiplied.

$$\begin{bmatrix} 2a & 6a \\ 1a & 4a \end{bmatrix} = \begin{bmatrix} x & 27 \\ y & z \end{bmatrix}$$

We can use the term 27 in the right side of the given equation to determine the value of a.

$$6a = 27$$

$$a = \frac{27}{6} = \frac{9}{2}$$

Find the values of x and z.

$$x = 2a = 2(\frac{9}{2}) = 9$$

$$z = 4a = 4(\frac{9}{2}) = 18$$

Find the sum of x and z.

$$9 + 18 = 27$$

46. Algebra & Functions >> Solving Equations

The correct answer is J. Let x be the volume of the container. Convert the word problem into an equation.

$$\frac{1}{8}x + 10 = \frac{3}{4}x$$

$$\frac{5}{8}x = 10$$

$$x = 16$$

47. Algebra & Functions >> Arithmetic: Ratios

The correct answer is B. Convert the 11th grade ratio to have a common right side with the 10th grade ratio by multiplying both sides by 5. 18:51 = 90:255. For every 255 students, therefore, 255 – 90 – 86 = 79 must be twelfth grade students. Tenth grade students have a ratio of 86:255, eleventh grade students have a ratio of 90:255, and twelfth grade students have a ratio of 79:255. Therefore, the random selection is most likely to include an eleventh grade student.

48. Algebra & Functions >> Exponents & Roots

The correct answer is G. To combine the terms, both must have a common denominator. Multiply the first fraction's numerator and denominator by $\sqrt{3}$, and multiply the second fraction's numerator and denominator by $\sqrt{2}$.

$$\frac{4}{\sqrt{2}} + \frac{2}{\sqrt{3}} = \frac{4\sqrt{3}}{\sqrt{6}} + \frac{2\sqrt{2}}{\sqrt{6}} = \frac{4\sqrt{3} + 2\sqrt{2}}{\sqrt{6}}$$

49. Algebra & Functions >> Function Graphs – Coordinate Plane

The correct answer is A. The shaded region is at all points *below* the line $y = -x + 2$, so we expect a *less than* sign associated with that equation. The shaded region is at all points *inside* the circle expressed by the other equation on the figure, so we should also expect a *less than* sign associated with that equation. (If it were a *greater than* sign, then the entire area *outside* the radius of the circle would be shaded.) Therefore, the correct system of inequalities is

$$\begin{cases} y < -x + 2 \\ (x-1)^2 + (y-2)^2 < 9 \end{cases}$$

50. Geometry >> Area, Perimeter, Volume & Circumference

The correct answer is F. Since the water level rose by 0.25 cm, a volume of water with dimensions 40 by 30 by 0.25 has been displaced. Find the volume of the water displaced.

$40 \cdot 30 \cdot 0.25 = 300$

Since the volume of the object is equal to the volume of the displacement, the volume of the object must be 300 cubic centimeters.

51. Algebra & Functions >> Arithmetic: Ratios

The correct answer is E. Manipulate the ratios so that y is equal in both ratios. $x{:}y = 5{:}2 = 15{:}6$ and $y{:}z = 3{:}2 = 6{:}4$. Now it is apparent that $x{:}y{:}z = 15{:}6{:}4$ and thus $x{:}z = 15{:}4$.

52. Algebra & Functions >> Inequalities & Absolute Value

The correct answer is H. Break the composite inequality into two separate inequalities. $-5 < 1 - 3x$ and $1 - 3x < 10$. Simplify both inequalities.

$-5 < 1 - 3x$	$1 - 3x < 10$
$-6 < -3x$	$-3x < 9$
$2 > x$	$x > -3$

Combine the two inequalities.

$-3 < x < 2$

53. Geometry >> Area, Perimeter, Volume & Circumference

The correct answer is B. Each term has two of the three variables l, w, and h. If each of these variables are doubled, then each term will be doubled twice, or four times the original value. Since each term making up A is multiplied by a factor of 4, A is also multiplied by a factor of 4.

54. Algebra & Functions >> Creating Expressions & Functions

The correct answer is K. If the dog eats 7 cans of food in 3 days, then it eats $\frac{7}{3}$ cans of food in 1 day. In 3 days, the dog eats 7 cans, and in d additional days, the dog eats $\frac{7d}{3}$ cans, so we can express the total number of cans as $7 + \frac{7d}{3}$.

55. Statistics & Probability >> Data Interpretation

The correct answer is E. A total of 65 students skied either cross-country or downhill. Since there were 28 students who skied downhill and 45 students who skied cross-country, there were $(28 + 45) - 65 = 8$ students who must have skied both cross-country and downhill.

56. Geometry >> Area, Perimeter, Volume & Circumference

The correct answer is K. Each row has equal area (and thus one third of the entire square), so the top A has an area of $\frac{1}{2} \cdot \frac{1}{3} = \frac{1}{6}$. The middle A has an area of $\frac{1}{3} \cdot \frac{1}{3} = \frac{1}{9}$. The bottom A has an area of $\frac{1}{4} \cdot \frac{1}{3} = \frac{1}{12}$. Add the fractions to find the total fractional area of the regions labeled A.

$$\frac{1}{6} + \frac{1}{9} + \frac{1}{12} = \frac{6}{36} + \frac{4}{36} + \frac{3}{36} = \frac{13}{36}$$

57. Algebra & Functions >> Trig Functions

The correct answer is A. The second line has the same maximum value as the first line, so there is no vertical shift in the second line. For that reason, b must equal 0. Choice A is the only choice that states that $b = 0$.

58. Algebra & Functions >> Inequalities & Absolute Value

The correct answer is K. There is no value for x which can cause the left side of the inequality to become negative, since the entire left side of the inequality is an absolute value. Therefore, the solution for x is an empty set (there are no solutions for x).

59. Statistics & Probability >> Probability

The correct answer is E. Since each event is independent, find the product of the probabilities of each event independently occurring.

$$\frac{1}{3} \cdot \frac{1}{3} \cdot \frac{1}{3} \cdot \frac{1}{3} = \frac{1}{81}$$

60. Algebra & Functions >> Trig Functions

The correct answer is J. We know the three sides of the triangle, but we do not know at least two of the angles, so we can only use the law of cosines. Plug in the known values into the law of cosines, using the shortest side as c and the smallest angle as θ.

$$14^2 = 18^2 + 20^2 - 2(18)(20)\cos\theta$$

ACT QUESTION INDEX

Category Breakdowns for ACT Math Test 72-C

MAIN CATEGORY	STANDARD FAMILY	QUESTION NUMBER
Statistics and Probability	Probability	1, 31, 59
	Averages, Mean, and Mode	2, 10, 37
	Data Interpretation	8, 55
Algebra and Functions	Arithmetic: Proportions	3, 33
	Solving Equations	4, 15, 24, 46
	Functions: Understanding and Evaluating	5, 42
	Arithmetic: Percent	6, 21, 25
	Patterns and Sequences	7
	Creating Expressions, Functions, and Equations	11, 54
	Arithmetic: Operations	16, 35
	Exponents and Roots	22, 48
	Expressions	23, 43
	Function Graphs: Coordinate Plane	28, 36, 38, 49
	Arithmetic: Ratios	47, 51
	Inequalites and Absolute Value	52, 58
	Trig Functions	57, 60

Geometry	Area, Perimeter, Volume, and Cicumference	9, 12, 34, 41, 50, 53, 56
	Angles and Shapes	13, 17, 20, 26
	Circles: Plane Geometry	14
	Triangles	27
	Trig Geometry	30
	Slope, Midpoint, and Distance	39, 44
	Translation, Rotation, Reflection, and Relative Equations	40
Number and Quantity	Fractions	18, 32
	Exponents and Place Value	19
	Complex Numbers	29
	Matrices	45

READING

The Reading section of this book is split into three segments that mirror the structure of the other sections of this book:

- **Reading Time Mastery**, which focuses on how to help students fully consider all four passages and answer the 40 questions that go with them in the span of 35 minutes.

- **Reading Test Mastery**, which centers on proven test-taking techniques and strategies that can help students get to the right answer, even if they don't understand some aspect of the passage, question, or answer choices. Much of this section addresses how to help students overcome a low reading level.

- **Reading Content Mastery**, which provides a guide on the skills and standards most likely to be tested on the ACT Reading test.

When you work with your students on the Reading test, consider taking a balanced approach. In each lesson, try helping your students improve in terms of Time Mastery, Test Mastery, and of course, Content Mastery.

READING TIME MASTERY

Time Management Strategies for the ACT Reading Test

It's Unfair

In some ways, the ACT Reading test is the most unfair of all the sections on the ACT.

Consider the English test. By the ninth grade, students have been introduced to most of the material they need to know in order to do well on this test.

In the Math test, students can achieve a near-perfect score solely based on what they have learned by junior year.

In the Science test, students have learned the most heavily tested fundamentals by their sophomore year if not earlier.

And yet, on the Reading test, the ACT consistently provides students with passages written at a collegiate level.

Desiring to predict how well students will be able to handle college texts, the ACT took the logical step of testing students with college-level materials. It is no coincidence that student reading levels are strongly correlated to ACT Reading test performance. The Reading test is, at its core, a literacy test.

ACT Reading passages routinely range between 11th grade and college reading levels. The questions associated with these reading passages are often even more complex. At the higher ranges of difficulty and complexity, your students will struggle to understand what is being discussed in the passage and what is being asked of them in the questions.

How do you get ACT Reading scores up? The simplest answer, and the hardest to actually accomplish, is to improve your students' reading levels. Students who read better score better on all sections of the ACT, not just Reading.

When you are coaching your students on the Reading test, it is important to keep this fact foremost in mind: students who answer questions incorrectly likely failed to understand either the question or the section of the passage that the question referred to. If your students missed a question about point of view, it may very well be the case that they need a brush-up on point of view, but it's far more likely that they simply did not understand the passage.

Pay particular attention to words, phrases, and concepts that students are likely to be unfamiliar with or misunderstand. If you teach your students strategies but ignore their misconceptions or trouble with vocabulary, you may find yourself working with some very frustrated pupils!

Many of the strategies in this book help students with reading levels lower than that of the ACT's passages understand and answer questions anyway. Students with high reading levels may find some or most of the strategies unnecessary; that's perfectly fine. Strategies are for when students don't know the answer or are unclear about how to proceed. If they know the answer, why use a strategy?

One of the most significant consequences of the high reading levels prevalent in ACT Reading passages is that most students struggle to complete the test in enough time. Some students only get through two or three passages before time runs out.

The more difficult a text, the more slowly a student naturally reads it. What's more, even if your students would read at the average adult's pace of 225 words per minute, they would barely have time to read the passages, questions, and answer choices, let alone figure out the answers!

For this reason, most students need a pacing strategy as well as specific coaching on time management techniques. By focusing on these skills, you can help your students level the playing field and have a massive impact on their scores.

3/5 Split

We call our most basic pacing strategy *the 3/5 split*.

Students who are scoring below a 24 would do well to adopt this strategy or a basic variation of it. In the 3/5 split, students spend 3 minutes reading or skimming the passage. They then spend 5 minutes answering the 10 questions that accompany the text. This gives a total of 8 minutes per passage, including questions.

8 minutes per passage adds up to 32 minutes. This pace provides students with 3 minutes at the end of the test to check their answers and work on any particular passage they feel might yield more points given a little more time.

With the *3/5 split*, the emphasis is on the questions. Students spend just enough time with the passage to become familiar with it, but they allocate most of their time to the questions. No student has ever earned a point on the ACT Reading test for reading a passage. All of the points reside with the questions, so the questions deserve emphasis.

This pace will not feel comfortable to most students. That's the point. If it felt comfortable, they would just do it, and then they would not need a strategy. (Believe it or not, this is a preview of an actual conversation you will have with some of your students when you work with them on this strategy). They need to practice the *3/5 split* until it feels like their natural pace.

Helping your students comfortably and reliably achieve the *3/5 split* is one of the most impactful things you can accomplish as a coach. Pacing improvements on the Reading test are often the largest sources of score gains. Some students have improved their Reading scores by as many as 10 points, just by getting their pacing straight.

Below is the basic pacing summary for Reading.

ACT READING
40 Questions
4 Passages
35 Minutes
Pace: 8 minutes per passage
(3 minutes to read text, 5 minutes to answer questions)
3 minutes for review at end

Advanced Pacing Guidelines

In ACT prep workshops for students, the *3/5 split* is the only pacing strategy presented to students scoring below 24. However, there are a few variations worth mentioning here. These have the disadvantage of being a little more complicated and less memorable, but if you have a good amount of time to work with your students in smaller groups or individually, and if they have enough time to practice, these guidelines might be a better fit for your students.

ACT READING SCORE	PASSAGE TEXT	10 QUESTIONS	LEFTOVER REVIEW TIME
Less than 20	3 to 3.5 minutes	5 to 5.5 minutes	1-3 minutes*
20 to 24	4 minutes	4 minutes 30 seconds	1 minute*
Greater than 24	Up to 5 minutes	At least 3 minutes 30 seconds	1 minute*

*Time allotment is flexible. Students may be able to complete one or two passages in less time than prescribed, which creates more review time at the end.

If you decide to use these advanced pacing guidelines, students scoring less than 20 should stick with the 3/5 split, although technically they can tack on an additional 30 seconds to either the passage text or the questions, depending on where they feel they need more time.

Students scoring between 20 and 24 can allow themselves a little extra time for reading the passage. Students in this range tend to benefit from the extra understanding they are able to gain from taking the passage a little more slowly.

High performing students should read thoroughly and at a comfortable pace. It's okay if they spend as many as five minutes on the passage. The rationale here is that their higher reading levels make it much more valuable to spend precious seconds on the passage text. They will be able to instantly answer many of the questions based on their recollection of the text. Not so with students at lower reading levels.

A note about the advanced pacing guidelines: your students will have little wiggle room in their allotted time. You run the risk of having your students (particularly your lower performing students) rush through the last passage with its questions . Advanced pacing guidelines should be accompanied by a healthy dose of extra practice.

Just Read

High performing students aiming to score 25 or higher should not concern themselves too much with how much time they spend reading a passage. Nor should they concern themselves with fancy reading sequences or note-taking strategies while they read. They should just read.

There are no reading tricks that will get students to the 99th percentile. To reach that bar, students must read thoroughly and attentively, challenging themselves to retain what they read on the first pass.

Tutoring companies have made vast businesses out of teaching high performing students extremely complicated reading strategies. In most cases, you can help these students improve their ACT scores by coaching them to ignore those crazy strategies and instead focus on the text itself.

If you're teaching a class full of high performing students, ask them to explain all of the ACT Reading pacing strategies they read in books or heard in classes, in tutoring, or on YouTube. Then tell them, "Don't do that."

In the end, the path to ACT Reading mastery is…reading. Who woulda thunk?

Passage Difficulty Distribution

It's worth noting that the distribution of difficulty among the Reading passages is essentially random.

This fact invalidates one of the most popular ACT Reading strategies circulating in the test prep world: telling underperforming students to blindly guess on the last one or two passages and focus their time on answering two or three passages correctly.

The reason this strategy is popular is that sometimes it works beautifully. If the last passage happens to be the most difficult of the four, with an advanced reading level and only one close reading question, then blind guessing may have been in order anyway. Having almost 12 minutes for each of the remaining passages can be a powerful boost.

But before you send your students off on their merry way to Guessland, consider the fact that this "strategy" has a 50/50 shot of forcing your students to blindly guess through one or two of the easier passages.

What's more, even the toughest passages typically have two or three "gimmes."

Your students will *feel* better emotionally if they focus on only three passages (since it lowers the difficulty of the work they are doing), but usually their scores will be the worse for it.

On about a quarter of ACT Reading tests, the last passage is the easiest. Students skip it at their peril.

Due to the random difficulty distribution, and the fact that even the most difficult of passages typically have two or three relatively simple questions, the optimum pacing strategy is to give yourself enough time to consider every single question.

Students who read (or at least skim) every passage and consider every question tend to score higher than students who ignore chunks of the test. Students who consider every question can afford to guess on some because they have a larger set of questions to answer and earn points from.

Reading Time Management Heat Map

Below is what we call a "heat map" showing the performance of over 20,000 students on an ACT Reading test. This is a powerful tool for understanding your students' level of time mastery.

Each vertical bar represents one of the 40 questions on the test. A light shade means that most of the students answered the question correctly. A darker shade means that fewer students answered right. When the color is completely black, it means that students would have done better on that item if they had just blindly guessed.

We use heat maps to understand at a glance how students in a class are handling time management.

On the ACT Math test, for example, we expect the heat map to get darker and darker as we read from left to right. There is a very clear reason for this: the questions become more and more complex.

On the Reading test, however, if students are managing their time correctly, there should be only a very minor shift in color from left to right. The stronger the shift, the more likely it is that students failed to manage their time and were rushing at the end of the test. We call this characteristic of the graph *color shift*. If you see a strong color shift with your students, you should work with them on their *pace*. By pace we mean your students developing a discipline to spend only a certain amount of time on a given section of the test (such as eight minutes per passage, including questions, in Reading).

This graphic tells us that the typical class of students has a relatively strong *color shift* in Reading. In the absence of any specific data about your students, you should assume they will run out of time before they complete the fourth passage (prompting them to blindly guess at the end), and you should work with them on correctly rationing time for each passage to avoid this outcome.

It should be noted here that students are a relatively bad judge of whether they felt rushed towards the end of the test. It's hard for anyone to give their all on a test and also analyze on the level of metacognition. For that reason, we recommend using the hard data, the color shift, rather than surveying students about whether or not they felt like they had enough time.

We also look for *contrast* when we read a time management heat map. There should be strong contrast in the colors between any two questions. The reason for this is that students who are managing their time correctly, and who are quickly moving past confusing questions to retain their time, are able to identify the easy questions sprinkled throughout the test and answer them correctly. Students who are unable to cherry-pick the easiest questions get rushed and guess on questions they should know how to solve. A class of students who are failing to cherry-pick (in other words, manage their time on individual questions) will have a heat map without much contrast. Each question will have a similar color, one to the next. Good time managers have very bright spots scattered throughout the test, even toward the end.

This graphic tells us that a typical group of students is not able to cherry-pick obviously easy questions towards the end of the test. These last few questions on this test in particular should look relatively bright when students attain a high degree of competence in time management.

MasteryPrep provides a very affordable practice testing service that can give you these pre-made heat maps specific to your students. You can also accomplish similar insights by gathering your student practice test data, looking at the percentage of students who correctly answered each question, and laying this information out in a spreadsheet. Use Excel's "Conditional Formatting / Color Scales" feature to visualize the data in a way similar to the graphic we have provided.

Passage Categories and Sequence

Categories and Sequence

ACT Reading passages fall into four major categories. These categories always appear in the same order. ACT Inc. provides guidelines about what topics could appear in each category.

Prose Fiction or Literary Narrative: Excerpts from short stories, novels, memoirs, or personal essays.

Social Science: Essay excerpts concerning anthropology, archaeology, biography, business, economics, education, geography, history, political science, psychology, or sociology.

Humanities: Essay or memoir excerpts concerning architecture, art, dance, ethics, film, language, literary criticism, music, philosophy, radio, television, or theater.

Natural Science: Essay excerpts concerning anatomy, astronomy, biology, botany, chemistry, ecology, geology, medicine, meteorology, microbiology, natural history, physiology, physics, technology, or zoology.

As previously discussed, there is no significant correlation between category and difficulty. In some cases, the Natural Science passage is the most difficult. In other cases, it is the easiest.

Familiarity

Students familiar with the topics listed above are at an advantage. A plethora of studies show that familiarity makes it easier to learn and retain new information. That being said, familiarity takes time.

Consider sharing this list of topics with the teachers at your school. If each teacher in each grade (from ninth to twelfth) were to provide an interesting introduction to one of these subjects throughout the school year, your students will be more well-rounded, find a variety of texts more accessible, and have more confidence when they take the ACT reading test—which will be reflected in their scores.

Varying Sequence

Some students find the ACT Reading test is not as intimidating if they change the order in which they attack the passages.

Since the difficulty of each passage is random, the major benefit of this strategy is that the student feels more confident going into the test with a definite game plan. For those students who are particularly adept at one or more passage category, this strategy will have a definite impact beyond the placebo effect.

The basic concept behind changing up the sequence is this:

If students prefer English as a subject and hate math and science, they should read and answer Passages I and III first, then go back to Passages II and IV.

If students are stronger in math and science than English, they should read and answer Passage IV, then Passage II, then Passage III, then finally Passage I.

If students are neutral in choosing from math, science, and English (or hate them all equally), they should answer questions in the order they appear on the test.

The rationale is that if students start with the categories with which they are most comfortable, they are more likely to retain a sense of confidence and perform better as they progress through the test. Furthermore, students are more likely to answer questions correctly in the categories with which they are familiar; by starting with these, students remove the risk of running out of time before they can answer these questions.

This strategy is viable, but it's important to consider how much time your students need in order to practice with it sufficiently. There is a certain value in the simplicity of just answering questions in sequence, so if you do not have adequate practice time, stick with going in order. If you do introduce this strategy, make sure your students are definite on their individual plans of attack and give them plenty of opportunities to practice and get comfortable with it before test day.

Refer to the Reading test on pages 32–39 of *Preparing for the ACT 2015-16*.

Check Your Understanding: Common topics that appear in each ACT reading passage category are listed above. Look through each of the four passages that appear on pages 32-39 and identify which topic applies to each.

Passage I: _____

Passage II: _____

Passage III: _____

Passage IV: _____

Brain Going Numb?

If you could hook your students up to some electrodes while they take the ACT Reading test and scan their brain activity, you would discover a curious fact: most students spend a significant amount of time mentally disengaged from the passages, the questions, or the answer choices. They're daydreaming. Their brain has gone numb.

For a vivid illustration of this theory, ask your students, "How many of you have ever made it down to the bottom of a page and all of a sudden realized that you have no idea what you had just read?" It's a rare room that doesn't have 100% of the students raising their hands.

Then ask, "How many of you had this happen on one of the ACT Reading passages?"

When students take on challenging passages that are at or above their reading levels, it is inevitable that their concentration will at least occasionally slip. It is not a question of *if* students will blank out. It's a question of *when*.

In other words, your students will daydream, even if only for a moment. They read a question five times and still it means nothing to them. They ponder thoughtfully into the distance, but the cogs of their minds turneth not. The real question is, "Will the student stop focusing on the test for a mere five seconds? Or a devastating five minutes?"

In other words, once a student's brain train has jumped tracks, how quickly does it take him or her to recognize it and take action to correct it?

If students are able to recognize (self-diagnose) when they have lost focus and then employ a coping mechanism, they will save a lot of time.

Simply by raising the question about blanking out while reading you are increasing awareness. A more effective strategy, though, is to have your students tackle Reading passages and questions and *highlight* the text at each point where they find themselves losing focus. This can greatly increase your students' abilities to recognize when they have lost concentration.

(Note: Use a highlighter whenever you instruct your students to practice something that you <u>don't</u> want them to do on the actual ACT Reading test. Since students can't use a highlighter in the real testing environment, it's less likely they will carry over this practice exercise into the actual test.)

There are many coping mechanisms that you can teach your students, but the common denominator of most of them is *taking control*. By *doing* something—anything—students jumpstart their brains. For example, students who find themselves stuck on a paragraph can simply and intentionally move to the next paragraph. Students stuck on a question can mark their best guess and move on. *Keep moving forward* is a good motto for many effective coping techniques. While this seems like a very basic point, it's worth reviewing with your students. The next time they get stuck or blank out during the ACT, they know there are definite actions they can take, which will reduce their anxiety and improve their confidence and resulting performance.

Pair Down

If students carefully consider the evidence for all four answer choices in each question, they will run out of time.

The ACT Reading test is an open-book test. Every single answer comes directly from evidence in the passage. Unfortunately, the 35-minute time limit massively inhibits students' ability to investigate. They must use their understanding of the passage to intuitively narrow down their choices.

With every question, try to pare down the answer choices to a *pair* of viable options. Then, scan the passage to find support for the best choice.

Eliminating two weak choices drastically reduces how much information needs to be considered and cuts in half the time spent digging through the passage.

Refer to Reading question #17 on page 35 of *Preparing for the ACT 2015-16.*

In question #17, if students can recall what they read about *the deepest waters of an ocean*, they might very well be able to narrow down their choices immediately to A and B. They should at least recall the phrase *about one thousand miles offshore*, and even if they don't remember the passage describing the *middle of the ocean*, it makes sense that people would assume the *middle* is also the *deepest*.

Students can now investigate these two choices and look for evidence that supports one or contradicts the other. Lines 11–13 clearly support choice B: *contrary to what one might guess, Atlantic's deepest waters, like those in other oceans, are along her edges.*

Digging through the passage to support or contradict choices C and D wastes time. Students should focus on the two strongest options.

Refer to Reading question #38 on page 39 of *Preparing for the ACT 2015-16.*

Question #38 is a good example of a question where *pairing down* can save significant time. It turns out that only one answer choice has any support from the passage at all, and nothing eats up time more than trying to find evidence that isn't there!

Students who were effective in their reading or skimming are likely able to eliminate choices G and H. *Cushioned edges* inside jaws sounds odd and would be memorable if it were mentioned in the passage, and if the jaws didn't close completely, this also would have stuck out while skimming. Choices F and J thus seem the most viable options to investigate.

Having *paired down* to two choices, students can now afford to scan for supporting evidence. Students would be wise to start with choice J since the word *decelerate* will probably be easier to scan for than the word *hinge* used in choice F.

Actually Look

When a question refers to a line number, *actually look*.

Unless your students have a photographic memory, it's impossible for them to understand the meaning of a question based on a line reference without looking.

> Refer to Reading question #3 on page 33 of *Preparing for the ACT 2015-16*.

Consider question #3:

In lines 25-31, the narrator muses over, then rejects, the notion that:

This question is meaningless without actually looking at the lines in the passage and figuring out what is being referred to.

This may seem like an overly obvious point, but the default for many students who aren't used to the format of the ACT Reading test is to think their way to the right answer. Eventually, they reach a logjam and finally realize they need to look at the line reference. This only takes a few seconds, but these are precious seconds that could be better spent answering other questions.

Model the correct behavior for your students. Read questions aloud and pause at the line references. "Okay, it just mentioned lines 25-31. Put your finger on the section of the passage being referenced." Point out to your students that they only want to read the question once. If they don't stop and find the reference, they're committing themselves to reading the question at least twice.

Not checking the line reference is a subconscious effort on the student's part to save time, but this bad habit always ends up costing time instead.

> Refer to Reading question #33 on page 39 of *Preparing for the ACT 2015-16*.

Question #33 asks for the meaning of a phrase and provides a clear line reference. If students resist the temptation to ponder the meaning of the phrase without context and instead *actually look*, they will see that the essential clue to the answer appears right next to the phrase in question.

Specifically, the verb *penetrate* gives a strong hint about the defenses the trap-jaw ant is able to overcome. Armor, like a *hard outer shell* in choice A, can be penetrated. An attack (choices B and C) or mobility (choice D) is not penetrated.

When given a line reference, students must *actually look*.

Don't Read the Passage Ten Times

Some test prep programs recommend skipping ACT Reading passages entirely. By looking at the questions first, they reason, students can establish a purpose for their reading.

Besides, if there are only eight minutes available to answer questions, why not spend all eight minutes on the questions, the things that can actually earn points? After all, no student has ever earned a point on the ACT Reading test just for reading the passage. Points come from right answers.

The problem is that although it might be perfectly legitimate for other standardized tests, this strategy doesn't carry water on the ACT.

The ACT test writers design the Reading test is designed by the ACT test writers to measure reading comprehension, and this assessment can't be considered valid if students don't actually read the passages. For this reason, the test is filled with questions that punish students for skipping the text. Students who skip reading will find that they have to refer back to the text *often* to find answers to even the simplest of questions.

If your students think they don't have time to read the passage once, then they *really* don't have time to read the passage ten times!

> Refer to Reading question #1 on page 33 of *Preparing for the ACT 2015-16.*

The very first question of the Reading test perfectly illustrates this concept. This question asks about the passage as a whole. Many students who skipped the passage will find themselves reading *the whole passage* to find the answer to this question! Where went all of that time they saved?

This eventuality is worse than it first appears. It doesn't put the student back to square zero: it puts him or her back to square negative three. When the student reads to find the answer to question #1, the purpose for reading is specialized to this particular question. Such a focused approach means that useful details relevant to other questions will be screened out , which increases the likelihood that students will need to do another read-through for question #2, another read-through for question #3, etc.

It's a much better strategy for your students to begin with an effective read-through of the passage. This allows you to coach them on maximizing their reading time and greatly reduces the likelihood that they'll need to do multiple read-throughs in order to answer questions.

> Refer to Reading question #40 on page 39 of *Preparing for the ACT 2015-16.*

The very last question of an ACT Reading test provides another suitable example of this concept. This question asks for a specific detail about a single sentence in the passage. Students who skipped the passage will have an experience akin to searching out a needle in a haystack.

To add insult to injury, the evidence that supports the correct answer appears on line 70, nearly at the end of the passage, one of the last places students will look.

Students who read the passage are at a natural advantage with these types of questions. They will remember the overall structure of the passage and have at least a vague idea of where certain details are discussed. This tiny difference could save students twenty seconds or more.

Students should read through the passage once and well to avoid reading it ten times.

Open-Book Tests

The ACT Reading test is formatted as an open-book test. This can be an advantage, but students who don't have experience with open-book tests may need extra coaching.

Students who have never had an open-book test before are likely to either over-do it or under-do it when it comes to making reference to the ACT passages. Some students may not look up supporting evidence at all and instead try to answer all questions from the memory of their initial read-through. Others might blow off reading the passage for comprehension, incorrectly thinking that with the passage right there, it won't be hard to find the answers. These students spend the entire test frantically searching the passages for the info they need. Without sufficient practice, students won't know how to use the provided passage effectively.

Consider adding the open-book test to your classroom assessment repertoire if you aren't doing so already. If you are already providing your students with open-book tests, you may want to encourage other teachers to do so as well.

Open-book tests are in many cases not appropriate for what you are trying to accomplish with a given assessment. That being said, there are a number of ways your class could be enhanced by open-book tests.

For example, some teachers introduce a new unit with a short, relevant passage and several multiple choice questions. They provide students a short time to read the passage and answer the questions.

If there is a section in your textbook that you want students to be able to analyze but not necessarily memorize, a *timed* open-book test is the best fit. The time limit causes students to familiarize themselves with the text in a prior study period. They can then use the supporting data in the passage to complete their analysis.

Likewise, if you have assigned a book or reading passage without plans for assessment, adding a timed open-book test gives your students an accountability factor and helps them prepare for the ACT.

We strongly recommend timing most open-book tests. This closely parallels the ACT Reading test's format and will benefit your students as they learn to quickly read and analyze.

Reading Mini-Test Coaching

Refer to page 35 of this book for general information about mini-tests.

While mini-tests can help students improve their pacing habits on every section of the ACT, they are most effective in boosting outcomes on the Reading and Science tests.

A Reading mini-test consists of one passage and 10 accompanying questions.

Before starting a mini-test, remind students of their pacing strategy. Depending on how you have coached them, allot either 8 or 8.5 minutes for each mini-test. Project a full-screen timer using a website such as online-stopwatch. com so that students can refer to it as they need. As students skim the passage, call out the line numbers they should have passed at each minute. For example:

"Seven minutes left. You want to be past line 35 by now."

"Six minutes left. You want to be past line 70."

"Five minutes left. Start the questions if you haven't already."

Continue to give verbal cues on progress at the three- and one-minute marks.

Once the mini-test is complete, immediately give the answers, discuss the passage, and explain any difficult questions students ask about. If students have a concern about a particular aspect of one question, consider taking the time to explain the question in full, from beginning to end, for the benefit of all students instead of just answering the specifics.

For the Reading test, the more mini-tests, the better. Most students aren't used to digesting so much difficult content so quickly. Familiarity with the format goes a long way toward boosting scores.

As you administer more and more mini-tests, reduce and then eventually eliminate the verbal cues. Students who are able to work through the mini-tests on pace without any prompts will usually be able to get through the whole Reading test with time to spare.

If most of your students have major pacing issues, consider gradually expanding the length of the mini-tests to two or even three passages (timed 16 or 24 minutes total) so that they get used to managing time over a longer period. That said, most students can gain sufficient benefit by working one passage at time.

Use mini-tests to help your students develop a strong sense of pace for the ACT Reading test.

Reading Mini-Tests

What follows are four Reading mini-tests. You are permitted to photocopy these mini-tests and provide them to your students.

Printable PDFs of these mini-tests with answer keys and explanations as well as links to four full-length ACT tests that you can use as fodder for additional mini-tests are available at this address: masteryprep.com/decode/resources.

Mini-Test 1

Passage I

LITERARY NARRATIVE: The following passage is an excerpt from *Peter and Wendy* by J.M. Barrie (©1911 by Charles Scribner's Sons).

All children, except one, grow up. They soon know that they will grow up, and the way Wendy knew was this: one day when she was two years old, she was playing in a garden, and she plucked another flower and ran with it to
5 her mother. I suppose she must have looked rather delightful, for Mrs. Darling put her hand to her heart and cried, "Oh, why can't you remain like this forever!" This was all that passed between them on the subject, but henceforth Wendy knew that she must grow up. You always know
10 after you are two. Two is the beginning of the end.

The Darlings lived at number 14, and until Wendy came, her mother had been the chief one. Mrs. Darling was a lovely lady with a romantic mind and such a sweet mocking mouth. Her romantic mind was like the tiny
15 boxes, one within the other, that come from the puzzling East; however, no matter how many you discover there is always one more, and her sweet mocking mouth had one kiss on it that Wendy could never get, though there it was, perfectly conspicuous in the right-hand corner.

20 The way Mr. Darling won her was this: the many gentlemen who had been boys when she was a girl discovered simultaneously that they loved her, and they all ran to her house to propose to her except Mr. Darling, who took a cab and nipped in first, so he got her. He got
25 all of her except the innermost box and the kiss. He never knew about the box, and in time he gave up trying for the kiss. Wendy thought Napoleon could have gotten it, but I can picture him trying and then going off in a passion, slamming the door.

30 Mr. Darling used to boast to Wendy that her mother not only loved him but respected him. He was one of those deep ones who knows about stocks and shares. Of course no one really knows, but he quite seemed to know, and he often said stocks were up and shares were down in a way
35 that would have made any woman respect him.

Mrs. Darling was married in white, and at first she kept the books perfectly, almost gleefully, as if it were a game. Not so much as a Brussels sprout was missing, but by and by whole cauliflowers dropped out, and instead
40 of them there were pictures of babies without faces. She drew them when she should have been totting up. They were Mrs. Darling's guesses.

Mrs. Darling loved to have everything just so, and Mr. Darling had a passion for being exactly like his neigh-
45 bors; so, of course, they had a nurse. As they were poor, owing to the amount of milk the children drank, this nurse was a prim Newfoundland dog called Nana, who had belonged to no one in particular until the Darlings engaged her. She had always thought children were im-
50 portant, and the Darlings had become acquainted with her in Kensington Gardens, where she spent most of her spare time peeping into baby carriages. She was much hated by careless nursemaids whom she followed to their homes and complained of to their mistresses. She proved to be
55 quite a treasure of a nurse. How thorough she was at bath-time, and she was up at any moment of the night if one of her charges made the slightest cry. Of course her kennel was in the nursery. She had a genius for knowing when a cough was a thing to have no patience with and when
60 it needed a stocking around your throat. She believed in old-fashioned remedies like rhubarb leaf to her last day, and she made sounds of contempt over all this new-fangled talk about germs and so on. It was a lesson in propriety to see her escorting the children to school, walking
65 sedately by their sides when they were well behaved and butting them back into line if they strayed.

No nursery could possibly have been conducted more correctly, and Mr. Darling knew it, yet he sometimes wondered uneasily whether the neighbors talked.

1. What does the author mean when he writes that Mrs. Darling's mind was like tiny boxes?

   A. Mrs. Darling is a complex and secretive person.
   B. Mrs. Darling is a deep and respectful person.
   C. Mrs. Darling is a simple-minded person.
   D. Mrs. Darling has a very good memory.

2. Mr. Darling can best be described as:

   F. a bold, pretentious man.
   G. a family man of great character.
   H. a strict authoritarian parent.
   J. a gentle and caring man.

GO ON TO THE NEXT PAGE

3. Why did Mrs. Darling begin shirking her book-keeping duties?

   A. She started growing vegetables instead.
   B. Someone was stealing cauliflower from their garden.
   C. She wanted children and couldn't focus.
   D. Mr. Darling decided to do the books instead.

4. Nana did all of the following EXCEPT:

   F. bring the children to school.
   G. give the children baths.
   H. sleep at the foot of the children's bed.
   J. cure the children when they were sick.

5. The narrator explains that women respected Mr. Darling because:

   A. he was rich and smart.
   B. he understood stocks and shares.
   C. he was a romantic.
   D. he demanded respect wherever he went.

6. It can be reasonably inferred from the passage that Wendy:

   F. is the center of attention in the house.
   G. is a neglected child.
   H. is adventurous and innocent.
   J. has been full of contempt since the age of two.

7. It is implied in lines 43–44 that:

   A. Mr. Darling valued his reputation a great deal.
   B. Mr. Darling felt it was important for the sake of his children's health to have a nurse.
   C. the neighbors did not have nurses for their children.
   D. Mr. Darling's neighbors envied him.

8. The narrator claims the Darlings are poor because:

   F. Mrs. Darling does not work.
   G. Mr. Darling lost his job.
   H. Mr. Darling's job is based on an unreliable market.
   J. the children drink too much milk.

9. Why is Mr. Darling worried about what the neighbors think?

   A. Because they are poor
   B. Because Mrs. Darling wears extravagant clothing
   C. Because their nurse is a dog
   D. Because their children drink too much milk

10. What does the author imply about Nana's care for the children?

   F. Nana is a more prominent character in the novel than the Darlings.
   G. Nana is going to be the main protagonist of the novel.
   H. Nana played a larger role in the children's lives than their parents did.
   J. The neighbors want to replace their nurses with a dog like Nana.

END OF MINI-TEST ONE
STOP! DO NOT GO ON TO THE NEXT PAGE
UNTIL TOLD TO DO SO.

Mini-Test 2

Passage II

SOCIAL SCIENCE: This passage is adapted from *Our Vanishing Wild Life* by William T. Hornaday (©1913 by Charles Scribner's Sons).

The preservation of animal and plant life and of the general beauty of nature is one of the foremost duties of men and women today. It is an imperative duty because it must be performed at once, for otherwise it will be too
5 late. Every possible means of preservation—sentimental, educational, and legislative—must be employed.

The present warning issues with no uncertain sound because this great battle for preservation and conservation cannot be won by gentle tones nor by appeals to the aes-
10 thetic instincts of those who have no sense of beauty or enjoyment of nature. It is necessary to sound a loud alarm, to present the facts in very strong language backed up by irrefutable statistics and by photographs that tell no lies, to establish the law, and to enforce it with a bludgeon if
15 needed.

This book is such an alarm. Its forceful pages remind me of the sounding of the great bells in the watchtowers of the cities during the Middle Ages. These bells called the citizens to arms to protect their homes, their liberties,
20 and their happiness. It is undeniable that the welfare and happiness of our own and of all future generations of Americans are at stake in this battle for the preservation of nature against the selfishness, the ignorance, and the cruelty of her destroyers.

25 We no longer destroy great works of art. They are treasured and regarded as priceless, but we have yet to attain the state of civilization in which the destruction of a glorious work of nature—whether it be a cliff, a forest, or a species of mammal or bird—is regarded with equal
30 abhorrence. The whole earth is a poorer place to live in when a colony of exquisite egrets or birds of paradise is destroyed so their plumes may decorate the hat of some lady of fashion and ultimately find their way into the rubbish heap. The people of all the New England states are
35 poorer when ignorant residents destroy the robins and other songbirds of the North for a mess of pottage.

Travels through Europe, as well as over a large part of the North American continent, have convinced me that nowhere is nature being destroyed so rapidly as in the
40 United States. Except within our conservation areas, an earthly paradise is being turned into an earthly hades; it is neither savages nor primitive men who are doing this but men and women who boast of their civilization. Air and water are polluted, rivers and streams serve as sewers
45 and dumping grounds, forests are swept away, and fish

are driven from the streams. Many birds are becoming extinct, and certain mammals are on the verge of extermination. Vulgar advertisements hide the landscape, and in all that disfigures the wonderful heritage of nature's beauty
50 today, we Americans are in the lead.

Fortunately the tide of destruction is ebbing, and the tide of conservation is coming in. Americans are practical. Like all other northern peoples, they love money and will sacrifice much for it, but they are also full of idealism and
55 moral and spiritual energy. The influence of the splendid body of Americans and Canadians, who have turned their best forces of mind and language into literature and into political power for the conservation movement, is becoming stronger every day. Yet we are far from the point where
60 the momentum of conservation is strong enough to arrest and roll back the tide of destruction, and this is especially true with regard to our quickly vanishing animal life.

11. What does the writer intend to accomplish with this passage?

   A. He wants to shock the reader with gruesome facts about the destruction of wildlife.
   B. He wants to introduce the reader to the concept of conserving wildlife.
   C. He wants to incite fear in the reader.
   D. He wants to provoke activism in the reader to conserve nature.

12. Who does the author blame most for the destruction of wildlife?

   F. People around the world
   G. Americans
   H. Southerners
   J. The reader

GO ON TO THE NEXT PAGE

13. The author specifically mentions all of the following means of preservation EXCEPT:

   A. sentimental.
   B. legislative.
   C. economical.
   D. educational.

14. The author compares nature to:

   F. fine jewelry.
   G. fine art.
   H. a feather for fashion wear.
   J. a great battle.

15. It is implied throughout the entire passage that the author believes:

   A. nature is not just a part of the world, but rather nature is the world.
   B. living in harmony with nature should be every living being's first priority.
   C. the main job of human beings should be to protect the world in which they live.
   D. human beings have no capacity for compassion when it comes to nature.

16. The author urges the reader to evoke action by:

   F. appealing directly to the opposition.
   G. traveling to conservation areas to see nature's beauty.
   H. enforcing legislation about conservation and by raising awareness.
   J. starting violent protests against people who destroy nature.

17. The author uses lines 37–40 to:

   A. develop context for the rest of the paragraph.
   B. establish credibility and reliability in his passage.
   C. boast about all the places he has traveled to.
   D. encourage the reader to see places all over the world.

18. The overall tone of the passage can best be described as:

   F. angry and anxious.
   G. defensive and disdainful.
   H. honest and educational.
   J. determined and direct.

19. The final paragraph is vital to the passage because:

   A. it describes how conservationism is on the rise but emphasizes there is much work left to be done.
   B. it explains that humans are smart and innovative.
   C. it details how far humans still have to go in conservation efforts.
   D. it shows what efforts have already been made toward conserving nature.

20. The author compares his call for action to:

   F. an alarm clock.
   G. the sounding of a medieval bell tower.
   H. a battle.
   J. an imperative duty.

END OF MINI-TEST TWO
STOP! DO NOT GO ON TO THE NEXT PAGE
UNTIL TOLD TO DO SO.

Attempts: _____   Correct: _____

Passage III

HUMANITIES: This passage is adapted from *Architecture and Democracy* by Claude Bragdon (©1918 by A.A. Knopf).

Broadly speaking, there are not five orders of architecture—nor fifty—but only two: arranged and organic. These correspond to the two terms of that "inevitable duality" which bisects life. Talent and genius, reason and
5 intuition, bromide and sulfite are some of the names we know them by.

Arranged architecture is reasoned and artificial produced by talent and governed by taste. Organic architecture, on the other hand, is the product of some obscure
10 inner necessity for self-expression, which is subconscious. It is as though nature herself, through some human organ of her activity, had addressed herself to the service of the sons and daughters of men.

Arranged architecture in its finest manifestations is
15 the product of a pride, a knowledge, a competence, a confidence staggering to behold. It seems to say of the works of nature, "I'll show you a trick worth two of that." For the subtlety of nature's geometry, and for her infinite variety and unexpectedness, arranged architecture substitutes a
20 Euclidian system of straight lines and (for the most part) circular curves, assembled and arranged according to a definite logic of its own. It is created but not creative; it is imagined but not imaginative. Organic architecture is both creative and imaginative. It is non-Euclidian in the
25 sense that it is higher-dimensional—that is, it suggests extension in directions and into regions where the spirit finds itself at home but of which the senses give no report to the brain.

To make the whole thing clearer, it may be said that
30 arranged and organic architecture bear much the same relation to one another that a piano bears to a violin. A piano is an instrument that does not give forth discords if one follows the rules. A violin requires absolutely an ear—an inner rectitude. It has a way of betraying the man of talent
35 and glorifying the genius, becoming one with his body and his soul.

Of course it stands to reason that there is not always a hard and fast differentiation between these two orders of architecture, but there is one sure way by which each may
40 be recognized and known. If the function appears to have created the form, and if everywhere the form follows the function, changing as that changes, the building is organic; if on the contrary "the house confines the spirit," if the building presents not a face but however beautiful a mask,
45 it is an example of arranged architecture.

But in so far as it is anything at all, aesthetically, our architecture is arranged, so if only by the operation of the law of opposites, or alternation, we might reasonably expect the next manifestation to be organic. There are
50 other and better reasons, however, for such expectancy.

Organic architecture is ever a flower of the religious spirit. When the soul draws near to the surface of life, as it did in the two mystic centuries of the Middle Ages, it organizes life; and architecture, along with the other arts,
55 becomes truly creative. The informing force comes not so much from man as through him. After the war that spirit of brotherhood, born in the camps and bred on the battlefields and in the trenches of Europe, is likely to take on all the attributes of a new religion of humanity, prompting
60 men to such heroisms and renunciations, exciting in them such psychic sublimations, as have characterized the great religious renewals of time past.

If this happens it is bound to write itself on space in an architecture beautiful and new; one which "takes
65 its shape and sun-color" from the opulent heart. This architecture will of necessity be organic, the product not of self-assertive personalities but the work of the "patient demon" organizing the nation into a spiritual democracy.

The author is aware that in this point of view there
70 is little of the "scientific spirit," but science fails to reckon with the soul. Science advances facing backward, so what prevision can it have of a miraculous and divinely inspired future—or for the matter of that, of any future at all? The old methods and categories will no longer answer; the or-
75 derly course of evolution has been violently interrupted by the earthquake of the war; igneous action has superseded aqueous action. The casements of the human mind look out no longer upon familiar hills and valleys, but on a stark, strange, devastated landscape, the ploughed land
80 of some future harvest of the years. It is the end of the age, the Kali Yuga—the completion of a major cycle—but all cycles follow the same sequence: after winter, spring; and after the Iron Age, the Golden.

The specific features of this organic, divinely in-
85 spired architecture of the Golden Age cannot of course be discerned by any one any more than the manner in which the Great Mystery will present itself anew to consciousness. The most imaginative artist can imagine only in terms of the already-existent; he can speak only the
90 language he has learned. And yet some germs of the future must be enfolded even in the present moment. The course of wisdom is to seek them neither in the old romance nor in the new rationalism but in the subtle and ever-changing spirit of the times.

GO ON TO THE NEXT PAGE

21. Which of the following questions is NOT answered in the passage?

   A. What are the two main orders of architecture?
   B. What are the qualities of arranged architecture?
   C. What was the name of the period before the Middle Ages?
   D. What are the qualities of organic architecture?

22. All of the following descriptions are used in the passage to characterize arranged architecture EXCEPT that it is:

   F. based on a Euclidian system of straight lines and circular curves.
   G. creative and imaginative.
   H. assembled and arranged.
   J. reasoned and artificial.

23. Paragraphs 1 through 4 (lines 1–36) establish all of the following about organic architecture EXCEPT its:

   A. origins.
   B. differences from arranged architecture.
   C. association with religion and spirituality.
   D. inevitably dual nature.

24. According to the passage, which of the following best describes the author's predictions about the architecture of the new "Golden Age"?

   F. The architecture of the future will likely be organic.
   G. The architecture of the future will likely be arranged.
   H. The architecture of the future will be for religious buildings.
   J. The architecture of the future will be the product of self-assertive personalities.

25. The author mentions the idea of how "the house confines the spirit" as part of his argument that:

   A. one can find clear signs to tell the difference between the two orders of architecture.
   B. the arranged form of architecture follows the law of opposites.
   C. the arranged form of architecture feels too closed in and claustrophobic.
   D. the arranged form of architecture is based on an outgrowth of spirit.

26. In the context of the passage, paragraph 9 (lines 69–83) is best described as presenting images of all of the following EXCEPT:

   F. disaster.
   G. devastation.
   H. war.
   J. mystery.

27. The author indicates that one reason he believed that the organic order of architecture was on the rise was that:

   A. since the current trend was arranged, it would alternate to being organic because of the law of opposites.
   B. a spiritual democracy would have a law that all architecture must be organic.
   C. organic architecture is best, so it is the wave of the future.
   D. the Iron Age was populated mainly with organic architecture.

28. Information in the passage suggests that the author believes the exact features of the future architectural style cannot be described primarily because:

   F. he is not sufficiently romantic or rational.
   G. we can only know what will come once the war is over.
   H. one can only imagine based on what already exists.
   J. even though he knows what it will look like, he cannot express it in words.

GO ON TO THE NEXT PAGE

29. Based on paragraphs 1 through 4 (lines 1–36), which of the following statements indicates the author's opinion of the relationship between organic and arranged architecture?

    A. Though they are both styles of architecture, the arranged style is more structured, while the organic style is more imaginative.

    B. Both the organic and the arranged styles of architecture will soon give way to a spiritual form of architecture.

    C. All architecture is both organic and arranged.

    D. For thousands of years, mankind has alternated between an arranged and an organic architectural style.

30. The passage indicates that the violin described in paragraph 4 (lines 29–36) represents:

    F. the human spirit.

    G. arranged architecture.

    H. organic architecture.

    J. a lack of discord.

END OF MINI-TEST THREE
STOP! DO NOT GO ON TO THE NEXT PAGE
UNTIL TOLD TO DO SO.

Passage IV

NATURAL SCIENCE: This passage is adapted from *The Life Story of Insects* by George H. Carpenter (©1913 by G.P. Putnam's Sons).

Insects as a whole are preeminently creatures of the land and the air. This is shown not only by the posses-sion of wings by a vast majority of the class but also by the mode of breathing through a system of branching air
5 tubes carrying atmospheric air with its combustion-sup-porting oxygen to all the insect's tissues. The air gains access to these tubes through a number of paired air holes or *spiracles* arranged segmentally in series.

It is of great interest to find that, nevertheless, a
10 number of insects spend much of their time under water. This is true of not a few in the perfect winged state, as for example aquatic beetles and water bugs ("boatmen" and "scorpions"), which have some way of protecting their spiracles when submerged and, possessing usually
15 the power of flight, can pass on occasion from pond or stream to upper air. But it is advisable in connection with our present subject to dwell especially on some insects that remain continually under water until they are ready to undergo their final molt and attain the winged state,
20 which they pass entirely in the air. The preparatory instars of such insects are aquatic; the adult instar is aerial. All mayflies, dragonflies, caddisflies, many beetles and two-winged flies, and a few moths thus divide their life story between the water and the air. For the present we confine
25 attention to the stoneflies, the mayflies, and the dragon-flies.

In the case of many insects that have aquatic larvae, the latter are provided with some arrangement for en-abling them to reach atmospheric air through the surface
30 film of the water. But the larva of a stonefly, a dragonfly, or a mayfly is adapted more completely than these for aquatic life; it can, by means of gills of some kind, breathe the air dissolved in water.

The aquatic young of a stonefly does not differ suf-
35 ficiently in form from its parent to warrant us in calling it a larva; the life history is like that of a cockroach, all the instars, however, except the final one—the winged adult or *imago*—live in the water. The young of one of our large species, a perla for example, has well-chitinized
40 cuticle, broad head, powerful legs, long feelers, and cerci like those of the imago; its wings arise from external rudi-ments, which are conspicuous in the later aquatic stages. But it lives completely submerged, usually clinging or walking beneath the stones that lie in the bed of a clear
45 stream, and examination of the ventral aspect of the thorax reveals six pairs of tufted gills, by means of which it is

able to breathe the air dissolved in the water wherein it lives. At the base of the tail-feelers or cerci also, there are little tufts of thread-like gills. An insect that is continually
50 submerged and has no contact with the upper air cannot breathe through a series of paired spiracles, and during the aquatic life period of the stonefly, these remain closed. Nevertheless, breathing is carried on by means of the or-dinary system of branching air-tubes, the trunks of which
55 are in connection with the tufted hollow gill-filaments, through whose delicate cuticle gaseous exchange can take place, though the method of this exchange is as yet very imperfectly understood. When the stonefly nymph is fully grown, it comes out of the water and climbs to some con-
60 venient eminence. The cuticle splits open along the back, and the imago, clothed in its new cuticle, as yet soft and flexible, creeps out. The spiracles are now open, and the stonefly breathes atmospheric air like other flying insects. But throughout its winged life, the stonefly bears memori-
65 als of its aquatic past in the little withered vestiges of gills that can still be distinguished beneath the thorax.

31. The author's purpose for writing this passage can best be explained as:

A. to create a literary manifestation of his love for insects.
B. to educate readers on the life cycle of insects.
C. to compare and contrast the stonefly with the dragonfly.
D. to convince the reader to conserve insect habitats.

32. From the passage, the reader can infer that spiracles are most similar to:

F. fins.
G. lungs.
H. gills.
J. snorkels.

GO ON TO THE NEXT PAGE

33. The overall tone of the passage is:

    A. informative and insipid.
    B. fascinated and educational.
    C. scholastic and indifferent.
    D. objective and pensive.

34. Which of the following insects is NOT described in this passage as adapting physical features necessary for breathing underwater?

    F. Dragonfly
    G. Stonefly
    H. Beetle
    J. Mosquito

35. Given that *molt* is a verb meaning "to lose feathers, hair, or skin to make way for new growth," the reader can infer that *instar* (lines 20–21) means:

    A. phase.
    B. scales.
    C. wings.
    D. life.

36. Lines 34–42 indicate that stoneflies:

    F. spend almost all of their instars underwater.
    G. prefer to lay their eggs underwater to protect them from non-aqueous prey.
    H. only spend the first half of their life phases underwater.
    J. hunt in the air but nest underwater.

37. The transformation of a stonefly from water insect to air insect is most like the transformation of:

    A. a human fetus to a grown adult.
    B. a caterpillar to a butterfly.
    C. a tadpole to a frog.
    D. a fish egg to a fish.

38. It can be reasonably inferred that "we confine attention" (lines 24–25) to three species of flies in order to:

    F. provide examples of how typical flies go through some phases of their lives underwater.
    G. prove that some flies are named incorrectly.
    H. teach students about the larvae of all insects.
    J. show that all insects fall into these three categories.

39. Based on the passage as a whole, it is implied that the author believes:

    A. insects that can live in both the air and the water have a better chance of survival.
    B. insects that mature underwater are more likely to develop wings than insects born above water.
    C. insects who have the ability to lay eggs under water have higher offspring success rates.
    D. the dual environments of these insects give them a varied life cycle.

40. In the first line of the passage, it can be inferred that the term *preeminently* is similar to all of the following definitions EXCEPT:

    F. mostly.
    G. primarily.
    H. greatly.
    J. predominantly.

END OF MINI-TEST FOUR
STOP! DO NOT GO ON TO THE NEXT PAGE
UNTIL TOLD TO DO SO.

Other Time Management Strategies

In addition to test-specific time management strategies covered in the Reading section, there are several time management strategies that can benefit students when applied to the ACT Reading test:

- Mark and Move (Page 33)

- Head Down (Page 34)

- Answer Awareness (Page 146)

READING TEST MASTERY

Test-Taking Strategies for the ACT Reading Test

Reading Orientation

The Reading test is always the third test section on the ACT.

The Reading and Science tests are entirely different in format from the ACT English and Math tests. To be successful, students must shift gears during the break between these two sections.

The ACT English and Math sections mainly test students on what they already know. Students who have developed some skill in grammar, composition, and high school math will do well on these first two tests.

In contrast, the ACT Reading test is entirely uninterested in what students already know. Correct answers don't come from previous knowledge, but from the text provided. The test assesses how rapidly and accurately students can digest information and use it to answer questions. In other words, the Reading test measures how well and how quickly students can *learn*.

One major throttle on learning ability is reading level, which is why students with low reading levels struggle on the ACT Reading test and often have scores stuck in the teens.

You can give your students the opportunity to improve their reading score despite their reading level woes by familiarizing them with the way the ACT asks questions and coaching them on how to focus on and analyze what is essential in a passage. However, it bears repeating that the number-one, long-term method for boosting ACT Reading scores is to improve individual reading levels.

There are eight major categories of questions on the ACT Reading test. Five of these question categories are far and away the most important. Students will benefit from being exposed to this structure since it helps them understand what they need to pay attention to as they read the passage. This information also makes the ACT Reading questions less of a surprise. Below is a summary of the top five categories. Advanced students may find it helpful to refer to our ACT Standards Family document masteryprep.com/decode/resources, which includes much more detail on each standard as well as how frequently each standard is tested.

TOP FIVE ACT READING CATEGORIES

Close Reading
(30-35% of Questions)

- Paraphrase
- Locate
- Draw Conclusions

An example of Close Reading is Reading question #3 on page 33 of *Preparing for the ACT 2015-16*.

What is another example of a Close Reading question on the Reading Test?

_____

_____

Central Ideas, Themes & Summaries (15-20% of Questions)

- Central Ideas & Themes
- Summarize Key Ideas and Details

An example of Central Ideas, Themes & Summaries is Reading question #1 on page 33 of *Preparing for the ACT 2015-16*.

What is another example of a Central Ideas, Themes & Summaries question on the Reading Test?

_____

_____

Word Meaning & Word Choice
(15-20% of Questions)

- Analyze Word & Phrase Choices
- Interpret Words & Phrases

An example of a Sentence Structure & An example of Word Meaning & Word Choice is Reading question #6 on page 33 of *Preparing for the ACT 2015-16*.

What is another example of a Word Meaning & Word Choice question on the Reading Test?

_____

_____

Purpose & Point of View
(10-15% of Questions)

- Intent & Purpose
- Point of View

An example of Purpose & Point of View is Reading question #11 on page 35 of *Preparing for the ACT 2015-16*.

What is another example of a Purpose & Point of View question on the Reading Test?

_____

_____

Text Structure
(5-10% of Questions)

- Analyze Structure
- Function
- Relate to Passage as a Whole

An example of Text Structure is Reading question #7 on page 33 of *Preparing for the ACT 2015-16*.

What is another example of a Text Structure question on the Reading Test?

_____

_____

Setting Goals

Below is the AVERAGED CONVERSION TABLE for the ACT Reading test. This is the average number of questions that must be answered correctly in order to achieve a given scale score. We developed this chart by averaging 30 actual ACT conversion tables for the Reading test.

Use the averaged conversion table to set goals for class progress on the ACT Reading test. Both teachers and students tend to visualize their objectives better when they think in terms of a number of questions answered correctly rather than a nebulous scaled score. While it is generally a good rule of thumb to say that one question answered correctly on the ACT Reading test is worth one scale point, there are many exceptions.

READING - AVERAGED CONVERSION TABLE			
Scale Score	**Correct Questions**	**Scale Score**	**Correct Questions**
36	39.84	18	19.08
35	38.63	17	17.82
34	37.93	16	16.48
33	36.97	15	15.10
32	35.98	14	13.63
31	35.07	13	12.03
30	34.03	12	10.34
29	32.87	11	8.65
28	31.81	10	7.18
27	30.64	9	6.14
26	29.56	8	5.24
25	28.48	7	4.44
24	27.26	6	3.75
23	25.92	5	3.04
22	24.55	4	2.13
21	23.19	3	1.92
20	21.77	2	1.00
19	20.35	1	0.00

We recommend against sharing this averaged conversion table with your students. Since this is an averaged table, there are many cases where students could answer the prescribed number of questions correctly and still *not* earn the score they need. Students should instead be shown our STUDENT CONVERSION TABLE.

In the student conversion table, we provide the number of questions a student needs to answer correctly in order to practically guarantee a given scale score. As an example, our database shows that students with a raw score of 27 on the reading test have NEVER scored less than a 22 on their scaled ACT score for Reading. Students should use the student conversion table to set their goals.

Once students have their "numbers," the number of questions they need to answer correctly, they should make a habit of writing these objectives at the top of their test sections. For instance, if the student wants to earn a 25 in Reading, he or she should write *33* at the top of the test section. He or she needs to answer 33 questions correctly (or only miss 7 questions) in order to achieve the target scaled score.

Please feel free to copy this page and distribute it to your students. An easy-to-print PDF is also available for you at masteryprep.com/decode/resources.

READING - STUDENT CONVERSION TABLE

Scale Score	Correct Questions	Scale Score	Correct Questions
36	40	18	21
35	39	17	19
34	39	16	18
33	38	15	16
32	37	14	15
31	37	13	13
30	36	12	12
29	35	11	10
28	34	10	8
27	33	9	7
26	32	8	6
25	31	7	5
24	30	6	4
23	29	5	4
22	27	4	3
21	26	3	2
20	24	2	1
19	22	1	0

Using the Break

The break between the ACT Math and Reading tests should be a reset moment for your students. The way they handle the break will be analogous to the way they handle the next two test sections.

If students use the 10-minute break to put their heads down and rest, they're going to start the ACT Reading test already feeling sleepy and tired.

How students *feel* has a major impact on their outcomes in Reading and Science. If students are *hungry*, if they feel *lifeless*, if they are still *stressed out* from the previous test sections, they aren't going to perform at their best.

Students should take with them a healthy snack that will keep them full through to the end of the Science test. It's worth taking the time to designate to your students exactly *what* a healthy snack is. A honey bun does not pass muster. Neither do Skittles nor Snickers bars.

A granola or protein bar and fruit is a great snack. Fruit by itself might not keep students full throughout the test period, but the protein in a health bar will keep them going.

Students should also *get up and move around* during the break. They need to be on their feet the whole time to get the blood flowing. They should *stretch*. Believe it or not, it's a really good idea to practice this with your students. Demonstrate a few effective stretches that will loosen them up and increase circulation. If you have a ninety-minute class, make a habit of taking a two-minute break halfway through to stretch as a group. This gives them a short mental break and will keep them alert to the end.

Students should also *go to the restroom* during the test break. Even if they don't need to, the walking is helpful. *Briskly* walking back and forth is even better.

Essentially, students should do the opposite of what they've been doing for the past two hours: sitting and thinking.

The start of the break is the last moment students are allowed to think about English or Math. Thoughts about those two tests—good or bad, productive or pointless—won't help them on the Reading or Science tests. They did their best: now it's time to move forward. They need to push lingering regrets from English or Math out of their minds.

Students should also take the last 30 seconds of the break to focus on their plan for Reading.

MAXIMIZE YOUR BREAK

- Eat a healthy snack.
- Get up and move.
- Go to the restroom.
- Clear your mind of the English and Math tests.
- Focus on your plan of attack for the Reading test.
- DON'T nap. DON'T sit. DON'T think about English or Math. DON'T eat honey buns.

Read the Questions Carefully

For students to maximize their scores, they must read the questions carefully.

Students typically lose several points for making the mistake of correctly answering a question that does not appear on the test. They move too quickly and make assumptions that kill their scores.

When I am tutoring high performing students, I often hear them say as we review the questions they missed, "Oh, I thought the question was asking for (*this* or *that*)…" They don't need any help with the question or how to answer it. What they really need is coaching on how to be more thorough.

Refer to Reading question #27 on page 37 of *Preparing for the ACT 2015-16.*

Question #27 asks how an image functions *figuratively*. But students who rush through the question might glance at lines 74–76 and choose the answer that matches what is being described: choice D. They miss that choice D describes what *literally* happened, the opposite of what the question asks.

In other words, some students miss question #27 because they are making up their own question and then answering that! Coach your students to read the questions *carefully* and answer the ACT's questions, not their own.

Refer to Reading question #36 on page 39 of *Preparing for the ACT 2015-16.*

While it is true that reading the questions carefully will help students avoid careless mistakes, students can also benefit from the clues that the questions provide upon close inspection.

In #36, the question itself highlights that the *bouncer-defense jump* is not like the *escape jump*. Facts that are called out in questions should be regarded as particularly important. If students use this cue to look for differences in the two jumps, they are more likely to avoid the trap answer, choice F, which actually describes the possible evolution of the bouncer-defense jump (not the *escape jump* actually being asked about).

Read the questions carefully to avoid trap answers and pick up clues about the right answer.

Get Technical

If you can eliminate an answer choice on a technicality, eliminate it. Don't even hesitate.

Strong test-takers have an inner geek inside of them that nudges his spectacles along his nose, points out his finger in the most annoying way possible, and screeches contradictorily, "Well, *technically speaking…*"

If an answer choice is only partially correct, it's partially wrong. A correct answer on the ACT is never partially wrong.

Refer to Reading question #15 on page 35 of *Preparing for the ACT 2015-16*.

Choice D in question #15 can be tempting. Lines 73-76 explain that scientists named the volcanic hills after *distant, lifeless planets*. Some of your students might have imagined a few names as they read: *Mars, Venus, Neptune*.

However, choice D can be eliminated on a technicality. Students don't even need to consider the broader question of whether or not listing names was the *main purpose* of these lines. The fact is, lines 71-76 *don't* list names. They only describe the category of names that were given.

Students should *get technical* to save time and avoid trap answers. There is no value to pondering an answer choice that contains a factual inaccuracy.

Refer to Reading question #23 on page 37 of *Preparing for the ACT 2015-16*.

In question #23, students can make one rapid elimination on a technicality. The question concerns Bradbury's writing sessions, which is a very general concept. Choice A insinuates that *all* of Bradbury's writing sessions were an attempt to understand John Huff, which seems obsessive and highly unlikely.

Some students might reason, "Well, that is ridiculous. The question didn't really mean *all* of his writing sessions." But it says *writing sessions*. Get technical and scoop up the easy eliminations.

This strategy ties in many ways with *paying attention to extremes* (page 281).

Get technical and eliminate factually inaccurate answer choices.

One of These Things Is Not Like the Other

There can only be one correct answer. If two or more answers seem equally valid, chances are that they are both wrong (see *Two Rights Make a Wrong* on page 42).

The main reason students find more than one correct answer is either because they misread the question or they considered the question with an invalid assumption.

Tell your students that when multiple answer choices seem possible, they need to take a step back, re-read the question, and challenge their assumptions. Students should be looking for unique answer choices, not choices that say the same thing as the rest.

Refer to Reading question #24 on page 37 of *Preparing for the ACT 2015-16*.

In this question, choices F, G, and H all seem viable to those students who missed an important detail in the seventh paragraph: the narrator is strolling through a *recollection* each day. It's happening in his memory, not with physical objects.

One of these things is not like the other. The fact that choice J is so different from the other three should immediately make it appealing as an answer. It's the only choice that discusses *thinking*, rather than physical objects.

Looking for what makes an answer choice unique can give focus to students' thought processes. If they are paying attention to what makes choice J unique, they will begin to question, "Wait, is paragraph seven about *thinking*, or is it about visiting places and looking at objects?" With this question in mind, students can quickly get to the answer.

There can only be one correct answer. Students should look for unique answer choices to eliminate incorrect answers and focus their thinking.

The Answers Are the Question

On the ACT Reading test, students should develop the habit of reading the answer choices *with* the question, particularly if the answer does not jump out at them right away.

The reason for this is that it's easier to answer the question when given four choices than as an open-ended constructed response. Students don't have to find the absolutely right answer: they just have to find the one choice that isn't terrible.

The question is always easier than it seems when the answer choices are considered.

Refer to Reading question #10 on page 33 of *Preparing for the ACT 2015-16*.

Question #10 ends with a colon and is quite meaningless without the answer choices that complete the sentence. Students should not stop at the colon and think, *Why did the father show him those pictures?* Instead, they should jump immediately to the answer choices and begin eliminating.

Students might find it helpful to rephrase the answers into *yes/no* questions. For example:

Did his father show him the photos to teach him about the commercial progress the people who work in Bombay made?

Was his father trying to convince him that Dayal and Haseler were Bombay's first great photographers?

Was his father clarifying his claim that his photo collection was not about modern-day Bombay but rather about the early twentieth century?

You'll notice that the focus quickly turns to the answer choices, not the question. To illustrate this concept to your students, pick a few questions like this (where the total amount of answer text far and away exceeds the amount of question text) and rephrase the question in a fashion similar to the example presented above. More students will likely answer correctly and see the value in tackling the question in this manner.

With question #10, the answers to the rephrased questions are clearly *no*, which leaves choice J as the best alternative.

Refer to Reading question #31 on page 39 of *Preparing for the ACT*.

This is another example of a question that is almost meaningless without also reading the answer choices. Students should move straight from the question to the answers. Chances are, an open response to the question won't be helpful in finding the right answer. As students consider each option, their thinking should run something like this:

Is the main purpose to provide an overview of the mechanics and key operations of the jaws of trap-jaw ants?

Or is it to analyze Patek and Baio's techniques for filming two defensive maneuvers of trap-jaw ants?

Or could it be that the passage is comparing the jaws of *Odontomachus bauri* to the jaws of other species of ants?

Or maybe the passage is describing the evolution of the ability of trap-jaw ants to perform an escape jump?

These questions are already a lot to consider. Students can't afford to waste time pondering the purpose of the passage without looking at the focus of this particular question.

Consider the answer choices as part of the question. Avoid making the question more difficult than it needs to be.

The Four S's: Skim

A typical ACT Reading passage contains 800 to 900 words. The questions that go with this passage add up to another 500 to 600 words. Since the average adult reading speed is between 200 and 250 words per minute, it would take a typical adult anywhere from 5 to 7 minutes *just to read* the content, not counting the time it takes to think about and answer the questions.

For this reason, many students need a *skimming* strategy for the ACT Reading test. If students thoroughly read at their natural, comfortable pace, many of them will run out of time.

When students *skim*, they have a different objective than perfect comprehension.

It's important that when you introduce the concept of skimming to your students, you point out that they are making a tradeoff. They can't try to skim and also try to understand everything. They are trading comprehension for speed.

How much comprehension they lose depends on their natural reading speed and how much practice they have skimming. If after many attempts at skimming, certain students are still unable to complete a passage in three minutes, you may need to coach them to read only the first and last sentences of each paragraph, or only the first sentence of each paragraph. In these instances, you're trading a lot of comprehension in order to obtain the desired speed. However, it's better to skim—even just if it's just the first sentences—than to skip the passage entirely.

Efficient skimmers try to understand everything they can but mainly focus on not missing essentials that will help them answer the questions they will soon be facing.

Give your students skimming practice by giving them ACT Reading passages and challenging them to read through the given passage's text in three minutes. Ask them to try to catch the important details and understand as much as they can within the time limit.

Students who have taken many ACT Reading practice tests are much better at skimming because they can anticipate the types of questions that will be asked. They can catch the information they need as they skim.

You can help this process along by emphasizing the major concepts covered in the following *While Reading* chapters (pages 277-282). These chapters provide tips you can use to coach your students on improving the quality and efficiency of their skimming.

Important note: If your students are aiming for higher than a 24 on the ACT Reading test, they need to read each passage in its entirety. They cannot skim and hope to attain a high score. In the end, there is no substitute for fluently reading and comprehending. Advise high performing students to skim at their own risk. Many will find that their scores, if already above 24, will go down when they try to skim. That said, students who are reading for comprehension and not skimming should still pay particular attention to the areas we describe in the following *While Reading* chapters.

While Reading: First Date

Most ACT Reading passages are very boring to students.

This is a huge problem. Emotions dramatically impact how the brain functions, for good or for ill. Boredom tells the brain that reading must be suffered through, but that there is very little essential information. Reading while bored means that most of the text is not retained.

Something is interesting to a reader if it is connected to his or her passions. It's difficult to maintain interest if the material is not related in some way to a reader's passions or day-to-day survival.

One of the simplest ways to improve retention while reading passages is to genuinely *get interested*. If students are interested and not bored, their brains are more likely to capture the important facts and details, and they're more likely to gain a solid conceptual understanding of the reading material.

That can be difficult to do when the passage is about some foreign country from fifty years ago, or all one ever wanted to know about eels, or a too logical dissertation on philosophy.

But it's all a matter of one's frame of mind. We like to explain this to students by describing the "first date" phenomenon:

Have you ever had a girlfriend or boyfriend who talked endlessly about sports, or decorating, or clothes, or you-name-it, and it was *so* boring? Would they ever get mad at you for tuning them out?"

That's what happens on the reading passages. The ACT is like that boyfriend or girlfriend who won't shut up about football or whether maxi dresses are in season. You get bored. You're not interested. You can't help but zone out. If they talk long enough, you might fall asleep. If you're driving while they're talking, they might run you off the road.

But you know, it's your fault that this is happening. Because on your first date, you *weren't* bored. They probably talked about the same things, but it was the first date. You were interested! You were FASCINATED in what they had to say about the nickelback formation or decorative socks. *Please tell me more*, you said. You made yourself interested. You hung onto their every word. And what happened? You remembered what they said.

Students need to go on a *first date* with their reading passages. They need to tell themselves, "This is so interesting! So fascinating!" You can't wait to read them and learn what they have to say, not because they will get you points on the ACT, but because they are interesting in their own right. Students need to treat the reading passages right, or they'll never get a second date. If they get genuinely interested, they'll be amazed at how much more they retain.

Instead of dreading the unfamiliarity of these passages, look forward to them as a path to exploring new worlds. The mindset dramatically impacts retention level.

Avoid saying or thinking that the reading passages are extremely boring and stupid. The only way for this strategy to work is to *authentically* get interested in the material. Pretending to be interested in the passages will not help at all, just like pretending to be interested in a first date is unlikely to lead to a meaningful relationship. Muster as much interest as possible on each passage.

While Reading: One Question

When it comes to the ACT Reading passages, there is one question that students must be able to answer above all else: WHERE?

By *where*, we don't mean the setting of the passage. We mean literally, "*Where* does information occur on the page?"

Refer to Reading question #14 on page 35 of *Preparing for the ACT 2015-16.*

This question refers to the Grand Canyon. *Where* should students look?

Students who skimmed or read while paying attention to *where* information appeared will start their search in the middle of the right column. Those who didn't pay attention to *where* might have to start their search at the very beginning of the passage and scan through the whole thing!

The ACT Reading test is structurally an open-book test. Since all of the information that students need to answer the questions is in the passage, it's essential to know *where* information is located. Every second students spend on frantically searching for an excerpt they can't find is a missed opportunity for a higher score. Lines 66–67 contain the answer to question #14, but if students can't find it, it won't help them.

Two strategies can help students remember *where* to find information: *landmarks* and *bundling*.

A *landmark* is a particular word or phrase that stands out to a student. If students mentally note or underline landmarks as they read, they can use these to navigate the passage later when they answer questions. A landmark can be a unique name, a phrase that signals a shift in discussion, or a topic sentence. The more ACT Reading practice tests students work through, the better they will identify useful landmarks. *Grand Canyon* in line 64 is an example of a potential landmark.

Bundling is more applicable to reading than to skimming. This is an advanced technique that involves mentally grouping a set of data to make it easier to find. It's a lot harder to remember and locate one specific piece of information on one line than it is to find a set of related information across many lines. Since students can't predict what the ACT will ask about, and there's not enough time to memorize everything, bundling allows them to achieve a middle ground, where specific questions jog their memory about which area in the passage to look for answers.

For example, in Passage II on page 34 of *Preparing for the ACT 2015-16, Grand Canyon* can be bundled with *rift valley, 11,000 miles, subterranean fires, fresh lava,* and *lifeless planets.* When a bundle has enough items connected to it, the brain can quickly remember *where.*

The quickest way to *bundle* is to rapidly self-assess with questions like, "What are these paragraphs about?" or "What's connected here?" By paying attention to connections, students will naturally bundle concepts. Students who accomplish *bundling* while reading will readily be able to answer *where.*

Bundling and *landmarks* work hand in hand.

For example, imagine that a student reads a question with an answer choice that reads *11,000 miles.* This should trigger her memory from the read-through. She may not know where *11,000 miles* appears in the passage, but she does remember that it was bundled with *Grand Canyon,* and she knows exactly where that is located because it is one of her landmarks. Because she used bundling and landmarks, this student starts her search very close to where the answer appears.

One way to coach your student on *landmarks* is to have them underline words and phrases that stick out as they read the passage. Afterward, discuss with the class the merits of their landmarks. Teach them how to choose distinctive and helpful words and phrases. The direction, "Turn at the gas station," isn't helpful when there are five gas stations, and likewise bland, unthoughtful landmarks won't be help students because they can't be used to navigate the passage..

To help your students with bundling, choose a concept in a passage and ask your students to underline all the ideas that have a relationship to that concept. Discuss what they bundled and why. Then, have students convert a single ACT-length passage into 4 to 7 bundles. Students can highlight each bundle of concepts with a different color to better visualize this technique.

Refer to Reading question #20 on page 35 of *Preparing for the ACT 2015-16.*

Most passages include two or three questions based solely on this question of *where*. Often the last several questions in a set of ten involve *close reading* skills (finding answers in the text). For example, questions #19 and #20 are answered simply by finding the information word-for-word in the passage.

This fact alone should be enough to motivate students to pace themselves in such a way that they have time to consider all 40 questions on the test. At least 10 will be of the close reading variety. Answering just these questions and guessing on the rest would yield an ACT Reading score of 19!

Students who use landmarks and bundling are more likely to be able to answer question #20 quickly. If students start scanning on the fourth paragraph, they will find *skeletal remains* on line 57 in a matter of seconds.

Refer to Reading question #39 on page 39 of *Preparing for the ACT 2015-16.*

Towards the end of the ACT Reading test, time is at a premium. Students will feel tempted to skip the skimming step for the last passage and dive straight into the questions. Question #39 is a good illustration of why that could be a bad idea.

This question refers to lines 53–64, but it doesn't give a specific line reference. Many students who read this question will find themselves scanning *the entire passage* in order to find the supporting evidence they seek.

Students who noted the *escape jump* landmark during their skim, however, are able to easily navigate to lines 53–64 and can answer this question almost instantly. The correct answer is a paraphrase of the last two lines of the paragraph.

It's worth noting that questions #38, #39, and #40 all rely heavily on the student being able to answer this essential question of *where*. In each case, answers are found almost word-for-word in the passage.

If students skim using the techniques of *landmarks* and *bundling*, they will be able to quickly find the answers they seek in the text.

While Reading: Pay Attention to Emotions

Emotions are much more memorable than facts.

Or expressed another way, the brain gleans more information from an emoji than it does from a letter or word.

As students read, they should pay attention to the emotions that are described. If a question or answer choice mentions an emotion, they want to be able to be fairly confident about whether or not that emotion appeared in the text. If the emotion didn't appear, eliminating incorrect answers can be done quickly and easily. In some lucky instances, an emotion can bring a student all the way to a correct answer.

Emotions can also make memorable landmarks that allow students to quickly find answers while scanning. After your students read a passage, ask them what emotions they noticed in the passage. Where did those emotions appear? Why did the characters feel that way? What happened just before or as a result of those emotions?

> Refer to Reading question #8 on page 33 of *Preparing for the ACT 2015-16*.

Question #8 concerns itself entirely with emotions. How does the narrator feel about his parents' work?

If students pay attention to the emotions that appeared in the passage, they can quickly make a couple eliminations without having to refer back to the text. This can save valuable time.

For example, choice G can be eliminated right away. *Fear* is a strong feeling, and students should be confident that if they don't remember *fear* appearing in their read-through, it probably wasn't there.

In choice H, the word *jealousy* should be a trigger for students. Line 33 describes the narrator feeling *insanely jealous*, which is a powerful emotion and is in sharp contrast to the tone of the passage up to that point. Students who focused on emotions during their read-through will be able to scan quickly to where this emotion appears and verify that this choice is correct.

> Refer to Reading question #23 on page 37 of *Preparing for the ACT 2015-16*.

In the answer choices for question #23, *fear* once again rears its ugly head. Students who were paying attention to emotions during their read-through should be able to confidently eliminate choice C. What should run through their heads is, "Well, if he *only* wrote about words that *inspired his fears*, I would have remembered that. That sounds creepy and Edgar Allen Poe-ish!"

The time saved by using this strategy can be immense. Nothing eats up more time than looking for something that is not there. It's like looking in the house for your keys when you left them in the car.

While reading, students should do their best to pay attention to emotions and use them as landmarks.

While Reading: Pay Attention to Extremes

Students should give careful attention to extremes when they skim the passage as well as when they read the questions and answer choices.

During skimming, extremes—like emotions—serve as landmarks that can help students navigate when they scan for answers. Extremes stand out. They're memorable, and the questions are likely to ask about them.

What's more, because extremes *are* memorable if students focus on them, when an answer choice mentions an extreme that students *don't* remember, they can feel pretty confident that it is not supported by the passage.

This is important because the most time-consuming action a student can take on the ACT Reading test is verifying that something *does not* appear in the passage. To verify that something does not occur, students must scan the entire passage. If they are certain about an extreme not appearing, they can avoid this major time sink.

In the questions and answer choices, extremes must be taken literally. If an extreme answer is presented, in order to be correct it must be fully and explicitly supported by the passage. For this reason, most extreme answer choices are wrong. If students are looking for easy eliminations, they should gravitate toward considering and eliminating extreme choices.

For Reading questions, *take extremes literally. Eliminate them liberally.*

> Refer to Reading question #8 on page 33 of *Preparing for the ACT 2015-16.*

In question #8, choice F poses an extreme that allows for a quick elimination. If the narrator's family had an *extravagant* lifestyle, students would likely remember reading about it. Students who paid attention to extremes during their readthrough would not feel the need to scan the passage to verify that this elimination is warranted. They would have a gut feeling that it is incorrect and make this elimination in under a second.

Extremes often help you to *pair down* (see page 252).

> Refer to Reading question #25 on page 37 of *Preparing for the ACT 2015-16.*

If students pay attention to extremes, then certain answer choices will stand out as obviously incorrect. The extreme does not necessarily need to be in terms of whether or not it could appear in an action movie. An extreme scope is enough. In question #25, choice D advances the idea that *John Huff* is used *as a minor character in _many_ of the* narrator's *stories.*

When students read this choice, they should draw a blank, thinking, "I don't remember this essay saying anything about characters appearing again and again in Bradbury's stories."

Students who aren't paying attention to extremes will doubt themselves and say, "Well, I better go digging!" In the end, they will waste valuable time looking for evidence that isn't there.

Students who *are* paying attention to extremes will think, "If John is in *many* of Bradbury's stories, I would have remembered that. That's pretty extreme for an author as famous as Ray Bradbury to use the same character again and again." They will rightly make the elimination with confidence.

Pay attention to extremes when skimming and use extremes in answer choices to quickly arrive at the correct answer.

While Reading: Strategies for Higher Performing Students

While most test-taking strategies naturally center around ways to tackle the questions, high performing students should also spend some time improving their reading efficiency. The better they are able to read and understand the text, the easier the questions will be to answer.

Below are two strategies that have helped some students improve their reading of the text:

Self-Assess as You Read

When students read a text, they store information and their conclusions about it. When they are asked about the text, they attempt to *retrieve* this information. How quickly and completely they can retrieve the data is based on the *retrieval strength* of the memory.

When you read something, you store it, but you aren't doing anything to improve its retrieval strength.

How do students improve the *retrieval strength* of a memory? A simple yet effective way is *by attempting to retrieve it*.

In order to improve retention (read *retrieval strength*), students should self-assess as they read. "What was this paragraph about?" "What is that sentence in my own words?" "Now, who is John again?" This does not need to be a big production. Rapid self-assessment of key facts and details means that students will be much more ready for the questions that follow the text.

If your students are not already in the habit of doing this, it may take some practice to develop the skill beyond the point where it is a clumsy distraction. In the end, this strategy can make a huge difference in retention not only with the ACT but with academic reading of any kind.

Visualize as You Read

This strategy begins with a disclaimer. This recommendation has helped some of our students. However, the research is still unclear about whether visualization helps students become strong readers, or whether instead visualization is simply a consequence of students being strong readers.

The idea is that students should try to visualize what they read as much as they can. They should attempt to imagine the scene in their mind's eye. This provides several benefits. For one, students tend to be more interested in what they visualize, which improves retention. Also, if students are visualizing a "movie" in their mind, when they no longer understand what they are reading, it's obvious—the movie reel suddenly stops, and students have to pause and figure out what they don't get. Last but not least, to accomplish visualization students must engage with the text, which causes a deeper level of interaction and understanding than just doing a read-through. There may also be fewer instances of students "going through the motions," their eyes scrolling down the text without any comprehension, if visualization is the goal.

The Four S's: Scan

The second *S* in our 4S strategy stands for *scan*. When students *scan*, they lock in to the essence of a question, including key terms or unique phrasings in any answer choice that stand out, and rapidly search through the passage to find a match.

Skimming helps students develop familiarity with the passage and its paragraphs. Students who are good at *scanning* use this familiarity to begin their search close to their goal. Students who don't skim efficiently end up scanning the passage from stem to stern over and over again. In this case, scanning is still more efficient than re-reading, since the scanning can happen much more quickly, but skimming and scanning work best in conjunction with one another.

Scanning has a wide variety of applications. At a minimum, it can and should be used to accomplish the following:

- Find an exact answer.

- Find evidence in support of an answer.

- Verify that evidence supporting an answer does not appear.

- Verify that an answer is correct.

- Find a section referenced by a question in order to establish context.

The most obvious use of scanning is to find an exact answer for a close reading question. This can be a fruitful area of focus when coaching your underperforming students. That being said, *scanning* is not only a strategy for underperformers. High performing students must be able to scan in order to answer with certainty, using this method to quickly verify their answers.

One simple exercise to reinforce scanning is to select a unique phrase from the passage and ask your students to write on a piece of paper the line number where the phrase appears. Students should hold up their line number as quickly as they can. This can be a competition to see which side of the classroom can find the phrase faster. In order to complete the task quickly, students will need to scan rather than re-read.

> Refer to Reading question #2 on page 33 of *Preparing for the ACT 2015-16*.

Question #2 does not provide a line number, yet it refers to a specific section of the passage. The best way to answer this question is to refer to the relevant section in order to have context and supporting (or contradicting) evidence close at hand.

The key terms students should scan for are *Bombay's first great photographers* and *inspiring*. These actually appear word-for-word in the passage: lines 61–62 mention *Bombay's first great photographers*, and line 68 says these photographers *inspired* the narrator.

Students who were effective in skimming will start scanning in the last two paragraphs, since photography is not introduced until near the end of the text.

Now that students have scanned and found the relevant paragraph, if they have to read again to find the answer, they are re-reading only one paragraph and not the whole passage.

> Refer to Reading question #19 on page 35 of *Preparing for the ACT 2015-16*.

Question #19 includes two answer choices that are easy to scan for: *Mount St. Helens* and *Himalayas*. Choice A is quickly eliminated once students scan to where *Mount St. Helens* appears (line 59) and find that this particular comparison is about height, not surface area.

Likewise, *Himalayas* is easily found on line 51 and not only allows another elimination but also leads to the source of the correct answer: *it covers almost as much of the earth's surface as the dry land of continents* (lines 51–52).

Refer to Reading question #22 on page 37 of *Preparing for the ACT 2015-16*.

Half of the battle in scanning is selecting a good word or phrase to scan for.

 Check Your Understanding: In question #22, what would be a weak word to scan the passage for?

_____

What would be a strong word to scan for?

_____

Students should scan for unique words or phrases that help them zero in on the evidence they need in the passage.

The Four S's: Support

The third component of the 4S strategy is *support*.

The correct answer must be supported by the passage.

The most frequent reason an answer choice is incorrect is because it is not supported by the passage.

It doesn't matter if an answer choice is true. Its veracity is beside the point. On the ACT, an answer is correct only if it is supported.

The following lines of "reasoning" are major point killers on the Reading test:

Well, that choice could be right.

I can't find anywhere where it says that choice is wrong.

That's the right answer—I read about that in a book yesterday.

It doesn't matter if a choice *could* be correct. If it isn't directly supported by the text, it's wrong.

It doesn't matter if there's no particular point in the passage that contradicts the answer choice. A choice lacking support from the passage is reason enough to disqualify it.

It doesn't matter if outside information supports the answer choice. Support must come from the passage to be valid.

To help students understand and feel confident about this concept, we like to have them briefly put themselves in the shoes of an ACT test writer:

> *Imagine you have moved to Iowa and by some trick of fate you've ended up working for ACT Inc. Your boss is rather mean and won't let you leave work each day until you have written a Reading question that they can use on their test. It turns out there is one big rule that you have to follow in order for your question to be accepted: there can only be one correct answer. When you submit a question, you have to explain not only why the right answer is right but also why the wrong answers are wrong. Every answer choice has to have a hole in it except the correct answer. This is tricky. It's hard to make a question have only one right answer and still be challenging. If the reason the answers are wrong are obvious (for example, if they are directly contradicted by the passage) then your question will be too easy. After a few long nights, a colleague gives you a hint. This isn't just a little hint: it is the number-one way that ACT test writers make a wrong answer wrong. The right answer has to be SUPPORTED. You can say that the incorrect answers are incorrect "because they aren't supported by the passage." And that's enough. The number-one way to eliminate answer choices, the number-one thing that makes answer choices wrong, is a lack of support.*

Refer to Reading question #5 on page 33 of *Preparing for the ACT 2015-16*.

In question #5, two choices can be eliminated due to a lack of *support*.

Choice C mentions the *narrator's mother* taking *the narrator along to building sites*, but there is no support for this idea. It is true that the narrator's mother *could* have taken him along to building sites, but the passage does not indicate that she did so.

Likewise, choice D mentions a babysitter. Nowhere in the passage is a babysitter mentioned, so this claim is not supported by the passage.

Having a clear understanding of the concept of *support* can help students avoid overthinking.

Refer to Reading question #8 on page 33 of *Preparing for the ACT.*

In question #8, we have three unsupported choices, one of which might be particularly tempting for some students.

Choice J says that the narrator viewed his parents' work with *respect*. The reasoning provided, *his parents were known for their quality workmanship throughout the city*, echoes the narrator's statement in lines 23–24 that his *parents' construction firm of Merchant & Merchant had been prominent in* Bombay's *making*. Some students might argue, "The narrator's parents were accomplished. They helped create a great city. They're *prominent*. The quality of their work *must* be admirable if Bombay architecture is comparable to that of Rome. Of course he would be proud of his parents. Of course he would *respect* them. Don't most kids respect their parents?"

The problem is, there is no direct support for this idea. At no point are there any details that suggest the narrator respected his parents. Not only is it *possible*: it's *likely* that the narrator respected his parents, but that doesn't make this option correct.

On the ACT, students might need to read between the lines, but they must also ensure that there *are* lines to read through. *Support* provides the lines through which you make your conclusions.

If an answer choice is not supported by the passage, eliminate it.

The Four S's: Scope

The last element of our 4S strategy is *scope*. By scope, we mean its literal definition: *the extent of the area that something deals with or to which it is relevant.*

Every ACT Reading question has a scope.

Refer to Reading question #4 on page 33 of *Preparing for the ACT 2015-16.*

In some cases, the scope is quite obvious because particular line numbers are called out. The scope of question #4 is lines 32–43.

In other cases, the scope is less obvious but nonetheless inferred. The scope might be the entire passage, or it might only be a particular paragraph or part of a paragraph. In fact, the scope might be limited to a certain character who is mentioned in the question.

Answers must always match scope. Even if an answer choice is supported, if the choice does not fit the scope of the question, it's incorrect.

In the case of question #4, it doesn't matter if *alliteration*, *allusion*, or *simile* appear in any other part of the passage. Students can only concern themselves within the scope: lines 32–43.

Refer to Reading question #7 on page 33 of *Preparing for the ACT 2015-16.*

Question #7 asks about *the primary function of lines 6–10.* A strict interpretation of scope is quite important: students must limit their focus to lines 6–10.

One answer choice, B, mentions a potential function for lines 10-14: *help illustrate how the term "art deco" was derived.* Some students might be tempted to choose this because it's a more clear-cut choice: the key term *derived* even appears on line 12. This answer choice is designed to trip up those who aren't paying attention to *scope*. However, students who check for scope as part of their 4S strategy are less likely to run headlong into this trap.

Refer to Reading question #21 on page 37 of *Preparing for the ACT 2015-16.*

A word of warning about scope: if a line number is mentioned in a question, it does not automatically mean that students should go into tunnel-vision mode and only consider that one line. Consider question #21, where students are asked to interpret what the phrase *thus I fell into surprise* in line 46 refers to.

The scope *is* line 46. Students should answer specifically about *thus I fell into surprise*. But it turns out that this phrase is part of the author's conclusion of this passage. If students don't consider what they read up to that point and instead only seek an answer from line 46, they may have trouble making the correct choice.

Refer to Reading question #31 on page 39 of *Preparing for the ACT 2015-16.*

Scope is one of the primary factors to consider in answering question #31.

Check Your Understanding: What is the scope of the question?

_____

What is the scope assumed in each of the answer choices?

_____

_____

What answer choice(s) match scope with the question?

_____

An answer choice must be _supported_ and must match the _scope_ of the question in order to be correct.

Distractors and Outliers

Many sets of answer choices on the ACT Reading test include a *distractor* and an *outlier*.

A *distractor* is a choice that sounds a lot like what appeared in the passage but fails to answer the question or misinterprets the information provided in the text. A *distractor* makes students feel certain about an answer choice that they should actually avoid.

An *outlier* is a choice that comes completely out of left field and has nothing to do with anything in the text. The sheer crazy audacity of the choice gives students pause and may even make it appealing to them. If they forget that they must select a supported answer choice, the outlier tempts them because it's so outside the scope of the passage that there is nothing to contradict it. The student thinks, "Well, that might be true…I can't find anything that proves it wrong…"

Students who are aware of these common answer choice types can make eliminations more quickly and with more certainty. They can also develop the ability to avoid tempting trap answers as they work through the test.

> Refer to Reading question #13 on page 35 of *Preparing for the ACT 2015-16*.

In question #13, there are two subtle *distractors* as well as an *outlier*.

Choice A, a distractor, mentions the *wind rising*, which matches *waiting for the wind to rise,* on line 2. However, the general concept in choice A is not supported by the passage. It never says that the stillness *won't last long*. For all we know, the stillness could last for days.

Choice B, a distractor, mentions *oceanic islands that break the water's surface,* which matches the phrase *oceanic islands* on line 6. However, the first paragraph does not state that this *stillness* would make the islands *easy to spot*, so students cannot choose B even though it has similar language as the passage.

Choice D is a classic outlier. There is no mention of a *wake* in the text. There is no connection between a *wake* and the *stillness*. The answer creates a vivid image that has absolutely nothing to do with the text. In its lack of connection, it can be convincing. A student may think, "Hmm, well, boats typically make wakes. And if it's totally still, it would look like that! This sounds way cooler than the other choices." The student is stretching quite a bit here. That's how outliers work. Students have to stretch to reach them. There is a direct contradiction to this choice in lines 3–4—*nothing demarcates or divides the smooth expanse of water dissolving into the horizon*—but that won't stop some students from choosing the dreamy outlier.

> Refer to Reading question #34 on page 39 of *Preparing for the ACT 2015-16*.

If students can wade through the outlier and two distractors in question #34, they can arrive at the correct answer.

Choice F is an outlier. The passage does not mention the jaw hinge moving easily, but this is still a tempting choice. How could the jaw move quickly if its hinge *didn't* move easily? Students must avoid overthinking and remember that an answer without support is an incorrect answer.

Choice G is a distractor. Line 48 does mention *firing* of mandibles, but not in a *continuous, steady* way. There is no support for this aspect of the answer choice. Still, the appearance of words that *seem* to support part of the answer might cause students to select the incorrect response.

Choice H is a distractor. The jaws' light weight is mentioned in lines 18–19, but there is no clear connection between weight and speed.

When students learn to look for outliers and distractors, they can avoid many of the trap answers that the ACT puts in their way.

Meaning, Not Just Word Match

When students don't understand a passage selection or a question, they tend to choose answers that have matching words appearing in the passage, regardless of meaning.

Students in a rush fall prey to the same mistake. High-performing students seem to be particularly prone to this error.

The ACT test writers seem to be aware of this, and so they provide answer choices that fit the *words* in the passage but not the meaning. In this way, the ACT can assess whether students are actually comprehending the text.

The Reading test may build this trap by providing literal interpretations to figurative language, by giving answers that ignore the meaning of key transition words, or any of a dozen other tricks and devices.

> Refer to Reading question #12 on page 34 of *Preparing for the ACT 2015-16.*

In this question, students who are in a rush might be tempted by choices G and H. The evidence for the correct answer does not appear until the next paragraph, on lines 48–49, and impatient students might only look close to where the highly visible terms *Middle Ground*, *Telegraph Plateau*, and *Dolphin Rise* appear.

Transatlantic telegraph cable appears on line 36 and seems to offer support for choice G. However, further consideration would reveal that it is unlikely a single telegraph cable caused a shoal in the Atlantic Ocean.

Likewise, students who miss the key verb *assumed* on line 33 think that the passage is saying that the shoal was an *ancient and drowned land bridge.* Even though the sentence later states that *sailors repairing transatlantic telegraph cable unknowingly produced evidence to prove otherwise,* the fact that the passage provides a word-for-word match for choice H can cause students to read a false positive.

A word match can create a false "aha" moment for students, which causes them to move too quickly without considering the meaning and miss out on points.

> Refer to Reading question #25 on page 37 of *Preparing for the ACT 2015-16.*

In question #25, students in a rush can fall for a word match rather than finding the choice that aligns with the passage's meaning. *Arizona* is a rather obvious trap to avoid, but a subtler word match trips up many students.

Check Your Understanding: In your opinion, what word in the answer choices is most likely to cause students to fall for the *word match* trap? Why?

Students should seek the answer that matches meaning, not just the words.

_____

_____

_____

_____

The Least Horrible Answer

Students tend to overthink ACT Reading questions. This is because if students had to provide their own response to one of the test questions (rather than choosing from the multiple choices), chances are they would create a correct answer that does not exactly match *any* of the choices provided.

In other words, the answer choices don't fit what the students are looking for. In these cases, there is no "Aha!" moment, no rush of revelation. None of the choices feel right, and students who haven't been coached on this matter tend to think they are doing something wrong or have missed something crucial. It's at this moment that they erase the (correct) answer they had selected and choose another (wrong) one, or agonize for minutes over a question that should take seconds.

The fact of the matter is that the ACT is *not* a constructed response test. It doesn't ask for an absolute answer or even a subjective answer. It asks students to select the choice that, relative to the other choices, is best.

At least, that's how the ACT explains it. We recommend another way to think about it that can help your students avoid overthinking and propel them to the correct answer.

Find the least horrible answer choice.

This directive emphasizes that the correct choice might not *feel* like the correct choice. It might only feel like the least terrible one.

Refer to Reading Question #11 on page 34 of *Preparing for the ACT 2015-16.*

When tackling question #11, most students will feel tentative about selecting choice A. After all, *awe* and *fascination* are strong emotions, and it is difficult to find a piece of hard evidence directly supporting this concept.

If you were to ask your students to answer question #11 without looking at the choices, they would most likely say something along the lines of "strong interest" or "curiosity." It is unlikely that many of them will proffer "awe" or "fascination."

When students feel unsure and start to overthink, they should opt for determining the *least horrible answer choice*. They do this by reviewing each choice and eliminating it if it is a worse fit than the choice they are considering.

This passage's tone is quite clearly positive and interested, so students should be able to eliminate choices B and D as horrible choices right away. Choice C also has problems because the passage does not contain any humor at all.

In the end, choice A is correct because it is the least horrible choice. It could possibly be right, and the others are quite obviously wrong. That is enough reason to choose A and move forward. Sure, strong interest isn't quite the same as *awe*. But choices B, C, and D are much worse.

Refer to Reading question #32 on page 39 of *Preparing for the ACT 2015-16.*

ACT test writers have a habit of calling selections or passages *lighthearted* or *amusing* when they are really just *slightly less dry or boring* than the rest of their passages.

Question #32 is a good example of this concept. The correct answer is choice G, but this answer feels only halfway right. The last sentence of the passage—*such a serendipitous event would have been a rare instance in which banging one's head against the ground got good results*—is lighthearted, especially in relief to the rest of the passage. However, lines 73–75—*in the wild, gangs of defending ants team up to attack hostile strangers, sending them head over heels out of the nest*—reads more as a colorful description and less as a lighthearted interjection.

Students can be certain about choice G not by the quality of the answer but because they can eliminate the other choices. There are no moments of sarcasm (choice F), combativeness (choice H), or personal anecdotes (choice J), so they are stuck with the least horrible answer choice, G.

Students should avoid overthinking by seeking the *least horrible answer choice.*

Find All of the Wrong Answers

Many ACT Reading questions appear to have no correct answers.

Students will especially feel this way if there is a concept or passage excerpt that they did not fully understand.

If a question does not seem to have a right answer, students should immediately switch their technique to *finding all of the wrong answers*. In many cases, it is easier to feel certain about an answer being incorrect than it is to find support for a correct answer. This technique is closely related to the *least horrible answer* technique found on page 292.

Students who switch to finding all of the wrong answers should use the concepts of *support* and *scope* to make eliminations.

The point of this technique is for students to quickly recognize when they aren't sure about the correct answer and to instantly transition to "process of elimination" mode.

Refer to Reading question #16 on page 35 of *Preparing for the ACT 2015-16.*

Question #16 can pose quite a challenge for students because of the vocabulary involved in the last paragraph of the passage. Furthermore, some students may have been unable to skim all the way to this paragraph before running out of time, so they may be completely unfamiliar with what is being asked. Even in the absence of these complicating factors, students tend to struggle with finding a definite answer to questions about *purpose*.

If students switch to *finding all of the wrong answers*, however, they can quickly eliminate everything they need to. While choices F, G, and J all include word matches, they clearly don't match the meaning of the paragraph (see *Meaning, Not Just Word Match* on page 291). There are gashes, but no support for them *increasing* in width (choice F); the Earth is cooling, but nowhere does it say that the seafloor *has cooled* (choice G); and the entire paragraph concerns the underwater rift valley, not *dry land* (choice J). These are basic eliminations related mainly to *support*.

Even if students are unable to make sense of why choice H is the best answer, they can *find all the wrong answers* and earn a point.

If you would like to help your students develop this skill, split them into groups of three. Assign each student in the group a different wrong answer. Their job is to find a reason why the wrong answer is indeed wrong. Each student discusses what he or she found with the group. Then the group discusses whether or not they feel more certain about the correct answer after they have found all the wrong ones.

Synthesis Passages

One of the newest and most visible changes to the ACT is the presence of the *synthesis passage* in the ACT Reading test. By *synthesis passage* we mean a two-for-one set of passages that tests the student's ability to synthesize from two sources of information and compare two texts.

This is one of the few ways that ACT has started to conform to the Common Core State Standards rather than the other way around.

This new passage type has a predictable pattern that students should use to their advantage. Students who aren't expecting to see this passage type will waste precious time and might get thrown off by the format.

Refer to Reading Passage III and questions #21–30 on pages 36–38 of *Preparing for the ACT 2015-16.*

The questions associated with this passage on pages 37–38 are split into three clearly labeled parts. The first part includes questions that only pertain to Passage A. The second part contains questions pertaining only to Passage B. The final part asks questions that require students to synthesize from both Passages A and B.

This structure lends itself to a unique reading strategy. Students should first read or skim Passage A. Then they should answer the questions that pertain only to Passage A. In this example, those are questions #21–25.

After answering questions #21–25, students should return to the text and read or skim Passage B. They will then be able to answer the remaining questions (in this example, questions #26–30).

Attacking the passage in this way allows students to answer half of the questions with a fresh take on the part of the passage most relevant.

The strategies covered throughout the Reading Test Mastery section can apply to most of the questions in a synthesis passage. Seven out of ten questions related to Passage III, for instance, only concern one passage. That being said, roughly three questions on each ACT Reading test will concern two passages, and so we have included below a couple tips for answering this question type.

One Passage at a Time

Refer to Reading question #29 on page 37 of *Preparing for the ACT 2015-16.*

Students may feel bewildered by how much text they need to consider at once in order to answer a question like #29. It seems that they must identify a writing process in Passage A and compare it to a story in Passage B.

Students should consider one piece at a time. It's often the case that only one passage has the answer they seek.

For example, in question #29, before thinking specifically about the story that appears in Passage B, students should consider which of the answer choices provided actually conforms to the writing process that Bradbury describes in Passage A. It turns out that only choice C accurately describes the writing process, so there is no need to refer to Passage B.

The descriptor above this set of questions, which reads *Questions 28–30 ask about both passages*, is somewhat misleading. Yes, question #29 does ask about both passages, but only one passage is needed to arrive at an answer.

New Excerpt

Refer to Reading question #30 on page 38 of *Preparing for the ACT 2015-16*.

It seems to be a trend for synthesis passages to have a question formatted like question #30. This question type introduces an additional excerpt so that students must consider *three* sources in order to answer the question.

One thing to keep in mind about this question type is that the text introduced in the question tends to be *much more important* than either of the passages. For example, in question #30 only choice G is clearly supported by the new excerpt. The other choices can be eliminated without much reference to Passages A and B.

The Death of ALL EXCEPT

A quick note to those of you who have provided ACT Reading test preparation in the past.

For a long time, there had been a prominent question wording that required particular coaching with students: "All of the following…EXCEPT:"

In this question type, students had to find the three details that were supported in order to determine the one detail that wasn't. The negative wording often tripped students up. They found a supported answer instead of an unsupported one if they didn't read the question carefully.

It appears that the ALL EXCEPT question category has died a quick, quiet death.

We are still waiting on an additional year of data to officially declare the demise of ALL EXCEPT, but no released Reading test since December of 2014 has featured this question type.

The most likely reason for this disappearance is an effort on the part of the ACT to compete with the SAT and simplify its verbiage, making its test more approachable for students.

All is not lost for the negative question type, however. A relatively ancient format has reappeared in at least one test in the past two years: "Which of the following questions does the passage NOT answer?"

In any event, the ACT is staying true to its pattern of putting in ALL CAPS the indicators that a question is in the negative format. Unfortunately, people have a subconscious tendency to skip text in ALL CAPS!

In light of this information, we recommend that you spend time coaching your students on *carefully reading the questions* (especially anything capitalized), but you should avoid specifically addressing the ALL EXCEPT syntax.

For now, we advise against telling your students that ALL EXCEPT has disappeared entirely. We don't have enough data to support that statement, and the ACT can always change its mind. We do have enough data, however, to impact what we recommend for you to focus on.

Vocabulary Substitution

Vocabulary is important on the ACT, mainly because students who have insufficient vocabularies also have insufficient reading levels, and reading levels are strongly correlated to performance on the ACT Reading test.

The ACT will never ask students for an isolated definition of a vocabulary term, so reviewing flashcards of esoteric terms is unlikely to produce ACT score gains. Vocabulary will be tested several times on each Reading test, but the questions always ask for the meaning of a word or phrase *in context*.

For this reason, students who learn the strategy of *substitution*, maximizing the value of context clues, can work their way to a correct answer even when they are unsure of a certain term or unfamiliar with how it's being used.

This strategy allows students to use the ACT Reading test like a dictionary!

Refer to Reading question #6 on page 33 of *Preparing for the ACT 2015-16.*

In this question, four potential meanings for the term *sweep* are provided. All of these choices are valid definitions of *sweep*, but only one fits the context of the sentence. Students who struggle with this question should stop thinking about the word *sweep* entirely and instead consider the item from another angle: which of these choices is the best fit in line 9?

Mentally, students should consider four sentences (from lines 6–10):

> Malabar and Cumballa hills were our Capitol and Palatine, the Brabourne Stadium was our Colosseum, and as for the glittering Art Deco <u>overwhelming victory</u> of Maine Drive, well, that was something not even Rome could boast.

> Malabar and Cumballa hills were our Capitol and Palatine, the Brabourne Stadium was our Colosseum, and as for the glittering Art Deco <u>wide-ranging search</u> of Maine Drive, well, that was something not even Rome could boast.

> Malabar and Cumballa hills were our Capitol and Palatine, the Brabourne Stadium was our Colosseum, and as for the glittering Art Deco <u>complete removal</u> of Maine Drive, well, that was something not even Rome could boast.

> Malabar and Cumballa hills were our Capitol and Palatine, the Brabourne Stadium was our Colosseum, and as for the glittering Art Deco <u>broad area</u> of Maine Drive, well, that was something not even Rome could boast.

In this question, it doesn't really matter what *sweep* means; all of the choices are valid definitions for the term.

As a matter of fact, we could say that the ACT is a dictionary that has already provided four definitions of *sweep*. What matters is which definition fits the *sentence*. Even if students had a real dictionary on hand, it might not help them select the correct answer.

Viewed in this way, the question becomes much simpler, even if we didn't know beforehand that *broad area* was a possible definition. *Victory*, *removal*, and *search* just don't make sense in the context of the sentence when substituted for *sweep*.

Another way to explain this to your students is that on the ACT, the choices for the meaning of vocabulary words will probably all be valid definitions. If a choice fits the sentence, then it is correct, even if the student isn't sure that the word in question can have that particular meaning. The ACT is testing suitability to the sentence, not the definition of the term.

In other words, the actual question being asked in #6 is:

Below are four correct definitions for the word sweep. *Which of these definitions fits the use of this word in line 9?*

Refer to Reading question #9 on page 33 of *Preparing for the ACT 2015-16.*

In question #9, substitution can get students all the way to the correct answer. It's worth pointing out to your students that all four possible meanings of *drew up* are correct definitions of the phrase, but only one fits the sentence as it is used in the passage. Below are the four possible sentences:

> It was on account of their romance with the city that they <u>extended</u> that weekly rota (list) of shared parental responsibilities.

> It was on account of their romance with the city that they <u>prepared</u> that weekly rota (list) of shared parental responsibilities.

> It was on account of their romance with the city that they <u>approached</u> that weekly rota (list) of shared parental responsibilities.

> It was on account of their romance with the city that they <u>straightened</u> that weekly rota (list) of shared parental responsibilities.

Through substitution, students can see that *prepared* is the most natural fit.

Refer to Reading question #18 on page 35 of *Preparing for the ACT 2015-16.*

Question #18 breaks form by requiring students to determine the meaning of a phrase instead of a word. Two of the choices are *not* definitions of the phrase. However, substitution can still be used to find the most appropriate choice.

Check Your Understanding: Use the *vocabulary substitution* method to verify the correct answer for question #18.

What choice is most likely to distract students from the correct answer? Why?

_____

_____

_____

_____

Lock Box

Confusing terms make for confusing passages, questions, and answer choices.

Most students have an incorrect reaction to a confusing term and do the exact opposite of what they should. They allow the term to freeze them up, or they gravitate toward the choice that uses the term because it sounds fancy or complicated, even though there is a perfectly acceptable alternative staring them in the face. And when all but a confusing choice have been eliminated, students tend to avoid it and pick a suboptimal answer.

All of these pitfalls can be avoided by using the *lock box*.

When students use the lock box technique, they *lock away* confusing terms and don't think about them at all. They ignore the term completely and try to answer without it. By doing this, they avoid freezing up and are still able to determine whether or not the word is key to the answer.

This strategy is best understood through a few examples.

Refer to Reading Question #18 on page 35 of *Preparing for the ACT 2015-16.*

In question #18, one answer choice in particular might throw students for a loop: choice G, *ascertained*. Students unsure of this word's meaning should lock it away and for the time being imagine that there are only three choices available.

Most students can quickly eliminate choices H and J since one does not usually *suggest* or *compensate eight miles of rope*. Since choice G is in the lock box, students should select choice F and move on. No further consideration is needed.

If, however, students had been able to eliminate choices F, H, and J, they should confidently select choice G. However, they should still keep it in the lock box. They should not allow themselves to doubt their choice because they don't know its meaning. Based on their process of elimination, choice G is the only viable option. All they need to do next is move on.

Put simply, the lock box is a mental mechanism that students can utilize to isolate their confusion from unfamiliar terms so that they can continue to answer questions.

Refer to Reading question #28 on page 37 of *Preparing for the ACT 2015-16.*

Students with relatively low reading levels will be extremely challenged by question #28. Here are some of the terms that may cause these students to panic: *omniscient, satire, irony, allegory, philosophical, sensory, convey.*

The truth is that by using the lock box technique, students can wade through the unknown to get to the correct answer. It turns out that they don't need to know what these words mean to select choice J. But if they don't mentally lock away the confusing terms, they'll spend their time thinking about what they *don't* know instead of what they *do*.

Students at low reading levels who have trouble with all of the terms listed above can apply the lock box technique to realize that choices F, G, and H are locked away entirely. The meanings of the choices depend entirely on these key, difficult words.

Furthermore, there are two words in choice J that aren't familiar, but the conjunction *and* indicates that if the student understands *imaginative description*, he or she might still be able to get to the correct answer.

Below is what question #28 looks like to students with low reading levels who have locked away confusing terms:

28. Both Passage A and Passage B highlight Bradbury's use of:

F. a first person omniscient narrator to tell a story.

G. satire and irony to develop characters.

H. allegory to present a complex philosophical question.

J. sensory details and imaginative description to convey ideas.

Before deliberating on any other choice, students should investigate choice J and leave everything else in the lock box. As it turns out, there is an enormous amount of support for Bradbury using imaginative description. Students can now unlock a couple of the boxes and use context clues and word roots to further verify their suspicions that J is the correct choice.

J. sensory details and imaginative description to convey ideas.

Sensory is similar to *senses*. Bradbury is giving details that involve the *senses*? If so, then students can find support for that.

Furthermore, *convey* is similar to *conveyor belt*. Perhaps Bradbury is sending along ideas using imaginative description? That would make sense.

At this point, students can choose J and move forward. By using the lock box, students contain the confusion and consider one tough element at a time.

In this question, the students applying the lock box luck out. If the correct answer were F, G, or H, it is unlikely that the students would be able to get there.

Refer to Reading question #37 on page 39 of *Preparing for the ACT 2015-16*.

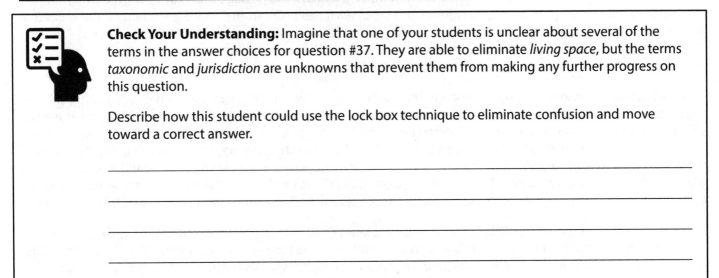

Check Your Understanding: Imagine that one of your students is unclear about several of the terms in the answer choices for question #37. They are able to eliminate *living space*, but the terms *taxonomic* and *jurisdiction* are unknowns that prevent them from making any further progress on this question.

Describe how this student could use the lock box technique to eliminate confusion and move toward a correct answer.

_____

_____

_____

_____

Context Clues 2.0

The high reading level of some passages makes it difficult for students to understand the meaning of certain sentences or paragraphs. Often, difficult vocabulary that is essential to understanding a sentence prevents students from answering a question.

One way to check if reading level was the reason students missed a particular question is to provide them with the definitions of the key terms that appear in the question, answers, and referenced selection from the passage. If students are suddenly able to answer the question, you have a reading level problem on your hands.

For students who are below a 12th-grade reading level, every twentieth word in an ACT reading passage may as well be in Greek.

While the long-term solution to such a problem is obviously to help students increase their reading level (through reading high quantities of quality texts while also learning relevant vocabulary in context), there are several short-term solutions that can boost scores on the ACT Reading test.

One involves giving your students an artificial reading level boost by familiarizing them with the language the ACT uses to ask its questions. In this way you can ensure that your students understand what is being asked of them, which will alleviate much of the confusion they typically suffer. We discuss this strategy further on page 306.

Another solution is to coach students to pay careful attention to *transitions* and *relationships* in order to decode meaning of terms. This allows students to take the concept of *context clues* to the next level, using several sentences or even entire paragraphs to lend context to unfamiliar terms, rather than just the sentence where the word appears.

Refer to Reading question #7 on page 33 of *Preparing for the ACT 2015-16.*

In this question, it may be difficult for students to determine *the primary function of lines 6-10* if they don't understand what is being discussed. Besides the difficult but often overlooked terms *context, primary,* and *function* that appear in the question, there is also the matter of the key terms in the passage that may as well be Greek for most students. *Grandeur, permanence, peninsular,* and *perennial* (lines 3–6) can all throw the student off the trail. What follows is a discussion of landmarks that very few students are familiar with: *Malabar, Cumballa hills, Capitol, Palatine, Brabourne Stadium, Colosseum, Art Deco, sweep, Marine Drive.* Even *Bombay* and *Rome* might contribute to the student's confusion.

However, if students know to pay attention to the relationship between sentences, they can begin to piece this together. In the first sentence of the passage, the narrator says that he thinks of the *great city* he grew up in as *eternal.* The next sentence reinforces this concept: *always there.* The following sentence carries this thought and mentions an *illusion of permanence* created by the *grandeur of the metropolis.* Some students may be lost at this point. Ask them, "Never mind if you're unsure about what they mean by *grandeur* or *permanence.* Do you think that the narrator is trying to elaborate his point, contradict himself, or go off subject?" He's elaborating his point. Based on this, students can infer that *permanence* is related to *always was there, always will be.* The context lends the unfamiliar term meaning.

The key to answering question #7 is the term *perennial.* Lines 6–10 reinforce the concept that Bombay seemed *perennial* to the author by comparing the landmarks of Bombay to the timeless, classic landmarks of Rome. Students who don't understand what is meant by *perennial* may not understand what the narrator is trying to accomplish in the sentences that follow. Again, they can use the relationship of the sentence to preceding sentences in order to lend context.

The peninsular Bombay into which I was born certainly seemed perennial to me.

Certainly seemed tells students that this sentence reinforces and adds onto the preceding sentences. The way that Bombay *seems* in the previous sentences is the same way Bombay *seems* to the narrator here. *Eternal, always...there, permanence.* These are the terms the narrator has used to describe Bombay up to this point. So *perennial* likely has a meaning closely related to these concepts.

With this sorted out, it becomes more obvious that the function of lines 6–10 is to compare Bombay architectural landmarks to Roman landmarks in order to illustrate the perennial quality of the city of Bombay, not to provide examples of "Bombay-style" architecture in Rome. Thus, choice A is a better pick than choice D.

If students pay attention to the relationship and transitions between sentences, they can use these sentences to provide context for unfamiliar terms. This is much more effective than looking for context clues only in the sentence where the term appears.

Dictionary

The most daunting task associated with improving ACT Reading scores is improving your students' reading levels.

Improvement reading levels is not a battle, but a war.

In reading, the rich get richer and the poor tend to get poorer. Strong readers tend to love to read. They read more and more. They get better and better. Poor readers have difficulty reading. It's less likely to be a fun activity for them. They fall further and further behind.

How do you reverse this trend? How do you get students to outperform their peers and boost their reading levels by more than one level per year?

First of all, there is the matter of how much your students read. If you can improve *quantity*, they will make gains.

That being said, there is also the question of *how* they read. Here is where the dictionary comes into play. *Vocabulary* is an essential part of reading level and has the tendency to hold students back.

Most students use "context clues" when they encounter terms they are unfamiliar with, which is to say that they are in the habit of skipping over words they don't understand. I'm only halfway joking here. Even students who apply context clues correctly need repeated encounters with unfamiliar terms before they can master them.

Instead of struggling to figure out unfamiliar words, students should look them up in a dictionary. Then, they should take it one step further and create their own sentences using the term. They should try to really understand the words they look up.

If students develop this habit, there will be a noticeable improvement in their reading level and their progress will accelerate past their peers.

Students should take care to use an appropriate dictionary. Collegiate dictionaries and the dictionary Google uses when you type a word in the search box rely on students having a college reading level. A much more appropriate dictionary can be found at www.yourdictionary.com, for instance. Many high school students would do well to start with a middle school dictionary.

Students should make notes of terms they have looked up and take the time to review them. They can use sites like www.cram.com to create online flashcards and review the words they learn.

The name of the school game is *reading*, but many students don't know the rules. One of the fundamentals is vocabulary. If students make a dedicated effort to improve their vocabulary each and every day, they will find that school gets easier and easier. And so does the ACT.

Read!

The equivalent chapter to this in our *ACT Boot Camp* book is entitled, *Read, Please, Pretty Please!*

We hate to beg, but there is no skill more influential to ACT scores or success in school than reading.

Reading is a learned skill that is mainly enhanced by reading. The more students read texts of an appropriate reading level, the higher their reading level rises.

More reading is better than less reading. There is no real qualification to that statement. Students who want to get ahead, who want to improve their ACT scores, who want to succeed in college and in life, must read more than the average student. How much more? Students who want to be wildly successful should attempt to read at least five times more than their peers.

Where does one find all of that time to read?

Only about 50% of Americans have read a book for pleasure in the past year. If your students don't read for pleasure, they will never be able to read enough. Reading has to be a fun activity, not a drag. It has to be something your students look forward to.

Unfortunately, the deluge of canned entertainment makes it difficult for most students to find the entertainment factor in books. One could say that the entire modern entertainment industry is built around the concept of selling things more interesting than books. Anyone who has found themselves 10 consecutive hours into a Netflix binge will attest to the fact that many shows have been scientifically engineered to be addictive and engaging in ways that books find hard to rival.

But—and it's a giant *but*—the book readers of the world will tell you that many books are far more addictive, engaging, and entertaining than *Lost* could ever be. How is it that the book lovers see this but so many people do not? One of the major reasons is that the experience obtained from reading a book is largely dependent upon the *reader*. The reader is the cameraman, the actors, the audio, the CGI. Everything but the script rests with the reader. Skilled readers bring a lot to the table, and their enjoyment factor is greatly amplified. Unskilled readers (or those who don't read frequently as a habit) only have a script, and a rather dry and difficult one at that if its reading level causes every line to be an epic battle for comprehension.

The barrier to entry to some of the greatest novels ever written is orders of magnitude greater than the barrier to entry to the most successful films or television series. People naturally learn the spoken word, how to read faces, how to perceive emotions. Just by living they become skilled TV and movie viewers. No one has to watch a hundred movies to be able to appreciate *Titanic* or *Star Wars*. Not so with books. One may have to read a thousand books before Hemingway's short stories or Shakespeare's *King Lear* comes to life. The skill and experience required is much greater, even if the reward is commensurate.

Students must continue to read, even if the instant gratification is small, until they can reach the point where the instant gratification from reading is greater than that from consuming other media.

One way to accomplish this is for students to limit the amount of digital entertainment they consume. Canned entertainment is like a gas: it will completely fill any container it's placed in. Make the container small and leave room for reading. If there is nothing to do, if there is actually a moment of boredom in your students' lives, then in relief to that moment a book seems to be a wonderful and interesting thing.

One of the best things you can do for your students is bring them to the level of reading skill where they can actively and intentionally choose reading for pleasure. These students will out-read and eventually outperform their peers.

On the ACT, and in academics, to the bookworms go the spoils.

Artificial Reading Level Boost

Since reading level is one of the biggest contributors to success or failure on the ACT Reading test, is there any way to improve it in a hurry? Is there a path to improving the reading level of students who are taking the ACT in a month?

The short answer is *no*. Reading level is improved by reading. Unless the student reads a lot, things aren't going to get better. It's like asking for a way to turn a beginner into a concert pianist in a month.

That being said, you can accomplish an *artificial reading level boost* in a short timespan by improving your students' vocabulary and fluency with the questions the ACT is likely to ask.

For example, the ACT Reading test likes to use the term *primarily*. If students are taught the meaning of this term and practice using it in the same context as the ACT does, they will perform at a higher reading level with respect to those questions. They are more likely to get to the correct answer. Since the language of the questions tend to be the most important (as all points flow from the questions, not from the text), this artificial reading level boost can have a significant impact.

Although terms in the questions may not seem confusing to you, if you consider that the average high school student reads at a 7th-grade level, you can imagine how they can wreak havoc with student comprehension. What follows is a detailed analysis of the terms that are most likely to appear. By working with your students on these terms, you can make the ACT reading test much more approachable.

Please note that your students may already be familiar with some of these terms. A few of the words, like *best*, are rather obvious, but it's still worth talking with your students about them because they have a specialized meaning on the ACT. For example, *best* asks the students to select the top alternative, although none of the answers might actually be *good* answers in the student's mind.

TERMS		PHRASES
• passage	• theory	• reasonably be inferred from the passage that
• best	• context	• which of the following words best describes
• following	• transition	• which of the following statements best describes
• narrator	• present	• of the following best describes
• author	• intend	• which of the following questions is not answered
• according	• image	• in the context of the passage the statement
• reasonably	• expresses	• as it is used in line
• main	• establish	• when the narrator says
• indicates	• determining	• which of the following words
• inferred	• details	• which of the following questions
• statements	• specifically	• the main function of the
• primarily	• increase	• which of the
• suggest	• emphasize	• according to the
• based	• develop	• the passage indicates
• refers	• demonstrate	• the author uses
• purpose		• point of view
		• indicates that the
		• the main function of
		• the main purpose of
		• the author most likely
		• the following except
		• passage suggests that
		• passage states that
		• passage most strongly

Common Errors to Avoid in Reading

Careless errors can kill an ACT score. Three mistakes can drop a scale score by 3 points! It doesn't help students when they go through the effort of reading the text and understanding the questions only to fall for trap answers. If your students choose an incorrect answer choice because of one of these common mistakes, it's worth taking the time to clear it up.

You'll notice that many of these common errors are resolved by a unique strategy outlined in this book.

1. Not reading the question; answering a different question than what was actually asked.

2. Answering with a word match instead of a meaning match.

3. Choosing an unsupported outlier because it can't be proven wrong.

4. Answering a figurative question with a literal answer or vice versa.

5. Not looking at the text when a question refers to a line number.

6. Choosing an answer supported by only one paragraph when the question asks about the passage as a whole.

7. Choosing an answer because it has a big, unfamiliar word.

8. Avoiding the only answer choice not eliminated because it has a big, unfamiliar word.

9. Skipping the text and going straight to the questions.

10. Staring blankly at a question or section of text.

Check Your Understanding: What three errors are *your* students most likely to make? What will you do to help your students avoid these errors?

_____

_____

_____

_____

READING CONTENT MASTERY

Content Strategies for the ACT Reading Test

Difficulty Distribution Within Passages

Within each set of 10 questions on the ACT reading test, there is a noticeable difficulty pattern which your students should be aware of. We detected these patterns by analyzing 800,000 student responses on retired ACT Reading tests.

Specifically, questions #4 and #6 tend to be the most challenging. The last question in any set of 10 is also frequently missed, but this may be due to the fact that when students run out of time, they end up guessing on the last question.

Questions #1, #5, and #7 tend to be the easiest.

This pattern's existence is probably due to the sequence in which the ACT prefers to ask questions. For example, the first question for any passage is usually a general comprehension question.

Below is the average percentage of correct responses for each question in any set of 10.

Please note that the 1st applies to any first question in the test (i.e., questions #1, #11, #21, and #31).

QUESTION NUMBER	AVERAGE PERCENTAGE OF CORRECT RESPONSES
1st	41.5%
2nd	40.25%
3rd	41.375%
4th	34.875%
5th	41.75%
6th	35.75%
7th	42%
8th	41%
9th	41.125%
10th	36.875%

Complexity of ACT Reading Passages

Below you will find the word counts, estimated grade levels, and ATOS complexity levels of the four Reading passages that comprise the released test provided in Preparing for the ACT 2015-16. An analysis of this test's questions and answer choices follows, since a significant portion of the text appearing in the test is in the questions rather than the passage.

One interesting result of our analysis is that the reading level and complexity of the questions and answer choices on the ACT Reading test are reliably higher than that of the passages the questions refer to. This fact may have a part in explaining the value of helping students develop an artificial reading level by familiarizing them with the terms and syntax of ACT Reading questions.

	GRADE LEVEL	WORD COUNT	ATOS LEVEL
Passage 1 – Passage Text	12th Grade	848	9.4
Passage 1 – Question Text	College	544	11.1
Passage 2 – Passage Text	College	780	10.3
Passage 2 – Question Text	College	414	10.2
Passage 3 – Passage Text	12th Grade	912	6.5
Passage 3 – Question Text	College	763	9.8
Passage 4 – Passage Text	College	784	9.9
Passage 4 – Question Text	College	525	9.8

Reading Passage Dates and Subjects

We have conducted an analysis of the ten most recently released ACT Reading tests in order to provide you with a picture of the dates and topics of Reading passages.

The average Reading passage has a copyright date 10 years prior to the test's release date. The median age of these passages is eight years. One could say that the most likely copyright date for a reading passage provided in 2016 would be 2008.

For this reason, even though Chaucer, Shakespeare, and *The Rise and Fall of the Roman Empire* might make for good introductions to complex literature, they may not serve well to improve student familiarity with the typical, modern language structure that shows up so frequently on the ACT.

Below is a breakdown of copyright dates and subjects by passage category.

It's interesting to note that the Natural Science passages are strongly related to life sciences. Natural Science and Social Science passages tend to be somewhat fresher (average 7 and 9.2 years old, respectively) compared to Prose and Humanities passages (average 11.6 and 13 years). A significant percentage of Prose and Humanities passages are over a decade old. The Social Science passages have a marked tendency toward topics about geography.

One item not included in this analysis but that should be noted is that the themes of environmentalism and conservation have shown up in *many* Social Science and Natural Science passages throughout the past few years. If your students are unfamiliar with the fundamentals of these two subjects, it's well worth providing them a brief introduction. Familiarity helps students retain information during the test and thereby improves scores.

Passage I – Literary Narrative or Prose Fiction

Average Age: 11.6 years	Median Age: 10 years	Oldest Passage: 21 years	Newest Passage: 5 years
Novel Excerpts: 90%		**Short Story Excerpts:** 10%	

Passage II – Social Science

Average Age: 9.2 years	Median Age: 8 years	Oldest Passage: 14 years	Newest Passage: 4 years
Geography: 40%	Social Science/ Anthropology: 30%	History/Biography: 20%	Other: 10%

Passage III – Humanities

Average Age: 13 years		Median Age: 7 years		Oldest Passage: 38 years		Newest Passage: 4 years	
Memoir: 30%	Literary Criticism: 30%	Art: 20%	Film: 10%	Music: 10%			

Passage III – Natural Science

Average Age: 7 years	Median Age: 7 years	Oldest Passage: 11 years	Newest Passage: 4 years
Life Sciences: 60%	Geology: 20%	Astronomy/Physics: 20%	

Content Area #1: Locate

Two of the most heavily weighted ACT Reading Standard Families belong to the Close Reading category: Locate (#1) and Draw Conclusions (#3).

Refer to Reading question #3 on page 33 of *Preparing for the ACT 2015-16* for an example of this standard family.

On *locate* questions, students must quickly find answers that are spelled out practically word-for-word in the passage while also avoiding trap answers. If students are having trouble with this standard family, focus on these skills covered in the *Test Mastery* section:

- The Four S's: Skim (page 276)

- The Four S's: Scan (page 283)

- Meaning, Not Just Word Match (page 291)

CATEGORY: CLOSE READING

Family: Locate

Weight: 16+%

Standards:
CLR 201. Locate basic facts (e.g., names, dates, events) clearly stated in a passage
CLR 301. Locate simple details at the sentence and paragraph level in somewhat challenging passages
CLR 401. Locate important details in somewhat challenging passages
CLR 501. Locate and interpret minor or subtly stated details in somewhat challenging passages
CLR 502. Locate important details in more challenging passages
CLR 601. Locate and interpret minor or subtly stated details in more challenging passages
CLR 602. Locate important details in complex passages
CLR 701. Locate and interpret minor or subtly stated details in complex passages
CLR 702. Locate important details in highly complex passages

Example: Reading question #12 on page 34 of *Preparing for the ACT 2015-16.*

Content Area #2: Summarize Key Ideas & Details

Students who successfully answer questions in this standard family demonstrate mastery of an interesting mix of skills.

In order to answer these questions effectively, students must be able to easily "zoom in" on the portion of the passage referenced by the question. In this regard, the skill is similar to *close reading*. Once there, however, students must comprehend and analyze what they find in order to get to the correct answer.

If your students are challenged by this type of question, focus on these skills covered in the *Test Mastery* section:

- Distractors and Outliers (page 289)

- The Least Horrible Answer (page 292)

CATEGORY: CENTRAL IDEAS, THEMES, AND SUMMARIES

Family: Summarize Key Ideas & Details

Weight: 8-15%

Standards:
IDT 403. Summarize key supporting ideas and details in somewhat challenging passages
IDT 503. Summarize key supporting ideas and details in more challenging passages
IDT 602. Summarize key supporting ideas and details in complex passages
IDT 702. Summarize key supporting ideas and details in highly complex passages

---

Example: Reading question #2 on page 33 of *Preparing for the ACT 2015-16*.

Content Area #3: Draw Conclusions

Questions in this standard family tend to be more challenging than their *locate* kin. Students must still find relevant evidence for their answer choice, but the text never exactly matches up with the correct answer. Students are forced to make their own conclusions.

For this reason, students having difficulty with this standard family should review these skills:

- The Four S's: Support (page 285)

- The Four S's: Scope (page 287)

Students typically miss questions in this standard family because they choose an unsupported response or select an answer choice that does not match the scope of the question.

CATEGORY: CLOSE READING

Family: Draw Conclusions

Weight: 8-15%

Standards:
CLR 202. Draw simple logical conclusions about the main characters in somewhat challenging literary narratives
CLR 302. Draw simple logical conclusions in somewhat challenging passages
CLR 402. Draw logical conclusions in somewhat challenging passages
CLR 403. Draw simple logical conclusions in more challenging passages
CLR 503. Draw subtle logical conclusions in somewhat challenging passages
CLR 504. Draw logical conclusions in more challenging passages
CLR 603. Draw subtle logical conclusions in more challenging passages
CLR 604. Draw simple logical conclusions in complex passages
CLR 703. Draw logical conclusions in complex passages
CLR 704. Draw simple logical conclusions in highly complex passages
CLR 705. Draw complex or subtle logical conclusions, often by synthesizing information from different portions of the passage

---

Example: Reading question #10 on page 33 of *Preparing for the ACT 2015-16.*

Content Area #4: Interpret Words & Phrases

Although the ACT prides itself on never asking students to define terms in isolation, the Reading test does assess the definition of terms *within context* quite heavily.

How to coach students on this standard family is covered thoroughly in the section entitled *Vocabulary Substitution* (page 298). The segment *Context Clues 2.0* (page 302) may also be helpful.

CATEGORY: WORD MEANINGS & WORD CHOICE

Family: Interpret Words & Phrases

Weight: 8-15%

Standards:
WME 302. Interpret basic figurative language as it is used in a passage
WME 402. Interpret most words and phrases as they are used in somewhat challenging passages, including determining technical, connotative, and figurative meanings
WME 503. Interpret virtually any word or phrase as it is used in somewhat challenging passages, including determining technical, connotative, and figurative meanings
WME 504. Interpret most words and phrases as they are used in more challenging passages, including determining technical, connotative, and figurative meanings
WME 602. Interpret virtually any word or phrase as it is used in more challenging passages, including determining technical, connotative, and figurative meanings
WME 603. Interpret words and phrases in a passage that makes consistent use of figurative, general academic, domain-specific, or otherwise difficult language
WME 702. Interpret words and phrases as they are used in complex passages, including determining technical, connotative, and figurative meanings
WME 703. Interpret words and phrases in a passage that makes extensive use of figurative, general academic, domain-specific, or otherwise difficult language

---

Example: Reading question #6 on page 33 of *Preparing for the ACT 2015-16*.

Content Area #5: Intent & Purpose

The ACT Reading test frequently requires students to put themselves in the shoes of the author by asking, "Why did the author write this?"

The following skills covered in the *Test Mastery* section can help your students master some of the challenges offered by this question type:

- The Three Toughest Reading Questions and Why (page 317)

- The Answers are the Question (page 275)

- Find All of the Wrong Answers (page 294)

CATEGORY: PURPOSE & POINT OF VIEW

Family: Intent & Purpose

Weight: 8-15%

Standards:
PPV 201. Recognize a clear intent of an author or narrator in somewhat challenging literary narratives
PPV 301. Recognize a clear intent of an author or narrator in somewhat challenging passages
PPV 401. Identify a clear purpose of somewhat challenging passages and how that purpose shapes content and style
PPV 501. Infer a purpose in somewhat challenging passages and how that purpose shapes content and style
PPV 502. Identify a clear purpose of more challenging passages and how that purpose shapes content and style
PPV 601. Infer a purpose in more challenging passages and how that purpose shapes content and style
PPV 701. Identify or infer a purpose in complex passages and how that purpose shapes content and style

Example: Reading question #13 on page 35 of *Preparing for the ACT 2015-16.*

The Three Toughest Reading Questions and Why

Please refer to Preparing for the ACT 2013-14. *For the bulk of this book, we have been referring to a later edition of* Preparing for the ACT, *but in this chapter we are referring to the earlier* 2013-14 *edition so that we can provide information about student response data that we have gathered. Please note that if you refer to the* Preparing for the ACT 2015-16 *booklet, this chapter won't make sense.*

At this point, we have discussed the five most important question categories on the ACT Reading test. In this section, we discuss three questions on a released test that give students the most trouble. This information provides insight into the biggest challenges on the ACT Reading test and illuminates gaps in students' skills.

Sequence of Events

The most difficult question on ACT Reading test 67-C concerns a sequence of events.

> Refer to Reading question #22 on page 36 of *Preparing for the ACT 2013-14.*

On this question, the most popular choices are F and G, with choice J, the correct answer, earning just 16% of responses. Students would have done better by randomly guessing on this question.

Test items that involve sequences of events tend to have trap answers. Students who rush through these questions will answer them incorrectly. Surprisingly, many high performing students struggle with this question type not because they don't understand the concept of sequence but because it is so easy to make an error. Particularly, students pressed for time will choose the answer that appears first in the passage, rather than what comes first *chronologically.*

The subjects *drumming* and *philosophy* appear in the passage before the subject of *butterflies,* so they win the lion's share of responses. *Butterflies* is actually mentioned last, but it is clear that this interest was the narrator's earliest: *I had had a similar passion for chemistry when I was ten, and for butterflies and lizards before that* (lines 53–54).

If you coach your students that when it comes to sequence questions, the ACT is looking for *chronological* sequence, they should be able to avoid this common mistake.

Draw Conclusions

While appearing somewhat less frequently than its sibling *locate* in the Close Reading category, *draw conclusions* can be a vehicle for some of the ACT's most challenging content.

> Refer to Reading question #4 on page 35 of *Preparing for the ACT 2013-14.*

Only 27% of students responded correctly (choice G), which is practically the same as blind guessing. Choice F was much more popular, winning 38% of responses. This fact tells us that this item succeeded in testing what the ACT was aiming for: can the student *draw complex or subtle logical conclusions, often by synthesizing information from different portions of the passage (CLR 705)*?

Students who chose F completely missed the subtleties of the passage and took the changes described in lines 49–60 (*one-hour photo, tanning salon, pizza parlor, Las Vegas-style gambling*) as improvements. They did not catch the narrator's tone or point.

This question highlights the fact that students who are aiming for high ACT Reading scores must read and understand the passage. This is not the sort of question that can be answered by skipping to the questions and then scanning the passage for answer choices. A question like this demands that students actually "get the point."

Intent & Purpose

The question of *why* can be the most challenging to answer, and this is certainly this case on the ACT.

Refer to Reading question #14 on page 35 of *Preparing for the ACT 2013-14.*

Although the correct answer is G, this choice only garnered 28% of responses (compared to a 25% blind guess rate). The most popular choice was F.

The crux of student difficulties with this question has to do with selecting *details* discussed in the paragraph rather than focusing on the *purpose* of the paragraph. This item tests a higher-level skill, requiring students to ask themselves, "Why did the writer include this in the essay?"

Choice F is apparently supported by the facts that *the Amazon is one of the most rapidly urbanizing regions of the world* (lines 6–7) and *the city of Manaus, for example, has grown in the past decade from 850,000 to 1.5 million* (lines 9–10). However, the purpose of the paragraph concerns Gomes and his workshop school. Lines 6–10 state facts and make arguments in order to lay a foundation for discussing Gomes's work.

Again, *subtlety* causes many of the difficulties.

Students may improve on this question category if they're reminded that *purpose* describes *why* writers say what they say. It doesn't describe *what* they say.

Reading Standard Families

ACT provides College Readiness Standards that are essential to understanding the structure of the test. At MasteryPrep, we have taken it one step further by grouping these standards into logical, teachable categories and providing data on how frequently each standard family is assessed on the ACT. Below is a preview of one of the standard families. Feel free to download this resource, print it, and use it as you see fit.

CLOSE READING (33%)	
PARAPHRASE (2-4%)	**DRAW CONCLUSIONS (8-15%)**
CLR 404. Paraphrase some statements as they are used in somewhat challenging passages	CLR 202. Draw simple logical conclusions about the main characters in somewhat challenging literary narratives
CLR 505. Paraphrase virtually any statement as it is used in somewhat challenging passages	CLR 302. Draw simple logical conclusions in somewhat challenging passages
CLR 506. Paraphrase some statements as they are used in more challenging passages	CLR 402. Draw logical conclusions in somewhat challenging passages
CLR 605. Paraphrase virtually any statement as it is used in more challenging passages	CLR 403. Draw simple logical conclusions in more challenging passages
CLR 706. Paraphrase statements as they are used in complex passages	CLR 503. Draw subtle logical conclusions in somewhat challenging passages
	CLR 504. Draw logical conclusions in more challenging passages
LOCATE (>15%)	CLR 603. Draw subtle logical conclusions in more challenging passages
CLR 201. Locate basic facts (e.g., names, dates, events) clearly stated in a passage	CLR 604. Draw simple logical conclusions in complex passages
CLR 301. Locate simple details at the sentence and paragraph level in somewhat challenging passages	CLR 703. Draw logical conclusions in complex passages
CLR 401. Locate important details in somewhat challenging passages	CLR 704. Draw simple logical conclusions in highly complex passages
CLR 501. Locate and interpret minor or subtly stated details in somewhat challenging passages	CLR 705. Draw complex or subtle logical conclusions, often by synthesizing information from different portions of the passage
CLR 502. Locate important details in more challenging passages	
CLR 601. Locate and interpret minor or subtly stated details in more challenging passages	
CLR 602. Locate important details in complex passages	
CLR 701. Locate and interpret minor or subtly stated details in complex passages	
CLR 702. Locate important details in highly complex passages	

Visit masteryprep.com/decode/resources to download a printable PDF of MasteryPrep's ACT Reading Standard Families.

Common Core Alignment

Visit masteryprep.com/decode/resources to find the Common Core alignment to ACT standards.

DECODING READING TEST 72-C

Answer Explanations and Standard Families

1. Central Ideas, Themes, and Summaries >> Central Ideas & Themes

Choice B is incorrect because while many paragraphs mention important buildings and locations in Bombay, the passage as a whole concerns the narrator, his family, and their relationship with Bombay; it does not center around a discussion of buildings.

Choice C is incorrect because most paragraphs don't discuss Bombay's prominence in the world of architecture.

Choice D is incorrect because only the third paragraph (lines 32–51) discusses the narrator's emotional environment, and it does so only obliquely.

The correct answer is A. Every paragraph in the passage discusses *the relationship the narrator* and/or *his parents had with the city of Bombay*, so this choice is the best fit. There is strong evidence throughout the passage that supports this choice. Lines 5–14 show that the narrator considered that Bombay had the best architecture in the world. Lines 22–25 explain the role the narrator's parents had in the construction of the city. Lines 32–34 describe how the narrator was *insanely jealous of the city* because it was his *parents' other love*. Lines 70–76 describe the parts of the city and its people that inspired the narrator's art.

2. Central Ideas, Themes, and Summaries >> Summarize Key Ideas & Details

Choice F is incorrect because it contradicts the passage, which indicates in lines 84–87 indicate that the narrator has not given up photography and is, in fact, a photographer.

Choice G is incorrect because the passage describes panoramic pictures as examples of what the narrator *did not want to do* in lines 64–65.

Choice H is incorrect because the passage does not support the concept that the narrator wanted to create pictures that would be added to his father's collection.

The correct answer is J. Lines 67–69 state that *their images were awe-inspiring, unforgettable, but they also inspired in me a desperate need to get back down to ground level*. The narrator then describes what *ground level* meant to him: *I yearned for the city streets…I yearned for life* (lines 70–77). This evidence supports the claim that the narrator was inspired to *photograph subjects that depict everyday life on Bombay's streets*.

3. Close Reading >> Paraphrase

Choice A is incorrect because lines 25–31 do not refer to Merchant & Merchant.

Choice B is incorrect because these lines are talking about the time *before* the narrator was born, not about what he paid attention to at a young age.

Choice D is incorrect because lines 29–31 reject the way of thinking that the narrator is describing, *not* the fact that Bombay was a *gigantic building site* during that time period.

The correct answer is C. Lines 25–26 make reference to the ten years before the narrator's birth as a time of much construction and productivity. Lines 27–29 at first proposes that this was so that the city would be *in finished condition by the time* the narrator began *paying attention to it*. The narrator then contradicts himself in lines 29–30 by saying, *no, no, I don't really think along such solipsistic lines*. *Solipsism* is the philosophy that one's own existence is the only thing that is real. Choice C effectively paraphrases this information.

4. Relationships >> Comparative Relationships

Choice F is incorrect because *alliteration* means *to use words beginning with the same sound*, which does not occur in this selection.

Choice G is incorrect because *allusion* means *referring to something without mentioning it directly*, but the entire selection is direct and explicit.

Choice J is incorrect because *simile* means *a comparison of one thing to another*, but these lines do not show a comparison.

The correct answer is H. Lines 36 and 42 refer to Bombay as *her*. Because the narrator discusses Bombay as though it were a person, *personification* is the best fit.

5. Close Reading >> Paraphrase

Choice A is incorrect because this contradicts the passage, which indicates in line 47 that the mother would also help take care of the narrator.

Choice C is incorrect because the passage does not describe the narrator being taken *to building sites*.

Choice D is incorrect because there is no mention of a *babysitter* in the passage.

The correct answer is B. The passage describes *shared parental responsibilities* (lines 38–39), with the narrator alternately spending time with his father while his mother *was out there with* her, *with Bombay* (line 42) or with his mother while his father went *to dig in the foundations of building sites* (line 49). This evidence supports the concept that the *narrator's parents traded off responsibility* in raising the narrator and *working at the construction company*.

6. Word Meanings & Word Choice >> Interpret Words & Phrases

Choice F is incorrect because a street (Marine Drive) typically cannot have an *overwhelming victory*.

Choice G is incorrect because the concept of *searching* does not fit the meaning of this sentence. It is unclear who is *searching*.

Choice H is incorrect because a street cannot normally be *completely removed*.

The correct answer is J. It makes the most sense for *sweep* to mean *broad area* in this sentence, since it is possible for the Art Deco buildings on Marine Drive to represent a *broad area*.

7. Text Structure >> Function

Choice B is incorrect because there is no information about the derivation of *the term "art deco"* in lines 6–10. The narrator does speculate on the term's possible derivation in lines 10–14, but that is beyond the scope in the question.

Choice C is incorrect because the narrator says he grew up in Bombay during its *golden age* (line 2), and he does not later contradict himself on this point.

Choice D is incorrect because the narrator uses figurative language to compare Bombay's architecture to Rome's. He is not literally saying that Rome had Bombay–style architecture.

The correct answer is A. The narrator says that the architectural achievements of Bombay seemed everlasting (*perennial*) to him, much like Roman architecture. He then goes on to compare architectural landmarks in Bombay to those in Rome: *Malabar and Cumballa hills* are compared to *Capitol and Palatine* (lines 6–7), and *Brabourne Stadium* is compared to the *Colosseum* (line 8).

8. Relationships >> Comparative Relationships

Choice F is incorrect because there is no support in the passage for the family having an *extravagant* lifestyle.

Choice G is incorrect because there is no evidence in the passage that the narrator felt fear about his parents' work or their well–being.

Choice J is incorrect because although the narrator *might* have felt respect for his parents, there is no direct support for this in the passage.

The correct answer is H. The narrator says that he *was insanely jealous* of Bombay because he viewed it as his *parents' other love* (lines 32–34). His parents would spend their time working with their *construction firm of Merchant & Merchant* (line 24) out in Bombay building the city (lines 42–51).

9. Word Meanings & Word Choice >> Interpret Words & Phrases

Choices A, C, and D are incorrect because a weekly list of responsibilities is probably not *extended*, *approached*, or *straightened*, so these meanings of the phrase *drew up* are not logical.

The correct answer is B. It is more likely that a *list* of *shared parental responsibilities* was *prepared*. Following line 38 are examples of the narrator spending time with one parent while the other continued construction work, which is consistent with this meaning.

10. Close Reading >> Drawing Conclusions

[Justification: we are asked to make a conclusion about the narrator's father's rationale, given specific information to consider]

Choice F is incorrect because the father says these photos showed *where people lived and worked and shopped* (lines 80–81). He does not use them to teach his son about commercial progress.

Choice G is incorrect because these specific photos are not related to the photographers Dayal and Haseler.

Choice H is incorrect because the narrator's father does not make a claim about his photo collection being from the early twentieth century.

The correct answer is J. The narrator says that he *yearned for life* (lines 76–77), but his father insists the photos of storefronts and piers showed *where people lived and worked and shopped* and that in these photos *it becomes plain what they were like* (lines 80–83). The narrator's father is saying that pictures of places can tell you about the *people who spent time there*.

11. Purpose & Point of View >> Point of View

Choice B is incorrect because there is no support that the author has *disbelief* or *cynicism* toward the main subject, the seafloor of the Atlantic Ocean. Both *disbelief* and *cynicism* are negative attitudes, but there is no negativity in the passage.

Choice C is incorrect because there is no support for the author being *amused* or *nostalgic*. If the author had an attitude of *amusement*, she would think the subject is funny, and if she had an attitude of *nostalgia*, she would be thinking affectionately about the past.

Choice D is incorrect because the author's tone throughout the passage is definitely interested, not *bored* or *indifferent*. If the author were *indifferent*, she would be uninterested in her subject.

The correct answer is A. Many of the author's dramatic word choices convey an attitude of *awe* and *fascination*: lines 6–8 state, *the unperturbed surface offers no hint of the grand and sweeping energies hidden below* (lines 5–8); lines 41–43 emphasize that this underwater terrain has *some of the youngest, freshest rock on earth… torn not from a piece of continent sunk beneath the waves, but from the very foundation of the sea*; and lines 77–79 dramatize that *what had seemed so foreign to scientists is an integral part of earth's very being, for at the ridge our own planet gives birth*.

12. Close Reading >> Locate

Choice F is incorrect because an *island* is land that is surrounded by water, but the basin named in lines 33–34 is at the bottom of the ocean, largely submerged in water.

Choice G is incorrect because line 36 only mentions a telegraph cable to describe its part in dredging up a chunk of the ocean's floor.

Choice H is incorrect because *people assumed that* it *was an ancient and drowned land bridge* (lines 32–35), but that was not the *actual* nature of what people had named the *"Middle Ground"*—sailors *unknowingly produced evidence to prove otherwise* (lines 36–37).

The correct answer is J. Lines 48–49 state that *hidden beneath the waves is an immense submerged mountain range, the backbone of the sea*. This adequately describes the actual reason the Atlantic basin shoaled in its center.

13. Purpose & Point of View >> Intent & Purpose

Choice A is incorrect because there is no support within the scope of the first paragraph that the stillness will not *last long*.

Choice B is incorrect because the first paragraph does not mention whether stillness makes spotting *oceanic islands* easier or harder.

Choice D is incorrect because this paragraph does not describe the ship's *wake*.

The correct answer is C. The last sentence of the first paragraph (lines 6–8) states that *the unperturbed surface offers no hint of the grand and sweeping energies hidden below*. The author uses the stillness of the surface to show how dramatically different it is underwater.

14. Relationships >> Comparative Relationships

Choice F is incorrect because the canyons have *similar depth* (line 66).

Choice G is incorrect because the passage contains no evidence that the ocean canyon is older.

Choice H is incorrect because there is no support for *the rift valley* being wider than the *Grand Canyon*.

The correct answer is J. Lines 66–67 states that the ocean canyon has *considerably greater length* than the Grand Canyon.

15. Purpose & Point of View >> Intent & Purpose

Choice A is incorrect because within the scope of lines 71–76, there is no discussion of scientist expectations.

Choice C is incorrect because there are no statistics in these lines.

Choice D is incorrect because although lines 73–76 say that scientists *named the volcanic hills in this otherworldly setting after distant, lifeless planets*, this part of the passage does not actually list the names given.

The correct answer is B. Lines 71–76 describe the *rift valley* as *bleak, forbidding,* and *otherworldly.* These word choices give the valley the quality of being alien and barren.

16. Purpose & Point of View >> Intent & Purpose

Choice F is incorrect because although line 80 mentions *gashes,* the *main purpose* of the entire paragraph does not concern *gashes* and whether they increase in width.

Choice G is incorrect because although line 82 states that *Earth is still cooling,* it does not support the statement that the Atlantic seafloor has cooled.

Choice J is incorrect because the paragraph does not discuss any volcanoes on dry land, only the underwater volcano in the Atlantic.

The correct answer is H. The beginning of the paragraph states that *at the ridge our own planet gives birth* (lines 78–79). It also explains that *from the gashes has sprung the seafloor underlying all of Atlantic* (lines 80–81). This evidence supports that one main purpose of this paragraph is to explain from where the Atlantic seafloor has issued.

17. Close Reading >> Summarize Key Ideas & Details

Choice A is incorrect because lines 9–11 explain that one ship has *sailed through some of Atlantic's deepest waters, only one thousand miles offshore.* The word *only* indicates that this distance is not very far from the shore.

Choice C is incorrect because although line 6 mentions *a few lonely oceanic islands,* the passage does not indicate that people assume the deepest waters of an ocean are dotted with islands.

Choice D is incorrect because the trenches described in the sixth paragraph are unrelated to where people assume the deepest waters of an ocean are located.

The correct answer is B. Lines 11–13 state that *contrary to what one might guess, Atlantic's deepest waters, like those in other oceans, are along her edges.* Since the narrator says that this fact is against *what one might guess,* she implies that a common assumption is that an ocean's deepest waters are in the middle.

18. Word Meanings & Word Choice >> Interpret Words & Phrases

Choice G is incorrect because *ascertain* means *to find out,* but it does not make sense that the *naval officer found out eight miles… of hemp rope.*

Choice H is incorrect because the officer did not *suggest* eight miles of rope.

Choice J is incorrect because one cannot *compensate* eight miles of hemp rope.

The correct answer is F. In the context of plumbing the Atlantic's depths, *paid out* means *to let out (a line or rope) by slackening*, which is close in meaning to *dispensed*.

19. Close Reading >> Locate

Choice A is incorrect because line 59 compares the heights of the peaks of the Atlantic basin to those of Mount St. Helens, not the surface areas.

Choice B is incorrect because the Himalayas are used to describe how *extensive, rugged,* and *imposing* the *submerged mountain range* is in lines 48–51, but it does not describe its surface area.

Choice C is incorrect because the passage does not mention the Pacific Ocean, much less use it as a comparison to the Atlantic's mountain range.

The correct answer is D. Lines 51–52 state that the mountain range *covers almost as much of earth's surface as the dry land of continents.*

20. Close Reading >> Locate

Choices G, H, and J are incorrect because there is no support in the passage for the *white cover on the peaks* being the result of *volcanic ash, ice,* or *salt deposits.*

The correct answer is F. Lines 55–59 describe the mountain range as *lit only at their peaks by a thin, patchy covering of white, the skeletal remains of tiny microscopic animals.*

21. Arguments >> Identify Claims

Choice B is incorrect because the narrator is using his memory, sending himself back *to open the memories out and see what they had to offer* (lines 28–29). He is not meeting with old acquaintances in person.

Choice C is incorrect because lines 38–45 clearly refer to the narrator's past, not his current experiences.

Choice D is incorrect because the narrator *came on the old and best ways of writing through ignorance and experiment* (lines 46–48), not through methods that other writers taught him.

The correct answer is A. The word *thus* on line 46 means *in this way* and summarizes the many paragraphs that came before it. The main topic of Passage A is about how the narrator *floundered into a word–association process* (line 8) and its beneficial effect on his craft.

22. Close Reading >> Paraphrase

Choices F, H, and J are incorrect because the narrator only mentions beginning writers in the first paragraph, and in this context he does not discuss learning the nature of surprises, using one word as a catalyst for a story, or experimenting one's way to being a good writer.

The correct answer is G. The narrator states in lines 2–4 that *like every beginner,* he *thought you could beat, pummel, and thrash an idea into existence.* This is similar to the idea of forcing an idea into creation.

23. Arguments >> Identify Claims

Choice A is incorrect because Bradbury's writing sessions were not only about understanding John Huff. In lines 44–45, he states that his writing let him sit down *with the long dead and much loved*, which is plural.

Choices B and C are incorrect because there is no support in the passage that the narrator either rejected a word during his writing sessions or selected only words that inspired his fears.

The correct answer is D. Lines 13–14 make it clear that the narrator did this to *bring on an assortment of characters to weigh the word and show me its meaning in my own life*. This information supports the concept of the narrator struggling to find the significance of a particular word.

24. Central Ideas, Themes, and Summaries >> Central Ideas & Themes

Choice F, G, and H are incorrect because they all describe physically looking at objects from the narrator's past, but the seventh paragraph concerns the narrator's *recollections* (memories).

The correct answer is J. Lines 30–32 state that *hardly a day passed when I didn't stroll myself across a recollection of my grandparents' northern Illinois grass*. The narrator then goes on to describe how he tries to remember objects from his childhood there. This evidence closely supports choice J.

25. Close Reading >> Paraphrase

Choice A is incorrect because in one story, the narrator placed John away from Arizona, in Green Town (lines 40–41).

Choices B and D are incorrect because there is no evidence in the passage that the narrator used John in multiple stories, either in Arizona or as a minor character.

The correct answer is C. Lines 39–42 say that the narrator *borrowed* John *and shipped him East to Green Town*. This closely supports the concept that the narrator "moved" John to a town other than the one *in which the real-life John Huff had grown up*.

26. Word Meanings & Word Choice >> Analyze Word & Phrase Choices

Choice F is incorrect because the phrase *that Douglas Spaulding knew of* (line 63) indicates that this paragraph is from the point of view of Douglas, not John Huff.

Choice H is incorrect because although the paragraph does include some details about John Huff that might lead you to characterize him as *reckless*, there is not much support for him being *rebellious* or for the narrator being *most fond* of that aspect of John's character.

Choice J is incorrect because there is no mention in this paragraph of children and adults admiring John.

The correct answer is G. Douglas considers John to be *the only god living in the whole of Green Town* (lines 61–62), which is best expressed as an idolization. The descriptions of John are also exaggerations; this paragraph uses hyperbole to give a glimpse of how Douglas viewed John.

27. Text Structure >> Function

Choice A is incorrect because the image of a cloud covering the sun does not provide supporting evidence that there would be a stormy night.

Choice B is incorrect because line 74 says it had been *such a fine day*, so it is inaccurate to say that John's disappointment was *reflected in his mood all day*.

Choice D is incorrect because the question asks how the image *functions figuratively*, but this answer choice describes what occurred literally.

The correct answer is C. The image on lines 74–76 describes a dramatic and permanent change from a *fine day* to a cloudy one. This supports the expression that the mood of the day was changed dramatically and irreversibly after John said he was moving.

28. Multiple Texts >> Compare Two Texts

Choice F is incorrect because *first person omniscient* narration would provide insight into the thoughts of other characters besides the narrator, but there is no supporting evidence for this in the passages.

Choice G is incorrect because there is little supporting evidence of *satire* or *irony* in either passage. *Satire* uses humor, exaggeration, or ridicule to criticize. *Irony* occurs when the full significance of a character's words or deeds are clear to the audience but not to himself.

Choice H is incorrect because neither passage poses a complex philosophical question. Furthermore, an *allegory* is a work that can be interpreted to reveal a typically moral or political meaning, which is not present in these passages.

The correct answer is J. Both passages lean heavily on sensory details and imaginative description, such as *any decent idea folds up its paws, turns on its back, fixes its eyes on eternity, and dies* (lines 5–6) and *could leap from the sky like a chimpanzee from a vine* (lines 54–55). *Sensory details* are descriptions of sights, sounds, touches, smells, and tastes used to engage the reader's interest.

29. Multiple Texts >> Conclusions Two Texts

Choices A, B, and D are incorrect because *taking notes, forming…characters*, and *outlining…plot* are three writing techniques that do not conform with the writing process that Bradbury described in Passage A.

The correct answer is C. Passage A details a *word–association process* (line 8) that Bradbury used *from the age of twenty–four to thirty–six* (line 30), during which time he came up with a story that involved John Huff, one of the central characters in Passage B. Choice C describes what may have occurred in the word-association process that became the basis of Passage B.

30. Multiple Texts >> Conclusions Two Texts

Choice F is incorrect because the lines given in the question do not concern *surprise*.

Choice H is incorrect because there is no support in the passage or lines provided in the question for the idea that *Bradbury felt such pain* or the concept that reversing *events* would somehow relieve that pain.

Choice J is incorrect because the fact that there really was a John Huff directly contradicts the claim that *Bradbury rarely used his life experiences to create fiction*.

The correct answer is G. The quote in the question supports the claim that Bradbury used his life experiences in his writing because John Huff really existed. It also supports the claim that Bradbury would alter his experiences in the writing process, because he switches which childhood friend moves away from the other.

31. Purpose & Point of View >> Intent & Purpose

Choice B is incorrect because the passage only mentions Patek and Baio filming the ants' defensive maneuvers in line 46, so analyzing filming techniques cannot be the primary purpose of the passage.

Choice C is incorrect because this passage describes the jaws of *Odontomachus bauri* but does not compare them to the jaws of other ant species.

Choice D is incorrect because although the last paragraph speculates the evolution of the escape jump, this is not the primary purpose of the entire passage.

The correct answer is A. The passage as a whole provides an overview of how the jaws in trap-jaw ants operate. The first paragraph introduces trap-jaw ants and their *unique ability to jump with their jaws* (lines 6–7), and the last paragraph speculates how this function evolved.

32. Word Meanings & Word Choice >> Analyze Word & Phrase Choice

Choice F is incorrect because lines 73–75 and lines 86–89 do not contain sarcasm. Furthermore, this passage is mostly technical, not casual or playful.

Choice H is incorrect because lines 73–75 and 86–89 are not combative, which means *eager to fight*.

Choice J is incorrect because these lines do not give personal anecdotes. A *personal anecdote* would be a short and amusing or interesting story involving the narrator.

The correct answer is G. The last sentence of the passage is lighthearted, joking about *banging one's head against the ground*, and lines 73–75 do present a somewhat amusing image of intruders being propelled *head over heels* from the ants' habitat.

33. Word Meanings & Word Choice >> Interpret Words & Phrases

Choices B, C, and D are incorrect because the context of the phrase in question explains that trap–jaw ants store *energy in their jaws to penetrate well–defended prey* (lines 80–82). The verb *penetrate* means *to force through*, which would not apply to prey that attack with lethal bites, travel in groups, or move quickly.

The correct answer is A. It is logical that the ants' jaws can *penetrate* prey that have hard outer shells.

34. Close Reading >> Locate

Choices F and G are incorrect because there is no support in the passage that the jaw's speed comes from easily moving the jaw hinge or steadily firing the jaw's mandibles.

Choice H is incorrect because although line 19 does say the jaw is lightweight, this characteristic is not associated with its speed.

The correct answer is J. Lines 22–25 explain that the speed of the jaws *comes from stored energy produced by the strong but slow muscles of the jaw.*

35. Word Meanings & Word Choices >> Analyze Word & Phrase Choices

Choice A is incorrect because the author's mention of *hot popcorn* in lines 40–41 is figurative, not literal. The ants are not actually becoming hot.

Choice B is incorrect because although the passage does describe how the ants can jump to *a new vantage point from which to relaunch an attack* (lines 63–64), this is not necessarily analogous to grabbing popcorn as it pops.

Choice C is incorrect because the passage's reference to throwing intruders out of their nest in lines 74–75 is not connected to the *popping popcorn* reference.

The correct answer is D. *The insects bounced around in a dizzying frenzy…when biologists or smaller intruders approached them* (lines 43-5) closely supports the claim presented by choice D. Furthermore, this choice includes wording most analogous to *popcorn as it pops*.

36. Close Reading >> Locate

Choice F is incorrect because the paragraph states in lines 82–84 that what evolved out of trap-jaw ants' attempts to bite intruders was the bouncer-defense jump, not the escape jump.

Choices G and J are incorrect because the paragraph does not support the concept that the escape jump came about because of a change in mandible structure or because of positive outcomes in group attacks.

The correct answer is H. The passage states in lines 84–86 that the escape jump *must have arisen from a different, perhaps accidental kind of behavior*, which is best expressed by this choice.

37. Word Meanings & Word Choice >> Interpret Words & Phrases

Choice A is incorrect because it does not make sense to say that the *biomechanics of energy storage* are a *living space* for scientists.

Choice C is incorrect because it would designate scientists to a taxonomic category (a classification of organisms) called *biomechanics of energy storage*. This is illogical because scientists are humans, not biomechanics.

Choice D is incorrect because a science subject cannot have a *local jurisdiction*.

The correct answer is B. It is logical to assume that the *biomechanics of energy storage* would be an *area of expertise* for two *biomechanists* (lines 31–32). *Expertise* means *expert skill or knowledge*.

38. Close Reading >> Locate

Choices F, G, and H are incorrect because their claims are not supported by the passage. There is no evidence of hinges preventing mandibles from snapping together, mandibles with cushioned inner edges, or latch mechanisms preventing the mandibles from closing completely.

The correct answer is J. This choice is supported by lines 49–51: *They also observed that mandibles started to decelerate before they met—possibly to avoid self-inflicted damage.*

39. Close Reading >> Paraphrase

Choice B is incorrect because the escape jump described in lines 53–55 involves the ant releasing its jaws into the ground, not into a predator.

Choice C is incorrect because this maneuver is described as *unpredictable* (line 60).

Choice D is incorrect because with the escape jump, *the ant doesn't seem to go in any particular direction* (lines 58–59), which contradicts the claim that the ant points itself in a determined direction.

The correct answer is A. This answer choice paraphrases lines 63–64, which state that the escape jump can give trap-jaw ants *a new vantage point from which to relaunch an attack.*

40. Close Reading >> Locate

Choices F, G, and J are incorrect because they contradict the description of the bouncer defense detailed in lines 66–70.

The correct answer is H. Lines 66–70 describe the bouncer defense in detail: *one of the ants bangs its jaws against the intruder, which triggers the trap-jaw and propels the interloper…in one direction, out of the nest, and the ant in the other.*

ACT QUESTION INDEX

Category Breakdowns for ACT Reading Test 72-C

MAIN CATEGORY	STANDARD FAMILY	QUESTION NUMBER
Central Ideas, Theme, and Summaries	Central Ideas and Themes	1, 24
	Summarize Key Ideas and Details	2
Close Reading	Paraphrase	3, 5, 22, 25, 39
	Drawing Conclusions	10
	Locate	12, 19, 20, 34, 36, 38, 40
	Summarize Key Ideas and Details	17
Relationships	Comparative Relationships	4, 8, 14
Word Meanings and Word Choice	Interpret Words and Phrases	6, 9, 18, 33, 37
	Analyze Words and Phrase Choices	26, 32, 35
Text Structure	Function	7, 27
Purpose and Point of View	Point of View	11
	Intent and Purpose	13, 15, 16, 31
Arguments	Identify Claims	21, 23
Multiple texts	Compare Two Texts	28, 29, 30

SCIENCE

The Science section, like the other sections, is split into three segments:

- **Science Time Mastery**, which focuses on how to help students fully consider all six passages and answer the 40 questions that go with them in the time span of 35 minutes.

- **Science Test Mastery**, which centers on proven test-taking techniques and strategies that can help students get to the right answer, even if they don't understand some aspect of the passages, graphs, questions, or answer choices.

- **Science Content Mastery**, which provides a guide on the skills and standards are most likely to be tested on the ACT Science test.

When you work with your students on the ACT Science test, consider taking a balanced approach. In each lesson, try helping your students improve in terms of Time Mastery, Test Mastery, and of course Content Mastery.

SCIENCE TIME MASTERY

Time Management Strategies for the ACT Science Test

The Science Sprint

The ACT Science test can be likened to the end of a long marathon.

We call it the *Science Sprint*.

For many students, the Science test is as much an assessment of endurance as it is of skill in scientific reasoning. Science is always the last assessment on the ACT, so students tend to be tired, if not exhausted, going into it.

Some students run hard throughout the ACT marathon only to walk it in at the end. Peers who these students were out-performing the entire time will beat them in the final leg of the race.

Other students, the *sprinters*, have known that the Science test was coming since the very beginning. They are mentally prepared. After the Reading test is complete, they stand up, stretch, and clear their minds. They focus on the task at hand. For these students, the test has only begun. It all comes down to this. Even if they have fallen a little behind their target score, they aren't discouraged. They know they can close the distance in Science.

Of all the ACT sections, Science tends to be the one where the largest score gains (or losses) are made.

It's easier to sprint if you slept well the night before. It's easier to sprint if you had a good breakfast, brought a healthy snack for the break between Math and Reading, and have practiced full-length ACT tests before.

Just getting your students into the *sprinter* mindset can create a small lift in their scores. There is a moment of truth for every student when they could either expend the extra effort and work out a problem or just guess C. Sprinters expend the energy. Walkers Charlie out.

In the end, the ACT is a competitive test. Students are competing for limited spots in colleges and scholarship dollars. Other students across the country are taking the test at the same time, trying to win the same prize. Encourage your students to keep this in mind during the Science test so they can *sprint* to gain the competitive edge.

Students who are prepared for the *Science Sprint* have the best shot at maximizing their scores.

4-7 Minutes Per Passage

Science tests usually include six passages. They used to always have seven passages, but that has changed in the past few years, and there's evidence to suggest that the ACT has made a permanent switch. However, we need to see a few more tests before we can make that pronouncement. Students should plan on spending 4–7 minutes on each passage. There are three major passage types that appear on the ACT, and each type requires a different amount of time. You'll learn more about these passage types later in the Time Mastery section.

DATA REPRESENTATION	4-5 minutes
RESEARCH SUMMARY	5-6 minutes
CONFLICTING VIEWPOINTS	6-7 minutes

Students must be very disciplined about how they spend their time on each passage. Science questions are not sorted by difficulty in the same way the math questions are. The last Science questions might include some gimmes, and the first questions might be the most difficult. Students have to give themselves enough time to consider every question, even if it means *marking and moving* past the last question on a particularly time-consuming passage.

Refer to Science question #37 on page 51 of *Preparing for the ACT 2015-16*.

Most students assume that question #37 is one of the most difficult on the test, since it appears at the end. And many students *do* miss this question. However, it's not because it is difficult, but rather because they run out of time.

Actually, question #37 is arguably the easiest question on the entire ACT Science test. The text above Figure 2 states that temperature is read every five seconds. Since there are 60 seconds in a minute, all students must do is divide 60 by five to find that the sensor took 12 readings per minute.

When you introduce the concept of pacing to your students, show them this question to make the point that even the last passage has questions that can be answered if students give themselves enough time.

Below is the basic pacing summary for Science.

ACT SCIENCE
40 Questions
6 Passages
35 Minutes
Pace: 4-7 minutes per passage

Data Representation

Data representation passages provide students with a valuable opportunity to pick up time and points. Unlike research summaries and conflicting viewpoints passages, data representation questions are almost entirely dependent upon tables and graphs.

Students can usually spot a data representation passage by noticing that the text does not have italicized headers (e.g., *Study 1*, *Experiment 2*, etc.). Furthermore, data representations focus on presenting data and tend to be unconcerned tend to be unconcerned with explaining the methods used to obtain the data..

Another giveaway of a data representation is the number of questions that accompany the passage. On Science tests with six passages, the two data representation passages have the shortest question sets, with six questions each. On Science tests with seven passages, there are three data representation passages with five questions each (also the shortest question sets).

The sequence in which data representation passages appear is relatively random, which means that all of them could be stacked at the end of the test. This is part of the reason why it is so important for students to stay disciplined with their pace and give themselves sufficient time for each question.

Refer to Science Passage III on pages 44–45 of *Preparing for the ACT 2015-16*.

Passage III is an excellent example of a data representation. The passage makes no mention of the experimental methods that were used to collect the data. Rather, the text serves as a glorified key to the graphs. Furthermore, this test has six passages, and this particular passage has six questions. There are no italicized text headers.

On a data representation such as this, students can safely *skip* the text and go straight to reading the graphs before finally settling on answering the questions. Students will find that they can usually answer all or all but one of the questions in a data representation passage without any reference to the text.

Refer to Science question #15 on page 45 of *Preparing for the ACT 2015-16*.

Question #15 is a classic example of a data representation question. Students only need to reference the figure to find their answer. Once they find the *x*-axis point that corresponds to 8,000 years, they can find the height of the solar radiation line on the *y*-axis, and there's the answer. Not only is the text unhelpful in this situation, it can only serve to slow the student down.

Refer to Science question #20 on page 45 of *Preparing for the ACT 2015–16*.

Question #20 breaks the rule of data representation passages; the *text* helps answer the question. The first sentence in the text allows two answers to be eliminated immediately. The format of the question and its answers (and how different they are compared to the rest of the items) should be a strong clue to students that they need to shift gears and look for information beyond what they find in the graphs.

Refer to Passage IV on pages 46-47 of *Preparing for the ACT 2015-16*.

Check Your Understanding: What type of passage is Passage IV?

_____

_____

What features tell you this is the case?

_____

_____

Answer the questions without reading the text. After you finish, review the text. Were there any questions in this passage where the text would have helped your students?

_____

_____

Research Summaries

Research summary passages strike a middle ground between the graph-obsessed *data representation* passages and the text-focused *conflicting viewpoints* passages.

There are always three research summaries on any ACT Science test.

The usual tell on a research summary is the italicized headers above the text. It typically (but not always) describes a series of experiments or studies. The questions tend to focus on experimental design and scientific investigation.

When the Science test is comprised of seven passages, each research summary has six questions. When the Science test is made up of six passages, the research summaries each have seven questions, just like the conflicting viewpoints passage.

Students must be able to understand the rationale behind experiments and think scientifically in order to succeed on research summary passages. Students should expect to use the text in conjunction with the graphs and tables in order to answer the questions.

When students first encounter a research summary, they should focus their efforts on *understanding* the experiment. They do not need to remember facts or details about the experiment; this is an open-book test, so memorization is unnecessary. However, students should be able to answer the following questions after they finish reading the passage, graphs, and tables:

- What happened in the experiment series?

- What were the scientists trying to prove or understand?

- What changed from experiment to experiment?

- How did those major changes help the scientists understand something?

This very basic, functional understanding of the passage is necessary for students to answer research summary questions. This fact is what separates research summaries from their simpler *data representation* cousins.

Consider asking students these questions after each research summary mini-test you provide. Students who internalize the above questions are more likely to answer research summary questions quickly and correctly.

Refer to Science Passage I on pages 40-41 of *Preparing for the ACT 2015-16.*

Passage I is an example of a research summary. It has italicized headers, describes a series of studies, and does not describe conflicting points of view. Because this Science test has six passages, this research summary has seven questions. All of these clues point to the fact that the test begins with a research summary passage. The text and the graphs are both necessary to answer the questions.

Refer to Science question #7 on page 41 of *Preparing for the ACT 2015-16.*

Question #7 is a typical research summary question. To answer correctly, students must be able to identify the essential features of each study as described in the text. They must also be able to infer that the 5% SY medium represents a *reduced calorie diet*, which for some students may not be immediately apparent.

Even students who did not fully understand the experiments as they read can answer this question by comparing the studies. However, those students who build an understanding as they read will think more sharply and move more quickly.

One of the simplest ways to improve student comprehension is to ask your students the questions listed above and scaffolding with simpler comprehension questions when they miss. Once students have considered and understood enough experiments, they will develop the ability to do so without scaffolding.

Refer to Science Passage V and question #27 on pages 48-49 of *Preparing for the ACT 2015-16.*

Check Your Understanding:

What clues could you point out to your students to help them categorize Passage V?

_____

_____

Of the four questions above, which is most important for students to have paid attention to in order to be able to answer question #27?

_____

_____

Conflicting Viewpoints

Each ACT Science test contains one, and only one, conflicting viewpoints passage. In this passage type, either multiple theories or hypotheses are presented, or multiple scientists disagree on a topic. While it used to be the case that just two points of view tended to be explored, in recent years passages featuring three and four viewpoints have been predominant. As a matter of fact, our analysis of the 10 most recently released ACT Science tests shows the average number of points of view discussed in the conflicting viewpoints passage to be 3.5, with more than half of the passages featuring 4 points of view and only one passage including just two points of view.

The conflicting viewpoints passage tends to follow a definite structure. First, an introduction (typically 1–3 paragraphs) provides background information relevant to all points of view discussed. Then, different points of view follow, each one separated by an italicized header.

This passage is completely different from the other ACT Science passages, so much so that students should always save it for last, no matter when they encounter it. The conflicting viewpoints passage is where students are likely to run into time trouble.

The conflicting viewpoints passage can appear anywhere in the test, from Passage I to Passage VI (or VII).

Students should treat this passage like an ACT Reading passage, reading through the text and gaining a basic understanding of what is being discussed *before* attempting the questions.

As with research summaries, students don't need to memorize any facts (since it's an open-book test), but they do need to glean a basic comprehension of what is being discussed. Particularly, students should be able to answer these basic questions:

- What is known and indisputable? (In other words, what's the five-second summary of the intro?)

- What is the major difference between the points of view?

- Are there any similarities between the points of view?

- Why do the scientists disagree?

Students should try to understand as much as they can during the read-through, but they should not be discouraged if they don't comprehend everything the first time. The maxim is that the questions in conflicting viewpoints are always easier than the passage. Understanding the nuances of the different points of view can be extremely challenging, but this nuanced understanding is unnecessary to answer the questions correctly.

We recommend that you give your students several conflicting viewpoints mini-tests and ask them the above questions after they read each passage. By focusing their attention on these elements, you can improve their retention and prepare them for the questions that follow.

Refer to Science Passage II on page 42 of *Preparing for the ACT 2015-16.*

Passage II is the conflicting viewpoints passage in this ACT test. This passage involves three points of view. Students should not despair, however, if their conflicting viewpoints passage includes three or even four points of view. In fact, the more points of view, the simpler and more clearly differentiated they tend to be.

The passage follows the basic format of all conflicting viewpoints passages.

Refer to Science question #11 on page 43 of *Preparing for the ACT 2015-16.*

Question #11 is typical of the more challenging questions that appear in this passage type. To answer it correctly, students must understand the major differences between each hypothesis (what happens with lipid storage) and integrate that with the new information provided in the question.

Students who skip the text will be challenged to juggle understanding the statement made in the question while also attempting to find the relevant evidence in the passage.

Passage Difficulty Distribution

While it tends to be the case with the ACT Science test that the first two passages are somewhat simpler than the final two passages, it's also true that the increase in difficulty from passage to passage is all but indiscernible for most students. Some students are stronger in biology or chemistry, and it is these differences that play a larger role in the perceived difficulty of any one passage.

More noticeable is the increase in difficulty *within* each passage. The first few questions of each passage tend to be easier than the last two. Students might notice that each set of questions seems to "reset" in terms of difficulty at the start of each passage, then gradually become more difficult up to the last question in the set. (More detail on this in the next chapter.)

In all cases, there will be at least one or two "gimme" questions in each passage, including the last passage. These gimme questions tend to be among the first four questions in each set.

With regard to pacing, students should aim to give themselves time to consider every single question. They have to give themselves the opportunity to succeed.

It is somewhat in vogue in test prep circles to coach students to try fewer passages than all six or seven. The "logic" behind this advice is that if students spend more time on fewer passages, they are more likely to correctly answer the questions they *do* consider.

However, if you coach students to skip one or more passages, you're coaching them to reduce the number of chances they have to reach their points goal.

If you are concerned about your students running out of time, it's a far better idea to teach them how to differentiate between passage types so they can use effective strategies on each passage. For instance, if they can recognize a data representation passage, they'll save time by skipping the text and going straight to the questions. Likewise, if they can tell the next passage is conflicting viewpoints, they know to save it for last so that their pacing stays on track.

Every passage has easy and difficult questions.

Difficulty Distribution Within Passages

On average, within each ACT Science passage, question difficulty noticeably increases from beginning to end. The simpler questions tend to be at the front of each set, and the more difficult questions tend toward the back.

For this reason, if students are following your pacing guidelines and run out of time on the last question of a passage, it's a far better idea to *mark and move* than to allow that final question to eat up time. Students should never risk the opportunity to make it to the end of the test and consider every question. The first question of the last passage is likely to be easier than the last question of the first passage.

Below is our analysis of the percentage of questions answered correctly in five-question, six-question, and seven-question passages. You'll notice in each case that students have an easier time with earlier questions than with later ones.

5-QUESTION PASSAGES	
1	45%
2	41%
3	35%
4	38%
5	29%

6-QUESTION PASSAGES	
1	47%
2	47%
3	39%
4	34%
5	31%
6	31%

7-QUESTION PASSAGES	
1	39%
2	33%
3	27%
4	28%
5	28%
6	31%
7	25%

Science Time Management Heat Map

Below is what we call a "heat map" showing the performance of over 20,000 students on an ACT Science test. This is a powerful tool for understanding your students' level of time mastery.

Each vertical bar represents one of the 40 questions on the test. A light shade means that most of the students answered the question correctly. A darker shade means that fewer students answered right. When the color is completely black, it means that students would have done better on that item if they had just blindly guessed.

We use heat maps to understand at a glance how students in a class are handling time management.

On the ACT Math test, for example, we expect the heat map to get darker and darker as we read from left to right. There is a very clear reason for this: the questions become more and more complex.

On the Science test, however, if students are managing their time correctly, there should be only a very minor shift in color from left to right. The stronger the shift, the more likely it is that students failed to manage their time and were rushing at the end of the assessment. We call this characteristic of the graph *color shift*. If you see a strong color shift with your students, you should work with them on their *pace*. By pace we mean your students developing the discipline to spend only a certain amount of time on a given section of the test (such as 4–7 minutes per passage, including questions, in Science).

This graphic tells us that the typical class of students has a relatively strong color shift in Science. In the absence of any specific data about your students, you should assume they will run out of time before they complete the last passage (prompting them to blindly guess at the end), and you should work with them on correctly rationing time for each passage to avoid this outcome.

It should be noted here that students are a relatively bad judge of whether they felt rushed toward the end of the test. It's hard for anyone to give their all on a test and also analyze on the level of metacognition. For this reason, we recommend using the hard data, the color shift, rather than surveying students about whether or not they felt like they had enough time.

The Science test tends to be the most heavily impacted by color shift because students are often exhausted by the time they reach this final section of the ACT.

Also look for *contrast* when reading a time management heat map. There should be strong contrast in the colors between any two questions. The reason for this is that students who are managing their time, and who are quickly moving past confusing questions to retain their time, are able to identify the easy questions sprinkled throughout the test and answer them correctly. Students who are unable to cherry-pick the easiest questions get rushed and guess on questions they should know how to solve. A class of students who are failing to cherry-pick (in other words, manage their time on individual questions) will have a heat map without much contrast. Each question will have a similar color, one to the next. Good time managers have very bright spots scattered throughout the test, even toward the end.

This graphic tells us that a typical group of students is not able to cherry-pick obviously easy questions toward the end of the test. The last few questions on this test, particularly, should look relatively bright when students attain a high degree of competence in time management.

MasteryPrep provides a very affordable practice testing service that can give you these pre-made heat maps specific to your students. You can also accomplish similar insights by gathering your student practice test data, looking at the percentage of students who correctly answered each question, and laying this information out in a spreadsheet. Use Excel's "Conditional Formatting/Color Scales" feature to visualize the data in a way similar to the graphic we have provided.

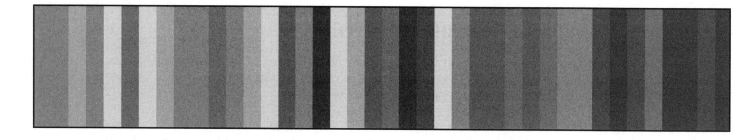

Science Passage Categories

The major subjects touched upon in the ACT Science test include the following:

- Biology
- Chemistry
- Earth/Space sciences
- Physics

Earth/Space sciences can include geology, astronomy, and meteorology.

Passage topics are selected in such a way that each major subject appears at least once but no more than twice.

The variety of topics that can appear on any one Science test is yet another reason why students must be disciplined about pacing. Just because the first two passages were difficult and unfamiliar doesn't mean that the next one won't be about the student's favorite science subject.

Below is a list of the specific topics that can be included in the Science test. Students who are familiar with these topics will find it easier to understand the Science passages and answer questions correctly. These topics appear in the ACT College Readiness Standards. We have sorted them according to the four major categories above. Some of these topics are much more important than others. See masteryprep.com/decode/resources for our full analysis.

Biology	Chemistry	Physics	Earth/Space Sciences
• Animal behavior • Animal development and growth • Body systems • Cell structure and processes • Ecology • Evolution • Genetics • Homeostasis • Life cycles • Molecular basis of heredity • Origin of life • Photosynthesis • Plant development, growth, structure • Populations • Taxonomy	• Chemical bonding, equations, nomenclature, reactions • Elements, compounds, mixtures • Periodic table • Properties of solutions • States, classes, and properties of matter	• Atomic structure • Force and motion • Gravitation • Kinetic and potential energy • Magnetism • Momentum • Waves • Sound and light • Heat and work • Electrical circuits	• Earthquakes and volcanoes • Earth's atmosphere • Earth's resources • Fossils and geological time • Geochemical cycles • Groundwater • Lakes, rivers, and oceans • Mass movements • Plate tectonics • Rocks and minerals • Solar system • Stars, galaxies, and the universe • Water cycle • Weather and climate • Weathering and erosion

Brain Going Numb?

This strategy has an important place in a student's approach to the ACT Reading test, and it becomes even more relevant during the Science test. The closer students come to the end of the ACT, the more mental exhaustion is likely to cause them to blank out or disengage.

The Science test is full of potential triggers for spacing out: unfamiliar terms, complex sentences, and high-level reasoning questions. Students must be prepared for these moments and have a coping mechanism ready. Otherwise, they risk wasting a minute or more staring blankly at a question or off into space.

A simple, effective coping mechanism for blanking out on a Science question is to find something in the text or passage that is referenced by the question. For example, if the question mentions Figure 1, students should force themselves to look at Figure 1. If the question mentions DNA, students must find where DNA appears in the relevant graph.

Likewise, if students find themselves blanking out as they read through the passage text or graphs, they should immediately move to the questions and begin working the test from that angle.

The act of *doing something* causes students to get back on track and continue making progress.

When you need to wake someone up, you nudge them. When you need your brain to wake up, you give it a nudge as well. When students feel like they have spaced out, they must *do something* to continue and regain focus.

Pair Down

The *pair down* strategy appears in both our Reading and Science sections, and it's equally important in both. With roughly five or six minutes to spend on each passage in the Science test, there is no time to investigate every possible answer choice. Students must use their understanding of the passage and its graphs to quickly narrow down to a *pair* of potentially viable answer choices they can explore.

Refer to Science question #3 on page 41 of *Preparing for the ACT 2015-16.*

Question #3 asks students to compare Study 1 to Study 2 and identify a crucial difference. This question is challenging first because the answer choices comprise 10 lines of text. For some students, this alone is intimidating. Secondly, the answer choices present two topics that apparently require investigation: the gender of the fruit flies and the sugar concentration of the SY medium.

If students are willing to trust their memory, however, they can quickly narrow down to just one line of investigation. In order to answer the previous question, #2, students had to ascertain that the experiment involved *female* fruit flies. If they remember this going into question #3, they can immediately *pair down* by eliminating choices A and B out of hand.

The trick here is for students to trust their instincts and resist the urge to spend a ton of time verifying this elimination. The truth is, if they make an incorrect elimination on the front end, they will soon figure it out because the remaining two choices they investigate won't work. Students should not be anxious about moving quickly; they can always correct their mistakes.

Once choices A and B are eliminated, students are faced with a radically simpler question: was the sugar content of the SY medium higher or lower going from Study 1 to Study 2?

Refer to Science question #36 on page 51 of *Preparing for the ACT 2015-16.*

In question #36, two answer choices can be rapidly eliminated while two choices require a bit of squinting in the general direction of Figure 1.

Check Your Understanding: How should your students apply *pair down* to quickly focus on the two potentially viable answer choices in question #36?

_____

_____

_____

_____

Answer Awareness

Some Science questions sound more difficult than they really are. Until you look at the answer choices, you can't be sure what the question is asking you to do.

Refer to Science question #4 on page 41 of *Preparing for the ACT 2015-16*.

Question #4 is asking us to do something quite challenging, something not even the best biologists can do accurately, even armed with molecular models and supercomputers: predict the average lifespan of an organism consuming a new diet.

If students take the question at face value, they'll immediately launch into doing work that is entirely unnecessary. They'll find the *Strain X* rows in Table 1 and see that 12% lies between 10% and 15% on the chart. They will calculate that 12% is two-fifths of the difference between 10% and 15%, then multiply this fraction by the difference between 58.6 and 55.6, which gives them 1.2. Finally, they'll subtract *that* from the 10% lifespan and arrive at their prediction: 57.4 days. Unfortunately, in spite of so much clever mathematical reasoning, this number is not even accurate because biological processes do not typically follow direct proportionality. However, whether the prediction of 57.4 days is accurate or not is entirely beside the point.

In fact, none of the above calculations are necessary. After all, this is not the Math test. At the outset, students could realize that a 12% SY medium would generate a lifespan between those of 10% and 15%. Based on Table 1, this lifespan would fall between 58.6 and 55.6 days. Choice G spells out what students are looking for word for word, so no further calculation is necessary.

If students are aware of their answer choices, they can save time and avoid frustration.

Refer to Science question #19 on page 45 of *Preparing for the ACT 2015-16*.

Question #19 asks for the average distance between crests in the dotted line in Figure 1. Taken literally, students would need to estimate the distance between each crest, add them all up, and then divide by the number of cycles to find the correct answer.

Check Your Understanding: *How would you teach your students to apply the* answer awareness *strategy in order to radically simplify question #19?*

_____

_____

_____

_____

Open-Book Tests

The ACT Science test is an open-book test. 85–90% of the Science questions can be answered using only the information provided in the passages.

At face value, an open-book test should be easier than a closed-book test in all respects and not require any special preparation. In actual practice, however, students who do not have much experience with open-book tests will be at a major disadvantage to students who do.

For one, facts from charts, graphs, and texts being readily accessible means that students need only focus on comprehending certain aspects of the information. The passage is there as an assistant. But just like how one has to practice a bit to use an iPhone's Siri to its full potential, students also must practice before they can use an open-book passage to *its* full potential.

Until students have practiced with many open-book tests, they will still try to retain information they don't need. Furthermore, they will miss concepts that might not be important for a declarative knowledge, retention-focused closed-book test, but that make all the difference in a reasoning-focused, open-book one.

Students who are conversant with open-book tests don't pause their reading if they realize they missed a minor detail. They *do* pause and investigate when they find themselves not comprehending the big picture.

Students who only have experience with closed-book tests tend to do the opposite.

Consider the value of introducing a number of timed, reasoning-focused, open-book science tests to your class throughout the year. Not only will this help your students prepare for the ACT, but it will also expose your students to a different method of assessment and enhance their comprehension of the materials.

Science Mini-Test Coaching

Refer to page 35 of this book for general information about mini-tests.

While mini-tests can help students improve their pacing habits on every section of the ACT, mini-tests are most effective in boosting outcomes on the Reading and Science tests.

A mini-test in Science is one passage and the 5–7 questions that come with it.

Before starting the timer on the mini-test, remind students about their pacing strategy. Ask them to identify what type of passage the mini-test is. Assign a time limit based on the passage type:

DATA REPRESENTATION	4 minutes, 30 seconds
RESEARCH SUMMARY	5 minutes, 30 seconds
CONFLICTING VIEWPOINTS	6 minutes, 30 seconds

Give your students verbal cues every couple minutes to remind them about the time they have remaining.

Once the mini-test is complete, immediately call out the answers, discuss the passage, and explain any difficult questions that they are curious about. If students have a concern about a particular aspect of one question, consider taking the time to explain the question in full, from beginning to end, for the benefit of all students instead of just answering the specifics asked about.

Students will glean much benefit from practicing Science tests. It takes an enormous amount of practice just to get students to the point where they have seen most graph types and been exposed to most of the topics that the ACT tests on. Familiarity with the format can go a long way toward boosting scores.

As you administer more and more mini-tests, reduce and then eventually eliminate the verbal cues. Students who are able to work through the mini-tests on pace without any prompts will usually be able to get through the whole Science test with time to spare.

If the majority of your students have serious pacing issues, you may want to consider gradually expanding the length of the mini-tests to two or even three passages (with commensurate time) so that students get used to managing time over a longer period. That said, most students can gain sufficient benefit by working on the basis of one passage at time.

Use mini-tests to help your students develop a strong sense of pace on the ACT Science test.

Science Mini-Tests

What follows are five Science mini-tests. You are permitted to photocopy these mini-tests and provide them to your students.

Printable PDFs of these mini-tests with answer keys and explanations, as well as links to four full-length ACT tests that you can use as fodder for additional mini-tests are available at this address: masteryprep.com/decode/resources.

Passage I

A group of researchers attempted to develop a new technique for vertical farming by constructing three artificially heated and humidified chambers. The researchers found the weekly average air temperature in Celsius (°C) and the weekly average humidity in percent water vapor in each of the three chambers. The results for the first six weeks of their measurements are given in Table 1 and Table 2.

Table 1			
	Weekly average air temperature (°C)		
Week	Chamber 1	Chamber 2	Chamber 3
1	20.01	19.12	18.87
2	20.13	19.13	18.85
3	20.36	19.13	18.88
4	20.68	19.15	18.92
5	20.95	19.22	18.98
6	21.02	19.20	19.03

Table 2			
	Weekly average humidity (%)		
Week	Chamber 1	Chamber 2	Chamber 3
1	84%	83%	78%
2	84%	82%	77%
3	85%	81%	76%
4	86%	82%	76%
5	88%	80%	78%
6	87%	79%	79%

Attempts: _____ Correct: _____

1. The highest weekly average humidity recorded during the first six weeks of the study was:

   A. 86%
   B. 87%
   C. 88%
   D. 89%

2. What was the average air temperature in the three chambers in Week 4?

   F. 18.15
   G. 18.59
   H. 19.58
   J. 20.69

3. Which of the following statements best describes the relative conditions of the three chambers in the first six weeks of the study?

   A. Chamber 1 had high average air temperature and high average humidity, Chamber 2 had low average air temperature and low average humidity, and Chamber 3 had medium average air temperature and medium average humidity.
   B. Chamber 1 had low average air temperature and medium average humidity, Chamber 2 had medium average air temperature and low average humidity, and Chamber 3 had high average air temperature and high average humidity.
   C. Chamber 1 had high average air temperature and low average humidity, Chamber 2 had medium average air temperature and high average humidity, and Chamber 3 had low average air temperature and medium average humidity.
   D. Chamber 1 had high average air temperature and high average humidity, Chamber 2 had medium average air temperature and medium average humidity, and Chamber 3 had low average air temperature and low average humidity.

GO ON TO THE NEXT PAGE

4. Which of the following statements best describes the change in weekly average air temperature in Chamber 2?

F. The weekly average air temperature increased or stayed the same consistently from Week 1 to Week 6.

G. The weekly average air temperature decreased from Week 1 to Week 3 and increased or stayed the same from Week 3 to Week 6.

H. The weekly average air temperature increased or stayed the same from Week 1 to Week 5, and the weekly average air temperature decreased from Week 5 to Week 6.

J. The weekly average air temperature decreased or stayed the same from Week 1 to Week 4 and increased from Week 4 to Week 6.

5. Suppose the rate of growth of crops in each of the vertical farming chambers is determined by either weekly average air temperature, weekly average humidity, or both. If the growth rate in Chamber 2 greatly exceeds the growth rate of Chambers 1 and 3, which of the following conclusions would be justified?

A. High weekly average air temperature and high weekly average humidity are ideal for plant life growth rate.

B. Medium weekly average air temperature and medium weekly average humidity are ideal for plant life growth rate.

C. Low weekly average air temperature and low weekly average humidity are ideal for plant life growth rate.

D. None of the above conclusions can be justified.

END OF MINI-TEST ONE
STOP! DO NOT GO ON TO THE NEXT PAGE
UNTIL TOLD TO DO SO.

Mini-Test 2

Passage II

Solar panels are assemblies of connected photovoltaic cells that harness solar energy to produce electricity. Photovoltaic cells can produce electricity from a range of light frequencies at varying efficiencies; however, current solar panel technology is incapable of capturing the entire solar range. Scientists have determined that illuminating photovoltaic cells with monochromatic light enables higher efficiency, but they have yet to develop the technology necessary to split light into its various wavelength ranges to make use of this higher efficiency.

Experiment 1

Photovoltaic cells show a decrease in efficiency at increased temperatures. A group of scientists wanted to determine which frequency of light might produce the best efficiency in photovoltaic cells and how temperature might affect this efficiency. The results of their experiment are given in Table 1.

Experiment 2

With mathematical models, the same group of scientists attempted to project the efficiencies of photovoltaic cells coupled with techniques that allowed for the splitting of wavelength ranges. They projected uniform increases in efficiencies for all frequencies, but they noted the continued decrease in efficiency at increased temperatures. The theoretical results of their models are given in Table 2.

Table 1			
Temp. (°C)	Photovoltaic cell efficiency (%)		
	Frequency 1	Frequency 2	Frequency 3
25	20.2%	20.0%	20.4%
26	19.7%	19.7%	19.7%
27	19.2%	19.4%	19.0%
28	18.7%	19.1%	18.3%
29	18.2%	18.8%	17.6%

Table 2			
Temp. (°C)	Theoretical photovoltaic cell efficiency w/ wavelength splitting (%)		
	Frequency 1	Frequency 2	Frequency 3
25	47.2%	45.0%	50.4%
26	46.1%	44.3%	48.6%
27	45.0%	43.6%	46.8%
28	43.9%	42.9%	45.0%
29	42.8%	42.2%	43.2%

6. Do the results from Experiment 1 support the claim that photovoltaic cells capturing different frequencies function at varying efficiencies with changes in temperature?

   F. Yes, because as temperature increases, so does efficiency.
   G. Yes, because as temperature increases, efficiency decreases.
   H. No, because there is no uniform change in efficiency as related to temperature.
   J. No, because all photovoltaic cells function at the same efficiency regardless of frequency.

7. Based on the results from Experiment 1, photovoltaic cells capturing which frequency of light would function best in environments that keep the cell temperatures at roughly 29°C?

   A. Frequency 1
   B. Frequency 2
   C. Frequency 3
   D. All frequencies will function the same.

GO ON TO THE NEXT PAGE

8. Based on the results from Experiment 1, photovoltaic cells capturing which frequency of light would function best in environments that keep the cell temperatures at roughly 26°C?

   F. Frequency 1
   G. Frequency 2
   H. Frequency 3
   J. All frequencies will function the same.

9. One of the scientists suggests that he can build a cooling system for the theoretical photovoltaic cells in Experiment 2, which will keep the cells 1°C cooler than normal but decrease their efficiency by 1%. The theoretical photovoltaic cells capturing which frequencies, if any, would benefit from this cooling system?

   A. Frequencies 1 and 2
   B. Frequencies 1 and 3
   C. Frequencies 2 and 3
   D. None of the theoretical photovoltaic cells would benefit.

10. In Experiment 1, which of the following variables is held constant?

    F. The temperature of the environment
    G. The amount of sunlight shone on the photovoltaic cells
    H. The photovoltaic cells used
    J. The frequency of light captured by the photovoltaic cells

11. Suppose the scientists note the temperature sensitivity of the photovoltaic cells in both experiments, defining sensitivity as the amount of change in efficiency as temperature increases. Which of the following best describes the changes in efficiency and temperature sensitivity of the photovoltaic cells in Experiment 1 to the theoretical photovoltaic cells with wavelength splitting in Experiment 2?

    A. Efficiency increases from Experiment 1 to Experiment 2, and sensitivity to temperature increases from Experiment 1 to Experiment 2.
    B. Efficiency increases from Experiment 1 to Experiment 2, but sensitivity to temperature decreases from Experiment 1 to Experiment 2.
    C. Efficiency decreases from Experiment 1 to Experiment 2, and sensitivity to temperature decreases from Experiment 1 to Experiment 2.
    D. Efficiency decreases from Experiment 1 to Experiment 2, but sensitivity to temperature increases from Experiment 1 to Experiment 2.

END OF MINI-TEST TWO
STOP! DO NOT GO ON TO THE NEXT PAGE
UNTIL TOLD TO DO SO.

Passage III

Stars begin their lives composed of roughly 70% hydrogen. Nuclear fusion of hydrogen atoms at the cores of stars drives the majority of energy and luminosity. After the majority of hydrogen has been exhausted from the star's core, the star enters into the red giant branch and begins the fusion of hydrogen in the surrounding shell, as well as the fusion of helium in its core. The hydrogen in the surrounding shell is quickly exhausted, as is the helium in the core, and near the end of the star's life, it begins to fuse hydrogen and then helium in its outermost shell until all of it is exhausted. The figure below shows the percentage of hydrogen present in a star over the course of its life cycle.

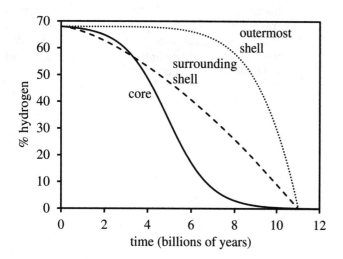

12. Based on the figure, the percentage of hydrogen in the surrounding shell after 8 billion years will be closest to which of the following:

    F. 30%
    G. 35%
    H. 40%
    J. 45%

13. Based on the figure, at how many billions of years will there be roughly 0% hydrogen remaining in the core?

    A. Between 7 and 8
    B. Between 8 and 9
    C. Between 9 and 10
    D. Between 10 and 11

14. After the fusion of hydrogen is exhausted in the core and fusion of hydrogen begins in the surrounding shell, the fusion of helium begins in the core. Which of the following is most likely true about the percentage of helium in the core as time increases?

    F. The percentage of helium decreases over time.
    G. The percentage of helium increases over time.
    H. The percentage of helium does not change over time.
    J. The percentage of helium over time cannot be determined.

GO ON TO THE NEXT PAGE

15. A star's core is approximately 28% helium at the beginning of its lifetime. A scientist theorizes that the amount of helium present begins to drop only after the percentage of hydrogen present in the core drops below 20%. According to this theory, which of the following is the best graphical representation of the percentage of helium over time?

A.

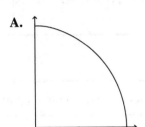

B.

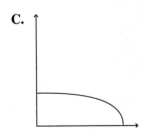

C.

D.

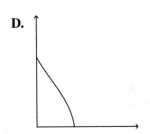

16. After 11 billion years, the star will shed nearly all of its mass and become a white dwarf, surviving for billions of years before fading out. Which of the following most likely catalyzes the transition from red giant to white dwarf?

F. The exhaustion of hydrogen in the core

G. The exhaustion of hydrogen and helium in the core

H. The exhaustion of hydrogen in the core and the exhaustion of helium in the shells

J. The exhaustion of hydrogen in the shells and the exhaustion of helium in the shells and core

END OF MINI-TEST THREE
STOP! DO NOT GO ON TO THE NEXT PAGE
UNTIL TOLD TO DO SO.

Passage IV

Human blood cells allow for the influx and efflux of H_2O molecules through semipermeable membranes. Osmotic pressure is the phenomenon that drives this influx and efflux of water. Depending on the concentration of solutes in the blood plasma, it may be hypertonic, isotonic, or hypotonic when compared to the cells themselves.

The plasma is *hypertonic* when it has a higher concentration of solute present outside of the cell than within the cell. Water flows out of the cell as it attempts to achieve homeostasis. This causes the cell to shrink and shrivel.

The plasma is *isotonic* when it has the same concentration of solute present both within the cell and outside it. This causes the cell to remain in equilibrium, or homeostasis, with water flowing both into and out of the cell evenly.

The plasma is *hypotonic* when it has a lower concentration of a solute present outside the cell than within the cell. Water flows into the cell as it attempts to achieve homeostasis. This causes the cell to bloat and burst.

A group of scientists is attempting to create synthetic plasma for hospital patients in need of transfusions. They realize a certain solute is key in the development of this synthetic plasma and use an initial set of solutions to approximate the amount of solute necessary for blood cells to achieve homeostasis. The composition of the four solutions (A, B, C, and D) in ppm (parts per million) are found in Table 1.

Table 1	
Solution	Solute concentration (ppm)
Solution A	980
Solution B	1,150
Solution C	1,245
Solution D	1,350

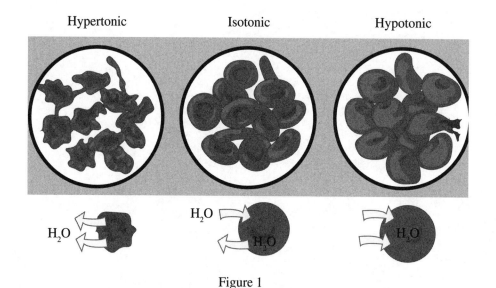

Figure 1

GO ON TO THE NEXT PAGE

17. If a cell is placed within a hypertonic solution, it will shrink and shrivel because:

A. water flows into the cell.
B. water flows out of the cell.
C. solutes flow out of the cell.
D. solutes flow into the cell.

18. If a cell is placed in an isotonic solution, it will remain in homeostasis because:

F. water flows into and out of the cell.
G. solutes flow into and out of the cell.
H. solutes flow into the cell, and water flows out of the cell.
J. solutes flow out of the cell, and water flows into the cell.

19. Which of the following solutions will best maintain homeostasis for a blood cell with a solute concentration of 1,250 ppm?

A. Solution A
B. Solution B
C. Solution C
D. Solution D

20. If a blood cell with a solute concentration of 1,250 ppm is placed within Solution D, the plasma will be which type of tonicity compared to the cell, and how will this affect the cell?

F. Hypertonic; it will shrink and shrivel.
G. Hypertonic; it will bloat and burst.
H. Isotonic; it will remain in homeostasis.
J. Hypotonic; it will bloat and burst.

21. If a blood cell with a solute concentration of 1,250 ppm is placed within Solution B, which type of tonicity will occur, and how will this affect the cell?

A. Hypertonic; it will shrink and shrivel.
B. Hypertonic; it will bloat and burst.
C. Isotonic; it will remain in homeostasis.
D. Hypotonic; it will bloat and burst.

22. Suppose one of the scientists has a blood sample from a patient but only needs a sample of the plasma. She places the blood sample in one side of a U-shaped tube, separated from the other side of the tube with a semipermeable membrane through which the blood cells cannot pass. She uses a device to produce slight pressure on the filled side of the tube and watches the plasma flow through the semipermeable membrane to the other side, which increases the concentration of the remaining plasma. This process caused the remaining plasma in the blood sample to be which type of tonicity compared to the blood cells?

F. Hypertonic
G. Hypotonic
H. Isotonic
J. The type of tonicity cannot be determined.

END OF MINI-TEST FOUR
STOP! DO NOT GO ON TO THE NEXT PAGE
UNTIL TOLD TO DO SO.

Mini-Test 5

Passage V

A particular area's soil horizons can be broken down into three distinct layers: permeable topsoil, highly plastic clay, and limestone bedrock. A company engineer is attempting to collect calcium carbonate, $CaCO_3$, from the area in order to produce a range of industrial materials. He projects calcium carbonate to be present in varying levels throughout the various soil horizons, as shown below in Table 1. In order to ensure stable mining conditions, he additionally collects information on the average water capacity of the various soil horizons, as shown in Table 2.

Table 1	
Soil texture	% $CaCO_3$
permeable topsoil	5%
highly plastic clay	32%
limestone bedrock	88%

Table 2	
Soil texture	Water capacity (in^3/ft^3)
permeable topsoil	0.9
highly plastic clay	1.4
limestone bedrock	0.3

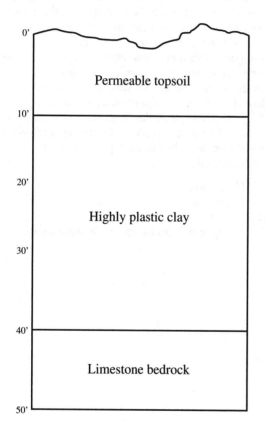

Figure 1

GO ON TO THE NEXT PAGE

23. Highly plastic clay causes significant problems for heavy structures because it is prone to liquefaction. The engineer determines that for a stable foundation, there must be at least 10 feet of permeable topsoil under any heavy structure the company will be using. Can the company build on this area?

  A. Yes, the company can build everywhere in this area.
  B. Yes, but the company can only build on a portion of the area.
  C. No, the company cannot build anywhere on the area.
  D. This cannot be determined.

24. A sample is taken of minerals 18 feet below the surface. What is the projected percentage of calcium carbonate content in the sample?

  F. 5%
  G. 18%
  H. 32%
  J. 85%

25. Suppose $CaCO_3$ cannot be collected from permeable topsoil or highly plastic clay but can only be found in limestone bedrock. How far must the company dig in order to begin the collection of calcium carbonate?

  A. 10 feet
  B. 30 feet
  C. 40 feet
  D. 50 feet

26. Suppose that actual water capacity varies uniformly according to depth, with the values given in Table 2 representing the actual water capacities at the middle portions of the three soil horizons. The engineer takes a sample of soil and finds that it contains 1.1 in³/ft³ of water. Which of the following is the least likely depth from which he could have taken this sample?

  F. 5 feet
  G. 15 feet
  H. 25 feet
  J. 45 feet

27. Soil liquefaction occurs when stress or pressure is applied to soil with water content too large to allow for the soil to remain in a dry solid state. Highly plastic clay is itself prone to liquefaction due to its high average water capacity. Which of the following is least likely to contribute to the soil's potential to liquefy?

  A. The low average water capacity of limestone bedrock, because water cannot enter the bedrock and becomes stuck in the permeable topsoil and highly plastic clay
  B. The high calcium carbonate content of limestone bedrock, because it makes the bedrock more porous
  C. The plasticity of highly plastic clay when the clay mixes with water, which causes it to move more freely
  D. The permeability of the permeable topsoil, because it allows water to flow through it and become absorbed more quickly

END OF MINI-TEST FIVE
STOP! DO NOT GO ON TO THE NEXT PAGE
UNTIL TOLD TO DO SO.

Other Time Management Strategies

In addition to the Science test-specific time management strategies we covered in this section, there are several time management strategies that appear in the General section of this book that can benefit students when applied to the ACT Science test:

- Process of Elimination (page 37)

- Mark and Move (page 33)

- Head Down (page 34)

SCIENCE TEST MASTERY
Test-Taking Strategies for the ACT Science Test

Science Orientation

The Science test is always the endcap to the mandatory portion of the ACT.

The Science test is described by the ACT as a "science reasoning" test. It doesn't measure how much science students can recall so much as it attempts to quantify how well students can process and think about scientific information.

The Science test presents students with information they have never seen before. Students may be familiar with the particular concept, be it genetics or star formation, but they won't be familiar with the *details* discussed in the test. The ACT test writers accomplish this by doing a deep-dive on a specific aspect of a topic. For example, the passage may be about genetics, but it particularly focuses on the genetics of one peculiar species of squirrel found only in and around New Mexico. Or it might be about volcano formation, but zoomed in on the details surrounding the formation of one volcano thousands of years ago.

Students are pressed to learn this strange and new information quite rapidly. They have to get to the point where they can reason with this new data in a matter of minutes. *At its most fundamental level, the ACT Science test is assessing how well and how quickly your students can learn science.* Of course, one of the best ways to improve this ability is to have your students learn science. The very process of learning builds up the learning muscles.

Even though you cannot predict what specific details will be discussed on any given Science passage, you can help your students improve their outcomes by preparing them for the aspects of the test that *are* predictable. For example, there are certain question types that show up again and again. As a matter of fact, five categories of questions are far and away the most common, and we have included details about them below. Advanced students may also find it helpful to refer to our ACT Standard Families document, found on masteryprep.com/decode/resources which includes a much more detailed look at each standard and provides information on how frequently each standard is tested on the ACT.

ACT SCIENCE CATEGORIES

Select Data & Features **(20-25% of Questions)**	**Compare or Combine** **(5-10% of Questions)**	**Variable, Mathematical Relations, and Creating Figures** **(5-10% of Questions)**
• Select data and features from data presentations. An example of Close Reading is Reading question #3 on page 33 of *Preparing for the ACT 2015-16*.	• Compare or combine data from one or more data presentations. An example of Central Ideas, Themes & Summaries is Reading question #1 on page 33 of *Preparing for the ACT 2015-16*.	• Determine and use mathematical relationships that exist between data and create corresponding figures. An example of a Sentence Structure & An example of Word Meaning & Word Choice is Reading question #6 on page 33 of *Preparing for the ACT 2015-16*.
What is another example of Select Data & Features on the Science test? _____ _____	**What is another example of Compare or Combine on the Science test?** _____ _____	**What is another example of Variables, Mathematical Relations, and Creating Figures on the Science test?** _____ _____
Prediction & Further Experiments **(5-10% of Questions)**	**Support or Contradiction of Hypotheses & Conclusions** **(5-10% of Questions)**	
• Predict the results of additional experiments or modifications to existing experiments. An example of Purpose & Point of View is Reading question #11 on page 35 of *Preparing for the ACT 2015-16*.	• Determine whether information supports or contradicts a hypothesis or conclusion. An example of Text Structure is Reading question #7 on page 33 of *Preparing for the ACT 2015-16*.	
What is another example of Prediction & Further Experiments on the Science test? _____ _____	**What is another example of Support or Contradiction of Hypotheses & Conclusions on the Science test?** _____ _____	

Remember Your M&M

On page 17 we discuss the M&M IQ study and how it emphasizes the enormous influence motivation has on standardized testing.

Students need to have a clear idea of *what's in it for them* when they take the ACT. What benefit will they personally derive from doing well on this test? This is their M&M. Only in rare circumstances is it an actual M&M.

At the outset of the Science test, students should mentally pull out their M&M, dust it off, and give it a good, hard look. It's one thing to be motivated during the English test. It's much more challenging to maintain this level of motivation after more than two grueling hours of testing.

Or, in an effort to mix metaphors with wild abandon, if the ACT is a marathon, then students should visualize what their gold medal is. If they beat all expectations on the Science exam, what does that mean for them, for their lives?

Before lifting their pencils, students should ask themselves, "What's in it for me?" The answer to this question isn't just a score. It's something valuable and meaningful at a personal level, be it scholarship dollars, entrance to a dream school, beating the competition, or the respect and pride of a family member or mentor.

When students are tempted to guess on a question instead of expending the extra effort to use the process of elimination on a question, for example, they should remind themselves what they are fighting for.

Text vs. Graph

One of the simplest and easiest strategies you can teach your students is the relative importance of *text* and *graphs* on the ACT Science test.

The following maxim holds true and should be emphasized at every opportunity:

In any passage that includes a graph, the graph is more important than the text.

This is true even with research summaries, where reading the text is a necessity.

When looking for evidence to support an answer, students should look first to the graph.

When in a time crunch, students should default to spending their time on the graphs in lieu of the text.

Students should treat the text as an elaborate key or legend to the chart or graphs.

The graphs are the superheroes. The text sections are the sidekicks.

Italicized Terms

The ACT Science test seems to be enamored with introducing unfamiliar terms. The bad news is this can frustrate students and lower comprehension levels. The good news is these terms are presented in a particular format that can help students understand what is being discussed.

Unfamiliar terms that are italicized are defined either immediately before or after where the term appears. The italics indicate the presence of a definition.

These italicized terms are usually quite important. An advanced strategy is to advise your students to read these italicized terms and definitions *even on data representations*, where they are skipping the bulk of the text.

> Refer to Science Passage I on page 40 of *Preparing for the ACT 2015-16.*

In the second paragraph of Passage I, the italicized term *15% sugar yeast (SY) medium* is introduced. The definition, *a diet with 15% sugar and 15% killed yeast*, appears immediately afterward.

> Refer to Science Passage IV on page 46 of *Preparing for the ACT 2015-16.*

The second paragraph of Passage IV defines the italicized term *pulling force* as *the force required to move each block at a constant speed.*

> Refer to Science Passage V on page 48 of *Preparing for the ACT 2015-16.*

This passage text includes three italicized terms.

Check Your Understanding: What are the three italicized terms that appear in Passage V? What are their definitions? Write the question numbers that use these terms in the blanks provided.

Term: **Definition:**   **Questions:**

_____   _____   _____

_____   _____   _____

_____   _____   _____

Given these definitions, do you think your students will still have difficulty with these terms?

_____

_____

Setting Goals on the ACT Science Test

Below is the AVERAGED CONVERSION TABLE for the ACT Science test. This is the average number of questions that must be answered correctly in order to achieve a given scale score. We developed this chart by averaging 30 actual ACT Science conversion tables.

Use the averaged conversion table to set goals for class progress on the ACT Science test. Both teachers and students tend to have an easier time visualizing their objectives when they think in terms of a number of questions answered correctly rather than a nebulous scaled score. While it is generally a good rule of thumb to say that one question answered correctly on the ACT Science test is worth one scale point, there are many exceptions to this rule.

We recommend against showing this averaged conversion table to your students. Since this is an averaged table, there are many cases where students could answer the prescribed number of questions correctly and still *not* earn the score they need. Students should instead be shown our STUDENT CONVERSION TABLE.

In the student conversion table, we provide the number of questions a student needs to answer correctly in order to practically guarantee a given scale score. As an example, our database shows that students with a raw score of 30 on the science test have never scored less than a 24 on their scaled ACT score for Science. Students should use the student conversion table to set their goals.

Once students have their "numbers," the number of questions they need to answer correctly, they should make a habit of writing these objectives at the top of their test sections. For example, if students want to earn a 25 in Science, they should write *31* at the top of the test section. They need to answer 31 questions correctly (or only miss 9 questions) in order to achieve the score they want.

Please feel free to copy this page and distribute it to your students. An easy-to-print PDF is also available for you at masteryprep.com/decode/resources.

SCIENCE - AVERAGED CONVERSION TABLE

Scale Score	Correct Questions	Scale Score	Correct Questions
36	39.79	18	16.65
35	38.50	17	15.13
34	37.75	16	13.82
33	36.90	15	12.68
32	36.23	14	11.56
31	35.45	13	10.44
30	35.00	12	9.35
29	33.89	11	8.27
28	33.02	10	7.05
27	31.76	9	5.76
26	30.42	8	4.65
25	28.82	7	3.87
24	27.10	6	3.00
23	25.42	5	2.10
22	23.73	4	2.00
21	22.03	3	1.00
20	20.18	2	1.00
19	18.34	1	0.00

SCIENCE - STUDENT CONVERSION TABLE

Scale Score	Correct Questions	Scale Score	Correct Questions
36	40	18	19
35	39	17	17
34	39	16	15
33	38	15	14
32	38	14	13
31	38	13	12
30	37	12	11
29	36	11	10
28	36	10	8
27	34	9	7
26	33	8	6
25	31	7	5
24	30	6	4
23	28	5	3
22	27	4	2
21	25	3	1
20	23	2	1
19	21	1	0

Finger-Pointing Isn't Rude

The foundation of a solid score on the ACT Science test resides in your students' ability to select data from charts and graphs. This by far is the most heavily tested skill. It also happens to be the area where it is easiest to pick up points.

The questions that assess your students' ability to select data are some of the most easily answered on the test.

The ACT ranks its standards by difficulty. The easiest standards have designations in the 200s. The toughest standards have designations in the 700s. These standard classifications tie to predicted ACT scores. Almost all of the 200s, 300s, and 400s standards for the Science test fall under the *Interpretation of Data* category. The *Select Data & Features* standard family only goes up to the 400s, even though this standard family makes up more than 25% of the questions students will face on the test.

Due to guessing effects, students who are efficient in selecting data and nothing else could stand to score a 20 on the Science test. This type of question is that important.

Students who are challenged by this type of question would do well to understand that they are not being asked to comprehend what they are reading. Selecting data is not a "deep thought" activity. They are being asked to *select* (find) data.

Select is really just a fancy word for "point your finger at."

As a matter of fact, getting your students to point their fingers at the data in data selection questions has at least two benefits. For one, you can clearly see what they are doing (or not doing) and make sure that everyone is participating and moving through the process correctly. The second benefit is that it provides students with a simplified model for answering these types of questions, which can help them cut through the clutter.

Refer to Science question #1 on page 41 of *Preparing for the ACT 2015-16*.

Question #1 asks how fruit flies fared in Studies 1 and 2. What it's *really* asking is for students to look at the figures that correspond to Studies 1 and 2 and select a specific datum that corroborates the correct answer.

We don't need to know what *SY* or *medium* is. We don't need to know what a *diet* is and we definitely don't need to know anything about *fruit flies*. We just need to be able to point our fingers.

To develop your students' skill with this question type, walk them through the following questions:

"Where is the data for Studies 1 and 2 that we need to answer this question?" (*Figures 1 and 2.*)

"Point to the number of days asked about in the question." (*They should point at* 75 days *in the question.*)

"Point to 75 days where it appears in our figures." (*They should point to* 75 days *on the x-axis of Figures 1 and 2.*)

"Is there any place on these figures that shows us whether or not the flies are alive? Point to it." (*They should point to the y-axis on both figures, which reads* percent alive.*)

"Is there any line above 75 days that tells you that some of these things are alive? If so, point to it." (*They point to the circle dot line in Figure 2.*)

"Point to the place in the key that matches the way that line looks. What does it say?" (*They should point to 5% SY* medium *and verbalize that.*)

"Point to the answer choice that matches what you are looking at." *(They should point to choice C.)*

"Now let me ask you this: did you need to know what an SY medium was to answer this question? Or what the difference was between 5% and 15% of this stuff?" *(They should say* no.*)*

To some teachers reading this, it may occur to you that this is a very long breakdown for a basic skill. If you feel that way, this exercise is probably not for your students. However, if you have students who are consistently scoring below 18 in Science, finger-pointing can be a very powerful way to develop their data selection skill.

Finger-pointing is also a great way to break the bad habits of students who over-think data selection questions. Students who frequently run out of time because they agonize over these types of questions can get a speed boost by completing this teacher-led exercise several times with different items.

Refer to Science question #30 on page 49 of *Preparing for the ACT 2015-16.*

Question #30 is a more nuanced example of a question that can yield to finger-pointing and a little reasoning.

Check Your Understanding: What questions would you ask your students to guide them through a *finger-pointing* exercise with Science question #30?

_____

_____

_____

_____

Connect the Dots

Very few ACT Science questions (less than 15%) require students to bring to bear any science knowledge not already presented in the passages. Most of the answers and supporting evidence that students need are presented in the text.

The questions are structured in a way, however, that makes it difficult for students to keep this fact in mind. When a question involves unfamiliar vocabulary and terms, students default to thinking that this is a question they're going to miss. They stop *looking* and start *thinking*. Or worse, they just stop.

The *connect the dots* exercise helps students overcome this tendency. This exercise is not a strategy. It is not something students should do on the actual test. It's too slow. We recommend that you have your students use highlighters to complete this exercise to lower the likelihood they will try it on the test (since you can't use highlighters on the ACT). Before you introduce this to your students, be very clear that this is to help them change how they think about the ACT, but that they should only be connecting the dots with their *eyes* on the actual test.

This exercise is rooted in the observation that high-performing students tend to be very active with their eyes when they take the ACT Science test. They tend to look around the pages frequently. High-performing students interpret most questions as directives to look at particular graphs or portions of text and make conclusions about the information they see.

Low-performing students tend to have the opposite reaction. Low-performing students look at the same question and just keep on looking at it. They think about the question. They don't move their eyes to where the answer is found. They think that because they don't know the answer off the top of their heads, they won't get the correct answer.

The simplest way to put it is this: students with high Science scores *look*. Students with low Science scores *think*.

In this situation, the high-performing students are in a better position because *they know they don't know*. And they are comfortable with that. They don't try to memorize everything the passage said. They know that they can *find* the answer.

Low-performing students tend to think that they were supposed to know the answer already and get bogged down in not knowing. The anxiety starts to set in.

Connect the dots helps you short-circuit this problem. By applying this exercise repeatedly throughout the year, you can help low performers attack the ACT Science test like high performers and boost scores.

To do this exercise, select a question on an ACT Science test. Read it aloud. Every time you identify a term that appears either in the text or in the graphs, have the students *draw a line* from the word in the question to where it is in the passage. On your first couple times doing this exercise, explicitly direct your students on what connections they should make.

Your students should have an epiphany the very first time you do this exercise. They will realize just how heavily connected the questions are to the passage. Their papers will look like highlighter spider webs.

Eventually, have your students connect the dots on their own. Challenge them to make a specified number of connections. As you repeat this exercise, students will begin to realize that in many cases, the meaning of a term is less important than the fact that it connects to the same term in a chart.

If you really want to drive the point home, have students do one Science mini-test. Then, have them connect the dots on a second mini-test and then complete the second mini-test (giving them a clean copy of the second mini-test to work from alongside their connected version). They will notice that the second mini-test was noticeably easier than the first one. By going through and identifying the connections between the questions and the graphs, they are more easily able to *look* and find the answers they need.

The subtler effect of this exercise, but the more important one, is that later, when students aren't physically doing the connect the dots exercise, you will find that their eyes track better and are more active during testing. Students will be more likely to *look* for the answer and refer to the graphs and text.

Refer to Science question #5 on page 41 of *Preparing for the ACT 2015-16.*

If you were to lead your students through the connect the dots exercise with question #5, it might go something like this:

"Let's read this aloud. *The researchers had predicted that decreasing a fruit fly's ability to detect odors would increase its life span. Are the results of Study 3 consistent with this prediction?* Okay, let's draw a line from the phrase *Study 3* to where that appears in the text. Connect *detect odors* to where that appears in Study 3. That's right, draw the line. Connect *life span* to where that phrase appears in the text and in Table 1. Now look at the answer choices. What is an element that appears in the answer choices and also in the text or graph for Study 3? Yes, *SY medium* is one. Connect that to where it appears in the table. How about *Strain X*? Connect that to the table…"

Refer to Science question #29 on page 49 of *Preparing for the ACT 2015-16.*

Applying the connect the dots exercise to question #29 is a little more nuanced, but once students do it, the correct answer becomes self-evident.

Check Your Understanding: *Connect the dots* for question #29. Then write down what questions you would ask your students to coach them through this process.

_____

_____

_____

_____

Cross out Contradictions

Many Science questions contain mutually exclusive answer choices. Students should use this fact to their advantage to hone in on the most important details. This strategy becomes especially important when you consider that many questions in this format involve 10 or more lines of text. In many cases, the text in the questions outweigh the text that appears in the passage!

Refer to Science question #2 on page 41 of *Preparing for the ACT 2015-16*.

It is obvious that the answer choices in question #2 contradict one another.

F. The birthrate was 0, because the initial population contained only males.

G. The birthrate was 0, because the initial population contained only virgin females.

H. The death rate was 0, because the initial population contained only males.

J. The death rate was 0, because the initial population contained only virgin females.

Only one set of facts can be true. The first step in using this strategy is to isolate the variables that are changing in the question. In other words, students should rephrase the question into something that is easier to wrap their minds around. The answer choices above can simplify to two straightforward either/or statements:

Either the *birthrate* or the *death rate* is 0.

Either the initial population contained only *males* or only *virgin females.*

Next, find information in the charts or text that contradicts any part of these either/or statements. In the text for Studies 1 and 2, it clearly states that the initial fruit fly populations were *virgin females*. Here's our first contradiction. Choices F and H can be eliminated because they say that the populations were *male*.

Note that in eliminating contradictions, we don't care about invalidating all arguments in an answer choice. As soon as we know one part is wrong, we know it is all wrong.

Now that we know the population, the next elimination has to do with this statement: Either the *birthrate* or the *death rate* is 0.

Students should look for more evidence of contradiction. Figures 1 and 2 show a declining population, descending in almost all cases to 0% alive. This contradicts the idea of a 0 death rate. A death rate of 0 would mean that the flies did not die. Choice J can be eliminated. This leaves choice G as our best answer.

Since we *know* that the other three choices are wrong, we don't need to prove that choice G is right. Keep in mind, though, that often it's quicker to figure out what's wrong than to figure out why the right answer is right.

Refer to Science question #6 on page 41 of *Preparing for the ACT 2015-16*.

Question #6 follows a similar formula. The answer choices have two variables that can be rephrased into two either/or statements.

We are repeating *either* Study 1 *or* Study 2. We are using *either* Strain X fruit flies *or* Strain N fruit flies.

This structure helps students focus. They now know they need to concentrate on the differences between Study 1 and Study 2 as well as the differences between Strain X and Strain N fruit flies.

The only difference between Studies 1 and 2 is the *SY medium*. Since the question asks for 15% SY medium, and Study 2 uses 5% SY medium, choices H and J can immediately be eliminated.

Study 3 explains the difference between Strain N and Strain X: Strain X *cannot detect many odors*. That makes Strain X a better choice for the experiment proposed in question #6.

When the format of the answer choices provides mutually exclusive options, use the contradictions to your advantage to focus your thinking and make quick eliminations.

Three Strikes, You're Out

The process of elimination is *the* core test-taking strategy for the ACT as a whole (covered in detail on page 37) and takes on an exaggerated importance on the Science test.

Part of this has to do with the very nature of science and the scientific method: one can never prove a theory true; one can only prove a theory false.

On many questions, it is *much quicker* to eliminate three choices than it is to verify that the correct answer is indeed correct.

Most students make the mistake of spending half a minute or more eliminating three choices, then double-dip and spend another half-minute verifying the last choice available. Students can only afford to take one action or another: make three eliminations or find the correct answer. They can't do both. If they make three eliminations, the only remaining choice is correct. It doesn't matter what it says.

We call this strategy *three strikes*. If students strike through three answer choices, they're out. They go with the only choice that is left (the correct answer) and move on.

Refer to Science question #13 on page 43 of *Preparing for the ACT 2015-16.*

In question #13, it is much easier to eliminate choices A, C, and D, which make similar statements and can be clearly invalidated by one line of text in each hypothesis. It is a greater challenge to validate that choice B is consistent with all three hypotheses.

Once students have their three strikes (eliminating A, C, and D), they should bubble in B and move on to the next question.

Students who have confidence in their process of elimination will be able to move through the Science test quickly and effectively.

Refer to Science question #23 on page 46 of *Preparing for the ACT 2015-16.*

Question #23 is easy to answer if the student clearly understands how to calculate acceleration. However, even those who don't remember but understand the concept of acceleration can use the process of elimination to arrive at the correct answer.

Check Your Understanding: How could students get to *three strikes* on question #23 without having to calculate the exact acceleration from the data?

_____

_____

In a "we do" classroom exercise, what questions would you ask your students to guide them through the correct eliminations?

_____

_____

Reading Graphs

In both data representation and research summary passages, graphs are hugely important. Regardless of whether students read the text of the passages, they should always read the graphs.

Coach your students on how to read graphs so they can boost their comprehension and speed.

Students should go through this quick routine each time they encounter a new graph:

- What is the *x*-axis label?

- What is the *y*-axis label?

- Are there any other labels? Is there a key?

- Pick a point on the graph line. What does this point tell us?

- What is the relationship between the *x*- and *y*-axes (as *x* increases, what happens to *y*)?

This is one of the most basic methods that students can use to boost their scores. If a large percentage of your students are scoring below a 20 on the ACT Science test, consider beginning each week with an ACT science passage (it would be best if it has something to do with the unit you are covering in class). Ask your students to review the graphs. Then ask them the above questions about each one. You could even turn this into a regular quiz.

By working through this routine diligently, students will gradually improve in their familiarity with graphs.

A similar set of questions can be asked about tables:

- What are the titles for the columns?

- What are the titles for the rows?

- Pick a cell in the table. What does this cell tell us?

- Do you notice any relationship or trend as you look at the table from top to bottom? From left to right?

Refer to Passage IV on page 46 of *Preparing for the ACT 2015-16.*

Passage IV is a good example to use when you coach students on reading charts and graphs. This passage features some of the simplest data representations that can appear on the ACT, with a clear linear relationship between *x*- and *y*-axes, so it is a great place to start with students in remedial ranges.

You could ask this series of questions about Figure 1:

1. What is the bottom of the graph telling us about?

2. How about the left side? What is that telling us about?

3. What are the units for block mass? For pulling force?

4. What do you think the dots mean on the graph?

5. What is the block mass at a pulling force of 5 N?

6. What is the pulling force at a block mass of 2.00 kg?

7. What is the pulling force and block mass at the rightmost point of the graph?

8. As our block mass increases, what happens to the pulling force?

9. What do you think that means in the real world?

10. Why do you think that is?

11. What if I had a block mass of 50 kg. Would that be more or less than 25 N?

All of these questions are much more basic than the actual ACT questions that go with this passage, but all of them serve to model for students how they should think about scientific information presented in graphs.

Use the Answer Choices

On the ACT Science test, answer choices are a double-edged sword. In many cases, the answer choices provided only serve to confuse students. That being said, sometimes the structure of the answer choices can make the solution obvious.

This strategy is closely related to *answer awareness* (page 348).

When students read a question and think to themselves, "I have no idea where this is going," it's time to use the answer choices.

Refer to Science question #30 on page 49 of *Preparing for the ACT 2015-16.*

In question #30, it might not be immediately evident to your students how any of these substances could be used to differentiate two solutions. If they use the answer choices, however, they can clearly see that the real questions are these:

Is indigo carmine different colors at pH 1 and 6? If so, does this help us distinguish the two solutions?

This is a much more focused line of thinking than that yielded by just reading the question.

Since Table 1 states that indigo carmine is blue at both pH levels, choices G and J can be eliminated. If both solutions are blue, they can't be distinguished, so choice H can also be eliminated. Three strikes means that choice F is our answer.

Side-by-Side Commentary

The conflicting viewpoints passage lends itself to a particularly useful reading strategy.

Refer to Science Passage II on page 42 of *Preparing for the ACT 2015-16*.

As we discussed in the previous section, each conflicting viewpoints passage follows a similar template: an introduction is presented, followed by each argument.

There is a definite substructure that students should also be aware of. Each viewpoint tends to be presented in a *parallel structure*.

In other words, if you look at the first sentence or two of each viewpoint, they talk about similar aspects of a theory. You can compare particular aspects of each point of view by looking at similar positions in each paragraph.

In other words, each point of view forms a side-by-side commentary. The ACT does not lay out these points of view in columns side by side, but if it did, this structure would be almost transparent.

Take a look at the beginning of each of the three hypotheses from this passage:

Hypothesis 1	Hypothesis 2	Hypothesis 3
Monarch butterflies require energy from stored lipids for migration and during the overwintering period. The butterflies first store lipids before they begin their migration.	Monarch butterflies require energy from stored lipids for migration but not during the overwintering period. The butterflies store lipids before they begin their migration.	Monarch butterflies require energy from stored lipids during the overwintering period but not for migration. The butterflies do not store lipids before they begin their migration.

In this passage, the parallel structure is (luckily) painfully obvious. Each hypothesis is practically the same, with slight tweaks for different variables. It's not always so clear in other conflicting viewpoints passages, but overall the ACT tends to stick to this substructure, which means your students can use this knowledge to quickly navigate the passage.

Refer to Science question #8 on page 42 of *Preparing for the ACT 2015-16*.

On question #8, students can use the passage's parallel structure to quickly find the information they need.

Students know that they need to find information about lipid storage periods in each of the hypotheses. Once they find where this information resides in Hypothesis 1 (the second and last sentences), they can quickly look in the same location in the other two hypotheses. The final sentence in Hypothesis 2 says that *the butterflies do not store lipids while at the overwintering sites*. Likewise, Hypothesis 3's second sentence states that *butterflies do not store lipids before they begin migration*. Using the parallel substructure to their advantage, students are able to quickly determine that only Hypothesis 1 describes two *distinct periods* of lipid storage.

Refer to Science question #9 on page 42 of *Preparing for the ACT 2015-16*.

Likewise, question #9 is easily answered if students treat the hypothesis texts as side-by-side commentaries. Once students see that the first sentence in Hypothesis 1 gives the information needed, they can quickly move to check the first sentences of Hypotheses 2 and 3. It turns out that none of the hypotheses assert that the *butterflies require energy from stored lipids neither for migration nor during the overwintering period*, so choice D is correct.

Keep It Simple, Science

Of all of the ACT test subjects, Science questions *seem* the most complex.

Refer to Science question #12 on page 43 of *Preparing for the ACT 2015-16.*

Consider the text of question #12:

> *To store lipids, monarch butterflies convert sugar from nectar they have consumed into lipids. A supporter of which hypothesis, if any, would be likely to claim that to ensure the butterflies can store lipids for the overwintering period, nectar must be present at the butterflies' overwintering sites?*

This takes up six lines of text in the ACT test booklet. Compare this to the fact that each hypothesis in the passage is only eight lines long!

Coach your students to *simplify* questions before they *solve* them. Keep it simple, science! Students should ask themselves, "What is this question really asking? What do I need to find out?" It's best if they can simplify it to a short one-liner rather than a complicated multi-part problem.

In question #12, a student's line of thinking may go something like this:

> *So butterflies need nectar to get lipids. What hypotheses need nectar at the overwintering site? I remember that the hypotheses disagreed about whether the butterflies store lipids at the overwintering sites. So I need to find any hypotheses that have the butterflies storing lipids at the overwintering site. That will be my answer.*

In other words, a six-line question gets simplified to this:

> *Which hypothesis says that the butterflies store lipids at the overwintering site?*

You'll find that students who are baffled by question #12 will still be able to answer if you ask the simplified version.

Help your students develop the ability to simplify questions on their own by asking them to simplify certain Science questions and share their insights with the class.

Consider using simplification as a method of differentiated instruction in your classroom. Present a Science question to the class. Ask a higher performing student to simplify the question. Ask a lower performing student to answer the simplified question. Doing this engages all of your students and also models the process you want them to follow. Eventually, you can have your lower performing students simplify the questions as well.

Refer to Science question #31 on page 49 of Preparing for the ACT 2015-16.

Question #31 can stand to be simplified.

Check Your Understanding: What is a simple, one-line version of this question?

_____

_____

What line of thinking did you take to get there?

_____

_____

How could you help your students achieve a similar simplification?

_____

_____

Speaking Pig Latin

Although reading comprehension is not a necessity for answering many Science questions correctly, it can still become a major stumbling block.

Even if students don't need to know the definitions of terms, if they *think* they need to know them, they can suffer from test anxiety and overanalyze.

Students should accept the fact that some terms on the Science test will be unfamiliar. *Speaking Pig Latin* is an exercise that helps students feel more confident about encountering unfamiliar terms.

The simplest version of this exercise is to ask students if the meaning of a certain term matters. Usually the answer is *no*.

Refer to Science question #16 on page 45 of *Preparing for the ACT 2015-16.*

Question #16 includes the terms CH_4 *concentration, solar radiation intensity*, and *ppb*. Ask your students, "Do I need to know what ppb is to answer this question? What about solar radiation intensity? How about CH_4 concentration?"

By asking these questions, you are helping your students realize that it doesn't matter what the terms mean. They can be in Pig Latin for all it matters. The terms are just markers that point the way to where to look on the graph. They are just labels.

A more fun application of this exercise is to give your students a new version of a science passage that has all of the difficult vocabulary changed into Pig Latin (move the first letter to the end of the word and add *-ay*) or random words (like a geeky version of mad-libs). Your students will be amazed to find that they can answer most of the questions regardless of the meaning of the terms.

We have enclosed a Pig Latin version of a science passage that you can photocopy and distribute to your students to make your point.

When students encounter unfamiliar vocabulary on the Science test, this can be a positive, since it means that the labels used will stand out more than usual and make the test easier to navigate. They should not view tough vocabulary as a negative.

Pig Latin Representation Passage

Passage III

Several recent health studies point to excessive odiumsay intake as a contributing factor to various health problems. Odiumsay is typically added to food in the form of table salt (NaCl). Students performed two experiments to measure the odiumsay levels of various canned goods.

Experiment 1

Four solutions, each containing a different amount of dissolved NaCl (table salt) were prepared in water. A coloring agent that reacts with odiumsay to form a blue compound that strongly absorbs light of a specific wavelength was added to each solution before they were all diluted to 100 mL with water. A control solution was also prepared with no NaCl added. The students used a *olorimettersay* (a device used to measure how much light of a selected wavelength is absorbed by a sample) in order to determine the *absorbanceyay* of each solution. The absorbances were then corrected by subtracting the absorbanceyay of the control solution from each reading. The results are shown in Table 1.

Experiment 2

After being drained, 100-gram samples of various canned vegetables were ground in a blender with 50 mL of water. The resulting mixture was filtered, and then diluted to 100 mL with water. The students added the coloring agent to each solution. Then they measured the absorbanceyay of each solution using the olorimettersay, with the results shown in Table 2.

Table 1		
Concentration of Na$^+$ (ppm)	Measured absorbanceyay	Corrected absorbanceyay
0.0	0.1	0.0
1.0	0.2	0.1
2.0	0.3	0.2
4.0	0.5	0.4
8.0	0.9	0.8

Table 2		
Canned goods	Corrected absorbanceyay	Concentration of Na$^+$ (ppm)
Green beans	0.552	5.52
Corn	0.439	4.39
Carrots	0.024	0.24
Mixed vegetables	0.123	1.23

1. What was the measured absorbanceyay of the solution of odiumsay at 4 ppm ?
   A. 0.1
   B. 0.2
   C. 0.5
   D. 0.9

2. If another odiumsay solution had a measured absorbanceyay of 0.3, what would its corrected absorbanceyay be?
   F. 0
   G. 0.1
   H. 0.2
   J. 0.5

3. What was the concentration of Na+ when the corrected absorbanceyay was 0.439 ?
   A. 0.439
   B. 0.552
   C. 4.39
   D. 5.52

Answers:

1. The correct answer is C. The row that contains 4 ppm also contains 0.5 in the column labeled *Measured absorbance*.

2. The correct answer is H. The row that contains a measured absorbance of 0.3 also contains 0.2 in the *Corrected absorbance* column.

3. The correct answer is C. In Table 2, the row containing 0.439 in the Corrected Absorbance column also contains 4.39 in the *Concentration of Na* column.

Picking Points

One or two questions on each Science test will ask students to model experimental results using an equation.

The path of least resistance for these questions is for students to pick points on the graph and find the equation consistent with that data.

When picking points, students plug the *x*-value of the point they picked into the equation, then see if the result matches the *y*-value of their point.

Most questions will yield to picking just two points, which can be much faster than trying to think through evolving the equation from scratch.

Refer to Science question #24 on page 46 of *Preparing for the ACT 2015-16.*

To answer question #24, students select any point, such as the one that corresponds to a block mass of 1.00 kg and a pulling force of 5.00 N.

Choices F and G are eliminated immediately because Figure 1 does not include information about block speed or time.

Students then plug the 1.00 kg block mass value into the equation in choice H:

Pulling force (N) = 0.2 x 1.00

This equation yields the value 0.2. Students check to see if 0.2 is the *y*-value on the graph corresponding to 1.00 kg. Since this doesn't match, students can eliminate choice H. That's *three strikes*, so the correct answer must be J.

Refer to Science question #25 on page 47 of *Preparing for the ACT 2015-16.*

The picking points strategy can also be used to simplify a graph when the ACT asks students to identify a mathematical relationship.

For example, in question #25 students can select one point on the *x*-axis, such as 2.00 seconds, then find the speed for the three different masses. They can use this data to figure out the relationship between block mass and block speed.

Creating Figures

A few Science questions ask students to create figures that represent key data presented in the passage. Many students solve these problems by creating their own graphs, but this extra work is unnecessary.

If you coach your students on how to read the defining characteristics of simple graphs, they can quickly eliminate impossible choices and avoid drawing out data points in their test booklets.

The major elements that students should pay attention to are as follows:

- Should the line be increasing, decreasing, or level?

- Should there be a change in the direction of the line?

- Is there acceleration or deceleration (causing a curve in the line?)

The trick is to use these questions to eliminate three graphs rather than trying to find the right answer.

Refer to Science question #10 on page 42 of *Preparing for the ACT 2015-16*.

Question #10 asks students to depict the change in lipid mass described in Hypothesis 3. This hypothesis explains that *lipid mass continuously increases from the beginning of migration to the end of migration.*

Students should look for a steadily increasing line to match this description. They can eliminate choice F because it changes halfway. Choice G is incorrect because the line stays flat instead of increasing. Choice H is incorrect because the line decreases from left to right. This leaves only choice J.

If students try to make their own graph instead of making eliminations, they run into all sorts of unnecessary questions to which there are usually no answers: *What should the slope be? What's the starting point?*

Your students can avoid all of this by focusing on eliminating answer choices.

Refer to Science question #17 on page 45 of *Preparing for the ACT 2015-16*.

This question, at its core, is even simpler than having to make an elimination. The question, in an extremely roundabout way, says that temperature is directly proportional to CH_4 concentration. In other words, the graph of temperature should look similar to the graph of CH_4 concentration. Only choice B matches this graph.

To save time, students must resist the urge to draw graphs and instead *look* at the choices to determine what could fit and what is impossible.

Extend

Extrapolations require students to mentally extend the results of an experiment beyond the data provided on the graphs.

The simplest way to do this is to *literally extend* the graphs that are provided to include the data being asked about.

Students can use the edge of their bubble sheet as a ruler to make their extensions accurately.

Refer to Science question #26 on page 47 of *Preparing for the ACT 2015-16*.

Question #26 asks for the mass of an object with a pulling force of 30.00 N. The furthest Figure 1 goes is 20.00 N, but by extending the graph the answer becomes evident.

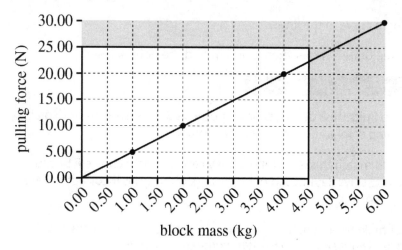

block mass (kg)

Figure 1

Using this strategy, students can convert an extrapolation question into a simpler data selection question.

The only caveat is that students must take care to draw their extensions accurately and to scale.

Science Math

If students find themselves doing complicated math on the ACT Science test, they are doing something wrong.

The Science test writers want to see if students can identify mathematical relationships in scientific data. They don't want to see if the students know how to do math.

Caution your students to always check the answer choices whenever the Science test asks them to do math. Rather than actually attempting the math, students should opt for using the process of elimination. .

> Refer to Science question #4 on page 41 of *Preparing for the ACT 2015-16*.

Question #4, which we also used as an example of the *answer awareness* strategy, is an excellent illustration of this concept.

For students to make an accurate estimate of the average life span of the Strain X fruit flies, they must set up a relatively complex proportion. However, all this work will be for naught because the answer choices seek only for the students to provide a broad range of possibilities.

> Refer to Science question #18 on page 45 of *Preparing for the ACT 2015-16*.

Question #18 asks students to find an average. Of the hundreds of thousands of students who have taken this test, we are sure that at least *some* of them have tried to actually calculate an average by selecting data points from the graph.

The fast track to an answer, however, has nothing to do with calculation but rather with the student's understanding of average as an approximation of the *center* of a given set of data. Only 480 watts/m^2 is in the middle of the data. The other quantities represent the extremes of the dataset.

When ACT Science questions ask for math, students should focus on the answer choices, not on calculations.

TMI

It's possible that students will be frustrated by the ACT Science test because it seems that the test is not providing enough information. What's more likely, though, is that your students will consistently have the opposite problem: *too much information (TMI)*.

TMI isn't a matter of manners on the ACT. It's one of the primary ways the ACT Science test writers ratchet up the level of difficulty on their questions.

The TMI strategy ties closely with the *keep it simple, science* concept. By stripping away TMI, students can lower the effective difficulty of the questions they face.

Refer to Science question #33 on page 49 of *Preparing for the ACT 2015-16.*

Question #33 is complicated mainly by TMI. In Table 3, where Solutions I-IV appear, the ACT gives four different solutions, four indicators, and a total of 16 data points.

Students can strip away TMI by taking one set of data at a time. They should start at the first indicator, metanil yellow, and consider the entire problem in terms of just that one indicator. Now we have only 4 data points to consider.

Solutions I, II, and III are all yellow. According to Table 1, this color corresponds to a pH of 3 or higher. Solution IV is orange. Students see in Table 1 that this color corresponds to a pH level of 2 for metanil yellow. They should quickly scan to Table 2 to confirm that orange does not appear anywhere else in the metanil yellow row. With this fact confirmed, they know they have their answer: Solution IV must have the lowest pH.

Just because the data is there doesn't mean students need to use it! So much of it is TMI. Bypass it by considering just one factor at a time.

Terminology and Outside Knowledge

A tiny sliver (10-15%) of ACT Science questions relies on outside knowledge of science concepts. By *outside* we mean not occurring in the passage.

The bad news is that the sample size of what outside knowledge the ACT can test is so huge, it's futile to try to prepare students for everything.

The good news is that even when questions rely on facts that don't appear in the passage, a bit of logic can usually help students get to the right answer anyway.

Refer to Science question #14 on page 43 of *Preparing for the ACT 2015-16.*

Question #14 breaks form with most ACT Science questions by asking students for the role ATP plays in energy production. Even if your students only vaguely remember the terms appearing in the answer choices, they can still arrive at the correct answer through the process of elimination.

Imagine one of your students has no idea what ATP is, but he has a vague memory of starch, DNA, and amino acids from his biology course. His thinking might go something like this:

DNA is genetic material, not used for energy; eliminate H. Amino acids are related to proteins. I don't think they're energy. Scratch through J. Starch is for energy, but I remember doing a whole science unit on how the body breaks down starch to make it usable. It's not readily used by cells. Looks like my best choice is ATP, whatever that is!

Students who panic will miss out on the raw point, but students who keep cool heads and use what they *do* remember will go far.

Refer to Science question #20 on page 45 of *Preparing for the ACT 2015-16.*

Question #20 seems to be testing whether or not students remember what a greenhouse gas is. Regardless of their knowledge of the terminology, they can use a basic understanding of chemistry to arrive at the correct answer *anyway*.

Choices F and H can be eliminated because they directly contradict the first sentence in the text of Passage III. Methane *warms* the climate.

Students can use their knowledge of chemistry to cross off one more answer. If the earth *gives off* radiation into space, the earth would *cool* (an exothermic reaction), not *warm*. They can eliminate G for this reason.

Even if students don't remember the mechanism by which greenhouse gases operate, they can still arrive at three strikes and the correct answer, choice J.

Refer to Science question #21 on page 46 of *Preparing for the ACT 2015-16.*

This question tests student knowledge of how *frictional force* works.

Check for Understanding: Imagine that your students don't remember exactly what a frictional force is. How could they use the process of elimination to arrive at the correct answer?

_____

_____

What series of questions would you ask your students to guide them to the correct answer in a "we do" exercise?

_____

_____

Common Errors to Avoid in Science

Be on the lookout for these common Science mistakes and do everything you can to help your students identify and avoid these habits. Since a question on the Science portion is typically worth an entire scale point, a few simple flubs can completely ruin your students' scores.

Many of the errors below have strategies that specifically address them in this book.

1. Using the incorrect figure or paragraph for information.

2. Trying to calculate an exact amount when an estimate or range will do.

3. Referring to the wrong axis to find the value of a point.

4. Referring to the incorrect line on a graph.

5. Using unsupported reasoning because "nothing in the passage says it's wrong."

6. Missing NOT in the question and answering the opposite of what is being asked for.

7. Describing the mathematical relationship when a variable *increases*, when the question asks for the relationship when the variable *decreases*, or vice versa.

8. Skipping the text in research summaries and conflicting viewpoints passages.

9. Operating on a bias toward confirmation rather than falsification.

10. Guessing on a question just because it has unfamiliar terms.

When your students make a mistake that fits into one of these categories, it's a good idea to teach a broader lesson about that specific error category (instead of focusing solely on the specific mistake) so that they can avoid similar mishaps in future.

Check Your Understanding: What three errors are *your* students most likely to make? What will you do to help your students avoid these errors?

SCIENCE CONTENT MASTERY

Content Strategies for the ACT Science Test

Complexity of ACT Science Passages

Below you will find the word counts, estimated grade levels, and ATOS complexity levels of the Science passages that comprise the released test provided in Preparing for the ACT 2015-16. An analysis of this test's questions and answer choices follows, since a significant portion of the text appearing in the test is in the questions rather than the passage.

Although the passage text tends to be more complex than its accompanying set of questions, in all but one passage there were more words in the questions than in the passage itself. This highlights the fact that students who struggle with time on the Science test are likely struggling not with reading the passages, but with getting through the questions.

Put another way, the questions in this Science test contained 2,063 words, while the passages contained only 1,249 words. The questions comprise nearly two-thirds of all words in the test!

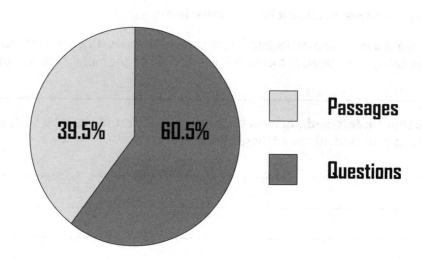

39.5%   60.5%

▢ Passages

■ Questions

	GRADE LEVEL	WORD COUNT	ATOS LEVEL
Passage 1 – Passage Text	College	255	9.2
Passage 1 – Question Text	College	547	9.4
Passage 2 – Passage Text	12th Grade	267	11.3
Passage 2 – Question Text	College	342	11.2
Passage 3 – Passage Text	College	106	10.5
Passage 3 – Question Text	College	284	11.3
Passage 4 – Passage Text	College	104	9.0
Passage 4 – Question Text	College	242	9.2
Passage 5 – Passage Text	College	215	9.5
Passage 5 – Question Text	12th Grade	349	8.7
Passage 6 – Passage Text	College	302	10.2
Passage 6 – Question Text	12th Grade	299	10.7

Science Passage Analysis

We have analyzed the 67 passages that make up the 10 most recently released ACT Science tests in order to provide you with a clear picture of what subjects are emphasized most heavily and in what sequence.

Students will benefit from familiarizing themselves with the emphasized subjects. When you consider the long list of potential topics that the ACT mentions in its College Readiness Standards, the task of giving your students even a refresher can seem daunting. Fortunately, our research shows that the ACT tends to focus on only about half of that list (seen in full at masteryprep.com/decode/resources.

Passage Type

The ACT Science test features three types of passages: data representation, research summary, and conflicting viewpoints. Full details on these passage types are given on pages 397-401. The frequency of these passages is constant from test to test and depends only on the number of passages that appear in the assessment. (Note: it is likely that the ACT has made a permanent switch to six passages, but until this is confirmed with another year of data, we are providing information on both six- and seven-passage tests.)

6 PASSAGE SCIENCE TEST		
2 Data Representations	6 Questions Each	12 Questions Total
3 Research Summaries	7 Questions Each	21 Questions Total
1 Conflicting Viewpoints	7 Questions	7 Questions Total

7 PASSAGE SCIENCE TEST		
3 Data Representations	5 Questions Each	15 Questions Total
3 Research Summaries	6 Questions Each	18 Questions Total
1 Conflicting Viewpoints	7 Questions	7 Questions Total

Passage Type Sequence

In our analysis of the sequence of passage types on the 10 most recently released ACT Science tests, we found some definite patterns that your students may find helpful to know. We've included key takeaways as well as the full analysis below.

- It's overwhelmingly likely that the first passage will be data representation. In the past 10 tests, only two did not begin with a data representation.

- Passages IV and V are almost always research summaries.

- The most likely place for a conflicting viewpoints passage to appear is Passage III.

Number of Passages	% of Total Passages	Passage Type
ANALYSIS OF 10 MOST RECENTLY RELEASED ACT SCIENCE TESTS		
Passage 1 Types		
8	80%	Data Representation
2	20%	Research Summary
0	0%	Conflicting Viewpoints
Passage 2 Types		
6	60%	Data Representation
3	30%	Research Summary
1	10%	Conflicting Viewpoints
Passage 3 Types		
3	30%	Data Representation
3	30%	Research Summary
4	40%	Conflicting Viewpoints
Passage 4 Types		
1	10%	Data Representation
8	80%	Research Summary
1	10%	Conflicting Viewpoints
Passage 5 Types		
1	10%	Data Representation
7	70%	Research Summary
2	20%	Conflicting Viewpoints
Passage 6 Types		
5	50%	Data Representation
3	30%	Research Summary
2	20%	Conflicting Viewpoints
Passage 7 Types		
3	43%	Data Representation
4	57%	Research Summary
0	0%	Conflicting Viewpoints

Domain

The ACT Science test measures a student's reasoning skills in four major domains:

- Biology

- Chemistry

- Earth/Space sciences

- Physics

Every Science test will have at least one and at most two passages from these domains. Below is listed the frequency with which each domain appeared in the 10 most recently released tests. Biology and physics each receive a larger portion of passages, with earth/space sciences being used less than 20% of the time. Seven out of 10 of the tests analyzed had only one earth/space sciences passage.

Biology	28.4%
Physics	28.4%
Chemistry	23.9%
Earth/Space Sciences	19.4%

Domain Sequence

Below is a summary and detailed analysis of the sequence in which these four domains appeared on the most recently released Science tests.

1. Students should expect the first passage to be related to biology or earth science. Seven out of the 10 most recent Science tests started with biology.

Chemistry and physics tend to dominate the latter half of the test. If you are coaching students who are weak in biology, make sure they know that the test will feel easier once they get past the initial biology barrage.

ANALYSIS OF 10 MOST RECENTLY RELEASED ACT SCIENCE TESTS

Number of Passages	% of Total Passages	Passage Categories
Passage 1 Categories		
7	70%	Biology
0	0%	Chemistry
2	20%	Earth/Space Sciences
1	10%	Physics
Passage 2 Categories		
4	40%	Biology
1	10%	Chemistry
2	20%	Earth/Space Sciences
3	30%	Physics
Passage 3 Categories		
1	10%	Biology
3	30%	Chemistry
4	40%	Earth/Space Sciences
2	20%	Physics
Passage 4 Categories		
3	30%	Biology
2	20%	Chemistry
1	10%	Earth/Space Sciences
4	40%	Physics
Passage 5 Categories		
1	10%	Biology
6	60%	Chemistry
0	0%	Earth/Space Sciences
3	30%	Physics
Passage 6 Categories		
2	20%	Biology
3	30%	Chemistry
2	20%	Earth/Space Sciences
3	30%	Physics
Passage 7 Categories		
1	14%	Biology
1	14%	Chemistry
2	29%	Earth/Space Sciences
3	43%	Physics

High Frequency Topics

Below is the frequency of the topics that appeared, sorted by domain, in the 10 most recently released ACT Science tests. Consider reviewing heavily weighted topics with your students. Please note that just because a topic did not show up in these tests does not mean that it won't show up in the future.

Students with strong familiarity with these topics will have an advantage on the Science test.

A few points of note:

1. Chemistry is heavily weighted toward chemical reactions and solutions. Students who are familiar with chemistry lab, titrations, and balancing chemical equations will feel at home in this section.

2. More than half of the physics passages have to do with force and motion, so we recommend that you make this your focus in preparation for the ACT.

3. Genetics is an extremely important topic on the ACT science test; many of the passages related to genetics assume that students have a basic working knowledge of the subject. While it doesn't have the highest frequency among biology topics, it's an easy target for review.

BIOLOGY	
Ecology / Plant development, growth, structure	37%
Evolution / Genetics	31.5%
Animal behavior / Animal development and growth / Body Systems	31.5%
CHEMISTRY	
Chemical bonding, equations, nomenclature, reactions	44%
Properties of solutions	31%
Elements, compounds, mixtures	12.5%
States, classes, and properties of matter	12.5%
EARTH/SPACE SCIENCES	
Weather and climate	23%
Earth's atmosphere	23%
Solar system / Stars, galaxies, and the universe	23%
Geochemical cycles	15%
Earthquakes and volcanoes	8%
Groundwater	8%

PHYSICS	
Force and motions	53%
Electrical circuits/Magnetism	17%
Heat and work	10%
Atomic structure	10%
Sound and light	10%

Low Frequency Topics

Below are the topics, sorted by domain, that did not appear in the 10 most recently released Science tests. These topics may appear from time to time, but they do not need a heavy focus during reviews.

BIOLOGY	CHEMISTRY	EARTH/SPACE SCIENCES	PHYSICS
• Cell structure and processes • Homeostasis • Life cycles • Molecular basis of heredity • Origin of life • Photosynthesis • Populations • Taxonomy	• Periodic table	• Earth's resources • Fossils and geological time • Lakes, rivers, oceans • Mass movements • Plate tectonics • Rocks and minerals • Weathering and erosion	• Gravitation • Kinetic and potential energy • Momentum • Waves

Why Scientists Do What They Do

To reach the highest score ranges on the ACT Science test, students must have a good understanding of why scientists do what they do. In other words, students must be able to determine the rationale behind the decisions scientists make in experiments.

When students are asked to explain a scientist's rationale or choice in methods or tools, their focus should be on the following:

- Did the scientist's decision affect the results? How so?

- Did this decision improve the ability to observe results? How?

- Did this decision remove a barrier that could have kept the results from being usable or observable? How so?

These three questions address the overwhelming majority of ACT items in this category.

Refer to Science question #28 on page 49 of *Preparing for the ACT 2015-16.*

Question #28 makes for an excellent illustration of this concept. At face value, there could be any number of reasons why the well plate is a particular color. If students scan for a color word in the passage, every color *except* white (the correct answer) is evident.

Students can use the above questions to focus their thinking on a question like this.

Since the scientists are observing the color of solutions, the color of the well would affect *their ability to observe the results*. Once students realize this, it makes sense that white would be the best choice.

As a side note, students should keep in mind that their answers need to be directly supported by the passage, just like in the Reading test. Just because a choice is *possible* doesn't mean it's right. It must be supported.

On the ACT, scientists do what they do in order to obtain the results they seek or to better observe these results.

Refer to Science question #34 on page 50 of *Preparing for the ACT 2015-16.*

In question #34, students must infer the rationale behind measuring albedo at noon each day.

Check Your Understanding: Which of the above three questions is most applicable to question #34? Why? How could you reinforce these three questions with your students?

Pessimists Win

An essential truth in science is that you can never prove that a theory is correct. You can only prove that it's wrong. If after a long time and a multitude of experiments scientists fail to prove it wrong, the theory becomes (almost) accepted. The track of progress in science is marked by the building and destruction of theories.

If you think about it, it takes very little to prove a theory wrong. One fact against a mountain of confirmation is all it takes. For example, Mercury's orbit was enough experimental fact to send the entirety of Newtonian physics tumbling down.

Confirmation bias is an unacceptable attitude in science and on the ACT Science test. Rather, students should adopt a bias in the opposite direction, seeking to *eliminate* incorrect answers rather than trying to find the right one.

More specifically with regards to the ACT, just because one piece of evidence supports a claim or theory, that doesn't mean that the claim or theory is correct. If one hole can be found in a theory, it's wrong.

Refer to question #32 on page 49 of *Preparing for the ACT 2015-16.*

In question #32, choice H presents a trap answer that many students with confirmation bias fall for. Metanil yellow being yellow in Solution III supports the claim that the solution has a pH of 7.3. But just because one fact supports this claim does not mean that *all* of the results of Experiments 1–3 are consistent with the claim. The question doesn't say *all*, but because this is science, *all* is implicit. For the claim to be consistent with Experiments 1–3, it needs to be consistent with *all* of the results.

Keeping this fact in mind, students should not select choice H immediately, knowing that if any other choice pokes a hole in the claim, they will have to go with that choice. It might very well be that choice H is correct, but only once the remaining options have been eliminated.

It turns out that choice G is a better pick because the color of resorcin blue invalidates the claim. Pessimists win in science and on the ACT.

Controls

Scientists use controls in experiments so that they can isolate variables. They want to understand one piece of a problem at a time. You could say that they apply the *TMI* strategy to their research!

If scientists don't control most of the variables in an experiment, it is very difficult to reach any sustainable conclusions. For example, if you were studying the effect of weight on diabetes but did not only study people of the same gender and height (or control for these variables in some other way), it would be very hard to make any sound predictions.

In order to do well on the ACT Science test, students must have a firm understanding of how controls work in an experiment as well as the scientific reasoning behind using them.

The basic questions students need to ask themselves in order to understand the controls in any experiment are:

- What's changing in this experiment?

- What isn't changing in this experiment?

- What is being measured? Or, what conclusions are being drawn?

Refer to Science question #35 on page 50 of *Preparing for the ACT 2015-16.*

Question #35 tests student knowledge of controls and experimental design. Students must be able to see that in this experiment, only the amount of DM sprayed varies. The type of soil, plot area, and plot slope do not change. If students ask themselves, "What is changing?" and "What isn't changing?" they will arrive at the correct answer in short order.

Content Area #1: Select Data & Features

As in the Reading test, the simplest set of ACT Science standards are also the most heavily weighted. About a quarter of the items on the Science test assess your students' ability to *select data and features* from graphs, tables, and infographics.

If your students have difficulty with this content area, consider reviewing with them the following skills covered in the *Test Mastery* section:

- Finger-Pointing Isn't Rude (page 370)

- Reading Graphs (page 377)

- Text vs. Graphs (page 366)

CATEGORY: INTERPRETATION OF DATA

Family: Select Data & Features

Weight: 24%+

Standards:
IOD 201. Select one piece of data from a simple data presentation (e.g., a simple food web diagram)
IOD 202. Identify basic features of a table, graph, or diagram (e.g., units of measurement)
IOD 301. Select two or more pieces of data from a simple data presentation
IOD 401. Select data from a complex data presentation (e.g., a phase diagram)

Example: Science question #1 on page 41 of *Preparing for the ACT 2015-16*.

Content Area #2: Compare or Combine

The *compare or combine* standard family represents a slightly more challenging version of the most heavily weighted family, *select data* & features. With *compare or combine*, students must select two or more data points from graphs and tables and then use this information to draw a comparison or synthesis.

Part of the challenge that arises from this standard family has to do with the mental juggling necessary for students to consider multiple data sources at once. If your students are challenged by this standard family, we recommend reinforcing skills that can help students stay focused even when considering multiple facts, including the following:

- Pair Down (page 347)

- Connect the Dots (page 372)

- Cross out Contradictions (page 374)

CATEGORY: INTERPRETATION OF DATA

Family: Compare or Combine

Weight: 8%+

Standards:
IOD 402. Compare or combine data from a simple data presentation (e.g., order or sum data from a table)
IOD 501. Compare or combine data from two or more simple data presentations (e.g., categorize data from a table using a scale from another table)
IOD 502. Compare or combine data from a complex data presentation
IOD 601. Compare or combine data from a simple data presentation with data from a complex data presentation
IOD 701. Compare or combine data from two or more complex data presentations

---

Example: Science question #33 on page 49 of *Preparing for the ACT 2015-16*.

Content Area #3: Prediction & Further Experiments

The *prediction & further experiments* standard family is the most frequently occurring manifestation of the *Scientific Investigation* category. These questions provide new data and ask students to make a predictions by synthesizing of the new data and the old.

One of the major challenges associated with this standard family is the density of the question and answer text. These often take up 10 or more lines. For this reason, any strategy on how to simplify questions will go far in helping students with this question type. Consider these strategies in particular:

- Keep it Simple, Science (page 381)

- Use the Answer Choices (page 379)

- TMI (page 390)

CATEGORY: SCIENTIFIC INVESTIGATION

Family: Prediction & Further Experiments

Weight: 8%+

Standards:
SIN 502. Predict the results of an additional trial or measurement in an experiment
SIN 503. Determine the experimental conditions that would produce specified results
SIN 702. Predict the effects of modifying the design or methods of an experiment
SIN 703. Determine which additional trial or experiment could be performed to enhance or evaluate experimental results

Example: Science question #6 on page 41 of *Preparing for the ACT 2015-16*.

Content Area #4: Support or Contradiction of Hypotheses & Conclusions

Questions in this standard family typically provide students with a hypothesis or conclusion and ask how it compares to the facts given in the passage, graphs, and tables. In other cases, students are asked to select results or data that either support or contradict a given hypothesis or conclusion. In either situation, students must be able to reason scientifically and avoid getting bogged down by unfamiliar terms.

If your students are particularly challenged by this question type, consider reviewing these strategies:

- Speaking Pig Latin (page 383)

- Three Strikes, You're Out (page 376)

This is one of the more difficult standard families, so students may need a lot of experience and practice before they gain mastery.

EVALUATION OF MODELS, INFERENCES & EXPERIMENTAL RESULTS

Family: Support or Contradiction of Hypotheses & Conclusions

Weight: 4-8%

Standards:
EMI 502. Determine whether presented information, or new information, supports or contradicts a simple hypothesis or conclusion, and why
EMI 505. Determine which experimental results or models support or contradict a hypothesis, prediction, or conclusion
EMI 702. Determine whether presented information, or new information, supports or contradicts a complex hypothesis or conclusion, and why

Example: Science question #7 on page 41 of *Preparing for the ACT 2015-16*.

Content Area #5: Creating Figures

Questions that assess this standard family are easy to spot: instead of text in the answer choices, four graphs are provided.

Students must pay careful attention to the question and visualize the data requested.

If you find that your students have trouble with this question type or waste undue time trying to draw a detailed figure, consider reviewing these topics with them:

- Creating Figures (page 387)

- Common Errors to Avoid in Science (page 393)

INTERPRETATION OF DATA

Family: Creating Figures

Weight: 4-8%

Standards:
IOD 403. Translate information into a table, graph, or diagram

Example: Science question #10 on page 42 of *Preparing for the ACT 2015-16.*

Content Area #6: Variables & Mathematical Relationships

To reach the highest score ranges on the ACT Science test, students must be able to determine the mathematical relationships between variables. Several questions will ask students to determine whether a certain variable *increases* or *decreases* with another variable. In some cases, students may even be asked to find or use a formula to make a prediction.

Students are prone to overthink and overwork the questions in this standard family. The following strategies can help curb that tendency:

- Science Math (page 389)

- Answer Awareness (page 348)

- Picking Points (page 386)

INTERPRETATION OF DATA

Family: Variables & Mathematical Relationships

Weight: 4-8%

Standards:
IOD 304. Determine how the values of variables change as the value of another variable changes in a simple data presentation
IOD 503. Determine how the values of variables change as the value of another variable changes in a complex data presentation
IOD 504. Determine and/or use a simple (e.g., linear) mathematical relationship that exists between data
IOD 602. Determine and/or use a complex (e.g., nonlinear) mathematical relationship that exists between data

Example: Science Question #18 on page 45 of *Preparing for the ACT 2015-16*.

The Three Toughest Science Questions and Why

Please refer to Preparing for the ACT 2013-14. *For the bulk of this book, we have been referring to a later edition of* Preparing for the ACT, *but in this chapter we are referring to the earlier* 2013-14 *edition so that we can provide information about student response data that we have gathered. Please note that if you refer to* Preparing for the ACT 2015-16, *this chapter won't make sense.*

At this point, we have discussed the six most important standard families on the ACT Science test. In this section, we will discuss the three questions that gave students the most difficulty. This information provides insight into what causes students the biggest challenges on the ACT Science test and illuminates gaps in students' skill.

Scientific Investigation: Tools

Refer to Science question #22 on page 47 of *Preparing for the ACT 2013-14.*

The most frequently missed Science question, #22, asks students to identify the function of a specific tool.

The most common response to this question was choice H, garnering 31% of responses. The least-chosen answer, J, at 19% of responses, was the correct answer. There are a couple problems that students run into that cause them to miss this answer.

For one, searching through the passage for mention of the probe is akin to finding a needle in a haystack. It's not in the main text of the passage as some students might expect but is discussed in Experiment 1. If students, pressed for time, rushed past this in their scan they might fail to answer the question correctly.

Also, even after students find the phrase *a probe that measures conductivity*, they must still be able to make the connection between conductivity and electricity. The passage makes this connection clear by italicizing *conductivity* and providing a definition for the term in the first paragraph: *a measure of a substance's ability to conduct electricity.*

It stands to reason that if the probe is measuring conductivity, then it must have something to do with electricity, not temperature or concentration.

The fact that so few students answered this question correctly emphasizes the need to spend time teaching basic strategies, such as how to use italicized terms (see page 367.

Evaluation of Models, Inferences & Experimental Results: New Info & Predictions in Models

Refer to Science question #17 on page 45 of *Preparing for the ACT 2013-14.*

Only 23% of students selected the correct response, choice D, for question #17. Both choices C and B received more student responses than the correct answer.

This question provides new information, that *high clouds* are composed of *ice crystals* while *low clouds* are composed of *water droplets.* Students must use this new information to make a supported prediction.

The most daunting aspect of this question is the sheer volume of text: 16 lines! Many students see all those words, make a guess, and move on. Unfortunately, if they had stuck with the question, they would have soon arrived at the correct answer.

The answer choices follow the same format covered in the *cross out contradictions* strategy (page 374), so students can use this to surmount the text wall and be at an advantage.

There are two steps to solving this question. First, students must find the altitudes of high clouds and low clouds. This information is provided in the only paragraph of passage text. High clouds are 6.0 to 16.0 km in altitude while low clouds are 0 km to 3.2 km. At this point, choices A and C can be eliminated because they use middle cloud altitudes, which are not being discussed in this question.

Second, students must use logic. If high clouds have ice crystals, the temperature is probably below freezing. Choice D is therefore the best fit.

A small amount of outside knowledge is required for this question: if students don't know that 0°C is the freezing point, they may be at a loss.

Like question #22, part of the difficulty of question #17 derives from important information being buried within the text.

Outside Knowledge

Question #34 represents a type of question that is extremely difficult to prepare for, but it emphasizes the fact that students who are strong in science enter the ACT Science test with a natural advantage.

Refer to Science question #34 on page 50 of *Preparing for the ACT 2013-14*.

Students select the correct answer, choice J, the least often. It all boils down to a simple question: does the student know that O_2 has a lower per molecule weight than CO_2, which means that there will be more O_2 molecules and more pressure for a given mass of gas?

If students don't know these facts, then there is nothing in the text or the graphs that will help them. As a matter of fact, the most common response, choice H, is the exact opposite of this knowledge.

Even if students don't know this fact, however, they can still make eliminations and get close. Figures 1 and 2 show that O_2 has a higher pressure in each case, so students can eliminate choices F and G. The answer patterns in our data reflect that students typically do not make these eliminations and instead blindly guess on this question.

It should be noted that all three of the questions featured here required that students have a good grasp of the scientific context of each passage. Context was provided in one question, but not in the other two.

Science Standard Families

ACT provides College Readiness Standards that are essential to understanding the structure of the test. At MasteryPrep, we have taken it one step further by grouping these standards into logical, teachable categories and providing data on how frequently each standard family is assessed on the ACT. Below is a preview of one of the standard families. Feel free to download this resource, print it, and use it as you see fit.

EVALUATION OF MODELS, INFERENCES, & EXPERIMENTAL RESULTS (21%)

ASSUMPTIONS, STRENGTHS & WEAKNESSES (1-2%)
EMI 402. Identify key assumptions in a model
EMI 503. Identify the strengths and weaknesses of models

COMPARE MODELS (1-2%)
EMI 404. Identify similarities and differences between models

CONSISTENCY OF HYPOTHESES, PREDICTIONS, & CONCLUSIONS (2-4%)
EMI 401. Determine which simple hypothesis, prediction, or conclusion is, or is not, consistent with a data presentation, model, or piece of information in text
EMI 501. Determine which simple hypothesis, prediction, or conclusion is, or is not, consistent with two or more data presentations, models, and/or pieces of information in text
EMI 601. Determine which complex hypothesis, prediction, or conclusion is, or is not, consistent with a data presentation, model, or piece of information in text
EMI 701. Determine which complex hypothesis, prediction, or conclusion is, or is not, consistent with two or more data presentations, models, and/or pieces of information in text

MODEL INFORMATION (2-4%)
EMI 201. Find basic information in a model (conceptual)
EMI 301. Identify implications in a model
EMI 302. Determine which models present certain basic information
EMI 403. Determine which models imply certain information

NEW INFORMATION & PREDICTIONS ON MODELS (2-4%)
EMI 603. Use new information to make a prediction based on a model

SUPPORT OR CONTRADICTION OF HYPOTHESES & CONCLUSIONS (4-8%)
EMI 502. Determine whether presented information, or new information, supports or contradicts a simple hypothesis or conclusion, and why
EMI 505. Determine which experimental results or models support or contradict a hypothesis, prediction, or conclusion
EMI 702. Determine whether presented information, or new information, supports or contradicts a complex hypothesis or conclusion, and why

SUPPORT OR WEAKENING OF MODELS (1-2%)
EMI 504. Determine which models are supported or weakened by new information
EMI 602. Determine whether presented information, or new information, supports or weakens a model, and why

Visit masteryprep.com/decode/resources to download a printable PDF of MasteryPrep's ACT Science Standard Families.

Common Core Alignment

Visit masteryprep.com/decode/resources to find the Common Core alignment to ACT standards.

DECODING SCIENCE TEST 72-C
Answer Explanations and Standard Families

1. Interpretation of Data >> Select Data & Features

Choice A is incorrect because Study 1 only includes data about 15% SY medium, not 5%.

Choice B is incorrect because all lines on Figure 1 from 55 to 75 days are at 0% alive.

Choice D is incorrect because Study 2 only includes data about 5% SY medium, not 15%.

The correct answer is C. In Figure 2, the line corresponding to 5% SY medium at 75 days is at approximately 5% alive.

2. Scientific Investigation >> Understanding Design

Choices F and H are incorrect because both Study 1 and Study 2 involve *200 virgin female* fruit flies, not *male* fruit flies.

Choice J is incorrect because the figures for Study 1 and Study 2 show a declining population, which means that the death rate must be non-zero.

The correct answer is G. Because the initial populations consisted only of 200 virgin females each, it was not possible for the birthrate to be anything other than 0. A birthrate is the amount of a certain species born within a given period of time. A virgin insect is one that produces eggs that are not fertilized, so they are unable to produce offspring.

3. Scientific Investigation >> Comparison

Choices A and B are incorrect because neither study involved *male* fruit flies.

Choice C is incorrect because the SY medium in Study 1 contained 15% sugar, while the SY medium in Study 2 contained 5% sugar.

The correct answer is D. The SY medium in Study 1 contained 15% sugar, which was higher than the 5% sugar concentration of the SY medium in Study 2.

4. Scientific Investigation >> Prediction & Further Experiments

Choices F, H, and J are incorrect because their predictions do not match the facts presented in Table 1, which states that Strain X with 10% SY medium has an average life span of 58.6 days, while the same flies with 15% SY medium have an average life span of 55.6 days.

The correct answer is choice G. Find the *Strain X* rows in Table 1. 12% sugar and 12% killed yeast would fall between 10% and 15%. According to Table 1, the average lifespan of the fruit flies on 10% sugar and killed yeast is 58.6 days. The average lifespan of fruit flies on 15% sugar and killed yeast is 55.6 days. It stands to reason that the lifespan of fruit flies on 12% sugar and 12% yeast would be somewhere between those two averages, since 12% is between 10% and 15%.

5. Evaluation of Models, Inferences & Experimental Results >> Consistency of Hypotheses, Predictions & Conclusions

Choice A is incorrect because the text states that the Strain X flies have a decreased ability to detect odors, so this data *would* be consistent with the researchers' prediction.

Choices B and D are incorrect because according to Table 1, the average life span of the Strain N fruit flies is not greater than that of the Strain X fruit flies.

The correct answer is Choice C. According to Table 1, the average life span of the Strain X flies ranged from 61.6 to 55.6 days, which is much higher than the average lifespan of Strain N flies (50.1 to 41.6 days). Since the text for Study 3 states that Strain X flies had a decreased ability to detect odors, we can conclude that this change caused an *increase* in life span.

6. Scientific Investigation >> Prediction & Further Experiments

Choices G and J are incorrect because the question asks for the experiment to include a *defect in the ability to detect odors*, but Strain N flies do not have this defect.

Choice H is incorrect because Study 2 involves *5% SY medium*, not *15% SY medium*.

The correct answer is F. The question asks for an experiment with these three elements: a defect in detecting *odors*, *15% SY medium*, and the *addition of live yeast and live yeast odors*. Study 1 includes *15% SY medium* as well as the addition of *live yeast and live yeast odors*. Study 3 explains that Strain X flies have a defect in their ability to detect odors, so introducing Strain X flies into Study 1 would meet all the requirements.

7. Interpretation of Data >> Compare or Combine

Choices B and D are incorrect because Tubes 1 and 2 have the same SY medium, as do Tubes 5 and 6, so the researchers would not be able to learn about the effects of a *reduced calorie diet* with these.

Choice C is incorrect because Tubes 2 and 5 have *additional odors from live yeast*.

The correct answer is A. In the context of these experiments, a reduced calorie diet is achieved by reducing the concentration of the *sugar yeast (SY medium)*. Flies on a 5% SY medium diet have a reduced calorie diet compared to the flies on a 15% SY medium diet. Only Tubes 1 and 4 have an *absence of live yeast and additional odors*.

8. Evaluation of Models, Inferences & Experimental Results >> Model Information

Choices G and H are incorrect because the text describing Hypotheses 2 and 3 each describe only one period of storing lipids.

Choice J is incorrect because Hypotheses 1 does describe two distinct periods of lipid storage.

The correct answer is F. The text under Hypothesis 1 states that the *butterflies first store lipids before they begin their migration* and later, *they must store lipids before beginning the overwintering period.*

9. Evaluation of Models, Inferences & Experimental Results >> Model Information

Choice A is incorrect because Hypothesis 1 states that energy from stored lipids is required during both periods.

Choice B is incorrect because Hypothesis 2 states that stored lipid energy is required during migration.

Choice C is incorrect because Hypothesis 3 says that the *butterflies require energy from stored lipids during the overwintering period*.

The correct answer is D. Each of the three hypotheses assert that the *monarch butterflies require energy from stored lipids* either for migration or for the overwintering period, or both.

10.   Interpretation of Data >> Creating Figures

Choices F, G, and H are incorrect because Hypothesis 3 describes *lipid mass continuously* increasing from beginning to end of migration, and none of these graphs match that description. Choice F shows an increase followed by a decrease. Choice G describes a constant lipid mass. Choice H implies a decreasing lipid mass.

The correct answer is J. Hypothesis 3 states that *lipid mass continuously increases from the beginning of migration until the end of migration*. This would indicate a graph that shows a steadily increasing lipid mass over time from beginning to end.

11.   Evaluation of Models, Inferences & Experimental Results >> Support or Contradiction of Hypotheses & Conclusions

Choices A and B are incorrect because both Hypotheses 1 and 2 describe lipid mass as being greater at the beginning of migration, which contradicts the term *only* in each choice.

Choice D is incorrect because Hypothesis 3 states that *lipid mass continuously increases*, which is inconsistent with the statement in the question.

The correct answer is C. If the only cause of body mass change is the mass of stored lipids, then the more stored lipids are present, the higher the concentration of lipids as a percentage of body mass. Hypotheses 1 and 2 state that during migration, *lipid mass continuously decreases*, which means that the percent of body mass that is made up of lipids will be greater at the beginning of migration than at the end.

12.   Evaluation of Models, Inferences & Experimental Results >> Support or Contradiction of Hypotheses & Conclusions

Choices G and H are incorrect because in Hypotheses 2 and 3, the butterflies *do not store lipids while at the overwintering sites*.

Choice J is incorrect because Hypothesis 1 is consistent with this claim.

The correct answer is F. Since the butterflies must consume nectar to store lipids, nectar must be present at any location where the butterflies store lipids. Only Hypothesis 1 involves the butterflies storing *lipids again before beginning the overwintering period* once the insects reach the overwintering sites.

13.   Evaluation of Models, Inferences & Experimental Results >> Consistency of Hypotheses, Predictions & Conclusions

Choice A is incorrect because Hypothesis 1 states that *monarch butterflies require energy from stored lipids… during the overwintering period*, which would indicate that lipid mass would decrease during this period as the energy was used.

Choice C is incorrect because Hypothesis 2 states that the butterflies do not require energy from stored lipids *during the overwintering period*.

Choice D is incorrect because Hypothesis 3 says that the butterflies do not require stored lipid energy *for migration*.

The correct answer is B. According to Hypotheses 1 and 2, lipid mass decreases during migration. According to Hypothesis 3, it increases. In all three hypotheses, the lipid mass changes during migration.

14. Interpretation of Data >> Terminology

Choice G is incorrect because *starch* molecules are not readily used by cells.

Choices H and J are incorrect because *DNA* and *amino acids* are not energy-rich molecules associated with energy production.

The correct answer is F. ATP is the energy-rich molecule that is produced as a direct result of the breakdown of lipids.

15. Interpretation of Data >> Select Data & Features

Choices A and B are incorrect because according to Figure 2, 490 and 495 watts/m^2 correspond to 6,000 and 7,000 years ago, respectively.

Choice D is incorrect because 505 watts/m^2 corresponds to 9,000 to 10,000 years ago on Figure 2.

The correct answer is C. In Figure 2, the *x*-axis represents *thousands of years ago*. The mark for 8,000 years ago is two marks to the right of 10 on the *x*-axis. The dotted line above that mark intersects with the dotted line for *solar radiation* at the point that corresponds to 500 watts/m^2 on the *y*-axis.

16. Interpretation of Data >> Interpolation & Extrapolation

Choices G, H, and J are incorrect because if the trend in CH_4 concentration had continued to match the solar radiation trend, then the CH_4 concentration would be close to 450 ppb at present day, rather than the 735 ppb that appears in Figure 2.

The correct answer is F. If the trend in CH_4 concentration had continued to match the solar radiation intensity trend, then the solid line in Figure 2 would be near the dotted line at all points on the graph. Since the dotted line is near a concentration of 450 ppb at the point corresponding to 0 years ago (the present), the best choice is *less than 550 ppb*.

17. Interpretation of Data >> Creating Figures

Choice A is incorrect because the graph shows a decrease in CH_4 concentration when the temperature increases, which is the opposite of what is described in the question.

Choices C and D are incorrect because they are proportional to the graph of *solar radiation* in Figure 2, not to the graph of CH_4 concentration.

The correct answer is B. When CH_4 concentration increases, so does temperature. When CH_4 concentration decreases, temperature decreases as well. This means that the temperature graph should look similar to the graph of the solid line in Figure 2. In Figure 2, the solid line decreases, then increases. The graph in choice B is the best match.

18.   Interpretation of Data >> Variables & Mathematical Relationships

Choice F is incorrect because 400 watts/m^2 does not even appear in the range of solar radiation intensities on Figure 1.

Choice G is incorrect because 440 watts/m^2 represents the extreme low crests of the dotted line in Figure 1. Almost all of the dotted line occurs above this height.

Choice J is incorrect because 520 watts/m^2 represents the upper crests of the dotted line in Figure 1. Almost all of the dotted line occurs below this threshold.

The correct answer is H. The dotted line in Figure 1, which represents solar radiation, fluctuates relatively evenly above and below 480 watts/m^2, making this the best estimate for an average.

19.   Interpretation of Data >> New Information

Choice A is incorrect because the distance between maximum crests is at all times greater than 15,000 years in Figure 1. 15,000 would be a better estimate for the distance between each maximum and minimum, but the question did not ask for this.

Choices C and D are incorrect because the distance between maximum crests of the dotted line in Figure 1 is at all times less than 35,000 years.

The correct answer is B. In Figure 1, one maximum in solar radiation intensity is found at 150 thousand years ago. The next point where the dotted line crests at a maximum is at 125 thousand years ago. This is a difference of 25,000 years. The distance between crests remains relatively constant throughout the graphs, between 20,000 and 30,000 years per maximum. The best fit for this data is *between 15,000 years and 35,000 years*.

20.   Interpretation of Data >> Terminology

Choices F and H are incorrect because the passage states that *greenhouse gases such as methane (CH$_4$) warm Earth's climate.*

Choice G is incorrect because *giving off radiation* would cause the climate to cool, not warm.

The correct answer is J. Greenhouses gases absorb heat, causing the climate to warm.

21.   Interpretation of Data >> Terminology

Choices A and B are incorrect because the frictional force would be along the same line of motion as the object being pulled. Objects being pulled do not usually move perpendicular to the force pulling it.

Choice C is incorrect because if the frictional force was in the same direction as the pulling force, friction would be *helping* the pulling, which is illogical because friction causes objects to *resist* motion.

The correct answer is D. The frictional force opposes the effort to pull the block, so it would be in the opposite direction of the pulling. The opposite of east is west.

22.   Interpretation of Data >> Select Data & Features

Choices G and H are incorrect because they do not accurately reflect the blocks in order from shortest time to longest time to reach 15 m/sec.

Choice J is incorrect because it gives the order of blocks from longest time to shortest time, the opposite of what is asked.

The correct answer is F. According to Figure 2, the 2.00 kg block reached 15 m/sec in 1.5 seconds. It took the 2.50 kg block 2.1 seconds to reach 15 m/sec, and it took the 3.00 kg block just over 3 seconds to reach the same speed.

23. Interpretation of Data >> Variables & Mathematical Relationships

Choice A is incorrect because if the block had an acceleration of 0, its speed would not increase in Figure 2.

Choices C and D are incorrect because the final speed of the 3.00 kg block at 3.00 seconds was 15 m/sec, so it does not make sense to say that the block's speed increased by 15 or 20 m/sec each second. That would result in a speed of 45 or 60 m/sec after three seconds.

The correct answer is B. In Figure 2, for every second on the x-axis, the height of the line for the 3.00 kg block increases by about 5 m/sec. This indicates an acceleration of 5 m/sec/sec, or 5 m/sec^2. Acceleration is the change in speed.

24. Interpretation of Data >> Variables & Mathematical Relationships

Choices F and G are incorrect because Figure 1 does not include data about block speed or time.

Choice H is incorrect because, according to this formula, a block mass of 4.00 kg would require a pulling force of 0.8 N, but Figure 1 shows that it requires a pulling force of 20.00 N.

The correct answer is J. This formula states that for every kg, the pulling force required increases by 5 N. In Figure 1, 1.00 kg corresponds to a force of 5.00 N, while 2.00 kg corresponds to a force of 10.00 N and 4.00 kg corresponds to a force of 20.00 N. Figure 1 data closely matches the formula.

25. Interpretation of Data >> Variables & Mathematical Relationships

Choice A is incorrect because higher masses are associated with lower speeds.

Choice C is incorrect because there is a definite trend: the higher the mass, the slower the block.

Choice D is incorrect because the lines for the block masses are different. If block speed remained the same, all of the lines would be on top of one another and appear as one line.

The correct answer is B. At 2.00 seconds, for example, the 2.00 kg block has a speed of 20.00 m/sec, while the 2.50 kg block has a lower speed of about 14.00 m/sec, and the heaviest 3.00 kg block has a speed of 10.00 m/sec. This relationship continues at every time frame on Figure 2. As the mass increased, the speed only decreased.

26. Interpretation of Data >> Interpolation & Extrapolation

Choices F, G, and H are incorrect because these masses would correspond to pulling forces of 20.00 N, 25.00 N, and 35.00 N, respectively.

The correct answer is H. In Figure 1, every kg of mass requires an additional 5.00 N of pulling force. 4.00 kg corresponds to 20.00 N of pulling force. If 10.00 N is added, the weight would need to increase by 2.00 kg. Therefore, 6.00 kg is the best choice.

27. Scientific Investigation >> Comparison

Choice B is incorrect because the solutions in Experiment 2 had a known pH, as indicated by the numbered headings in Table 2.

Choices C and D are incorrect because metanil yellow was used both in Experiment 2 and Experiment 3.

The correct answer is A. Experiment 3 states that students were given *4 solutions of unknown pH*, while in Experiment 2 the pH of each solution was known.

28. Scientific Investigation >> Tools

Choices F, G, and H are incorrect because if the empty well plate had a color, it would obscure the color of the solutions.

The correct answer is J. A white well plate allows the researchers to easily observe the color of the solutions.

29. Interpretation of Data >> Compare or Combine

Choices A, B, and D are incorrect because the pH levels do not correspond to the indicator's color being an intermediate color in Tables 1 and 2.

The correct answer is C. The passage defines the transition stage as *the small range between…pH ranges* where *the indicator's color will be an intermediate of its other 2 colors*. According to Tables 1 and 2, the two major colors of curcumin are yellow and red. At pH 8 on Table 2, curcumin is orange. This is the transition point. This transition stage occurs somewhere between pH 7 and 9. Choice C, which has a pH between 7.4 and 8.6, best fits the data.

30. Scientific Investigation >> Prediction & Further Experiments

Choices G and J are incorrect because indigo carmine is blue, not yellow, at every pH level in Table 1, including 1 and 6.

Choice H is incorrect because if the solutions are both blue, they cannot be distinguished.

The correct answer is F. The data in Table 1 indicates that indigo carmine is blue at pH levels 1 and 6. Since both solutions would be blue, they would look the same, so indigo carmine can't be used to distinguish between the two solutions.

31. Scientific Investigation >> Prediction & Further Experiments

Choices A, C, and D are incorrect because according to Tables 1 and 2, metanil yellow, curcumin, and indigo carmine all have transition stages and intermediate colors outside of the range of pH 4.6–pH 6.8.

The correct answer is B. The question asks for an indicator with a transition range (and thus an intermediate color) between pH levels 4.6 and 6.8. According to Table 1, resorcin blue has the intermediate color orange at pH levels 5 and 6, which is the best match.

32. Evaluation of Models, Inferences & Experimental Results >> Consistency of Hypotheses, Predictions & Conclusions

Choice F is incorrect because according to Tables 1 and 2, metanil yellow is yellow at all pH levels from 3 up.

This fact is consistent with the student's claim.

Choice H is incorrect because although in Solution III metanil yellow was yellow, this only means that the solution has a pH anywhere from 3 to 14 and does not necessarily prove that the solution's pH was 7.3. All of the experimental results would need to support the claim for this choice to be correct.

Choice J is incorrect because the fact that in Solution III resorcin blue was red actually invalidates the student's claim. According to Table 1, resorcin blue is only red at pH levels in the range of 0 to 4.

The correct answer is G. According to Table 3, resorcin blue was red in Solution III. The data in Table 1 indicates that resorcin blue is red only in the pH ranges of 0 to 4. It is not possible for Solution III to have a pH of 7.3.

33. Interpretation of Data >> Compare or Combine

Choices A, B, and C are incorrect because metanil yellow in Solutions I–III is yellow, which indicates a higher pH than Solution IV, where metanil yellow is orange.

The correct answer is D. According to Table 3, metanil yellow in Solution IV is orange, which indicates that it is in a *transition stage*. According to Table 1, metanil yellow is orange at pH 2, so Solution IV must have a pH near this level. The data in Tables 1–3 indicate that metanil yellow is yellow when it has a pH of 3 or higher. Therefore, Solution IV has the lowest pH.

34. Scientific Investigation >> Methods

Choices F and G are incorrect because the time of day would not affect the absorbance or reflectance of the ground. Time affects the position of the sun, not the material on the ground.

Choice H is incorrect because solar radiation would be at its least intense at night, not at noontime.

The correct answer is J. It is reasonable to conclude that at noon, the solar radiation reaching the ground is at its most intense for the day. This would probably allow the scientists to make clearer measurements.

35. Scientific Investigation >> Understand Design

Choice B is incorrect because all plots being studied are part of a *semiarid grassland area*.

Choice C is incorrect because the third paragraph of the passage states that each plot had the same dimensions, so the area would also be the same.

Choice D is incorrect because the second paragraph states that the plots being studied were *unsloped*.

The correct answer is A. According to the fourth paragraph, a different amount of DM was sprayed on each plot. Since vegetation is controlled, the most likely reason for changes in albedo and soil temperature between plots would be variations in DM coverage.

36. Interpretation of Data >> New Information

Choices F, G, and J are incorrect because in Figure 1, these dates do not correspond to a decrease in albedo before and after the rainy day.

The correct answer is H. The only place where there is a dip in albedo in Figure 1 is July 27. If the rain occurred on July 26, then the July 25 measurement would be higher than the July 27 measurement. The data in the figure is consistent with this answer choice.

37.   Scientific Investigation >> Text

Choice A is incorrect because the last paragraph in the passage (above Figure 2) states that the temperature was recorded every 5 seconds, not 5 times per minute.

Choices C and D are incorrect because 50 or 60 times per minute is close to once per second, which contradicts information in the passage.

The correct answer is B. The last paragraph states that *for each plot, the sensor recorded the soil temperature every 5 sec over the study period.* If the temperature was recorded every 5 seconds, and there are 60 seconds in a minute, then the temperature was recorded 60/5 = 12 times per minute.

38.   Evaluation of Models, Inferences & Experimental Results >> Model Information

Choices G and J are incorrect because there is no icon above July 20 in Figure 1, which means that albedo data was not collected that day. Albedo data was only recorded on cloudless days, so July 20 must have been cloudy.

Choice H is incorrect because the fifth paragraph of the passage states that *albedo was calculated for each cloudless day.* Since no data was collected on July 20, it's unlikely that it was a cloudless day.

The correct answer is F. According to the fifth paragraph of the text, *albedo was calculated for each cloudless day.* The icons on the lines in Figure 1 represent each albedo data collection. Because there is no icon above July 20, no data was collected that day. This implies that July 20 was not cloudless.

39.   Interpretation of Data >> Variables & Mathematical Relationships

Choice A is incorrect because according to Figure 1, the plots covered in DM had lower albedo than Plot 1, not increased albedo.

Choices B and C are incorrect because according to Figure 2, the plots covered in DM had higher temperatures than Plot 1, not decreased temperatures.

The correct answer is D. According to the fourth paragraph of the passage, Plot 3 had the greatest amount of DM, and *no DM was sprayed on Plot 1.* In Figure 1, Plot 3 has much lower albedo than Plot 1, so it can be inferred that DM *decreased* albedo. In Figure 2, Plot 3 has a higher temperature than Plot 1, so it can be inferred that DM *increased* temperature.

40.   Interpretation of Data >> Variables & Mathematical Relationships

Choice F is incorrect because this gives the percentage that *was* reflected, but the question asks for the percentage *not* reflected.

Choices G and H are incorrect because Figure 1 gives an albedo of 0.2 for Plot 2 on August 3, which does not correspond to a non-reflectance of either 40% or 60%.

The correct answer is J. According to Figure 1, Plot 2 had an albedo of 0.2 on August 3. The second paragraph of the passage defines *albedo* as the *proportion of the total incoming solar radiation that is reflected from a surface.* If 0.2 is reflected, then that means 1 − 0.2 = 0.8 or 80% was not reflected.

ACT QUESTION INDEX

Category Breakdowns for ACT Science Test 72-C

MAIN CATEGORY	STANDARD FAMILY	QUESTION NUMBER
Interpretation of Data	Select Data and Features	1, 15, 22
	Compare or Combine	7, 29, 33
	Creating Figures	10, 17
	Terminology	14, 20, 21
	Interpolation and Extrapolation	16, 26
	Variables and Mathematical Relationships	18, 23, 24, 25, 39, 40
	New Information	19, 36
Scientific Investigation	Understanding Design	2, 35
	Comparison	3, 27
	Prediction and Further Experiments	4, 6, 30, 31
	Tools	28
	Methods	34
	Text	37
Evaluation of Models, Inferences, and Experimental Results	Consistency of Hypotheses, Predictions, and Conclusions	5, 13, 32
	Model Information	8, 9, 38
	Support or Contradiction of Hypotheses and Conclusions	11, 12

ACT® Mastery's effectiveness is driven by MasteryPrep's firm commitment to industry-leading research coupled with results-oriented product development. What follows are two reports that provide a small window into the results being obtained for students in over 500 schools and districts throughout the country.

An In-Class ACT Prep Initiative

MasteryPrep partnered with several Louisiana school districts to provide in-person ACT preparation services to 404 students in remedial ranges at 10 school sites throughout the state during the fall 2014 semester.

State Background Information

The state of Louisiana tested 100% of its high school graduates on the ACT in 2014. The average composite ACT score in Louisiana was 19.2, which was 47th in the nation.[1] The state's average subject scores are broken down as follows:

English	18.9
Math	18.9
Reading	19.5
Science	19.1
Composite	19.2

The Louisiana Department of Education served 697,223 students in 2013 across 1,407 school sites.

Delivery Model

MasteryPrep personnel delivered one to three ACT prep courses as half-credit electives on-site during the school day at each school. Most students participated in the MasteryPrep course for one semester (18 weeks). In schools that operate on a block schedule, which effectively doubles class instruction time, students participated for nine weeks. MasteryPrep instructors coordinated closely with school officials and stakeholders throughout the length of the course.

Course Content

Instructors used MasteryPrep's ACT Mastery curriculum for course content. The course included practice tests, remedial lessons designed to improve student mastery of fundamental content, and a review of test-taking strategies.

Data Source

Students participating in this initiative were administered a full-length retired ACT test as a pretest. At the end of the course, students took a second, different full-length retired ACT test as a post-test at the end of the course. Scores were calculated using the scaling rubrics for the tests released by ACT, Inc.

---

[1] "Average Scores by State." ACT Inc. Web. 13 Apr. 2015.

Summary of Results

In this report, we highlight results from 10 school sites with a sufficient level of program implementation fidelity from a cross-selection of score ranges, regions of the state, and demographics. The purpose of this analysis presents the possible results of using MasteryPrep's ACT Mastery program as a semester course during the school day.

Pre-Test Summary

At the 10 sites that are the focus of this report, the average ACT score of the 404 participating students ranged from 11.5 to 16.3, with a weighted mean ACT score of 14.3. According to pre-test data, the cohort of students at these 10 sites ranged in relative national performance from the 11th to the 21st percentile.

Post-Test Summary

The average post-test scores of the 404 participating students at these sites ranged from 14.8 to 19.8, with a weighted average of 16.9. According to post-test data, this cohort of students ranged in relative national performance from the 16th to the 48th percentile. The weighted mean change in student performance was +2.6.

Southeast Louisiana

In Southeast Louisiana, we look at the results of a total of 174 students at four sites: John Ehret High School and Bonnabel Magnet Academy High School in Jefferson Parish, and McKinley Senior High School and Mentorship Academy in Baton Rouge. The weighted mean composite score at these sites was 13.5 on the pretest and 15.8 on the posttest, with an increase of 2.3.

John Ehret High School

John Ehret High School serves approximately 1,718 students in Marrero. Of these students, 73% are eligible for free or reduced lunch.
The school offered two ACT Mastery courses, and 36 students participated, with an average teacher-to-student ratio of 1:18.

Pre-Test Composite Score: 14.3
Post-Test Composite Score: 17.3

+3.0

Bonnabel Magnet Academy High School

This school serves approximately 1,474 students in Kenner. Of these students, 64% are eligible for free or reduced lunch.
The school offered two ACT Mastery courses, and 41 students participated, with an average teacher-to-student ratio of 1:21.

Pre-Test Composite Score: 11.5
Post-Test Composite Score: 15.3

+3.8

McKinley Senior High School

McKinley Senior High School serves approximately 1,289 students in Baton Rouge. Of these students, 69% are eligible for free or reduced lunch.
The school offered two ACT Mastery courses, and 59 students participated, with an average teacher-to-student ratio of 1:30.

Pre-Test Composite Score: 14.8
Post-Test Composite Score: 15.9

+1.1

Mentorship Academy

Mentorship Academy serves approximately 444 students in Baton Rouge. Of these students, 88% are eligible for free or reduced lunch.
The school offered two ACT Mastery courses, and 38 students participated, with an average teacher-to-student ratio of 1:19.

Pre-Test Composite Score: 13.1
Post-Test Composite Score: 14.8

+1.7

Southwest Louisiana

In Southwest Louisiana, we look at the results of a total of 121 students at four sites: Breaux Bridge High School, Jeanerette Senior High School, Sam Houston High School, and Westlake High School. The weighted mean composite score at these sites was 14.3 on the pre-test and 17.0 on the post-test, reflecting an increase of 2.7.

Breaux Bridge High School

Breaux Bridge High School serves approximately 872 students in Breaux Bridge. Of these students, 62% are eligible for free or reduced lunch.
The school offered two ACT Mastery courses, and 42 students participated, with an average teacher-to-student ratio of 1:21.

Pre-Test Composite Score: 12.5
Post-Test Composite Score: 15.8

+3.3

Jeanerette Senior High School

Jeanerette Senior High School serves approximately 418 students in Jeanerette. Of these students, 88% are eligible for free or reduced lunch.
The school offered one ACT Mastery course, and 27 students participated, with an average teacher-to-student ratio of 1:27.

Pre-Test Composite Score: 14.0
Post-Test Composite Score: 16.4

+2.4

Sam Houston High School

Sam Houston High School serves approximately 1,190 students in Lake Charles. Of these students, 80% are eligible for free or reduced lunch.
The school offered one ACT Mastery course, and 26 students participated, with an average teacher-to-student ratio of 1:26.

Pre-Test Composite Score: 16.3
Post-Test Composite Score: 18.5

+2.2

Westlake High School

Westlake High School serves approximately 521 students in Westlake. Of these students, 47% are eligible for free or reduced lunch.
The school offered one ACT Mastery course, and 26 students participated, with a teacher-to-student ratio of 1:26.

Pre-Test Composite Score: 15.4
Post-Test Composite Score: 17.9

+2.5

North Louisiana

In North Louisiana, we look at the results of a total of 109 students at two sites: Ouachita Parish High School and West Ouachita High School. The weighted mean composite score at these sites was 15.6 on the pre-test and 18.6 on the post-test, reflecting an increase of 3.0.

Ouachita Parish High School

Ouachita Parish High School serves approximately 1,225 students in Monroe. Of these students, 27% are eligible for free or reduced lunch.
The school offered three ACT Mastery courses, and 75 students participated, with a teacher-to-student ratio of 1:25.

Pre-Test Composite Score: 15.3
Post-Test Composite Score: 18.0

+2.7

West Ouachita Parish High School

West Ouachita High School serves approximately 1,067 students in West Monroe. Of these students, 16% are eligible for free or reduced lunch.
The school offered two ACT Mastery courses, and 34 students participated, with a teacher-to-student ratio of 1:17.

Pre-test Composite Score: 16.3
Post-Test Composite Score: 19.8

+3.5

Summary and Conclusion

In-school semester-long courses led by MasteryPrep instructors using MasteryPrep's ACT Mastery curriculum can increase the mean composite ACT scores of participating students by one to four points. Among the 10 schools analyzed in this report, the weighted mean change in student composite ACT outcomes was +2.6. Despite the remedial score ranges of many of the 404 students examined in this report, and despite the wide geographical and demographic differences between the 10 school sites, all sites showed consistent progress.

Mean Pre-Test and Post-Test Scores, by School • Fall 2014

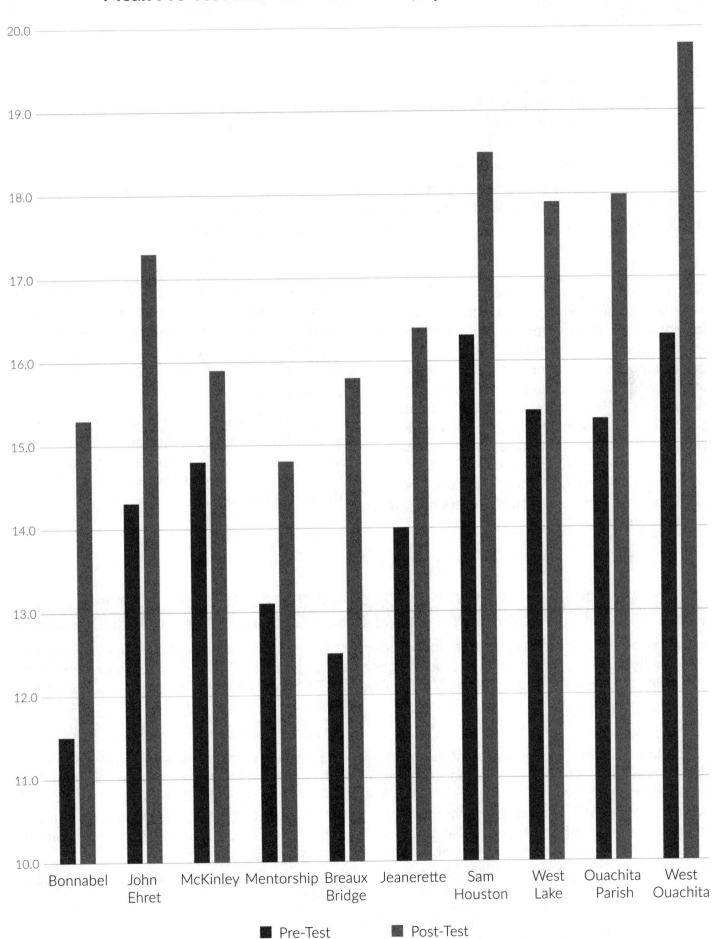

Pre-Test ▪ Post-Test ▪

A School-Based ACT Prep Initiative

MasteryPrep partnered with Dayton Public Schools to provide in-person ACT preparation services to 118 students at four high schools sites during the spring 2015 semester.

Dayton Public Schools Background Information

Dayton Public Schools is an urban district serving approximately 14,000 students at its 27 schools. The district's graduation rate is 72%. The percent of families certified to receive free and reduced price meals qualifies the district to provide free breakfast and lunch to all students.

Delivery Model

MasteryPrep personnel delivered six 2½-hour after-school ACT prep classes and one 6-hour in-school ACT Boot Camp class at four Dayton Public School high schools. Nearly all of the participating students were juniors. To encourage after-school participation students were provided food and bus tokens for transportation. Students who participated received a voucher provided by the district to take the ACT administered on April 18, 2015, or June 13, 2015, for free. MasteryPrep instructors coordinated closely with school officials and stakeholders throughout the course.

Course Content

Instructors used MasteryPrep's ACT Mastery curriculum for course content. The course included practice tests, remedial lessons designed to improve student mastery of fundamental content, and a review of test-taking strategies.

Data Source

Students participating in this initiative were administered a full-length retired ACT test as a pre-test. This was followed by an actual full-length ACT administration as a posttest at the end of the course.

Summary of Results

In this report, we highlight results from four school sites with a sufficient level of program implementation fidelity from a cross-selection of score ranges and demographics. The purpose of this analysis is to determine the possible results of using MasteryPrep's ACT Mastery course in an after-school setting.

Pre-Test Summary

At the four sites that are the focus of this report, the average ACT score of the 118 participating students ranged from 13.3 to 18.0, with a weighted mean ACT score of 15.3. According to pre-test data, the cohort of students at the four sites ranged in relative national performance from the 7th to the 36th percentile.

Post-Test Summary

The average post-test scores of the 118 participating students at these sites ranged from 16.2 to 21.7, with a weighted average of 18.4. According to post-test data, the cohort of students ranged in relative national performance from the 23rd to the 62nd percentile.

The weighted mean change in student performance was +3.1.

Dunbar High School

Dunbar High School serves approximately 481 students in Dayton. Of these students, 100% are considered economically disadvantaged.
The school offered the ACT Mastery program, and 40 students participated, with an average teacher-to-student ratio of 1:20.

Pre-Test Composite Score: 13.9
Post-Test Composite Score: 16.2

+2.3

Stivers School for the Arts

Stivers School for the Arts serves approximately 881 students in Dayton. Of these students, 100% are considered economically disadvantaged.
The school offered the ACT Mastery program, and 37 students participated, with an average teacher-to-student ratio of 1:19.

Pre-Test Composite Score: 18.0
Post-Test Composite Score: 21.7

+3.7

Meadowville High School

Meadowdale High School serves approximately 614 students in Dayton. Of these students, 100% are considered economically disadvantaged.
The school offered the ACT Mastery program, and 17 students participated, with an average teacher-to-student ratio of 1:9.

Pre-Test Composite Score: 15.5
Post-Test Composite Score: 18.1

+2.6

Thurgood Marshall High School

Thurgood Marshall High School serves approximately 653 students in Dayton. Of these students, 100% are considered economically disadvantaged.
The school offered the ACT Mastery program, and 24 students participated, with an average teacher-to-student ratio of 1:12.

Pre-Test Composite Score: 13.3
Post-Test Composite Score: 17.1

+3.8

Summary of Results

MasteryPrep's ACT Mastery curriculum led by MasteryPrep instructors can increase the mean composite ACT scores of participating students by one to four points. Among the 4 schools analyzed in this report, the weighted mean change in student composite ACT outcomes was +3.1. Despite the remedial score ranges of many of the 118 students examined in this report and the short format of the program, all 4 school sites demonstrated consistent progress.

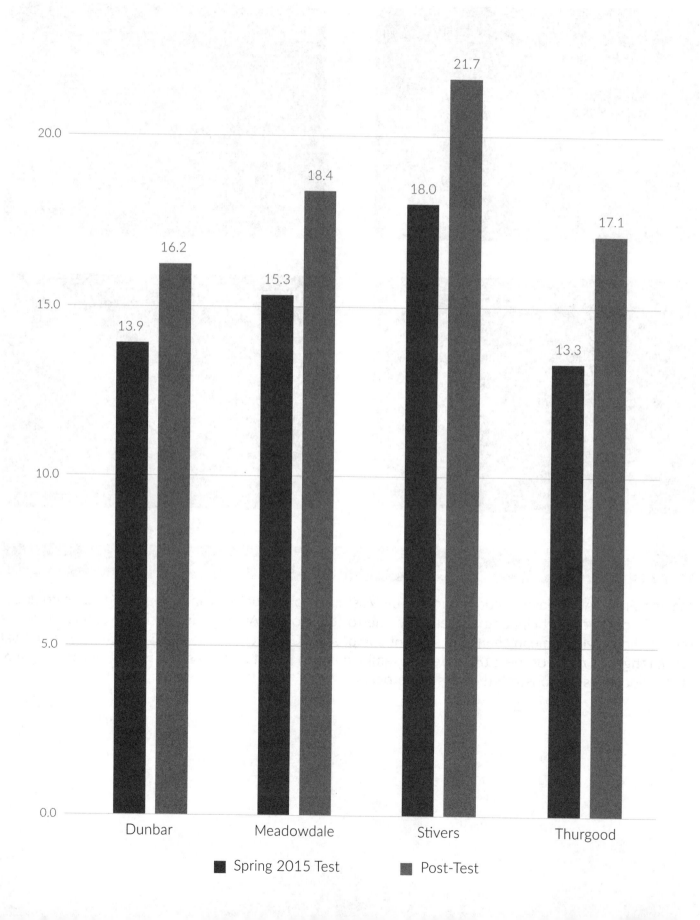

Mean Pre-Test and Post-Test Scores, by School • Fall 2014

Spring 2015 Test ■ Post-Test

Professional Development

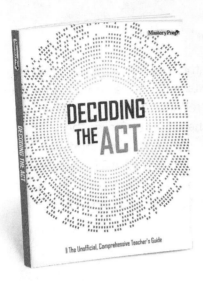

ACT Professional Development: Decoding the ACT

- **Motivation:** The unwritten first question on every standardized test is, "Do you give a flip?" We show you how to ensure that your students are motivated and care enough to perform well on the ACT.

- **Time Management:** MasteryPrep has helped over 100,000 students develop their time management skills on the ACT test. We share what works, and what doesn't, in getting students on-pace.

- **Process of Elimination:** By developing this one skill, you can turn a poor test-taker into a fantastic test taker. In Decoding the ACT, we show you how.

- **Guessing Strategies:** Every standardized test is susceptible to guessing strategies, and the ACT is no exception. We share the most effective techniques and how to present them to your students.

- **Test-Taking Skills:** Students will be taking tests for the rest of their lives. We break down what it means to develop test-taking skills that will help your students master standardized tests.

- **Subject Mastery:** Every PD session is designed specifically for a subject area (English, Math, Reading, and Science) and is packed with subject-specific tips and strategies. Content is key on the ACT, and we share strategies for content mastery, Common Core standard correlations, and a detailed analysis of what content the ACT treats as most important.

Every PD attendee receives the Decoding the ACT book to help their students succeed on the ACT.

1-DAY SESSIONS	**½-DAY SESSIONS**	**½-DAY WORKSHOPS**
English Math Reading Science	English Math Reading Science	English & Reading Math & Science

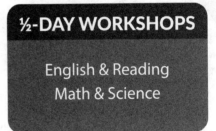

Product Training
Half-Day, On-Site Program

This program is designed for teachers who will be using the ACT Mastery program in the classroom.

In this half-day training program, a MasteryPrep trainer orients teachers to the ACT Mastery program and shows them how to use all of the tools the program provides in order to improve student outcomes. Furthermore, our trainer reviews essential test-taking strategies and content that teachers should particularly emphasize. Training on using MasteryPrep Online to access digital presentations and practice questions, as well as training on our TruScore practice test reports are included.

ACT Mastery

ACT Mastery Student Workbooks

The ACT Mastery program is the only ACT prep program designed specifically for students who score below College Readiness Benchmarks. ACT Mastery has been adopted by hundreds of schools throughout the United States because it produces profitable results with underperforming students. The program is a radically simplified approach to ACT preparation. Each workbook guides students to a thorough comprehension of the fundamental skills they need to succeed on the ACT.

ACT Mastery Key Features:

- **Entrance Tickets** engage students from the moment they sit down and allow teachers to assess student ability levels.

- **Self-Assessment** allows students to assess their confidence level about the upcoming lesson and re-evaluate their confidence after the lesson is completed.

- **Lesson Content** gradually increases in difficulty, building student confidence, and improving engagement level.

- **Lesson Summaries** review key content and definitions that students should master by the end of the lesson.

- **Test-Taking Strategies** give students an advantage by orientating them to the fast-paced ACT testing environment.

- **Practice Questions** (15 per lesson) bring students to a level of mastery in each skill.

- **Exit Tickets** at the end of each lessonimmediately review lesson content and hold students to be held accountable for what they've learned.

Teacher Manuals and Online Content

ACT Mastery Teacher Manuals

MasteryPrep follows a teacher-first design methodology, which means that in our courses, teacher manuals are written first. ACT Mastery Teacher Manuals are the most extensive teacher guides in the test prep industry. In addition to providing a step-by-step walk-through of the lesson, we also call out essential test-taking strategies, provide detailed explanations for every practice question, and give practical advice for coaching students through common errors. Teacher manuals provide extensive tools and tips derived from thousands of hours of research that will give your students major advantages on test day.

MasteryPrep Online

Every lesson in the ACT Mastery course is accompanied by a digital presentation, which helps teachers bring the program to life. Through MasteryPrep Online, teachers can access these presentations, and all of the practice questions provided in the ACT Mastery program.

Additionally, a student edition of MasteryPrep Online is available as a digital workbook replacement option. Students can access the student edition of MasteryPrep Online for both classwork, and homework, in lieu of the school purchasing student workbooks.

ACT Boot Camp

The ACT Boot Camp is a highly engaging & helpful one-day workshop.

- Students learn exactly what they need to boost their scores on the ACT, and receive live instruction by our expert ACT test advisors.

- ACT Boot Camp is the most helpful one-day ACT prep program, available during the school day or on the weekend.

Sample Agenda

ACT Test-Taking Strategies

- A million reasons to improve your ACT score
- How many correct answers do you need to get the score you want?
- Learn to guess twice as effectively in five minutes

English

- The difference between the right answer and the best answer
- What punctuation mark makes up 20% of your English score?

Math

- What to do when you draw a blank during the math test
- How to turn a word problem into something you can actually solve

Reading

- What question type determines over a third of your score?
- How to stop over-thinking?

Science

- The scientific method in 5 minutes
- How to spot contradictions

Elements

Student Workbooks

With ACT Elements, students can achieve better ACT scores in just five minutes a day. ACT Elements is a classroom warm-up program for middle school and high school designed to provide students with grade-level appropriate exercises that reinforce essential ACT College Readiness Standards.

Each week features a series of exercises related to one ACT College Readiness Standard, culminating in student proficiency. Our approach to the introducing and cultivating mastery in each standard reduces the amount of classroom time dedicated to explanations and increases student retention.

Our program includes English, math, reading, and science workbooks for middle and high school levels. We provide physical books and online access to a digital platform so that teachers can display questions on SMART Boards™ or projectors

Teacher Manuals

The ACT Elements teacher manuals include answers and explanations for all questions and best practices for running warm-up exercises (also known as "do nows" or "bell ringers"). It also explains how teachers can turn bell ringers into engaging games for your students.

Key Features

- Each week emphasizes a separate ACT College Readiness Standard todevelop student proficiency.

- Gradually increasing difficulty builds student confidence and improves engagement level.

- Hundreds of practice questions allow students to attain mastery of each skill.

- Answer explanations are provided at the end of each exercise.

- Simplified layout eliminates distractions and prevents students from feeling overwhelmed.

- Powerful test-taking strategies are integrated in the lessons and practice questions.

- A highly effective, content-centric approach to ACT prep.

ACT Essentials

In as little as 4-6 weeks, ACT Essentials covers important skills and strategies students need to master in order to make significant gains on the ACT. Lesson topics focus on the questions that are most often and most heavily tested on the ACT.

Students learn how the ACT is structured so that they can effectively manage their time in each subject. Practice questions exactly match the format and rigor of real ACT test questions, and each lesson includes five times more practice questions than traditional test prep books. Test-taking strategies give students the confidence to work through intimidating questions and guess twice as effectively as before. Also included are subject-specific tips and strategies, ensuring that students can make substantial gains in each section.

Each Workbook Includes:

- ACT practice items in the same format and with the same rigor as the ACT

- Time management strategies

- Constructed response practice

- Test-taking strategies

TruScore ACT Practice Testing and Scoring

Actionable data your teachers can use in the classroom

When teachers are asked to improve their students' ACT scores, what should they focus on first? The answer to that question is different for each class–and for each student.

MasteryPrep provides all necessary test documents for a no-hassle practice test administration. Answer sheets are scored and action-oriented reports are generated, giving insight into each student's strengths and weaknesses. TruScore provides industry-leading data assessments and is the most comprehensive and user-friendly ACT practice test system on the market.

TruScore can generate reports that break down information by district, school, class, and student. Professional development workshops present the data in such a way that allows can focus their curriculum on the most important skills for student success on the ACT.

With MasteryPrep's TruScore, the guessing game is over. Teachers can take effective action and get results.

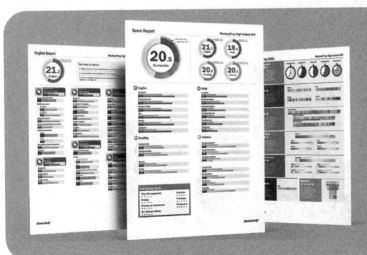

Data Analysis Professional Development

In this one-day professional development program, a MasteryPrep consultant will go on-site and provide a series of one-hour subject-specific sessions designed to help your instructors maximize the value of the TruScore ACT practice test data. In each session, the MasteryPrep consultant will call out important trends and helps your team develop an action plan that will result in improved student outcomes.

WorkKeys

Our MasteryKeys WorkKeys program is the most comprehensive WorkKeys test prep curriculum available and the only program specifically designed to help students earn their Silver National Career Readiness Certificate.

The MasteryKeys program consists of three workbooks, each geared to one of the three WorkKeys tests that count towards the NCRC: Applied Mathematics, Locating Information, and Reading for Information. Our program includes detailed lessons, thousands of practice questions, and full-length practice tests.

Also available as an online course.

MasteryKeys: Applied Mathematics

The MasteryKeys: Applied Mathematics unit focuses on the student's ability to solve problems, think critically, and calculate workplace mathematics. Lessons and practice questions involve setting up and solving a variety of problems as well as performing the types of calculations that occur in an actual workplace. Students will expand their knowledge and learn more about employing mathematical operations to solve word problems; converting numbers between fractions, decimals, and percentages; solving problems that deal with negative numbers, money, and time; learning how to apply operations by calculating averages, rates, ratios, and conversions; and essential test-taking tips.

MasteryKeys: Locating Information

In MasteryKeys: Locating Information, students will learn to decipher and analyze a variety of visual depictions that are likely to arise in a real-life work settings. Hundreds of practice questions improve student ability in understanding and explaining a wide range of real-world figures and graphics. Students will learn how to read and fill out complicated forms; practice reading maps, plans, tables, graphs, and diagrams; improve their ability to locate and use information; and experience a wide variety of information presentation styles.

MasteryKeys: Reading for Information

MasteryKeys: Reading for Information will improve student ability in reading and understanding written text from actual work situations. Lessons and practice questions emphasize comprehending letters, emails, instructions, memos, notices, policies, and regulations. Students will learn to pay attention to important details, how to follow step-by-step instructions, the importance of persistence and good "detective work," how to identify situations and then apply appropriate rules, how to filter a problem when dealing with too much information, and a variety of ways to decipher unfamiliar words.

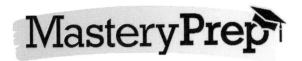

Professional Development Workshop Evaluation Form

1. On a scale of 1-5, with 1 being *unsatisfactory* and 5 being *excellent*, please fill in the bubbles below:

	1	2	3	4	5
Workshop overall	①	②	③	④	⑤
Presenter's expertise	①	②	③	④	⑤
Presenter's delivery style	①	②	③	④	⑤
The content of the workshop	①	②	③	④	⑤
The quality of the distributed materials	①	②	③	④	⑤

2. What was the most helpful part of the workshop?

    _____
    _____
    _____

3. What do you think we should improve about this workshop?

    _____
    _____
    _____

4. What information from this workshop are you going to apply?

    _____
    _____
    _____

5. What new topics should be included in the workshop?

    _____
    _____
    _____

6. Is there anything else you'd like to tell us?

    _____
    _____
    _____

7. Do we have your permission to use your quote anonymously in our publications?
    _____ Yes
    _____ No